SECOND EDITION

Linux System Programming

Robert Love

O'REILLY®

Beijing · Cambridge · Farnham · Köln · Sebastopol · Tokyo

Linux System Programming, Second Edition

by Robert Love

Published by O'Reilly Media, Inc., 1005 Gravenstein Highway North, Sebastopol, CA 95472.

O'Reilly books may be purchased for educational, business, or sales promotional use. Online editions are also available for most titles (*http://my.safaribooksonline.com*). For more information, contact our corporate/institutional sales department: 800-998-9938 or *corporate@oreilly.com*.

Editors: Andy Oram and Maria Gulick	**Indexer:** WordCo Indexing Services, Inc.
Production Editor: Rachel Steely	**Cover Designer:** Randy Comer
Copyeditor: Amanda Kersey	**Interior Designer:** David Futato
Proofreader: Charles Roumeliotis	**Illustrator:** Rebecca Demarest

May 2013:   Second Edition

Revision History for the Second Edition:

2013-05-10:   First release

See *http://oreilly.com/catalog/errata.csp?isbn=9781449339531* for release details.

ISBN: 978-1-449-33953-1

[LSI]

For Doris and Helen.

Table of Contents

Foreword

There is an old line that Linux kernel developers like to throw out when they are feeling grumpy: "User space is just a test load for the kernel."

By muttering this line, the kernel developers aim to wash their hands of all responsibility for any failure to run user-space code as well as possible. As far as they're concerned, user-space developers should just go away and fix their own code, as any problems are definitely not the kernel's fault.

To prove that it usually is not the kernel that is at fault, one leading Linux kernel developer has been giving a "Why User Space Sucks" talk to packed conference rooms for more than three years now, pointing out real examples of horrible user-space code that everyone relies on every day. Other kernel developers have created tools that show how badly user-space programs are abusing the hardware and draining the batteries of unsuspecting laptops.

But while user-space code might be just a "test load" for kernel developers to scoff at, it turns out that all of these kernel developers also depend on that user-space code every day. If it weren't present, all the kernel would be good for would be to print out alternating ABABAB patterns on the screen.

Right now, Linux is the most flexible and powerful operating system that has ever been created, running everything from the tiniest cell phones and embedded devices to more than 90 percent of the world's top 500 supercomputers. No other operating system has ever been able to scale so well and meet the challenges of all of these different hardware types and environments.

And along with the kernel, code running in user space on Linux can also operate on all of those platforms, providing the world with real applications and utilities people rely on.

In this book, Robert Love has taken on the unenviable task of teaching the reader about almost every system call on a Linux system. In so doing, he has produced a tome that will allow you to fully understand how the Linux kernel works from a user-space perspective, and also how to harness the power of this system.

The information in this book will show you how to create code that will run on all of the different Linux distributions and hardware types. It will allow you to understand how Linux works and how to take advantage of its flexibility.

In the end, this book teaches you how to write code that doesn't suck, which is the best thing of all.

—Greg Kroah-Hartman

Preface

This book is about system programming on Linux. *System programming* is the practice of writing *system software*, which is code that lives at a low level, talking directly to the kernel and core system libraries. Put another way, the topic of the book is Linux system calls and low-level functions such as those defined by the C library.

While many books cover system programming for Unix systems, few tackle the subject with a focus solely on Linux, and fewer still address the very latest Linux releases and advanced Linux-only interfaces. Moreover, this book benefits from a special touch: I have written a lot of code for Linux, both for the kernel and for system software built thereon. In fact, I have implemented some of the system calls and other features covered in this book. Consequently, this book carries a lot of insider knowledge, covering not just how the system interfaces *should* work, but how they *actually* work and how you can use them most efficiently. This book, therefore, combines in a single work a tutorial on Linux system programming, a reference manual covering the Linux system calls, and an insider's guide to writing smarter, faster code. The text is fun and accessible, and regardless of whether you code at the system level on a daily basis, this book will teach you tricks that will enable you to be a better software engineer.

Audience and Assumptions

The following pages assume that the reader is familiar with C programming and the Linux programming environment—not necessarily well-versed in the subjects, but at least acquainted with them. If you are not comfortable with a Unix text editor—Emacs and *vim* being the most common and highly regarded—start playing with one. You'll also want to be familiar with the basics of using *gcc*, *gdb*, *make*, and so on. Plenty of other books on tools and practices for Linux programming are out there; Appendix B at the end of this book lists several useful references.

I've made few assumptions about the reader's knowledge of Unix or Linux system programming. This book will start from the ground up, beginning with the basics, and winding its way up to the most advanced interfaces and optimization tricks. Readers of all levels, I hope, will find this work worthwhile and learn something new. In the course of writing the book, I certainly did.

Similarly, I make few assumptions about the persuasion or motivation of the reader. Engineers wishing to program (better) at the system level are obviously targeted, but higher-level programmers looking for a stronger foundation will also find a lot to interest them. Merely curious hackers are also welcome, for this book should satiate that hunger, too. This book aims to cast a net wide enough to satisfy most programmers.

Regardless of your motives, above all else, *have fun*.

Contents of This Book

This book is broken into 11 chapters and two appendices.

Chapter 1, Introduction and Essential Concepts
    This chapter serves as an introduction, providing an overview of Linux, system programming, the kernel, the C library, and the C compiler. Even advanced users should visit this chapter.

Chapter 2, File I/O
    This chapter introduces files, the most important abstraction in the Unix environment, and file I/O, the basis of the Linux programming mode. It covers reading from and writing to files, along with other basic file I/O operations. The chapter culminates with a discussion on how the Linux kernel implements and manages files.

Chapter 3, Buffered I/O
    This chapter discusses an issue with the basic file I/O interfaces—buffer size management—and introduces buffered I/O in general, and standard I/O in particular, as solutions.

Chapter 4, Advanced File I/O
    This chapter completes the I/O troika with a treatment on advanced I/O interfaces, memory mappings, and optimization techniques. The chapter is capped with a discussion on avoiding seeks and the role of the Linux kernel's I/O scheduler.

Chapter 5, Process Management
    This chapter introduces Unix's second most important abstraction, the *process*, and the family of system calls for basic process management, including the venerable *fork*.

Chapter 6, Advanced Process Management
    This chapter continues the treatment with a discussion of advanced process management, including real-time processes.

Chapter 7, Threading

This chapter discusses threads and multithreaded programming. It focuses on higher-level design concepts. It includes an introduction to the POSIX threading API, known as Pthreads.

Chapter 8, File and Directory Management

This chapter discusses creating, moving, copying, deleting, and otherwise managing files and directories.

Chapter 9, Memory Management

This chapter covers memory management. It begins by introducing Unix concepts of memory, such as the process address space and the page, and continues with a discussion of the interfaces for obtaining memory from and returning memory to the kernel. The chapter concludes with a treatment on advanced memory-related interfaces.

Chapter 10, Signals

This chapter covers signals. It begins with a discussion of signals and their role on a Unix system. It then covers signal interfaces, starting with the basic and concluding with the advanced.

Chapter 11, Time

This chapter discusses time, sleeping, and clock management. It covers the basic interfaces up through POSIX clocks and high-resolution timers.

Appendix A

The first appendix reviews many of the language extensions provided by *gcc* and GNU C, such as attributes for marking a function constant, pure, or inline.

Appendix B

This bibliography of recommended reading lists both useful supplements to this work, and books that address prerequisite topics not covered herein.

Versions Covered in This Book

The Linux system interface is definable as the application binary interface and application programming interface provided by the triplet of the Linux kernel (the heart of the operating system), the GNU C library (*glibc*), and the GNU C Compiler (*gcc*—now formally called the GNU Compiler Collection, but we are concerned only with C). This book covers the system interface defined by Linux kernel version 3.9, *glibc* version 2.17, and *gcc* version 4.8. Interfaces in this book should be forward compatible with newer versions of the kernel, *glibc*, and *gcc*. That is, newer versions of these components should continue to obey the interfaces and behavior documented in this book. Similarly, many of the interfaces discussed in this book have long been part of Linux and are thus backward compatible with older versions of the kernel, *glibc*, and *gcc*.

If any evolving operating system is a moving target, Linux is a rabid cheetah. Progress is measured in days, not years, and frequent releases of the kernel and other components constantly morph the playing field. No book can hope to capture such a dynamic beast in a timeless fashion.

Nonetheless, the programming environment defined by system programming is *set in stone*. Kernel developers go to great pains not to break system calls, the *glibc* developers highly value forward *and* backward compatibility, and the Linux toolchain generates compatible code across versions. Consequently, while Linux may be constantly on the go, Linux system programming remains stable, and a book based on a snapshot of the system, especially at this point in Linux's lifetime, has immense staying power. What I am trying to say is simple: don't worry about system interfaces changing and *buy this book*!

Conventions Used in This Book

The following typographical conventions are used in this book:

Italic
> Indicates new terms, URLs, email addresses, filenames, and file extensions.

`Constant width`
> Used for program listings, as well as within paragraphs to refer to program elements such as variable or function names, databases, data types, environment variables, statements, and keywords.

`Constant width bold`
> Shows commands or other text that should be typed literally by the user.

`Constant width italic`
> Shows text that should be replaced with user-supplied values or by values determined by context.

 This icon signifies a tip, suggestion, or general note.

 This icon signifies a warning or caution.

Most of the code in this book is in the form of brief, but reusable, code snippets. They look like this:

```
while (1) {
        int ret;

        ret = fork ();
        if (ret == -1)
                perror ("fork");
}
```

Great pains have been taken to provide code snippets that are concise but usable. No special header files, full of crazy macros and illegible shortcuts, are required. Instead of building a few gigantic programs, this book is filled with many simple examples. As the examples are descriptive and fully usable, yet small and clear, I hope they will provide a useful tutorial on the first read, and remain a good reference on subsequent passes.

Nearly all the examples in this book are self-contained. This means you can easily copy them into your text editor and put them to use. Unless otherwise mentioned, all the code snippets should build without any special compiler flags. (In a few cases, you need to link with a special library.) I recommend the following command to compile a source file:

```
$ gcc -Wall -Wextra -O2 -g -o snippet snippet.c
```

This compiles the source file *snippet.c* into the executable binary *snippet*, enabling many warning checks, significant but sane optimizations, and debugging. The code in this book should compile using this command without errors or warnings—although of course, you might have to build a skeleton program around the snippet first.

When a section introduces a new function, it is in the usual Unix manpage format, which looks like this:

```
#include <fcntl.h>

int posix_fadvise (int fd, off_t pos, off_t len, int advice);
```

The required headers, and any needed definitions, are at the top, followed by a full prototype of the call.

Using Code Examples

This book is here to help you get your job done. In general, you may use the code in this book in your programs and documentation. You do not need to contact us for permission unless you're reproducing a significant portion of the code. For example, writing a program that uses several chunks of code from this book does not require permission. Selling or distributing a CD-ROM of examples from O'Reilly books does require permission. Answering a question by citing this book and quoting example code does not require permission. Incorporating a significant amount of example code from this book into your product's documentation does require permission.

We appreciate, but do not require, attribution. An attribution usually includes the title, author, publisher, and ISBN. For example: "*Linux System Programming,* Second Edition, by Robert Love (O'Reilly). Copyright 2013 Robert Love, 978-1-449-33953-1."

If you feel your use of code examples falls outside fair use or the permission given above, feel free to contact us at *permissions@oreilly.com*.

Because the snippets in this book are numerous but short, they are not available in an online repository.

Safari® Books Online

 Safari Books Online is an on-demand digital library that delivers expert content in both book and video form from the world's leading authors in technology and business.

Technology professionals, software developers, web designers, and business and creative professionals use Safari Books Online as their primary resource for research, problem solving, learning, and certification training.

Safari Books Online offers a range of product mixes and pricing programs for organizations, government agencies, and individuals. Subscribers have access to thousands of books, training videos, and prepublication manuscripts in one fully searchable database from publishers like O'Reilly Media, Prentice Hall Professional, Addison-Wesley Professional, Microsoft Press, Sams, Que, Peachpit Press, Focal Press, Cisco Press, John Wiley & Sons, Syngress, Morgan Kaufmann, IBM Redbooks, Packt, Adobe Press, FT Press, Apress, Manning, New Riders, McGraw-Hill, Jones & Bartlett, Course Technology, and dozens more. For more information about Safari Books Online, please visit us online.

How to Contact Us

Please address comments and questions concerning this book to the publisher:

O'Reilly Media, Inc.
1005 Gravenstein Highway North
Sebastopol, CA 95472
800-998-9938 (in the United States or Canada)
707-829-0515 (international or local)
707-829-0104 (fax)

We have a web page for this book, where we list errata, examples, and any additional information. You can access this page at *http://oreil.ly/Linux_Sys_2E*.

To comment or ask technical questions about this book, send email to *bookquestions@oreilly.com*.

For more information about our books, courses, conferences, and news, see our website at *http://www.oreilly.com*.

Find us on Facebook: *http://facebook.com/oreilly*

Follow us on Twitter: *http://twitter.com/oreillymedia*

Watch us on YouTube: *http://www.youtube.com/oreillymedia*

Acknowledgments

Many hearts and minds contributed to the completion of this manuscript. While no list would be complete, it is my sincere pleasure to acknowledge the assistance and friendship of individuals who provided encouragement, knowledge, and support along the way.

Andy Oram is a phenomenal editor and human being. This effort would have been impossible without his hard work. A rare breed, Andy couples deep technical knowledge with a poetic command of the English language.

This book was blessed with phenomenal technical reviewers, true masters of their craft, without whom this work would pale in comparison to the final product you now read. The technical reviewers were Jeremy Allison, Robert P. J. Day, Kenneth Geisshirt, Joey Shaw, and James Willcox. Despite their toils, any errors remain my own.

My colleagues at Google remain the smartest, most dedicated group of engineers with whom I have had the pleasure to work. Each day is a challenge in the best use of that word. Thank you for the system-level projects that helped shape this text and an atmosphere that encourages pursuits such as this work.

For numerous reasons, thanks and respect to Paul Amici, Mikey Babbitt, Nat Friedman, Miguel de Icaza, Greg Kroah-Hartman, Doris Love, Linda Love, Tim O'Reilly, Salvatore Ribaudo and family, Chris Rivera, Carolyn Rodon, Joey Shaw, Sarah Stewart, Peter Teichman, Linus Torvalds, Jon Trowbridge, Jeremy VanDoren and family, Luis Villa, Steve Weisberg and family, and Helen Whisnant.

Final thanks to my parents, Bob and Elaine.

—Robert Love, Boston

## CHAPTER 1

Introduction and Essential Concepts

This book is about *system programming*, which is the practice of writing *system software*. System software lives at a low level, interfacing directly with the kernel and core system libraries. Your shell and your text editor, your compiler and your debugger, your core utilities and system daemons are all system software. But so are the network server, the web server, and the database. These components are entirely system software, primarily if not exclusively interfacing with the kernel and the C library. Other software (such as high-level GUI applications) lives at a higher level, delving into the low level only on occasion. Some programmers spend all day every day writing system software; others spend only part of their time on this task. There is no programmer, however, who does not benefit from an understanding of system programming. Whether it is the programmer's raison d'être, or merely a foundation for higher-level concepts, system programming is at the heart of all software that we write.

In particular, this book is about system programming on *Linux*. Linux is a modern Unix-like system, written from scratch by Linus Torvalds and a loose-knit community of programmers around the globe. Although Linux shares the goals and philosophy of Unix, Linux is not Unix. Instead, Linux follows its own course, diverging where desired and converging only where practical. The core of Linux system programming is the same as on any other Unix system. Beyond the basics, however, Linux differentiates itself—in comparison with traditional Unix systems, Linux supports additional system calls, behaves distinctly, and offers new features.

System Programming

Traditionally, all Unix programming was system-level programming. Unix systems historically did not include many higher-level abstractions. Even programming in a development environment such as the X Window System exposed in full view the core Unix system API. Consequently, it can be said that this book is a book on Linux programming in general. But note that this book does not cover the Linux programming *environment* —for example, there is no tutorial on *make* in these pages. What is covered is the system programming API exposed on a modern Linux machine.

We can compare and contrast system programming with application programming, which differ in some important aspects but are quite similar in others. System programming's hallmark is that the system programmer must have an acute awareness of the hardware and the operating system on which they work. Where system programs interface primarily with the kernel and system libraries, application programs also interface with high-level libraries. These libraries *abstract* away the details of the hardware and operating system. Such abstraction has several goals: portability with different systems, compatibility with different versions of those systems, and the construction of higher-level toolkits that are easier to use, more powerful, or both. How much of a given application uses system versus high-level libraries depends on the level of the stack at which the application was written. Some applications are written exclusively to higher-level abstractions. But even these applications, far from the lowest levels of the system, benefit from a programmer with knowledge of system programming. The same good practices and understanding of the underlying system inform and benefit all forms of programming.

Why Learn System Programming

The preceding decade has witnessed a trend in application programming away from system-level programming and toward very high-level development, either through web software (such as JavaScript), or through managed code (such as Java). This development, however, does not foretell the death of system programming. Indeed, someone still has to write the JavaScript interpreter and the Java VM, which are themselves system programming. Furthermore, the developer writing Python or Ruby or Scala can still benefit from knowledge of system programming, as an understanding of the soul of the machine allows for better code no matter where in the stack the code is written.

Despite this trend in application programming, the majority of Unix and Linux code is still written at the system level. Much of it is C and C++ and subsists primarily on interfaces provided by the C library and the kernel. This is traditional system programming—Apache, *bash*, *cp*, Emacs, *init*, *gcc*, *gdb*, *glibc*, *ls*, *mv*, *vim*, and X. These applications are not going away anytime soon.

The umbrella of system programming often includes kernel development, or at least device driver writing. But this book, like most texts on system programming, is unconcerned with kernel development. Instead, it focuses on user-space system-level programming, that is, everything above the kernel (although knowledge of kernel internals is a useful adjunct to this text). Device driver writing is a large, expansive topic, best tackled in books dedicated to the subject.

What is the system-level interface, and how do I write system-level applications in Linux? What exactly do the kernel and the C library provide? How do I write optimal code, and what tricks does Linux provide? What interesting system calls are provided in Linux compared to other Unix variants? How does it all work? Those questions are at the center of this book.

Cornerstones of System Programming

There are three cornerstones of system programming in Linux: system calls, the C library, and the C compiler. Each deserves an introduction.

System Calls

System programming starts and ends with *system calls*. System calls (often shortened to *syscalls*) are function invocations made from user space—your text editor, favorite game, and so on—into the kernel (the core internals of the system) in order to request some service or resource from the operating system. System calls range from the familiar, such as `read()` and `write()`, to the exotic, such as `get_thread_area()` and `set_tid_address()`.

Linux implements far fewer system calls than most other operating system kernels. For example, a count of the x86-64 architecture's system calls comes in at around 300, compared with the suspected thousands of system calls on Microsoft Windows. In the Linux kernel, each machine architecture (such as Alpha, x86-64, or PowerPC) can augment the standard system calls with its own. Consequently, the system calls available on one architecture may differ from those available on another. Nonetheless, a very large subset of system calls—more than 90 percent—is implemented by all architectures. It is this shared subset, these common interfaces, that we cover in this book.

Invoking system calls

It is not possible to directly link user-space applications with kernel space. For reasons of security and reliability, user-space applications must not be allowed to directly execute kernel code or manipulate kernel data. Instead, the kernel must provide a mechanism by which a user-space application can "signal" the kernel that it wishes to invoke a system call. The application can then *trap* into the kernel through this well-defined mechanism and execute only code that the kernel allows it to execute. The exact mechanism varies from architecture to architecture. On i386, for example, a user-space application executes a software interrupt instruction, `int`, with a value of `0x80`. This instruction causes a switch into kernel space, the protected realm of the kernel, where the kernel executes a software interrupt handler—and what is the handler for interrupt `0x80`? None other than the system call handler!

The application tells the kernel which system call to execute and with what parameters via *machine registers*. System calls are denoted by number, starting at 0. On the i386 architecture, to request system call 5 (which happens to be open()), the user-space application stuffs 5 in register eax before issuing the int instruction.

Parameter passing is handled in a similar manner. On i386, for example, a register is used for each possible parameter—registers ebx, ecx, edx, esi, and edi contain, in order, the first five parameters. In the rare event of a system call with more than five parameters, a single register is used to point to a buffer in user space where all of the parameters are kept. Of course, most system calls have only a couple of parameters.

Other architectures handle system call invocation differently, although the spirit is the same. As a system programmer, you usually do not need any knowledge of how the kernel handles system call invocation. That knowledge is encoded into the standard calling conventions for the architecture, and handled automatically by the compiler and the C library.

The C Library

The C library (*libc*) is at the heart of Unix applications. Even when you're programming in another language, the C library is most likely in play, wrapped by the higher-level libraries, providing core services, and facilitating system call invocation. On modern Linux systems, the C library is provided by *GNU libc*, abbreviated *glibc*, and pronounced *gee-lib-see* or, less commonly, *glib-see*.

The GNU C library provides more than its name suggests. In addition to implementing the standard C library, *glibc* provides wrappers for system calls, threading support, and basic application facilities.

The C Compiler

In Linux, the standard C compiler is provided by the *GNU Compiler Collection (gcc)*. Originally, *gcc* was GNU's version of *cc*, the *C Compiler*. Thus, *gcc* stood for *GNU C Compiler*. Over time, support was added for more and more languages. Consequently, nowadays *gcc* is used as the generic name for the family of GNU compilers. However, *gcc* is also the binary used to invoke the C compiler. In this book, when I talk of *gcc*, I typically mean the program *gcc*, unless context suggests otherwise.

The compiler used in a Unix system—Linux included—is highly relevant to system programming, as the compiler helps implement the C standard (see "C Language Standards" on page 8) and the system ABI (see "APIs and ABIs" on page 5).

C++

This chapter focuses on C as the lingua franca of system programming, but C++ plays a significant role.

To date, C++ has taken a backseat to C in system programming. Historically, Linux developers favored C over C++: core libraries, daemons, utilities, and of course the Linux kernel are all written in C. Where the ascendancy of C++ as a "better C" is all but universal in most non-Linux environments, in Linux C++ plays second fiddle to C.

Nonetheless, in much of this book, you can replace "C" with "C++" without issue. Indeed, C++ is an excellent alternative to C, suitable for any system programming task: C++ code can link to C code, invoke Linux system calls, and utilize *glibc*.

C++ programming adds two more cornerstones to the system programming foundation: the standard C++ library and the GNU C++ compiler. The *standard C++ library* implements C++ system interfaces and the ISO C++11 standard. It is provided by the *libstdc++* library (sometimes written *libstdcxx*). The *GNU C++ compiler* is the standard compiler for C++ code on Linux systems. It is provided by the *g++* binary.

APIs and ABIs

Programmers are naturally interested in ensuring their programs run on all of the systems that they have promised to support, now and in the future. They want to feel secure that programs they write on their Linux distributions will run on other Linux distributions, as well as on other supported Linux architectures and newer (or earlier) Linux versions.

At the system level, there are two separate sets of definitions and descriptions that impact portability. One is the *application programming interface* (API), and the other is the *application binary interface* (ABI). Both define and describe the interfaces between different pieces of computer software.

APIs

An API defines the interfaces by which one piece of software communicates with another at the source level. It provides abstraction by providing a standard set of interfaces——usually functions—that one piece of software (typically, although not necessarily, a higher-level piece) can invoke from another piece of software (usually a lower-level piece). For example, an API might abstract the concept of drawing text on the screen through a family of functions that provide everything needed to draw the text. The API merely defines the interface; the piece of software that actually provides the API is known as the *implementation* of the API.

It is common to call an API a "contract." This is not correct, at least in the legal sense of the term, as an API is not a two-way agreement. The API user (generally, the higher-level software) has zero input into the API and its implementation. It may use the API as-is, or not use it at all: take it or leave it! The API acts only to ensure that if both pieces of software follow the API, they are *source compatible*; that is, that the user of the API will successfully compile against the implementation of the API.

A real-world example of an API is the interfaces defined by the C standard and implemented by the standard C library. This API defines a family of basic and essential functions, such as memory management and string-manipulation routines.

Throughout this book, we will rely on the existence of various APIs, such as the standard I/O library discussed in Chapter 3. The most important APIs in Linux system programming are discussed in the section "Standards" on page 7.

ABIs

Whereas an API defines a source interface, an ABI defines the binary interface between two or more pieces of software on a particular architecture. It defines how an application interacts with itself, how an application interacts with the kernel, and how an application interacts with libraries. Whereas an API ensures source compatibility, an ABI ensures *binary compatibility*, guaranteeing that a piece of object code will function on any system with the same ABI, without requiring recompilation.

ABIs are concerned with issues such as calling conventions, byte ordering, register use, system call invocation, linking, library behavior, and the binary object format. The calling convention, for example, defines how functions are invoked, how arguments are passed to functions, which registers are preserved and which are mangled, and how the caller retrieves the return value.

Although several attempts have been made at defining a single ABI for a given architecture across multiple operating systems (particularly for i386 on Unix systems), the efforts have not met with much success. Instead, operating systems—Linux included—tend to define their own ABIs however they see fit. The ABI is intimately tied to the architecture; the vast majority of an ABI speaks of machine-specific concepts, such as particular registers or assembly instructions. Thus, each machine architecture has its own ABI on Linux. In fact, we tend to call a particular ABI by its machine name, such as *Alpha*, or *x86-64*. Thus, the ABI is a function of both the operating system (say, Linux) and the architecture (say, x86-64).

System programmers ought to be aware of the ABI but usually need not memorize it. The ABI is enforced by the *toolchain*—the compiler, the linker, and so on—and does not typically otherwise surface. Knowledge of the ABI, however, can lead to more optimal programming and is required if writing assembly code or developing the toolchain itself (which is, after all, system programming).

The ABI is defined and implemented by the kernel and the toolchain.

Standards

Unix system programming is an old art. The basics of Unix programming have existed untouched for decades. Unix systems, however, are dynamic beasts. Behavior changes and features are added. To help bring order to chaos, standards groups codify system interfaces into official standards. Numerous such standards exist but, technically speaking, Linux does not officially comply with any of them. Instead, Linux *aims* toward compliance with two of the most important and prevalent standards: POSIX and the Single UNIX Specification (SUS).

POSIX and SUS document, among other things, the C API for a Unix-like operating system interface. Effectively, they define system programming, or at least a common subset thereof, for compliant Unix systems.

POSIX and SUS History

In the mid-1980s, the Institute of Electrical and Electronics Engineers (IEEE) spear-headed an effort to standardize system-level interfaces on Unix systems. Richard Stallman, founder of the Free Software movement, suggested the standard be named *POSIX* (pronounced *pahz-icks*), which now stands for *Portable Operating System Interface.*

The first result of this effort, issued in 1988, was IEEE Std 1003.1-1988 (POSIX 1988, for short). In 1990, the IEEE revised the POSIX standard with IEEE Std 1003.1-1990 (POSIX 1990). Optional real-time and threading support were documented in, respectively, IEEE Std 1003.1b-1993 (POSIX 1993 or POSIX.1b), and IEEE Std 1003.1c-1995 (POSIX 1995 or POSIX.1c). In 2001, the optional standards were rolled together with the base POSIX 1990, creating a single standard: IEEE Std 1003.1-2001 (POSIX 2001). The latest revision, released in December 2008, is IEEE Std 1003.1-2008 (POSIX 2008). All of the core POSIX standards are abbreviated POSIX.1, with the 2008 revision being the latest.

In the late 1980s and early 1990s, Unix system vendors were engaged in the "Unix Wars," with each struggling to define its Unix variant as *the* Unix operating system. Several major Unix vendors rallied around The Open Group, an industry consortium formed from the merging of the Open Software Foundation (OSF) and X/Open. The Open Group provides certification, white papers, and compliance testing. In the early 1990s, with the Unix Wars raging, The Open Group released the Single UNIX Specification (SUS). SUS rapidly grew in popularity, in large part due to its cost (free) versus the high cost of the POSIX standard. Today, SUS incorporates the latest POSIX standard.

The first SUS was published in 1994. This was followed by revisions in 1997 (SUSv2) and 2002 (SUSv3). The latest SUS, SUSv4, was published in 2008. SUSv4 revises and combines IEEE Std 1003.1-2008 and several other standards. Throughout this book, I will mention when system calls and other interfaces are standardized by POSIX. I mention POSIX and not SUS because the latter subsumes the former.

C Language Standards

Dennis Ritchie and Brian Kernighan's famed book, *The C Programming Language* (Prentice Hall), acted as the informal C specification for many years following its 1978 publication. This version of C came to be known as *K&R C*. C was already rapidly replacing BASIC and other languages as the lingua franca of microcomputer programming. Therefore, to standardize the by-then quite popular language, in 1983 the American National Standards Institute (ANSI) formed a committee to develop an official version of C, incorporating features and improvements from various vendors and the new C++ language. The process was long and laborious, but *ANSI C* was completed in 1989. In 1990, the International Organization for Standardization (ISO) ratified *ISO C90*, based on ANSI C with a small handful of modifications.

In 1995, the ISO released an updated (although rarely implemented) version of the C language, *ISO C95*. This was followed in 1999 with a large update to the language, *ISO C99*, that introduced many new features, including inline functions, new data types, variable-length arrays, C++-style comments, and new library functions. The latest version of the standard is *ISO C11*, the most significant feature of which is a formalized memory model, enabling the portable use of threads across platforms.

On the C++ front, ISO standardization was slow in arriving. After years of development—and forward-incompatible compiler release—the first C `standard, ISO C98`, was ratified in 1998. While it greatly improved compatibility across compilers, several aspects of the standard limited consistency and portability. *ISO C++03* arrived in 2003. It offered bug fixes to aid compiler developers but no user-visible changes. The next and most recent ISO standard, *C++11* (formerly *C++0x* in suggestion of a more optimistic release date), heralded numerous language and standard library additions and improvements—so many, in fact, that many commentators suggest C++11 is a distinct language from previous C++ revisions.

Linux and the Standards

As stated earlier, Linux aims toward POSIX and SUS compliance. It provides the interfaces documented in SUSv4 and POSIX 2008, including real-time (POSIX.1b) and threading (POSIX.1c) support. More importantly, Linux strives to behave in accordance with POSIX and SUS requirements. In general, failing to agree with the standards is considered a bug. Linux is believed to comply with POSIX.1 and SUSv3, but as no official POSIX or SUS certification has been performed (particularly on each and every revision of Linux), we cannot say that Linux is officially POSIX- or SUS-compliant.

With respect to language standards, Linux fares well. The *gcc* C compiler is ISO C99-compliant; support for C11 is ongoing. The *g++* C++ compiler is ISO C++03-compliant with support for C++11 in development. In addition, *gcc* and *g++_* implement extensions to the C and C++ languages. These extensions are collectively called *GNU C*, and are documented in Appendix A.

Linux has not had a great history of forward compatibility,[1] although these days it fares much better. Interfaces documented by standards, such as the standard C library, will obviously always remain source compatible. Binary compatibility is maintained across a given major version of *glibc*, at the very least. And as C is standardized, *gcc* will always compile legal C correctly, although *gcc*-specific extensions may be deprecated and eventually removed with new *gcc* releases. Most importantly, the Linux kernel guarantees the stability of system calls. Once a system call is implemented in a stable version of the Linux kernel, it is set in stone.

Among the various Linux distributions, the Linux Standard Base (LSB) standardizes much of the Linux system. The LSB is a joint project of several Linux vendors under the auspices of the Linux Foundation (formerly the Free Standards Group). The LSB extends POSIX and SUS, and adds several standards of its own; it attempts to provide a binary standard, allowing object code to run unmodified on compliant systems. Most Linux vendors comply with the LSB to some degree.

This Book and the Standards

This book deliberately avoids paying lip service to any of the standards. Far too frequently, Unix system programming books must stop to elaborate on how an interface behaves in one standard versus another, whether a given system call is implemented on this system versus that, and similar page-filling bloat. This book, however, is specifically about system programming on a modern Linux system, as provided by the latest versions of the Linux kernel (3.9), gcc (4.8), and C library (2.17).

As system interfaces are generally set in stone—the Linux kernel developers go to great pains to never break the system call interfaces, for example—and provide some level of both source and binary compatibility, this approach allows us to dive into the details of Linux's system interface unfettered by concerns of compatibility with numerous other Unix systems and standards. This sole focus on Linux also enables this book to offer in-depth treatment of cutting-edge Linux-specific interfaces that will remain relevant and valid far into the future. The book draws upon an intimate knowledge of Linux and of the implementation and behavior of components such as *gcc* and the kernel, to provide an insider's view full of the best practices and optimization tips of an experienced veteran.

---

1. Experienced Linux users might remember the switch from *a.out* to ELF, the switch from *libc5* to *glibc*, *gcc* changes, C++ template ABI breakages, and so on. Thankfully, those days are behind us.

Concepts of Linux Programming

This section presents a concise overview of the services provided by a Linux system. All Unix systems, Linux included, provide a mutual set of abstractions and interfaces. Indeed, these commonalities *define* Unix. Abstractions such as the file and the process, interfaces to manage pipes and sockets, and so on, are at the core of a Unix system.

This overview assumes that you are familiar with the Linux environment: I presume that you can get around in a shell, use basic commands, and compile a simple C program. This is *not* an overview of Linux or its programming environment, but rather of the foundation of Linux system programming.

Files and the Filesystem

The file is the most basic and fundamental abstraction in Linux. Linux follows the *everything-is-a-file* philosophy (although not as strictly as some other systems, such as Plan 9).[2] Consequently, much interaction occurs via reading of and writing to files, even when the object in question is not what you would consider a normal file.

In order to be accessed, a file must first be opened. Files can be opened for reading, writing, or both. An open file is referenced via a unique descriptor, a mapping from the metadata associated with the open file back to the specific file itself. Inside the Linux kernel, this descriptor is handled by an integer (of the C type int) called the *file descriptor*, abbreviated *fd*. File descriptors are shared with user space, and are used directly by user programs to access files. A large part of Linux system programming consists of opening, manipulating, closing, and otherwise using file descriptors.

Regular files

What most of us call "files" are what Linux labels *regular files*. A regular file contains bytes of data, organized into a linear array called a byte stream. In Linux, no further organization or formatting is specified for a file. The bytes may have any values, and they may be organized within the file in any way. At the system level, Linux does not enforce a structure upon files beyond the byte stream. Some operating systems, such as VMS, provide highly structured files, supporting concepts such as *records*. Linux does not.

Any of the bytes within a file may be read from or written to. These operations start at a specific byte, which is one's conceptual "location" within the file. This location is called the *file position* or *file offset*. The file position is an essential piece of the metadata that the kernel associates with each open file. When a file is first opened, the file position

---

2. Plan9, an operating system born of Bell Labs, is often called the successor to Unix. It features several innovative ideas, and is an adherent of the everything-is-a-file philosophy.

---

is zero. Usually, as bytes in the file are read from or written to, byte-by-byte, the file position increases in kind. The file position may also be set manually to a given value, even a value beyond the end of the file. Writing a byte to a file position beyond the end of the file will cause the intervening bytes to be padded with zeros. While it is possible to write bytes in this manner to a position beyond the end of the file, it is not possible to write bytes to a position before the beginning of a file. Such a practice sounds nonsensical, and, indeed, would have little use. The file position starts at zero; it cannot be negative. Writing a byte to the middle of a file overwrites the byte previously located at that offset. Thus, it is not possible to expand a file by writing into the middle of it. Most file writing occurs at the end of the file. The file position's maximum value is bounded only by the size of the C type used to store it, which is 64 bits on a modern Linux system.

The size of a file is measured in bytes and is called its *length*. The length, in other words, is simply the number of bytes in the linear array that make up the file. A file's length can be changed via an operation called *truncation*. A file can be truncated to a new size smaller than its original size, which results in bytes being removed from the end of the file. Confusingly, given the operation's name, a file can also be "truncated" to a new size larger than its original size. In that case, the new bytes (which are added to the end of the file) are filled with zeros. A file may be empty (that is, have a length of zero), and thus contain no valid bytes. The maximum file length, as with the maximum file position, is bounded only by limits on the sizes of the C types that the Linux kernel uses to manage files. Specific filesystems, however, may impose their own restrictions, imposing a smaller ceiling on the maximum length.

A single file can be opened more than once, by a different or even the same process. Each open instance of a file is given a unique file descriptor. Conversely, processes can share their file descriptors, allowing a single descriptor to be used by more than one process. The kernel does not impose any restrictions on concurrent file access. Multiple processes are free to read from and write to the same file at the same time. The results of such concurrent accesses rely on the ordering of the individual operations, and are generally unpredictable. User-space programs typically must coordinate amongst themselves to ensure that concurrent file accesses are properly synchronized.

Although files are usually accessed via *filenames*, they actually are not directly associated with such names. Instead, a file is referenced by an *inode* (originally short for *information node*), which is assigned an integer value unique to the filesystem (but not necessarily unique across the whole system). This value is called the *inode number*, often abbreviated as *i-number* or *ino*. An inode stores metadata associated with a file, such as its modification timestamp, owner, type, length, and the location of the file's data—but no filename! The inode is both a physical object, located on disk in Unix-style filesystems, and a conceptual entity, represented by a data structure in the Linux kernel.

Directories and links

Accessing a file via its inode number is cumbersome (and also a potential security hole), so files are always opened from user space by a name, not an inode number. *Directories* are used to provide the names with which to access files. A directory acts as a mapping of human-readable names to inode numbers. A name and inode pair is called a *link*. The physical on-disk form of this mapping—for example, a simple table or a hash—is implemented and managed by the kernel code that supports a given filesystem. Conceptually, a directory is viewed like any normal file, with the difference that it contains only a mapping of names to inodes. The kernel directly uses this mapping to perform name-to-inode resolutions.

When a user-space application requests that a given filename be opened, the kernel opens the directory containing the filename and searches for the given name. From the filename, the kernel obtains the inode number. From the inode number, the inode is found. The inode contains metadata associated with the file, including the on-disk location of the file's data.

Initially, there is only one directory on the disk, the *root directory*. This directory is usually denoted by the path /. But, as we all know, there are typically many directories on a system. How does the kernel know *which* directory to look in to find a given filename?

As mentioned previously, directories are much like regular files. Indeed, they even have associated inodes. Consequently, the links inside of directories can point to the inodes of other directories. This means directories can nest inside of other directories, forming a hierarchy of directories. This, in turn, allows for the use of the *pathnames* with which all Unix users are familiar—for example, */home/blackbeard/concorde.png*.

When the kernel is asked to open a pathname like this, it walks each *directory entry* (called a *dentry* inside of the kernel) in the pathname to find the inode of the next entry. In the preceding example, the kernel starts at /, gets the inode for *home*, goes there, gets the inode for *blackbeard*, runs there, and finally gets the inode for *concorde.png*. This operation is called *directory* or *pathname resolution*. The Linux kernel also employs a cache, called the *dentry cache*, to store the results of directory resolutions, providing for speedier lookups in the future given temporal locality.[3]

A pathname that starts at the root directory is said to be *fully qualified*, and is called an *absolute pathname*. Some pathnames are not fully qualified; instead, they are provided relative to some other directory (for example, *todo/plunder*). These paths are called *relative pathnames*. When provided with a relative pathname, the kernel begins the pathname resolution in the *current working directory*. From the current working

---

3. *Temporal locality* is the high likelihood of an access to a particular resource being followed by another access to the same resource. Many resources on a computer exhibit temporal locality.

directory, the kernel looks up the directory *todo*. From there, the kernel gets the inode for *plunder*. Together, the combination of a relative pathname and the current working directory is fully qualified.

Although directories are treated like normal files, the kernel does not allow them to be opened and manipulated like regular files. Instead, they must be manipulated using a special set of system calls. These system calls allow for the adding and removing of links, which are the only two sensible operations anyhow. If user space were allowed to manipulate directories without the kernel's mediation, it would be too easy for a single simple error to corrupt the filesystem.

Hard links

Conceptually, nothing covered thus far would prevent multiple names resolving to the same inode. Indeed, this is allowed. When multiple links map different names to the same inode, we call them *hard links*.

Hard links allow for complex filesystem structures with multiple pathnames pointing to the same data. The hard links can be in the same directory, or in two or more different directories. In either case, the kernel simply resolves the pathname to the correct inode. For example, a specific inode that points to a specific chunk of data can be hard linked from */home/bluebeard/treasure.txt* and */home/blackbeard/to_steal.txt*.

Deleting a file involves *unlinking* it from the directory structure, which is done simply by removing its name and inode pair from a directory. Because Linux supports hard links, however, the filesystem cannot destroy the inode and its associated data on every unlink operation. What if another hard link existed elsewhere in the filesystem? To ensure that a file is not destroyed until *all* links to it are removed, each inode contains a *link count* that keeps track of the number of links within the filesystem that point to it. When a pathname is unlinked, the link count is decremented by one; only when it reaches zero are the inode and its associated data actually removed from the filesystem.

Symbolic links

Hard links cannot span filesystems because an inode number is meaningless outside of the inode's own filesystem. To allow links that can span filesystems, and that are a bit simpler and less transparent, Unix systems also implement *symbolic links* (often shortened to *symlinks*).

Symbolic links look like regular files. A symlink has its own inode and data chunk, which contains the complete pathname of the linked-to file. This means symbolic links can point anywhere, including to files and directories that reside on different filesystems, and even to files and directories that do not exist. A symbolic link that points to a nonexistent file is called a *broken link*.

Symbolic links incur more overhead than hard links because resolving a symbolic link effectively involves resolving two files: the symbolic link and then the linked-to file. Hard links do not incur this additional overhead—there is no difference between accessing a file linked into the filesystem more than once and one linked only once. The overhead of symbolic links is minimal, but it is still considered a negative.

Symbolic links are also more opaque than hard links. Using hard links is entirely transparent; in fact, it takes effort to find out that a file is linked more than once! Manipulating symbolic links, on the other hand, requires special system calls. This lack of transparency is often considered a positive, as the link structure is explicitly made plain, with symbolic links acting more as *shortcuts* than as filesystem-internal links.

Special files

Special files are kernel objects that are represented as files. Over the years, Unix systems have supported a handful of different special files. Linux supports four: block device files, character device files, named pipes, and Unix domain sockets. Special files are a way to let certain abstractions fit into the filesystem, continuing the everything-is-a-file paradigm. Linux provides a system call to create a special file.

Device access in Unix systems is performed via device files, which act and look like normal files residing on the filesystem. Device files may be opened, read from, and written to, allowing user space to access and manipulate devices (both physical and virtual) on the system. Unix devices are generally broken into two groups: *character devices* and *block devices*. Each type of device has its own special device file.

A character device is accessed as a linear queue of bytes. The device driver places bytes onto the queue, one by one, and user space reads the bytes in the order that they were placed on the queue. A keyboard is an example of a character device. If the user types "peg," for example, an application would want to read from the keyboard device the *p*, the *e*, and, finally, the *g*, in exactly that order. When there are no more characters left to read, the device returns end-of-file (EOF). Missing a character, or reading them in any other order, would make little sense. Character devices are accessed via *character device files*.

A block device, in contrast, is accessed as an array of bytes. The device driver maps the bytes over a seekable device, and user space is free to access any valid bytes in the array, in any order—it might read byte 12, then byte 7, and then byte 12 again. Block devices are generally storage devices. Hard disks, floppy drives, CD-ROM drives, and flash memory are all examples of block devices. They are accessed via *block device files*.

Named pipes (often called *FIFOs*, short for "first in, first out") are an *interprocess communication (IPC)* mechanism that provides a communication channel over a file descriptor, accessed via a special file. Regular pipes are the method used to "pipe" the output of one program into the input of another; they are created in memory via a system call and do not exist on any filesystem. Named pipes act like regular pipes but are accessed via a file, called a *FIFO special file*. Unrelated processes can access this file and communicate.

Sockets are the final type of special file. Sockets are an advanced form of IPC that allow for communication between two different processes, not only on the same machine, but even on two different machines. In fact, sockets form the basis of network and Internet programming. They come in multiple varieties, including the Unix domain socket, which is the form of socket used for communication within the local machine. Whereas sockets communicating over the Internet might use a hostname and port pair for identifying the target of communication, Unix domain sockets use a special file residing on a filesystem, often simply called a socket file.

Filesystems and namespaces

Linux, like all Unix systems, provides a global and unified *namespace* of files and directories. Some operating systems separate different disks and drives into separate namespaces—for example, a file on a floppy disk might be accessible via the pathname *A:\plank.jpg*, while the hard drive is located at *C:*. In Unix, that same file on a floppy might be accessible via the pathname */media/floppy/plank.jpg* or even via */home/captain/stuff/plank.jpg*, right alongside files from other media. That is, on Unix, the namespace is unified.

A *filesystem* is a collection of files and directories in a formal and valid hierarchy. Filesystems may be individually added to and removed from the global namespace of files and directories. These operations are called *mounting* and *unmounting*. Each filesystem is mounted to a specific location in the namespace, known as a *mount point*. The root directory of the filesystem is then accessible at this mount point. For example, a CD might be mounted at */media/cdrom*, making the root of the filesystem on the CD accessible at */media/cdrom*. The first filesystem mounted is located in the root of the namespace, /, and is called the *root filesystem*. Linux systems always have a root filesystem. Mounting other filesystems at other mount points is optional.

Filesystems usually exist physically (i.e., are stored on disk), although Linux also supports *virtual filesystems* that exist only in memory, and *network filesystems* that exist on machines across the network. Physical filesystems reside on block storage devices, such as CDs, floppy disks, compact flash cards, or hard drives. Some such devices are *partionable*, which means that they can be divided up into multiple filesystems, all of which can be manipulated individually. Linux supports a wide range of filesystems—certainly anything that the average user might hope to come across—including media-specific filesystems (for example, ISO9660), network filesystems (*NFS*), native filesystems (*ext4*), filesystems from other Unix systems (*XFS*), and even filesystems from non-Unix systems (*FAT*).

The smallest addressable unit on a block device is the *sector*. The sector is a physical attribute of the device. Sectors come in various powers of two, with 512 bytes being quite common. A block device cannot transfer or access a unit of data smaller than a sector and all I/O must occur in terms of one or more sectors.

Likewise, the smallest logically addressable unit on a filesystem is the *block*. The block is an abstraction of the filesystem, not of the physical media on which the filesystem resides. A block is usually a power-of-two multiple of the sector size. In Linux, blocks are generally larger than the sector, but they must be smaller than the *page size* (the smallest unit addressable by the *memory management unit*, a hardware component).[4] Common block sizes are 512 bytes, 1 kilobyte, and 4 kilobytes.

Historically, Unix systems have only a single shared namespace, viewable by all users and all processes on the system. Linux takes an innovative approach and supports *per-process namespaces*, allowing each process to optionally have a unique view of the system's file and directory hierarchy.[5] By default, each process inherits the namespace of its parent, but a process may elect to create its own namespace with its own set of mount points and a unique root directory.

Processes

If files are the most fundamental abstraction in a Unix system, processes are the runner up. Processes are object code in execution: active, running programs. But they're more than just object code—processes consist of data, resources, state, and a virtualized computer.

Processes begin life as executable object code, which is machine-runnable code in an executable format that the kernel understands. The format most common in Linux is called *Executable and Linkable Format* (*ELF*). The executable format contains metadata, and multiple *sections* of code and data. Sections are linear chunks of the object code that load into linear chunks of memory. All bytes in a section are treated the same, given the same permissions, and generally used for similar purposes.

The most important and common sections are the *text section*, the *data section*, and the *bss section*. The text section contains executable code and read-only data, such as constant variables, and is typically marked read-only and executable. The data section contains initialized data, such as C variables with defined values, and is typically marked readable and writable. The bss section contains uninitialized global data. Because the C standard dictates default values for global C variables that are essentially all zeros, there is no need to store the zeros in the object code on disk. Instead, the object code can simply list the uninitialized variables in the bss section, and the kernel can map the *zero page* (a page of all zeros) over the section when it is loaded into memory. The bss section was conceived solely as an optimization for this purpose. The name is a historic relic;

---

4. This is an artificial kernel limitation in the name of simplicity which may go away in the future.

5. This approach was first pioneered by Bell Labs' Plan 9.

---

it stands for *block started by symbol*. Other common sections in ELF executables are the *absolute section* (which contains nonrelocatable symbols) and the *undefined section* (a catchall).

A process is also associated with various system resources, which are arbitrated and managed by the kernel. Processes typically request and manipulate resources only through system calls. Resources include timers, pending signals, open files, network connections, hardware, and IPC mechanisms. A process's resources, along with data and statistics related to the process, are stored inside the kernel in the process's *process descriptor*.

A process is a virtualization abstraction. The Linux kernel, supporting both preemptive multitasking and virtual memory, provides every process both a virtualized processor and a virtualized view of memory. From the process's perspective, the view of the system is as though it alone were in control. That is, even though a given process may be scheduled alongside many other processes, it runs as though it has sole control of the system. The kernel seamlessly and transparently preempts and reschedules processes, sharing the system's processors among all running processes. Processes never know the difference. Similarly, each process is afforded a single linear address space, as if it alone were in control of all of the memory in the system. Through virtual memory and paging, the kernel allows many processes to coexist on the system, each operating in a different address space. The kernel manages this virtualization through hardware support provided by modern processors, allowing the operating system to concurrently manage the state of multiple independent processes.

Threads

Each process consists of one or more *threads of execution* (usually simplified to *threads*). A thread is the unit of activity within a process. In other words, a thread is the abstraction responsible for executing code and maintaining the process's running state.

Most processes consist of only a single thread; they are called *single-threaded*. Processes that contain multiple threads are said to be *multithreaded*. Traditionally, Unix programs have been single-threaded, owing to Unix's historic simplicity, fast process creation times, and robust IPC mechanisms, all of which mitigate the desire for threads.

A thread consists of a *stack* (which stores its local variables, just as the process stack does on nonthreaded systems), processor state, and a current location in the object code (usually stored in the processor's *instruction pointer*). The majority of the remaining parts of a process are shared among all threads, most notably the process address space. In this manner, threads share the virtual memory abstraction while maintaining the virtualized processor abstraction.

Internally, the Linux kernel implements a unique view of threads: they are simply normal processes that happen to share some resources. In user space, Linux implements threads in accordance with POSIX 1003.1c (known as *Pthreads*). The name of the current Linux thread implementation, which is part of *glibc*, is the *Native POSIX Threading Library* (*NPTL*). We'll discuss threads more in Chapter 7.

Process hierarchy

Each process is identified by a unique positive integer called the *process ID* (pid). The pid of the first process is 1, and each subsequent process receives a new, unique pid.

In Linux, processes form a strict hierarchy, known as the *process tree*. The process tree is rooted at the first process, known as the *init process*, which is typically the *init* program. New processes are created via the fork() system call. This system call creates a duplicate of the calling process. The original process is called the *parent*; the new process is called the *child*. Every process except the first has a parent. If a parent process terminates before its child, the kernel will *reparent* the child to the init process.

When a process terminates, it is not immediately removed from the system. Instead, the kernel keeps parts of the process resident in memory to allow the process's parent to inquire about its status upon terminating. This inquiry is known as *waiting on* the terminated process. Once the parent process has waited on its terminated child, the child is fully destroyed. A process that has terminated, but has not yet been waited upon, is called a *zombie*. The init process routinely waits on all of its children, ensuring that reparented processes do not remain zombies forever.

Users and Groups

Authorization in Linux is provided by *users* and *groups*. Each user is associated with a unique positive integer called the *user ID* (uid). Each process is in turn associated with exactly one uid, which identifies the user running the process, and is called the process's *real uid*. Inside the Linux kernel, the uid is the only concept of a user. Users, however, refer to themselves and other users through *usernames*, not numerical values. Usernames and their corresponding uids are stored in */etc/passwd*, and library routines map user-supplied usernames to the corresponding uids.

During login, the user provides a username and password to the *login* program. If given a valid username and the correct password, the *login* program spawns the user's *login shell*, which is also specified in */etc/passwd*, and makes the shell's uid equal to that of the user. Child processes inherit the uids of their parents.

The uid 0 is associated with a special user known as *root*. The root user has special privileges, and can do almost anything on the system. For example, only the root user can change a process's uid. Consequently, the *login* program runs as root.

In addition to the real uid, each process also has an *effective uid*, a *saved uid*, and a *filesystem uid*. While the real uid is always that of the user who started the process, the effective uid may change under various rules to allow a process to execute with the rights of different users. The saved uid stores the original effective uid; its value is used in deciding what effective uid values the user may switch to. The filesystem uid, which is usually equal to the effective uid, is used for verifying filesystem access.

Each user belongs to one or more groups, including a *primary* or *login group*, listed in */etc/passwd*, and possibly a number of *supplemental groups*, listed in */etc/group*. Each process is therefore also associated with a corresponding *group ID* (gid), and has a *real gid*, an *effective gid*, a *saved gid*, and a *filesystem gid*. Processes are generally associated with a user's login group, not any of the supplemental groups.

Certain security checks allow processes to perform certain operations only if they meet specific criteria. Historically, Unix has made this decision very black-and-white: processes with uid 0 had access, while no others did. Recently, Linux has replaced this security system with a more general *capabilities* system. Instead of a simple binary check, capabilities allow the kernel to base access on much more fine-grained settings.

Permissions

The standard file permission and security mechanism in Linux is the same as that in historic Unix.

Each file is associated with an owning user, an owning group, and three sets of permission bits. The bits describe the ability of the owning user, the owning group, and everybody else to read, write, and execute the file; there are three bits for each of the three classes, making nine bits in total. The owners and the permissions are stored in the file's inode.

For regular files, the permissions are rather obvious: they specify the ability to open a file for reading, open a file for writing, or execute a file. Read and write permissions are the same for special files as for regular files, although what exactly is read or written is up to the special file in question. Execute permissions are ignored on special files. For directories, read permission allows the contents of the directory to be listed, write permission allows new links to be added inside the directory, and execute permission allows the directory to be entered and used in a pathname. Table 1-1 lists each of the nine permission bits, their octal values (a popular way of representing the nine bits), their text values (as *ls* might show them), and their corresponding meanings.

Table 1-1. Permission bits and their values

Bit	Octal value	Text value	Corresponding permission
8	400	r--------	Owner may read
7	200	-w-------	Owner may write
6	100	--x------	Owner may execute
5	040	---r-----	Group may read
4	020	----w----	Group may write
3	010	-----x---	Group may execute

Bit	Octal value	Text value	Corresponding permission
2	004	- - - - - - r - -	Everyone else may read
1	002	- - - - - - - w -	Everyone else may write
0	001	- - - - - - - - x	Everyone else may execute

In addition to historic Unix permissions, Linux also supports access control lists (ACLs). ACLs allow for much more detailed and exacting permission and security controls, at the cost of increased complexity and on-disk storage.

Signals

Signals are a mechanism for one-way asynchronous notifications. A signal may be sent from the kernel to a process, from a process to another process, or from a process to itself. Signals typically alert a process to some event, such as a segmentation fault or the user pressing Ctrl-C.

The Linux kernel implements about 30 signals (the exact number is architecture-dependent). Each signal is represented by a numeric constant and a textual name. For example, SIGHUP, used to signal that a terminal hangup has occurred, has a value of 1 on the x86-64 architecture.

Signals *interrupt* an executing process, causing it to stop whatever it is doing and immediately perform a predetermined action. With the exception of SIGKILL (which always terminates the process), and SIGSTOP (which always stops the process), processes may control what happens when they receive a signal. They can accept the default action, which may be to terminate the process, terminate and coredump the process, stop the process, or do nothing, depending on the signal. Alternatively, processes can elect to explicitly ignore or handle signals. Ignored signals are silently dropped. Handled signals cause the execution of a user-supplied *signal handler* function. The program jumps to this function as soon as the signal is received. When the signal handler returns, the control of the program resumes at the previously interrupted instruction. Because of the asynchrony of signals, signal handlers must take care not to stomp on the code that was interrupted, by executing only *async-safe* (also called *signal-safe*) functions.

Interprocess Communication

Allowing processes to exchange information and notify each other of events is one of an operating system's most important jobs. The Linux kernel implements most of the historic Unix IPC mechanisms—including those defined and standardized by both System V and POSIX—as well as implementing a mechanism or two of its own.

IPC mechanisms supported by Linux include pipes, named pipes, semaphores, message queues, shared memory, and futexes.

Headers

Linux system programming revolves around a handful of headers. Both the kernel itself and *glibc* provide the headers used in system-level programming. These headers include the standard C fare (for example, `<string.h>`), and the usual Unix offerings (say, `<unistd.h>`).

Error Handling

It goes without saying that checking for and handling errors are of paramount importance. In system programming, an error is signified via a function's return value and described via a special variable, `errno`. *glibc* transparently provides `errno` support for both library and system calls. The vast majority of interfaces covered in this book will use this mechanism to communicate errors.

Functions notify the caller of errors via a special return value, which is usually –1 (the exact value used depends on the function). The error value alerts the caller to the occurrence of an error but provides no insight into why the error occurred. The `errno` variable is used to find the cause of the error.

This variable is declared in `<errno.h>` as follows:

```
extern int errno;
```

Its value is valid only immediately after an `errno`-setting function indicates an error (usually by returning –1), as it is legal for the variable to be modified during the successful execution of a function.

The `errno` variable may be read or written directly; it is a modifiable lvalue. The value of `errno` maps to the textual description of a specific error. A preprocessor `#define` also maps to the numeric `errno` value. For example, the preprocessor define `EACCES` equals 1, and represents "permission denied." See Table 1-2 for a listing of the standard defines and the matching error descriptions.

Table 1-2. Errors and their descriptions

Preprocessor define	Description
E2BIG	Argument list too long
EACCES	Permission denied
EAGAIN	Try again
EBADF	Bad file number
EBUSY	Device or resource busy
ECHILD	No child processes
EDOM	Math argument outside of domain of function
EEXIST	File already exists

Preprocessor define	Description
EFAULT	Bad address
EFBIG	File too large
EINTR	System call was interrupted
EINVAL	Invalid argument
EIO	I/O error
EISDIR	Is a directory
EMFILE	Too many open files
EMLINK	Too many links
ENFILE	File table overflow
ENODEV	No such device
ENOENT	No such file or directory
ENOEXEC	Exec format error
ENOMEM	Out of memory
ENOSPC	No space left on device
ENOTDIR	Not a directory
ENOTTY	Inappropriate I/O control operation
ENXIO	No such device or address
EPERM	Operation not permitted
EPIPE	Broken pipe
ERANGE	Result too large
EROFS	Read-only filesystem
ESPIPE	Invalid seek
ESRCH	No such process
ETXTBSY	Text file busy
EXDEV	Improper link

The C library provides a handful of functions for translating an errno value to the corresponding textual representation. This is needed only for error reporting, and the like; checking and handling errors can be done using the preprocessor defines and errno directly.

The first such function is perror():

```
#include <stdio.h>

void perror (const char *str);
```

This function prints to *stderr* (standard error) the string representation of the current error described by errno, prefixed by the string pointed at by str, followed by a colon. To be useful, the name of the function that failed should be included in the string. For example:

```
if (close (fd) == -1)
        perror ("close");
```

The C library also provides strerror() and strerror_r(), prototyped as:

```
#include <string.h>

char * strerror (int errnum);
```

and:

```
#include <string.h>

int strerror_r (int errnum, char *buf, size_t len);
```

The former function returns a pointer to a string describing the error given by errnum. The string may not be modified by the application but can be modified by subsequent perror() and strerror() calls. Thus, it is not thread-safe.

The strerror_r() function is thread-safe. It fills the buffer of length len pointed at by buf. A call to strerror_r() returns 0 on success, and –1 on failure. Humorously, it sets errno on error.

For a few functions, the entire range of the return type is a legal return value. In those cases, errno must be zeroed before invocation and checked afterward (these functions promise to only return a nonzero errno on actual error). For example:

```
errno = 0;
arg = strtoul (buf, NULL, 0);
if (errno)
        perror ("strtoul");
```

A common mistake in checking errno is to forget that any library or system call can modify it. For example, this code is buggy:

```
if (fsync (fd) == -1) {
        fprintf (stderr, "fsync failed!\n");
        if (errno == EIO)
                fprintf (stderr, "I/O error on %d!\n", fd);
}
```

If you need to preserve the value of errno across function invocations, save it:

```
if (fsync (fd) == -1) {
        const int err = errno;
        fprintf (stderr, "fsync failed: %s\n", strerror (errno));
        if (err == EIO) {
                /* if the error is I/O-related, jump ship */
                fprintf (stderr, "I/O error on %d!\n", fd);
                exit (EXIT_FAILURE);
        }
}
```

In single-threaded programs, errno is a global variable, as shown earlier in this section. In multithreaded programs, however, errno is stored per-thread, and is thus thread-safe.

Getting Started with System Programming

This chapter looked at the fundamentals of Linux system programming and provided a programmer's overview of the Linux system. The next chapter discusses basic file I/O. This includes, of course, reading from and writing to files; however, because Linux implements many interfaces as files, file I/O is crucial to a lot more than just, well, files.

With the preliminaries behind us, it is time to dive into actual system programming. Let's go!

## CHAPTER 2

File I/O

This and the subsequent three chapters cover files. Because so much of a Unix system is represented as files, these chapters discuss the crux of a Unix system. This chapter covers the basics of file I/O, detailing the system calls that comprise the simplest and most common ways to interact with files. The next chapter covers standard I/O from the standard C library; Chapter 4 continues the coverage with a treatment of the more advanced and specialized file I/O interfaces. Chapter 8 rounds out the discussion by addressing the topic of file and directory manipulation.

Before a file can be read from or written to, it must be opened. The kernel maintains a per-process list of open files, called the *file table*. This table is indexed via nonnegative integers known as *file descriptors* (often abbreviated *fds*). Each entry in the list contains information about an open file, including a pointer to an in-memory copy of the file's backing inode and associated metadata, such as the file position and access modes. Both user space and kernel space use file descriptors as unique cookies: opening a file returns a file descriptor, while subsequent operations (reading, writing, and so on) take the file descriptor as their primary argument.

File descriptors are represented by the C int type. Not using a special type is often considered odd, but is, historically, the Unix way. Each Linux process has a maximum number of files that it may open. File descriptors start at 0 and go up to one less than this maximum value. By default, the maximum is 1,024, but it can be configured as high as 1,048,576. Because negative values are not legal file descriptors, –1 is often used to indicate an error from a function that would otherwise return a valid file descriptor.

Unless the process explicitly closes them, every process by convention has at least three file descriptors open: 0, 1, and 2. File descriptor 0 is *standard in* (*stdin*), file descriptor 1 is *standard out* (*stdout*), and file descriptor 2 is *standard error* (*stderr*). Instead of referencing these integers directly, the C library provides the preprocessor defines STDIN_FILENO, STDOUT_FILENO, and STDERR_FILENO, respectively. Normally, stdin is connected to the terminal's input device (usually the user's keyboard) and stdout and stderr are connected to the terminal's display. Users can *redirect* these standard file descriptors and even pipe the output of one program into the input of another. This is how the shell implements redirections and pipes.

File descriptors can reference more than just regular files. Indeed, file descriptors are used for accessing device files and pipes, directories and futexes, FIFOs and sockets—following the everything-is-a-file philosophy, just about anything you can read or write is accessible via a file descriptor.

By default, a child process receives a copy of its parent's file table. The list of open files and their access modes, current file positions, and other metadata are the same, but a change in one process—say, the child closing a file—does not affect the other process's file table. While this is the typical behavior, as you'll see in Chapter 5, it is possible for the child and parent to share the parent's file table (as threads do).

Opening Files

The most basic method of accessing a file is via the read() and write() system calls. Before a file can be accessed, however, it must be opened via an open() or creat() call. Once done using the file, it should be closed using the system call close().

The open() System Call

A file is opened and a file descriptor is obtained with the open() system call:

```
#include <sys/types.h>
#include <sys/stat.h>
#include <fcntl.h>

int open (const char *name, int flags);
int open (const char *name, int flags, mode_t mode);
```

The open() system call maps the file given by the pathname name to a file descriptor, which it returns on success. The file position is to the start of the file (zero) and the file is opened for access according to the flags given by flags.

Flags for open()

The flags argument is the bitwise-OR of one or more flags. It must contain an access mode, which is one of O_RDONLY, O_WRONLY, or O_RDWR. Respectively, these arguments request that the file be opened only for reading, only for writing, or for both reading and writing.

For example, the following code opens */home/kidd/madagascar* for reading:

```
int fd;

fd = open ("/home/kidd/madagascar", O_RDONLY);
```

```
if (fd == -1)
        /* error */
```

A file opened only for reading *cannot* be written to, and vice versa. The process issuing the open() system call must have sufficient permissions to obtain the access requested. For example, if a file is read-only to a given user, then a process owned by that user can open that file O_RDONLY but not O_WRONLY or O_RDWR.

On top of the access mode, the flags argument may be bitwise-ORed with zero or more of the following values, modifying the behavior of the open request:

O_APPEND
> The file will be opened in *append mode*. That is, before each write, the file position will be updated to point to the end of the file. This occurs even if another process has written to the file after the issuing process's last write, thereby changing the file position (see "Append Mode" on page 38).

O_ASYNC
> A signal (SIGIO by default) will be generated when the specified file becomes readable or writable. This flag is available only for FIFOs, pipes, sockets, and terminals, not for regular files.

O_CLOEXEC
> Sets the close-on-exec flag on the opened file. Upon executing a new process, the file will automatically be closed. This obviates needing to call fcntl() to set the flag and eliminates a race condition. This flag is only available in Linux kernel 2.6.23 and later.

O_CREAT
> If the file denoted by name does not exist, the kernel will create it. If the file already exists, this flag has no effect unless O_EXCL is also given.

O_DIRECT
> The file will be opened for direct I/O (see "Direct I/O" on page 45).

O_DIRECTORY
> If name is not a directory, the call to open() will fail. This flag is used internally by the opendir() library call.

O_EXCL
> When given with O_CREAT, this flag will cause the call to open() to fail if the file given by name already exists. This is used to prevent race conditions on file creation. If O_CREAT is not also provided, this flag has no meaning.

O_LARGEFILE
> The given file will be opened using 64-bit offsets, allowing the manipulation of files larger than two gigabytes. This is implied on 64-bit architectures.

O_NOATIME+

The given file's last access time is not updated upon read. This flag is useful for backup, indexing, and similar programs that read every file on a system, to prevent significant write activity resulting from updating the inodes of each read file. This flag is only available in Linux kernel 2.6.8 and later.

O_NOCTTY

If the given name refers to a terminal device (say, */dev/tty*), it will not become the process's controlling terminal, even if the process does not currently have a controlling terminal. This flag is not frequently used.

O_NOFOLLOW

If name is a symbolic link, the call to open( ) will fail. Normally, the link is resolved, and the target file is opened. If other components in the given path are links, the call will still succeed. For example, if name is */etc/ship/plank.txt*, the call will fail if *plank.txt* is a symbolic link. It will succeed, however, if *etc* or *ship* is a symbolic link, so long as *plank.txt* is not.

O_NONBLOCK

If possible, the file will be opened in nonblocking mode. Neither the open( ) call, nor any other operation will cause the process to block (sleep) on the I/O. This behavior may be defined only for FIFOs.

O_SYNC

The file will be opened for synchronous I/O. No write operation will complete until the data has been physically written to disk; normal read operations are already synchronous, so this flag has no effect on reads. POSIX additionally defines O_DSYNC and O_RSYNC; on Linux, these flags are synonymous with O_SYNC (see "The O_SYNC Flag" on page 43).

O_TRUNC

If the file exists, it is a regular file, and the given flags allow for writing, the file will be truncated to zero length. Use of O_TRUNC on a FIFO or terminal device is ignored. Use on other file types is undefined. Specifying O_TRUNC with O_RDONLY is also undefined, as you need write access to the file in order to truncate it.

For example, the following code opens for writing the file */home/teach/pearl*. If the file already exists, it will be truncated to a length of zero. Because the O_CREAT flag is not specified, if the file does not exist, the call will fail:

```
int fd;

fd = open ("/home/teach/pearl", O_WRONLY | O_TRUNC);
if (fd == -1)
        /* error */
```

Owners of New Files

Determining which user owns a new file is straightforward: the uid of the file's owner is the effective uid of the process creating the file.

Determining the owning group is more complicated. The default behavior is to set the file's group to the effective gid of the process creating the file. This is the System V behavior, which is the behavioral model for much of Linux, and thus the standard Linux *modus operandi*.

To be difficult, however, BSD defined its own behavior: the file's group is set to the gid of the parent directory. This behavior is available on Linux via a mount-time option[1]— it is also the behavior that will occur on Linux by default if the file's parent directory has the set group ID (setgid) bit set. Although most Linux systems will use the System V behavior (where new files receive the gid of the creating process), the possibility of the BSD behavior (where new files receive the gid of the parent directory) implies that code that strongly cares about a newly created file's owning group needs to manually set said group via the fchown() system call (see Chapter 8).

Thankfully, you often need not care what group owns a file.

Permissions of New Files

Both of the previously given forms of the open() system call are valid. The mode argument is ignored unless a file is created; it is required if O_CREAT is given. If you forget to provide the mode argument when using O_CREAT, the results are undefined and often quite ugly—so don't forget!

When a file is created, the mode argument provides the permissions of the newly created file. The mode is not checked on this particular open of the file, so you can perform operations that contradict the assigned permissions, such as opening the file for writing but assigning the file read-only permissions.

The mode argument is the familiar Unix permission bitset, such as octal 0644 (owner can read and write, everyone else can only read). Technically speaking, POSIX says the exact values are implementation-specific, allowing different Unix systems to lay out the permission bits however they desired. Every Unix system, however, has implemented the permission bits in the same way. Thus, while technically nonportable, specifying 0644 or 0700 will have the same effect on any system you are likely to come across.

Nonetheless, to compensate for the nonportability of bit positions in the mode, POSIX introduced the following set of constants that may be binary-ORed together and supplied for the mode argument:

---

1. The mount options bsdgroups or sysvgroups.

S_IRWXU
> Owner has read, write, and execute permission.

S_IRUSR
> Owner has read permission.

S_IWUSR
> Owner has write permission.

S_IXUSR
> Owner has execute permission.

S_IRWXG
> Group has read, write, and execute permission.

S_IRGRP
> Group has read permission.

S_IWGRP
> Group has write permission.

S_IXGRP
> Group has execute permission.

S_IRWXO
> Everyone else has read, write, and execute permission.

S_IROTH
> Everyone else has read permission.

S_IWOTH
> Everyone else has write permission.

S_IXOTH
> Everyone else has execute permission.

The actual permission bits that hit the disk are determined by binary-ANDing the mode argument with the complement of the user's *file creation mask* (*umask*). The umask is a process-specific attribute that is usually set via the login shell but is modifiable by the umask() call, allowing the user to modify the permissions placed on newly created files and directories. The bits in the umask are turned *off* in the mode argument given to open(). Thus, the usual umask of 022 would cause a mode argument of 0666 to become 0644. As a system programmer, you normally do not take into consideration the umask when setting permissions—the umask exists to allow users to limit the permissions that their programs set on new files.

As an example, the following code opens the file given by `file` for writing. If the file does not exist, assuming a umask of 022, it is created with the permissions 0644 (even though the `mode` argument specifies 0664). If it does exist, it is truncated to zero length:

```
int fd;

fd = open (file, O_WRONLY | O_CREAT | O_TRUNC,
           S_IWUSR | S_IRUSR | S_IWGRP | S_IRGRP | S_IROTH);
if (fd == -1)
        /* error */
```

Trading portability (in theory at least) for readability, we could have written the following, to identical effect :

```
int fd;

fd = open (file, O_WRONLY | O_CREAT | O_TRUNC, 0664);
if (fd == -1)
        /* error */
```

The creat() Function

The combination of `O_WRONLY | O_CREAT | O_TRUNC` is so common that a system call exists to provide just that behavior:

```
#include <sys/types.h>
#include <sys/stat.h>
#include <fcntl.h>

int creat (const char *name, mode_t mode);
```

 Yes, this function's name is missing an *e*. Ken Thompson, the creator of Unix, once joked that the missing letter was his largest regret in the design of Unix.

The following typical `creat()` call,

```
int fd;

fd = creat (filename, 0644);
if (fd == -1)
        /* error */
```

is identical to

```
int fd;

fd = open (filename, O_WRONLY | O_CREAT | O_TRUNC, 0644);
if (fd == -1)
        /* error */
```

On most Linux architectures,[2] `creat()` is a system call, even though it can be implemented in user space as simply:

```
int creat (const char *name, int mode)
{
        return open (name, O_WRONLY | O_CREAT | O_TRUNC, mode);
}
```

This duplication is a historic relic from when `open()` had only two arguments. Today, `creat()` remains a system call for backward compatibility. New architectures can implement `creat()` as a library call invoking `open()` as shown.

Return Values and Error Codes

Both `open()` and `creat()` return a file descriptor on success. On error, both return −1, and set `errno` to an appropriate error value (Chapter 1 discussed `errno` and listed the potential error values). Handling an error on file open is not complicated, as generally there will have been few or no steps performed prior to the open that need to be undone. A typical response would be prompting the user for a different filename or simply terminating the program.

Reading via read()

Now that you know how to open a file, let's look at how to read it. In the following section, we will examine writing.

The most basic—and common—mechanism used for reading is the `read()` system call, defined in POSIX.1:

```
#include <unistd.h>

ssize_t read (int fd, void *buf, size_t len);
```

Each call reads up to `len` bytes into the memory pointed at by `buf` from the current file offset of the file referenced by `fd`. On success, the number of bytes written into `buf` is returned. On error, the call returns −1 and sets `errno`. The file position is advanced by the number of bytes read from `fd`. If the object represented by `fd` is not capable of seeking (for example, a character device file), the read always occurs from the "current" position.

Basic usage is simple. This example reads from the file descriptor `fd` into `word`. The number of bytes read is equal to the size of the `unsigned long` type, which (for Linux

---

2. Recall that system calls are defined on a per-architecture basis. Thus, while x86-64 has a `creat()` system call, Alpha does not. You can use `creat()` on any architecture, of course, but it may be a library function instead of having its own system call.

at least) is 4 bytes on 32-bit Linux systems, and 8 bytes on 64-bit systems. On return, nr contains the number of bytes read, or –1 on error:

```
unsigned long word;
ssize_t nr;

/* read a couple bytes into 'word' from 'fd' */
nr = read (fd, &word, sizeof (unsigned long));
if (nr == -1)
        /* error */
```

There are two problems with this naïve implementation: the call might return without reading all len bytes, and it could produce certain actionable errors that this code does not check for and handle. Code such as this, unfortunately, is very common. Let's see how to improve it.

Return Values

It is legal for read() to return a positive nonzero value less than len. This can happen for a number of reasons: less than len bytes may have been available, the system call may have been interrupted by a signal, the pipe may have broken (if fd references a pipe), and so on.

The possibility of a return value of 0 is another consideration when using read(). The read() system call returns 0 to indicate *end-of-file* (*EOF*); in this case, of course, no bytes were read. EOF is not considered an error (and hence is not accompanied by a –1 return value); it simply indicates that the file position has advanced past the last valid offset in the file and thus there is nothing else to read. If, however, a call is made for len bytes, but no bytes are available for reading, the call will *block* (sleep) until the bytes become available (assuming the file descriptor was not opened in nonblocking mode; see "Nonblocking Reads" on page 35). Note that this is different from returning EOF. That is, there is a difference between "no data available" and "end of data." In the EOF case, the end of the file was reached. In the case of blocking, the read is waiting for more data—say, in the case of reading from a socket or a device file.

Some errors are recoverable. For example, if a call to read() is interrupted by a signal before any bytes are read, it returns –1 (a 0 could be confused with EOF), and errno is set to EINTR. In that case, you can and should resubmit the read.

Indeed, a call to read() can result in many possibilities:

- The call returns a value equal to len. All len read bytes are stored in buf. The results are as intended.

- The call returns a value less than len, but greater than zero. The read bytes are stored in buf. This can occur because a signal interrupted the read midway; an error occurred in the middle of the read; more than zero, but less than len bytes' worth of data was available; or EOF was reached before `len` bytes were read. Reissuing the read (with correspondingly updated `buf` and `len` values) will read the remaining bytes into the rest of the buffer or indicate the cause of the problem.

- The call returns 0. This indicates EOF. There is nothing to read.

- The call blocks because no data is currently available. This won't happen in non-blocking mode.

- The call returns −1, and `errno` is set to `EINTR`. This indicates that a signal was received before any bytes were read. The call can be reissued.

- The call returns −1, and `errno` is set to `EAGAIN`. This indicates that the read would block because no data is currently available, and that the request should be reissued later. This happens only in nonblocking mode.

- The call returns −1, and `errno` is set to a value other than `EINTR` or `EAGAIN`. This indicates a more serious error. Simply reissuing the read is unlikely to succeed.

Reading All the Bytes

These possibilities imply that the previous trivial, simplistic use of `read()` is not suitable if you want to handle all errors and actually read all `len` bytes (at least up to an EOF). To do that, you need a loop, and a handful of conditional statements:

```
ssize_t ret;

while (len != 0 && (ret = read (fd, buf, len)) != 0) {
        if (ret == -1) {
                if (errno == EINTR)
                        continue;
                perror ("read");
                break;
        }

        len -= ret;
        buf += ret;
}
```

This snippet handles all five conditions. The loop reads `len` bytes from the current file position of `fd` into `buf`, which of course must be at least `len` bytes in length. It continues reading until it reads all `len` bytes, or until EOF is reached. If more than zero, but less than `len` bytes are read, `len` is reduced by the amount read, `buf` is increased by the amount read, and the call is reissued. If the call returns −1, and `errno` equals `EINTR`, the call is reissued without updating the parameters. If the call returns −1, and `errno` is set to anything else, `perror()` is called to print a description to standard error and the loop terminates.

Partial reads are not only legal, but common. Innumerable bugs derive from programmers not properly checking for and handling short read requests. Do not add to the list!

Nonblocking Reads

Sometimes, programmers do not want a call to read() to block when there is no data available. Instead, they prefer that the call return immediately, indicating that no data is available. This is called *nonblocking I/O*; it allows applications to perform I/O, potentially on multiple files, without ever blocking, and thus missing data available in another file.

Consequently, an additional errno value is worth checking: EAGAIN. As discussed previously, if the given file descriptor was opened in nonblocking mode (if O_NONBLOCK was given to open(); see "Flags for open()" on page 26) and there is no data to read, the read() call will return -1 and set errno to EAGAIN instead of blocking. When performing nonblocking reads, you must check for EAGAIN or risk confusing a serious error with the mere lack of data. For example, you might use code like the following:

```
char buf[BUFSIZ];
ssize_t nr;

start:
nr = read (fd, buf, BUFSIZ);
if (nr == -1) {
        if (errno == EINTR)
                goto start; /* oh shush */
        if (errno == EAGAIN)
                /* resubmit later */
        else
                /* error */
}
```

 Handling the EAGAIN case like we did the EINTR case (with a goto start) would make little sense. We might as well not have used nonblocking I/O. The point of nonblocking I/O is to catch the EAGAIN and do other, useful work.

Other Error Values

The other error codes refer to programming errors or (for EIO) low-level problems. Possible errno values after a failure on read() include:

EBADF
    The given file descriptor is invalid or is not open for reading.

EFAULT
    The pointer provided by buf is not inside the calling process's address space.

EINVAL
    The file descriptor is mapped to an object that does not allow reading.

EIO
    A low-level I/O error occurred.

Size Limits on read()

The size_t and ssize_t types are mandated by POSIX. The size_t type is used for storing values used to measure size in bytes. The ssize_t type is a signed version of size_t (the negative values are used to connote errors). On 32-bit systems, the backing C types are usually unsigned int and int, respectively. Because the two types are often used together, the potentially smaller range of ssize_t places a limit on the range of size_t.

The maximum value of a size_t is SIZE_MAX; the maximum value of an ssize_t is SSIZE_MAX. If len is larger than SSIZE_MAX, the results of the call to read() are undefined. On most Linux systems, SSIZE_MAX is LONG_MAX, which is 2,147,483,647 on a 32-bit machine. That is relatively large for a single read but nonetheless something to keep in mind. If you use the previous read loop as a generic super read, you might want to do something like this:

```
if (len > SSIZE_MAX)
        len = SSIZE_MAX;
```

A call to read() with a len of zero results in the call returning immediately with a return value of 0.

Writing with write()

The most basic and common system call used for writing is write(). write() is the counterpart of read() and is also defined in POSIX.1:

```
#include <unistd.h>

ssize_t write (int fd, const void *buf, size_t count);
```

A call to write() writes up to count bytes starting at buf to the current position of the file referenced by the file descriptor fd. Files backed by objects that do not support seeking (for example, character devices) always write starting at the "head."

On success, the number of bytes written is returned, and the file position is updated in kind. On error, -1 is returned and errno is set appropriately. A call to write() can return 0, but this return value does not have any special meaning; it simply implies that zero bytes were written.

As with read(), the most basic usage is simple:

```
const char *buf = "My ship is solid!";
ssize_t nr;

/* write the string in 'buf' to 'fd' */
nr = write (fd, buf, strlen (buf));
if (nr == -1)
        /* error */
```

But again, as with read(), this usage is not quite right. Callers also need to check for the possible occurrence of a partial write:

```
unsigned long word = 1720;
size_t count;
ssize_t nr;

count = sizeof (word);
nr = write (fd, &word, count);
if (nr == -1)
        /* error, check errno */
else if (nr != count)
        /* possible error, but 'errno' not set */
```

Partial Writes

The write() system call is less likely to return a partial write than the read() system call is to return a partial read. Also, there is no EOF condition for a write() system call. For regular files, write() is guaranteed to perform the entire requested write, unless an error occurs.

Consequently, for regular files, you do not need to perform writes in a loop. However, for other file types—say, sockets—a loop may be required to guarantee that you *really* write out all of the requested bytes. Another benefit of using a loop is that a second call to write() may return an error revealing what caused the first call to perform only a partial write (although, again, this situation is not very common). Here is an example:

```
ssize_t ret, nr;

while (len != 0 && (ret = write (fd, buf, len)) != 0) {
        if (ret == -1) {
                if (errno == EINTR)
                        continue;
                perror ("write");
                break;
```

```
        }

        len -= ret;
        buf += ret;
    }
```

Append Mode

When fd is opened in append mode (via O_APPEND), writes do not occur at the file descriptor's current file position. Instead, they occur at the current end of the file.

For example, assume that two processes intend to write to the end of the same file. This is common: consider a log of events shared among many processes. At the start, their file positions are correctly set to the end of the file. The first process writes to the end of the file. Without append mode, once the second process attempts the same, it will end up writing not to the end of the file, but to the offset that *was* the end of the file, before the data that the first process wrote. This means that multiple processes can never append to the same file without explicit synchronization between them because they will encounter race conditions.

Append mode avoids this problem. It ensures that the file position is always set to the end of the file so all writes always append, even when there are multiple writers. You can think of it as an atomic update to the file position preceding each write request. The file position is then updated to point at the end of the newly written data. This will not matter to the next call to write(), as it updates the file position automatically, but it might matter if you next call read() for some odd reason.

Append mode makes a lot of sense for certain tasks, such as the aforementioned writing out of log files, but little sense for much else.

Nonblocking Writes

When fd is opened in nonblocking mode (via O_NONBLOCK), and the write as issued would normally block, the write() system call returns –1 and sets errno to EAGAIN. The request should be reissued later. Generally, this does not occur with regular files.

Other Error Codes

Other notable errno values include:

EBADF
    The given file descriptor is not valid or is not open for writing.

EFAULT
    The pointer provided by buf points outside of the process's address space.

EFBIG

> The write would have made the file larger than per-process maximum file, or internal implementation, limits.

EINVAL

> The given file descriptor is mapped to an object that is not suitable for writing.

EIO

> A low-level I/O error occurred.

ENOSPC

> The filesystem backing the given file descriptor does not have sufficient space.

EPIPE

> The given file descriptor is associated with a pipe or socket whose reading end is closed. The process will also receive a SIGPIPE signal. The default action for the SIGPIPE signal is to terminate the receiving process. Therefore, processes receive this errno value only if they explicitly ask to ignore, block, or handle this signal.

Size Limits on write()

If count is larger than SSIZE_MAX, the results of the call to write() are undefined.

A call to write() with a count of zero results in the call returning immediately with a return value of 0.

Behavior of write()

When a call to write() returns, the kernel has copied the data from the supplied buffer into a kernel buffer, but there is no guarantee that the data has been written out to its intended destination. Indeed, write calls return much too fast for that to be the case. The disparity in performance between processors and hard disks would make such behavior painfully obvious.

Instead, when a user-space application issues a write() system call, the Linux kernel performs a few checks and then simply copies the data into a buffer. Later, in the background, the kernel gathers up all of the *dirty buffers*, which are buffers that contain data newer than what is on disk, sorts them optimally, and writes them out to disk (a process known as *writeback*). This allows write calls to occur relatively fast, returning almost immediately. It also allows the kernel to defer writes to more idle periods and batch many writes together.

The delayed writes do not change POSIX semantics. For example, if a read is issued for a piece of just-written data that lives in a buffer and is not yet on disk, the request will be satisfied from the buffer and not cause a read from the "stale" data on disk. This behavior further improves performance, as the read is satisfied from an in-memory cache without having to go to disk. The read and write requests interleave as intended, and the results are as expected—that is, if the system does not crash before the data makes it to disk! Even though an application may believe that a write has occurred successfully, in the event of a system crash, the data will never make it to disk.

Another issue with delayed writes is the inability to enforce *write ordering*. Although an application may take care to order its write requests in such a way that they hit the disk in a specific order, the kernel will reorder the write requests as it sees fit, primarily for reasons of performance. This is normally a problem only if the system crashes, as eventually all of the buffers are written back and the final state of the file is as intended. The vast majority of applications are not actually concerned with write ordering. Databases are a rare use case concerned with ordering; they want to ensure that write operations are ordered such that the database is never in an inconsistent state.

A final problem with delayed writes is the reporting of certain I/O errors. Any I/O error that occurs during writeback—say, a physical drive failure—cannot be reported back to the process that issued the write request. Indeed, dirty buffers inside the kernel are not associated with processes at all. Multiple processes may have dirtied the data contained in a single buffer, and processes may exit after writing data to a buffer but before that data is written back to disk. Besides, how would you communicate to a process that a write failed *ex post facto*?

Given these potential issues, the kernel attempts to minimize the risks of deferred writes. To ensure that data is written out in a timely manner, the kernel institutes a *maximum buffer age* and writes out all dirty buffers before they mature past the given value. Users can configure this value via */proc/sys/vm/dirty_expire_centisecs*. The value is specified in centiseconds (one hundredths of a second).

It is also possible to force the writeback of a given file's buffer, or even to make all writes synchronous. These topics are discussed in the next section, "Synchronized I/O".

Later in this chapter, "Kernel Internals" on page 62 will cover the Linux kernel's buffer writeback subsystem in depth.

Synchronized I/O

Although synchronizing I/O is an important topic, the issues associated with delayed writes should not be overstated. Buffering writes provides a *significant* performance improvement, and consequently, any operating system even halfway deserving the mark "modern" implements delayed writes via buffers. Nonetheless, there are times when applications want to control when data hits the disk. For those uses, the Linux kernel provides a handful of options that allow performance to be traded for synchronized operations.

fsync() and fdatasync()

The simplest method of ensuring that data has reached the disk is via the `fsync()` system call, standardized by POSIX.1b:

```
#include <unistd.h>

int fsync (int fd);
```

A call to `fsync()` ensures that all dirty data associated with the file mapped by the file descriptor `fd` are written back to disk. The file descriptor `fd` must be open for writing. The call writes back both data and metadata, such as creation timestamps and other attributes contained in the inode. It will not return until the hard drive says that the data and metadata are on the disk.

In the presence of hard disks with write caches, it is not possible for `fsync()` to know whether the data is physically on the disk. The hard drive can report that the data was written, but the data may in fact reside in the drive's write cache. Fortunately, data in a hard disk's cache should be committed to the disk in short order.

Linux also provides the system call `fdatasync()`:

```
#include <unistd.h>

int fdatasync (int fd);
```

This system call does the same thing as `fsync()`, except that it only flushes data and metadata required to properly access the file in the future. For example, a call to `fdata sync()` will flush a file's size, since you need that to read the file correctly. The call does not guarantee that nonessential metadata is synchronized to disk, and is therefore potentially faster. Most use cases do not consider metadata such as the file modification timestamp part of their essential transaction and thus `fdatasync()` is sufficient for their needs and potentially faster.

 `fsync()` always results in at least *two* I/O operations: one to write back the modified data and one to update the inode's modification timestamp. Because the inode and the file's data may not be adjacent on disk —and thus require an expensive seek operation—and most concerns over proper transaction ordering do not include metadata that isn't essential to properly access the file in the future (such as the modification timestamp), `fdatasync()` is an easy performance win.

Both functions are used the same way, which is very simple:

```
int ret;

ret = fsync (fd);
```

```
if (ret == -1)
        /* error */
```

or when using fdatasync()

```
int ret;

/* same as fsync, but won't flush non-essential metadata */
ret = fdatasync (fd);
if (ret == -1)
        /* error */
```

Neither function guarantees that any updated directory entries containing the file are synchronized to disk. This implies that if a file's link has recently been updated, the file's data may successfully reach the disk but not the associated directory entry, rendering the file unreachable. To ensure that any updates to the directory entry are also committed to disk, fsync() must also be called on a file descriptor opened against the file's directory.

Return values and error codes

On success, both calls return 0. On failure, both calls return -1 and set errno to one of the following three values:

EBADF
> The given file descriptor is not a valid file descriptor open for writing.

EINVAL
> The given file descriptor is mapped to an object that does not support synchronization.

EIO
> A low-level I/O error occurred during synchronization. This represents a real I/O error, and is often the place where such errors are caught.

In some versions of Linux, a call to fsync() may fail because fsync() is not implemented by the backing filesystem, even when fdatasync() is implemented. Paranoid applications may want to try fdatasync() if fsync() returns EINVAL. For example:

```
if (fsync (fd) == -1) {
        /*
         * We prefer fsync(), but let's try fdatasync()
         * if fsync() fails, just in case.
         */
        if (errno == EINVAL) {
                if (fdatasync (fd) == -1)
                        perror ("fdatasync");
        } else
                perror ("fsync");
}
```

Because POSIX requires `fsync()`, but labels `fdatasync()` as optional, the `fsync()` system call should always be implemented for regular files on any of the common Linux filesystems. Atypical file types (perhaps those in which there is no metadata to synchronize) or strange filesystems may implement only `fdatasync()`, however.

sync()

Less optimal, but wider in scope, the old-school `sync()` system call is provided for synchronizing *all* buffers to disk:

```
#include <unistd.h>

void sync (void);
```

The function has no parameters and no return value. It always succeeds and, upon return, all buffers—both data and metadata—are guaranteed to reside on disk.[3]

The standards do not require `sync()` to wait until all buffers are flushed to disk before returning; they require only that the call initiates the process of committing all buffers to disk. For this reason, it is often recommended to invoke `sync()` multiple times to ensure that all data is safely on disk. Linux, however, *does* wait until all buffers are committed. Therefore, a single `sync()` is sufficient.

The only real use for `sync()` is in the implementation of the *sync* utility. Applications should use `fsync()` and `fdatasync()` to commit to disk the data of only the requisite file descriptors. Note that `sync()` may take several minutes or longer to complete on a busy system.

The O_SYNC Flag

The O_SYNC flag may be passed to `open()`, indicating that all I/O on the file should be synchronized:

```
int fd;

fd = open (file, O_WRONLY | O_SYNC);
if (fd == -1) {
        perror ("open");
        return -1;
}
```

Read requests are always synchronized. If they weren't, the validity of the read data in the supplied buffer would be unknown. However, as discussed previously, calls to `write()` are normally not synchronized. There is no relation between the call returning

---

3. With the same caveat as before: the hard drive may lie and inform the kernel that the buffers reside on disk when they actually are still in the disk's cache.

and the data being committed to disk. The O_SYNC flag forces the relationship, ensuring that calls to write() perform synchronized I/O.

One way of looking at O_SYNC is that it forces an implicit fsync() after each write() operation, before the call returns. These are indeed the semantics provided, although the Linux kernel implements O_SYNC a bit more efficiently.

O_SYNC results in slightly worse *user* and *kernel times* (time spent in user and kernel space, respectively) for write operations. Moreover, depending on the size of the file being written, O_SYNC can cause an increase in total elapsed time of one or two orders of magnitude because all *I/O wait time* (time spent waiting for I/O to complete) is incurred by the process. The increase in cost is huge, so synchronized I/O should be used only after exhausting all possible alternatives.

Normally, applications that need guarantees that write operations have hit the disk use fsync() or fdatasync(). These tend to incur less cost than O_SYNC, as they can be called less often (i.e., only after certain critical operations have completed).

O_DSYNC and O_RSYNC

POSIX defines two other synchronized-I/O-related open() flags: O_DSYNC and O_RSYNC. On Linux, these flags are defined to be synonymous with O_SYNC; they provide the same behavior.

The O_DSYNC flag specifies that only normal data be synchronized after each write operation, not metadata. Think of it as causing an implicit fdatasync() after each write request. Because O_SYNC provides stronger guarantees, aliasing O_DSYNC to it involves no loss in functionality; there's only a potential performance loss from the stronger requirements provided by O_SYNC.

The O_RSYNC flag specifies the synchronization of read requests as well as write requests. It must be used with one of O_SYNC or O_DSYNC. As mentioned earlier, reads are already synchronized—they do not return until they have something to give the user, after all. The O_RSYNC flag stipulates that any side effects of a read operation be synchronized, too. This means that metadata updates resulting from a read must be written to disk before the call returns. In practical terms, this requirement most likely means only that the file access time must be updated in the on-disk copy of the inode before the call to read() returns. Linux defines O_RSYNC to be the same as O_SYNC, although this does not make much sense (one is not a subset of the other as with O_DSYNC and O_SYNC). There is currently no way in Linux to obtain the proper behavior of O_RSYNC; the closest a developer can come is invoking fdatasync() after each read() call. This behavior is rarely needed, though.

Direct I/O

The Linux kernel, like any modern operating system kernel, implements a complex layer of caching, buffering, and I/O management between devices and applications (see "Kernel Internals" on page 62). A high-performance application may wish to bypass this layer of complexity and perform its own I/O management. Rolling your own I/O system is usually not worth the effort, though, and in fact the tools available at the operating-system level are likely to achieve much better performance than those available at the application level. Still, database systems often prefer to perform their own caching and want to minimize the presence of the operating system as much as feasible.

Providing the O_DIRECT flag to open() instructs the kernel to minimize the presence of I/O management. When this flag is provided, I/O will initiate directly from user-space buffers to the device, bypassing the page cache. All I/O will be synchronous; operations will not return until completed.

When performing direct I/O, the request length, buffer alignment, and file offsets must all be integer multiples of the underlying device's sector size—generally, this is 512 bytes. Before the 2.6 Linux kernel, this requirement was stricter: in 2.4, everything must be aligned on the filesystem's logical block size (often 4 KB). To remain compatible, applications should align to the larger (and potentially less convenient) logical block size.

Closing Files

After a program has finished working with a file descriptor, it can unmap the file descriptor from the associated file via the close() system call:

```
#include <unistd.h>

int close (int fd);
```

A call to close() unmaps the open file descriptor fd and disassociates the file from the process. The given file descriptor is then no longer valid, and the kernel is free to reuse it as the return value to a subsequent open() or creat() call. A call to close() returns 0 on success. On error, it returns –1 and sets errno appropriately. Usage is simple:

```
if (close (fd) == -1)
        perror ("close");
```

Note that closing a file has no bearing on when the file is flushed to disk. To ensure that a file is committed to disk before closing it, an application needs to make use of one of the synchronization options discussed earlier in "Synchronized I/O" on page 40.

Closing a file does have some side effects, though. When the last open file descriptor referring to a file is closed, the data structure representing the file inside the kernel is freed. When this data structure is freed, it unpins the in-memory copy of the inode associated with the file. If nothing else is pinning the inode, it too may be freed from memory (it may stick around because the kernel caches inodes for performance reasons, but it need not). If a file has been unlinked from the disk but was kept open before it was unlinked, it is not physically removed until it is closed and its inode is removed from memory. Therefore, calling close() may also result in an unlinked file finally being physically removed from the disk.

Error Values

It is a common mistake to not check the return value of close(). This can result in missing a crucial error condition because errors associated with deferred operations may not manifest until later, and close() can report them.

There are a handful of possible errno values on failure. Other than EBADF (the given file descriptor was invalid), the most important error value is EIO, indicating a low-level I/O error probably unrelated to the actual close. Regardless of any reported error, the file descriptor, if valid, is always closed, and the associated data structures are freed.

Although POSIX allows it, close() will never return EINTR. The Linux kernel developers know better.

Seeking with lseek()

Normally, I/O occurs linearly through a file, and the implicit updates to the file position caused by reads and writes are all the seeking that is needed. Some applications, however, want to jump around in a file, providing random rather than linear access. The lseek() system call is provided to set the file position of a file descriptor to a given value. Other than updating the file position, it performs no other action, and initiates no I/O whatsoever:

```
#include <sys/types.h>
#include <unistd.h>

off_t lseek (int fd, off_t pos, int origin);
```

The behavior of lseek() depends on the origin argument, which can be one of the following:

SEEK_CUR
    The current file position of fd is set to its current value plus pos, which can be negative, zero, or positive. A pos of zero returns the current file position value.

SEEK_END
    The current file position of fd is set to the current length of the file plus pos, which can be negative, zero, or positive. A pos of zero sets the offset to the end of the file.

SEEK_SET

The current file position of fd is set to pos. A pos of zero sets the offset to the beginning of the file.

The call returns the new file position on success. On error, it returns –1 and errno is set as appropriate.

For example, to set the file position of fd to 1825:

```
off_t ret;

ret = lseek (fd, (off_t) 1825, SEEK_SET);
if (ret == (off_t) -1)
        /* error */
```

Alternatively, to set the file position of fd to the end of the file:

```
off_t ret;

ret = lseek (fd, 0, SEEK_END);
if (ret == (off_t) -1)
        /* error */
```

As lseek() returns the updated file position, it can be used to find the current file position via a SEEK_CUR to zero:

```
int pos;

pos = lseek (fd, 0, SEEK_CUR);
if (pos == (off_t) -1)
        /* error */
else
        /* 'pos' is the current position of fd */
```

By far, the most common uses of lseek() are seeking to the beginning, seeking to the end, or determining the current file position of a file descriptor.

Seeking Past the End of a File

It is possible to instruct lseek() to advance the file pointer past the end of a file. For example, this code seeks to 1,688 bytes beyond the end of the file mapped by fd:

```
int ret;

ret = lseek (fd, (off_t) 1688, SEEK_END);
if (ret == (off_t) -1)
        /* error */
```

On its own, seeking past the end of a file does nothing—a read request to the newly created file position will return EOF. If a write request is subsequently made to this position, however, new space will be created between the old length of the file and the new length, and it will be padded with zeros.

This zero padding is called a *hole*. On Unix-style filesystems, holes do not occupy any physical disk space. This implies that the total size of all files on a filesystem can add up to more than the physical size of the disk. Files with holes are called *sparse files*. Sparse files can save considerable space and enhance performance because manipulating the holes does not initiate any physical I/O.

A read request to the part of a file in a hole will return the appropriate number of zeros.

Error Values

On error, lseek() returns –1 and errno is set to one of the following four values:

EBADF
> The given file descriptor does not refer to an open file descriptor.

EINVAL
> The value given for origin is not one of SEEK_SET, SEEK_CUR, or SEEK_END, *or the* resulting file position would be negative. The fact that EINVAL represents both of these errors is unfortunate. The former is almost assuredly a compile-time programming error, whereas the latter can represent a more insidious runtime logic error.

EOVERFLOW
> The resulting file offset cannot be represented in an off_t. This can occur only on 32-bit architectures. Currently, the file position *is* updated; this error indicates just that it is impossible to return it.

ESPIPE
> The given file descriptor is associated with an unseekable object, such as a pipe, FIFO, or socket.

Limitations

The maximum file positions are limited by the size of the off_t type. Most machine architectures define this to be the C long type, which on Linux is always the *word size* (usually the size of the machine's general-purpose registers). Internally, however, the kernel stores the offsets in the C long long type. This poses no problem on 64-bit machines, but it means that 32-bit machines can generate EOVERFLOW errors when performing relative seeks.

Positional Reads and Writes

In lieu of using `lseek()`, Linux provides two variants of the `read()` and `write()` system calls. Both receive the file position from which to read or write. Upon completion, they do *not* update the file position.

The read form is called `pread()`:

```
#define _XOPEN_SOURCE 500

#include <unistd.h>

ssize_t pread (int fd, void *buf, size_t count, off_t pos);
```

This call reads up to `count` bytes into `buf` from the file descriptor `fd` at file position `pos`.

The write form is called `pwrite()`:

```
#define _XOPEN_SOURCE 500

#include <unistd.h>

ssize_t pwrite (int fd, const void *buf, size_t count, off_t pos);
```

This call writes up to `count` bytes from `buf` to the file descriptor `fd` at file position `pos`.

These calls are almost identical in behavior to their non-p brethren, except that they completely ignore the current file position; instead of using the current position, they use the value provided by `pos`. Also, when done, they do not update the file position. In other words, any intermixed `read()` and `write()` calls could potentially corrupt the work done by the positional calls.

Both positional calls can be used only on seekable file descriptors, which include regular files. They provide semantics similar to preceding a `read()` or `write()` call with a call to `lseek()`, with three differences. First, these calls are easier to use, especially when doing a tricky operation such as moving through a file backward or randomly. Second, they do not update the file pointer upon completion. Finally, and most importantly, they avoid any potential races that might occur when using `lseek()`.

Because threads share file tables and the current file position is stored in the shared file table, it is possible for one thread in a program to update the file position after a different thread's call to `lseek()` but before its read or write operation executed. In other words, `lseek()` is inherently racy when you have two or more threads in a process all manipulating the same file descriptor. Such race conditions can be avoided by using the `pread()` and `pwrite()` system calls.

Error Values

On success, both calls return the number of bytes read or written. A return value of 0 from pread() indicates EOF; from pwrite(), a return value of 0 indicates that the call did not write anything. On error, both calls return −1 and set errno appropriately. For pread(), any valid read() or lseek() errno value is possible. For pwrite(), any valid write() or lseek() value is possible.

Truncating Files

Linux provides two system calls for truncating the length of a file, both of which are defined and required (to varying degrees) by various POSIX standards. They are:

```
#include <unistd.h>
#include <sys/types.h>

int ftruncate (int fd, off_t len);
```

and:

```
#include <unistd.h>
#include <sys/types.h>

int truncate (const char *path, off_t len);
```

Both system calls truncate the given file to the length given by len. The ftruncate() system call operates on the file descriptor given by fd, which must be open for writing. The truncate() system call operates on the filename given by path, which must be writable. Both return 0 on success. On error, they return −1 and set errno as appropriate.

The most common use of these system calls is to truncate a file to a size smaller than its current length. Upon successful return, the file's length is len. The data previously existing between len and the old length is discarded and no longer accessible via a read request.

The functions can also be used to "truncate" a file to a larger size, similar to the seek plus write combination described earlier in "Seeking Past the End of a File" on page 47. The extended bytes are filled with zeros.

Neither operation updates the current file position.

For example, consider the file *pirate.txt* of length 74 bytes with the following contents:

```
Edward Teach was a notorious English pirate.
He was nicknamed Blackbeard.
```

From the same directory, running the following program:

```
#include <unistd.h>
#include <stdio.h>
```

```
int main()
{
        int ret;

        ret = truncate ("./pirate.txt", 45);
        if (ret == -1) {
                perror ("truncate");
                return -1;
        }

        return 0;
}
```

results in a file of length 45 bytes with the following contents:

```
Edward Teach was a notorious English pirate.
```

Multiplexed I/O

Applications often need to block on more than one file descriptor, juggling I/O between keyboard input (*stdin*), interprocess communication, and a handful of files. Modern event-driven graphical user interface (GUI) applications may contend with literally hundreds of pending events via their mainloops.[4]

Without the aid of threads—essentially servicing each file descriptor separately—a single process cannot reasonably block on more than one file descriptor at the same time. Working with multiple file descriptors is fine, so long as they are always ready to be read from or written to. But as soon as one file descriptor that is not yet ready is encountered —say, if a read() system call is issued, and there is not yet any data—the process will block, no longer able to service the other file descriptors. It might block for just a few seconds, making the application inefficient and annoying the user. However, if no data becomes available on the file descriptor, it could block forever. Because file descriptors' I/O is often interrelated—think pipes—it is quite possible for one file descriptor not to become ready until another is serviced. Particularly with network applications, which may have many sockets open simultaneously, this is potentially quite a problem.

Imagine blocking on a file descriptor related to interprocess communication while *stdin* has data pending. The application won't know that keyboard input is pending until the blocked IPC file descriptor ultimately returns data—but what if the blocked operation never returns?

---

4. Mainloops should be familiar to anyone who has written GUI applications—for example, GNOME applications utilize a mainloop provided by *GLib*, their base library. A mainloop allows multiple events to be watched for and responded to from a single blocking point.

Earlier in this chapter, we looked at nonblocking I/O as a solution to this problem. With nonblocking I/O, applications can issue I/O requests that return a special error condition instead of blocking. However, this solution is inefficient for two reasons. First, the process needs to continually issue I/O operations in some arbitrary order, waiting for one of its open file descriptors to be ready for I/O. This is poor program design. Second, it would be much more efficient if the program could sleep, freeing the processor for other tasks, to be woken up only when one or more file descriptors were ready to perform I/O.

Enter *multiplexed I/O*.

Multiplexed I/O allows an application to concurrently block on multiple file descriptors and receive notification when any one of them becomes ready to read or write without blocking. Multiplexed I/O thus becomes the pivot point for the application, designed similarly to the following activity:

1. Multiplexed I/O: Tell me when any of these file descriptors become ready for I/O.
2. Nothing ready? Sleep until one or more file descriptors are ready.
3. Woken up! What is ready?
4. Handle all file descriptors ready for I/O, without blocking.
5. Go back to step 1.

Linux provides three multiplexed I/O solutions: the *select*, *poll*, and *epoll* interfaces. We will cover the first two here, and the last, which is an advanced Linux-specific solution, in Chapter 4.

select()

The select() system call provides a mechanism for implementing synchronous multiplexing I/O:

```
#include <sys/select.h>

int select (int n,
            fd_set *readfds,
            fd_set *writefds,
            fd_set *exceptfds,
            struct timeval *timeout);

FD_CLR(int fd, fd_set *set);
FD_ISSET(int fd, fd_set *set);
FD_SET(int fd, fd_set *set);
FD_ZERO(fd_set *set);
```

A call to select() blocks until the given file descriptors are ready to perform I/O, or until an optionally specified timeout has elapsed.

The watched file descriptors are broken into three sets, each waiting for a different event. File descriptors listed in the readfds set are watched to see if data is available for reading (that is, if a read operation will complete without blocking). File descriptors listed in the writefds set are watched to see if a write operation will complete without blocking. Finally, file descriptors in the exceptfds set are watched to see if an exception has occurred, or if out-of-band data is available (these states apply only to sockets). A given set may be NULL, in which case select() does not watch for that event.

On successful return, each set is modified such that it contains only the file descriptors that are ready for I/O of the type delineated by that set. For example, assume two file descriptors, with the values 7 and 9, are placed in the readfds set. When the call returns, if 7 is still in the set, that file descriptor is ready to read without blocking. If 9 is no longer in the set, it is probably not readable without blocking. (I say *probably* here because it is possible that data became available after the call completed. In that case, a subsequent call to select() will return the file descriptor as ready to read.)[5]

The first parameter, n, is equal to the value of the highest-valued file descriptor in any set, plus one. Consequently, a caller to select() is responsible for checking which given file descriptor is the highest-valued and passing in that value plus one for the first parameter.

The timeout parameter is a pointer to a timeval structure, which is defined as follows:

```
#include <sys/time.h>

struct timeval {
        long tv_sec;        /* seconds */
        long tv_usec;       /* microseconds */
};
```

If this parameter is not NULL, the call to select() will return after tv_sec seconds and tv_usec microseconds, even if no file descriptors are ready for I/O. On return, the state of this structure across various Unix systems is undefined, and thus it must be reinitialized (along with the file descriptor sets) before every invocation. Indeed, current versions of Linux modify this parameter automatically, setting the values to the time remaining. Thus, if the timeout was set for 5 seconds, and 3 seconds elapsed before a file descriptor became ready, tv.tv_sec would contain 2 upon the call's return.

If both values in the timeout are set to zero, the call will return immediately, reporting any events that were pending at the time of the call, but not waiting for any subsequent events.

---

5. This is because select() and poll() are level-triggered and not edge-triggered. epoll(), which we'll discuss in Chapter 4, can operate in either mode. Edge-triggered operation is simpler but allows I/O events to be missed if care is not taken.

The sets of file descriptors are not manipulated directly, but are instead managed through helper macros. This allows Unix systems to implement the sets however they want. Most systems, however, implement the sets as simple bit arrays.

FD_ZERO removes all file descriptors from the specified set. It should be called before every invocation of select():

```
fd_set writefds;

FD_ZERO(&writefds);
```

FD_SET adds a file descriptor to a given set, and FD_CLR removes a file descriptor from a given set:

```
FD_SET(fd, &writefds);    /* add 'fd' to the set */
FD_CLR(fd, &writefds);    /* oops, remove 'fd' from the set */
```

Well-designed code should never have to make use of FD_CLR, and it is rarely, if ever, used.

FD_ISSET tests whether a file descriptor is part of a given set. It returns a nonzero integer if the file descriptor is in the set and 0 if it is not. FD_ISSET is used after a call from select() returns to test whether a given file descriptor is ready for action:

```
if (FD_ISSET(fd, &readfds))
        /* 'fd' is readable without blocking! */
```

Because the file descriptor sets are statically created, they impose a limit on the maximum number of file descriptors and the largest-valued file descriptor that may be placed inside them, both of which are given by FD_SETSIZE. On Linux, this value is 1,024. We will look at the ramifications of this limit later in this chapter.

Return values and error codes

On success, select() returns the number of file descriptors ready for I/O, among all three sets. If a timeout was provided, the return value may be 0. On error, the call returns −1, and errno is set to one of the following values:

EBADF
: An invalid file descriptor was provided in one of the sets.

EINTR
: A signal was caught while waiting, and the call can be reissued.

EINVAL
: The parameter n is negative, or the given timeout is invalid.

ENOMEM
: Insufficient memory was available to complete the request.

select() example

Let's consider an example program, trivial but fully functional, to illustrate the use of select(). This example blocks waiting for input on *stdin* for up to 5 seconds. Because it watches only a single file descriptor, it is not actually multiplexing I/O, but the usage of the system call is made clear:

```
#include <stdio.h>
#include <sys/time.h>
#include <sys/types.h>
#include <unistd.h>

#define TIMEOUT 5        /* select timeout in seconds */
#define BUF_LEN 1024     /* read buffer in bytes */

int main (void)
{
        struct timeval tv;
        fd_set readfds;
        int ret;

        /* Wait on stdin for input. */
        FD_ZERO(&readfds);
        FD_SET(STDIN_FILENO, &readfds);

        /* Wait up to five seconds. */
        tv.tv_sec = TIMEOUT;
        tv.tv_usec = 0;

        /* All right, now block! */
        ret = select (STDIN_FILENO + 1,
                      &readfds,
                      NULL,
                      NULL,
                      &tv);
        if (ret == -1) {
                perror ("select");
                return 1;
        } else if (!ret) {
                printf ("%d seconds elapsed.\n", TIMEOUT);
                return 0;
        }

        /*
         * Is our file descriptor ready to read?
         * (It must be, as it was the only fd that
         * we provided and the call returned
         * nonzero, but we will humor ourselves.)
         */
        if (FD_ISSET(STDIN_FILENO, &readfds)) {
                char buf[BUF_LEN+1];
                int len;
```

```
        /* guaranteed to not block */
        len = read (STDIN_FILENO, buf, BUF_LEN);
        if (len == -1) {
                perror ("read");
                return 1;
        }

        if (len) {
                buf[len] = '\0';
                printf ("read: %s\n", buf);
        }

        return 0;
    }

    fprintf (stderr, "This should not happen!\n");
    return 1;
}
```

Portable sleeping with select()

Because `select()` has historically been more readily implemented on various Unix systems than a mechanism for subsecond-resolution sleeping, it is often employed as a portable way to sleep by providing a non-NULL timeout but NULL for all three sets:

```
struct timeval tv;

tv.tv_sec = 0;
tv.tv_usec = 500;

/* sleep for 500 microseconds */
select (0, NULL, NULL, NULL, &tv);
```

Linux provides interfaces for high-resolution sleeping. We will cover these in Chapter 11.

pselect()

The `select()` system call, first introduced in 4.2BSD, is popular, but POSIX defined its own solution, `pselect()`, in POSIX 1003.1g-2000 and later in POSIX 1003.1-2001:

```
#define _XOPEN_SOURCE 600
#include <sys/select.h>

int pselect (int n,
             fd_set *readfds,
             fd_set *writefds,
             fd_set *exceptfds,
             const struct timespec *timeout,
             const sigset_t *sigmask);
```

```
/* these are the same as those used by select() */
FD_CLR(int fd, fd_set *set);
FD_ISSET(int fd, fd_set *set);
FD_SET(int fd, fd_set *set);
FD_ZERO(fd_set *set);
```

There are three differences between pselect() and select():

- pselect() uses the timespec structure, not the timeval structure, for its time out parameter. The timespec structure uses seconds and nanoseconds, not seconds and microseconds, providing theoretically superior timeout resolution. In practice, however, neither call reliably provides even microsecond resolution.

- A call to pselect() does not modify the timeout parameter. Consequently, this parameter does not need to be reinitialized on subsequent invocations.

- The select() system call does not have the sigmask parameter. With respect to signals, when this parameter is set to NULL, pselect() behaves like select().

The timespec structure is defined as follows:

```
#include <sys/time.h>

struct timespec {
        long tv_sec;            /* seconds */
        long tv_nsec;           /* nanoseconds */
};
```

The primary motivator behind the addition of pselect() to Unix's toolbox was the addition of the sigmask parameter, which attempts to solve a race condition between waiting on file descriptors and signals (signals are covered in depth in Chapter 10). Assume that a signal handler sets a global flag (as most do), and the process checks this flag before a call to select(). Now, assume that the signal arrives after the check, but before the call. The application may block indefinitely and never respond to the set flag. The pselect() call solves this problem by allowing an application to call pselect(), providing a set of signals to block. Blocked signals are not handled until they are unblocked. Once pselect() returns, the kernel restores the old signal mask.

Until the 2.6.16 kernel, the Linux implementation of pselect() was not a system call, but a simple wrapper around select(), provided by *glibc*. This wrapper minimized—but did not totally eliminate—the risk of this race condition occurring. With the introduction of a true system call, the race is gone.

Despite the (relatively minor) improvements in pselect(), most applications continue to use select(), either out of habit or in the name of greater portability.

poll()

The poll() system call is System V's multiplexed I/O solution. It solves several deficiencies in select(), although select() is still often used (most likely out of habit, or in the name of portability):

```
#include <poll.h>

int poll (struct pollfd *fds, nfds_t nfds, int timeout);
```

Unlike select(), with its inefficient three bitmask-based sets of file descriptors, poll() employs a single array of nfds pollfd structures, pointed to by fds. The structure is defined as follows:

```
#include <poll.h>

struct pollfd {
        int fd;            /* file descriptor */
        short events;      /* requested events to watch */
        short revents;     /* returned events witnessed */
};
```

Each pollfd structure specifies a single file descriptor to watch. Multiple structures may be passed, instructing poll() to watch multiple file descriptors. The events field of each structure is a bitmask of events to watch for on that file descriptor. The user sets this field. The revents field is a bitmask of events that were witnessed on the file descriptor. The kernel sets this field on return. All of the events requested in the events field may be returned in the revents field. Valid events are as follows:

POLLIN
> There is data to read.

POLLRDNORM
> There is normal data to read.

POLLRDBAND
> There is priority data to read.

POLLPRI
> There is urgent data to read.

POLLOUT
> Writing will not block.

POLLWRNORM
> Writing normal data will not block.

POLLWRBAND
> Writing priority data will not block.

POLLMSG

A SIGPOLL message is available.

In addition, the following events may be returned in the revents field:

POLLER

Error on the given file descriptor.

POLLHUP

Hung up event on the given file descriptor.

POLLNVAL

The given file descriptor is invalid.

These events have no meaning in the events field and you should not pass them in that field because they are always returned if applicable. With poll(), unlike select(), you need not explicitly ask for reporting of exceptions.

POLLIN | POLLPRI is equivalent to select()'s read event, and POLLOUT | POLLWR BAND is equivalent to select()'s write event. POLLIN is equivalent to POLLRDNORM | POLLRDBAND, and POLLOUT is equivalent to POLLWRNORM.

For example, to watch a file descriptor for both readability and writability, we would set events to POLLIN | POLLOUT. On return, we would check revents for these flags in the structure corresponding to the file descriptor in question. If POLLIN were set, the file descriptor would be readable without blocking. If POLLOUT were set, the file descriptor would be writable without blocking. The flags are not mutually exclusive: both may be set, signifying that both reads and writes will return instead of blocking on that file descriptor.

The timeout parameter specifies the length of time to wait, in milliseconds, before returning regardless of any ready I/O. A negative value denotes an infinite timeout. A value of 0 instructs the call to return immediately, listing any file descriptors with pending ready I/O, but not waiting for any further events. In this manner, poll() is true to its name, polling once, and immediately returning.

Return values and error codes

On success, poll() returns the number of file descriptors whose structures have non-zero revents fields. It returns 0 if the timeout occurred before any events occurred. On failure, -1 is returned, and errno is set to one of the following:

EBADF

An invalid file descriptor was given in one or more of the structures.

EFAULT

The pointer to fds pointed outside of the process's address space.

EINTR
  A signal occurred before any requested event. The call may be reissued.

EINVAL
  The nfds parameter exceeded the RLIMIT_NOFILE value.

ENOMEM
  Insufficient memory was available to complete the request.

poll() example

Let's look at an example program that uses poll() to simultaneously check whether a read from *stdin* and a write to *stdout* will block:

```c
#include <stdio.h>
#include <unistd.h>
#include <poll.h>

#define TIMEOUT 5        /* poll timeout, in seconds */

int main (void)
{
        struct pollfd fds[2];
        int ret;

        /* watch stdin for input */
        fds[0].fd = STDIN_FILENO;
        fds[0].events = POLLIN;

        /* watch stdout for ability to write (almost always true) */
        fds[1].fd = STDOUT_FILENO;
        fds[1].events = POLLOUT;

        /* All set, block! */
        ret = poll (fds, 2, TIMEOUT * 1000);
        if (ret == -1) {
                perror ("poll");
                return 1;
        }

        if (!ret) {
                printf ("%d seconds elapsed.\n", TIMEOUT);
                return 0;
        }

        if (fds[0].revents & POLLIN)
                printf ("stdin is readable\n");

        if (fds[1].revents & POLLOUT)
                printf ("stdout is writable\n");
```

```
        return 0;
    }
```

Running this, we get the following, as expected:

```
$ ./poll
stdout is writable
```

Running it again, but this time redirecting a file into standard in, we see both events:

```
$ ./poll < ode_to_my_parrot.txt
stdin is readable
stdout is writable
```

If we were using poll() in a real application, we would not need to reconstruct the pollfd structures on each invocation. The same structure may be passed in repeatedly; the kernel will handle zeroing the revents field as needed.

ppoll()

Linux provides a ppoll() cousin to poll(), in the same vein as pselect(). Unlike pselect(), however, ppoll() is a Linux-specific interface:

```
#define _GNU_SOURCE

#include <poll.h>

int ppoll (struct pollfd *fds,
           nfds_t nfds,
           const struct timespec *timeout,
           const sigset_t *sigmask);
```

As with pselect(), the timeout parameter specifies a timeout value in seconds and nanoseconds, and the sigmask parameter provides a set of signals for which to wait.

poll() Versus select()

Although they perform the same basic job, the poll() system call is superior to select() for a handful of reasons:

- poll() does not require that the user calculate and pass in as a parameter the value of the highest-numbered file descriptor plus one.

- poll() is more efficient for large-valued file descriptors. Imagine watching a single file descriptor with the value 900 via select()—the kernel would have to check each bit of each passed-in set, up to the 900th bit.

- select()'s file descriptor sets are statically sized, introducing a trade-off: they are small, limiting the maximum file descriptor that select() can watch, or they are inefficient. Operations on large bitmasks are not efficient, especially if it is not known whether they are sparsely populated.[6] With `poll()`, one can create an array of exactly the right size. Only watching one item? Just pass in a single structure.

- With `select()`, the file descriptor sets are reconstructed on return, so each subsequent call must reinitialize them. The `poll()` system call separates the input (`events` field) from the output (`revents` field), allowing the array to be reused without change.

- The `timeout` parameter to `select()` is undefined on return. Portable code needs to reinitialize it. This is not an issue with `pselect()`, however.

The `select()` system call does have a few things going for it, though:

- `select()` is more portable, as some Unix systems do not support `poll()`.

- `select()` provides better timeout resolution: down to the microsecond wheres `poll()` provides only millisecond resolution. Both `ppoll()` and `pselect()` theoretically provide nanosecond resolution but, in practice, none of these calls reliably provides even microsecond resolution.

Superior to both `poll()` and `select()` is the *epoll* interface, a Linux-specific multiplexing I/O solution that we'll look at in Chapter 4.

Kernel Internals

This section looks at how the Linux kernel implements I/O, focusing on three primary subsystems of the kernel: the *virtual filesystem* (VFS), the *page cache*, and *page writeback*. Together, these subsystems help make I/O seamless, efficient, and optimal.

 In Chapter 4, we will look at a fourth subsystem, the *I/O scheduler*.

The Virtual Filesystem

The virtual filesystem, occasionally also called a *virtual file switch*, is a mechanism of abstraction that allows the Linux kernel to call filesystem functions and manipulate filesystem data without knowing—or even caring about—the specific type of filesystem being used.

---

6. If a bitmask is generally sparsely populated, each word composing the mask can be checked against zero; only if that operation returns false need each bit be checked. This work is wasted, however, if the bitmask is densely populated.

The VFS accomplishes this abstraction by providing a *common file model*, which is the basis for all filesystems in Linux. Via function pointers and various object-oriented practices,[7] the common file model provides a framework to which filesystems in the Linux kernel must adhere. This allows the VFS to generically make requests of the filesystem. The framework provides hooks to support reading, creating links, synchronizing, and so on. Each filesystem then registers functions to handle the operations of which it is capable.

This approach forces a certain amount of commonality between filesystems. For example, the VFS talks in terms of inodes, superblocks, and directory entries. A filesystem not of Unix origins, possibly devoid of Unix-like concepts such as inodes, simply has to cope. Indeed, cope they do: Linux supports filesystems such as FAT and NTFS without issues.

The benefits of the VFS are enormous. A single system call can read from *any* filesystem on *any* medium; a single utility can copy from any one filesystem to any other. All filesystems support the same concepts, the same interfaces, and the same calls. Everything just works—and works well.

When an application issues a `read()` system call, it takes an interesting journey. The C library provides definitions of the system call that are converted to the appropriate trap statements at compile time. Once a user-space process is trapped into the kernel, passed through the system call handler, and handed to the `read()` system call, the kernel figures out what object *backs* the given file descriptor. The kernel then invokes the read function associated with the backing object. For filesystems, this function is part of the filesystem code. The function then does its thing—for example, physically reading the data from the filesystem—and returns the data to the user-space `read()` call, which then returns to the system call handler, which copies the data back to user space, where the `read()` system call returns and the process continues to execute.

To system programmers, the ramifications of the VFS are important. Programmers need not worry about the type of filesystem or media on which a file resides. Generic system calls—`read()`, `write()`, and so on—can manipulate files on any supported filesystem and on any supported media.

The Page Cache

The page cache is an in-memory store of recently accessed data from an on-disk filesystem. Disk access is painfully slow, particularly relative to today's processor speeds. Storing requested data in memory allows the kernel to fulfill subsequent requests for the same data from memory, avoiding repeated disk access.

---

7. Yes, in C.

The page cache exploits the concept of *temporal locality*, a type of *locality of reference*, which says that a resource accessed at one point has a high probability of being accessed again in the near future. The memory consumed to cache data on its first access therefore pays off, as it prevents future expensive disk accesses.

The page cache is the first place that the kernel looks for filesystem data. The kernel invokes the memory subsystem to read data from the disk only when it isn't found in the cache. Thus, the first time any item of data is read, it is transferred from the disk into the page cache, and is returned to the application from the cache. If that data is then read again, it is simply returned from the cache. All operations transparently execute through the page cache, ensuring that its data is relevant and always valid.

The Linux page cache is dynamic in size. As I/O operations bring more and more data into memory, the page cache grows larger and larger, consuming any free memory. If the page cache eventually does consume all free memory and an allocation is committed that requests additional memory, the page cache is *pruned*, releasing its least-used pages to make room for "real" memory usage. This pruning occurs seamlessly and automatically. A dynamically sized cache allows Linux to use all of the memory in the system and cache as much data as possible.

Often, however, it would make more sense to *swap* to disk a seldom-used page of process memory than it would to prune an oft-used piece of the page cache that could well be reread into memory on the next read request (swapping allows the kernel to store data on the disk to allow a larger memory footprint than the machine has RAM). The Linux kernel implements heuristics to balance the swapping of data versus the pruning of the page cache (and other in-memory reserves). These heuristics might decide to swap data out to disk in lieu of pruning the page cache, particularly if the data being swapped out is not in use.

The swap-versus-cache balance is tuned via */proc/sys/vm/swappiness*. This virtual file has a value from 0 to 100, with a default of 60. A higher value implies a stronger preference toward keeping the page cache in memory, and swapping more readily. A lower value implies a stronger preference toward pruning the page cache and not swapping.

Another form of locality of reference is *sequential locality*, which says that data is often referenced sequentially. To take advantage of this principle, the kernel also implements page cache *readahead*. Readahead is the act of reading extra data off the disk and into the page cache following each read request—in effect, reading a little bit ahead. When the kernel reads a chunk of data from the disk, it also reads the following chunk or two. Reading large sequential chunks of data at once is efficient, as the disk usually need not seek. In addition, the kernel can fulfill the readahead request while the process is manipulating the first chunk of read data. If, as often happens, the process goes on to submit a new read request for the subsequent chunk, the kernel can hand over the data from the initial readahead without having to issue a disk I/O request.

As with the page cache, the kernel manages readahead dynamically. If it notices that a process is consistently using the data that was read in via readahead, the kernel grows the readahead window, thereby reading ahead more and more data. The readahead window may be as small as 16 KB, and as large as 128 KB. Conversely, if the kernel notices that readahead is not resulting in any useful hits—that is, that the application is seeking around the file and not reading sequentially—it can disable readahead entirely.

The presence of a page cache is meant to be transparent. System programmers generally cannot optimize their code to better take advantage of the fact that a page cache exists—other than, perhaps, not implementing such a cache in user space themselves. Normally, efficient code is all that is needed to best utilize the page cache. Utilizing readahead, on the other hand, is possible. Sequential file I/O is always preferred to random access, although it's not always feasible.

Page Writeback

As discussed earlier in "Behavior of write()" on page 39, the kernel defers writes via buffers. When a process issues a write request, the data is copied into a buffer, and the buffer is marked *dirty*, denoting that the in-memory copy is newer than the on-disk copy. The write request then simply returns. If another write request is made to the same chunk of a file, the buffer is updated with the new data. Write requests elsewhere in the same file generate new buffers.

Eventually the dirty buffers need to be committed to disk, synchronizing the on-disk files with the data in memory. This is known as writeback. It occurs in two situations:

- When free memory shrinks below a configurable threshold, dirty buffers are written back to disk so that the now-clean buffers may be removed, freeing memory.

- When a dirty buffer ages beyond a configurable threshold, the buffer is written back to disk. This prevents data from remaining dirty indefinitely.

Writebacks are carried out by a gang of kernel threads named *flusher* threads. When one of the previous two conditions is met, the flusher threads wake up and begin committing dirty buffers to disk until neither condition is true.

There may be multiple flusher threads instantiating writebacks at the same time. This is done to capitalize on the benefits of parallelism and to implement *congestion avoidance*. Congestion avoidance attempts to keep writes from getting backed up while waiting to be written to any one block device. If dirty buffers from different block devices exist, the various flusher threads will work to fully use each block device. This fixes a deficiency in earlier kernels: the predecessor to flusher threads (*pdflush* and before that, *bdflush*) could spend all of its time waiting on a single block device, while other block devices sat idle. On a modern machine, the Linux kernel can now keep a very large number of disks saturated.

Buffers are represented in the kernel by the buffer_head data structure. This data structure tracks various metadata associated with the buffer, such as whether the buffer is clean or dirty. It also contains a pointer to the actual data. This data resides in the page cache. In this manner, the buffer subsystem and the page cache are unified.

In early versions of the Linux kernel—before 2.4—the buffer subsystem was separate from the page cache, and thus there was both a page and a buffer cache. This implied that data could exist in the buffer cache (as a dirty buffer) and the page cache (as cached data) at the same time. Naturally, synchronizing these two separate caches took some effort. The unified page cache introduced in the 2.4 Linux kernel was a welcomed improvement.

Deferred writes and the buffer subsystem in Linux enable fast writes at the expense of the risk of data loss on power failure. To avoid this risk, paranoid and critical applications can use synchronized I/O (discussed earlier in this chapter).

Conclusion

This chapter discussed the basics of Linux system programming: file I/O. On a system such as Linux, which strives to represent as much as possible as a file, it's very important to know how to open, read, write, and close files. All of these operations are classic Unix and are represented in many standards.

The next chapter tackles buffered I/O and the standard C library's standard I/O interfaces. The standard C library is not just a convenience; buffering I/O in user space provides crucial performance improvements.

## CHAPTER 3

Buffered I/O

Recall from Chapter 1 that the *block* is an abstraction representing the smallest unit of storage on a filesystem. Inside the kernel, all filesystem operations occur in terms of blocks. Indeed, the block is the lingua franca of I/O. Consequently, no I/O operation may execute on an amount of data less than the block size or that is not an integer multiple of the block size. If you only want to read a byte, too bad: you'll have to read a whole block. Want to write 4.5 blocks worth of data? You'll need to write 5 blocks, which implies reading that partial block in its entirety, updating only the half you've changed, and then writing back the whole block.

You can see where this is leading: partial block operations are inefficient. The operating system has to "fix up" your I/O by ensuring that everything occurs on block-aligned boundaries and rounding up to the next largest block. Unfortunately, this is not how user-space applications are generally written. Most applications operate in terms of higher-level abstractions, such as fields and strings, whose size varies independently of the block size. At its worst, a user-space application might read and write but a single byte at a time! That's a lot of waste. Each of those one-byte writes is actually writing a whole block.

The situation is exacerbated by the extraneous system calls required to read, say, a single byte 1,024 times rather than a single 1,024-byte block all at once. The solution to this pathological performance problem is *user-buffered I/O*, a way for applications to read and write data in whatever amounts feel natural but have the actual I/O occur in units of the filesystem block size.

User-Buffered I/O

Programs that have to issue many small I/O requests to regular files often perform user-buffered I/O. This refers to buffering done in user space, either manually by the application or transparently in a library, not to buffering done by the kernel. As discussed in

Chapter 2, for reasons of performance, the kernel buffers data internally by delaying writes, coalescing adjacent I/O requests, and reading ahead. Through different means, user buffering also aims to improve performance.

Consider an example using the user-space program *dd*:

```
dd bs=1 count=2097152 if=/dev/zero of=pirate
```

Because of the bs=1 argument, this command will copy two megabytes from the device */dev/zero* (a virtual device providing an endless stream of zeros) to the file *pirate* in 2,097,152 one-byte chunks. That is, it will copy the data via about two million read and write operations—one byte at a time.

Now consider the same two megabyte copy, but using 1,024 byte blocks:

```
dd bs=1024 count=2048 if=/dev/zero of=pirate
```

This operation copies the same two megabytes to the same file, yet issues 1,024 times fewer read and write operations. The performance improvement is huge, as you can see in Table 3-1. Here, I've recorded the time taken (using three different measures) by four *dd* commands that differed only in block size. Real time is the total elapsed wall clock time, user time is the time spent executing the program's code in user space, and system time is the time spent executing system calls in kernel space on the process's behalf.

Table 3-1. Effects of block size on performance

Block size	Real time	User time	System time
1 byte	18.707 seconds	1.118 seconds	17.549 seconds
1,024 bytes	0.025 seconds	0.002 seconds	0.023 seconds
1,130 bytes	0.035 seconds	0.002 seconds	0.027 seconds

Using 1,024 byte chunks results in an *enormous* performance improvement compared to the single byte chunk. However, the table also demonstrates that using a larger block size—which implies even fewer system calls—can result in performance degradation if the operations are not performed in multiples of the disk's block size. Despite requiring fewer calls, the 1,130 byte requests end up generating unaligned requests, and are therefore less efficient than the 1,024 byte requests.

Taking advantage of this performance boon requires prior knowledge of the physical block size. The results in the table show the block size is most likely 1,024, an integer multiple of 1,024, or a divisor of 1,024. In the case of */dev/zero*, the block size is actually 4,096 bytes.

Block Size

In practice, blocks are usually 512, 1,024, 2,048, 4,096, or 8,192 bytes in size.

As Table 3-1 demonstrates, a large performance gain is realized simply by performing operations in chunks that are integer multiples or divisors of the block size. This is because the kernel and hardware speak in terms of blocks. Thus, using the block size or a value that fits neatly inside of a block guarantees block-aligned I/O requests and prevents extraneous work inside the kernel.

Figuring out the block size for a given device is easy using the stat() system call (covered in Chapter 8) or the *stat*(1) command. It turns out, however, that you generally do not need to know the actual block size.

The primary goal in picking a size for your I/O operations is to not pick an oddball size such as 1,130. No block in the history of Unix has been 1,130 bytes, and choosing such a size for your operations will result in unaligned I/O after the first request. Using any integer multiple or divisor of the block size, however, prevents unaligned requests. So long as your chosen size keeps everything block-aligned, performance will be good. Larger multiples will simply result in fewer system calls.

Therefore, the easiest choice is to perform I/O using a large buffer size that is a common multiple of the typical block sizes. Both 4,096 and 8,192 bytes work great.

So perform all your I/O in 4 or 8KB chunks and everything is great? Not so fast. The problem, of course, is that programs rarely deal in terms of blocks. Programs work with fields, lines, and single characters, not abstractions such as blocks. User-buffered I/O closes the gap between the filesystem, which speaks in blocks, and the application, which talks in its own abstractions. How it works is simple, yet very powerful: as data is written, it is stored in a buffer inside the program's address space. When the buffer reaches a set size, called the *buffer size*, the entire buffer is written out in a single write operation. Likewise, data is read using buffer-sized, block-aligned chunks. The application's various-sized read requests are served not directly from the filesystem, but via the chunks of the buffer. As the application reads more and more, data is handed out from the buffer piece-by-piece. Ultimately, when the buffer is empty, another large block-aligned chunk is read in. In this manner, although the application reads and writes in whatever odd sizes it chooses, data is buffered such that only large, block-aligned reads and writes are actually issued to the filesystem. The end result is fewer system calls for larger amounts of data, all aligned on block boundaries. Huge performance benefits ensue.

It is possible to implement user buffering by hand in your own programs. Indeed, many mission-critical applications do just that. The vast majority of programs, however, make use of the popular *standard I/O library* (part of the *standard C library*) or the *iostream library* (part of the *standard C++ library*), which provides a robust and capable user-buffering solution.

Standard I/O

The standard C library provides the standard I/O library (often simply called *stdio*), which in turn provides a platform-independent, user-buffering solution. The standard I/O library is simple to use, yet powerful.

Unlike programming languages such as FORTRAN, the C language does not include any built-in support or keywords providing any functionality more advanced than flow control, arithmetic, and so on—there's certainly no inherent support for I/O. As the C programming language progressed, users developed standard sets of routines to provide core functionality, such as string manipulation, mathematical routines, time and date functionality, and I/O. Over time, these routines matured, and with the ratification of the ANSI C standard in 1989 (C89) they were eventually formalized as the standard C library. Although C95, C99, and C11 added several new interfaces, the standard I/O library has remained relatively untouched since its creation in 1989.

The remainder of this chapter discusses user-buffered I/O as it pertains to file I/O, and is implemented in the standard C library—that is, opening, closing, reading, and writing files via the standard C library. Whether an application will use standard I/O, a home-rolled user-buffering solution, or straight system calls is a decision that developers must make carefully after weighing their application's needs and behavior.

The C standards always leave some details up to each implementation, and implementations often add additional features. This chapter, as with the rest of this book, documents the interfaces and behavior as they are implemented in *glibc* on a modern Linux system. Where Linux deviates from the standard, this is noted.

File Pointers

StandardI/O routines do not operate directly on file descriptors. Instead, they use their own unique identifier, known as the *file pointer*. Inside the C library, the file pointer maps to a file descriptor. The file pointer is represented by a pointer to the FILE typedef, which is defined in <stdio.h>.

FILE: Why the Caps?

The FILE name is often derided for its ugly use of all-caps, which is particularly egregious given that the C standard (and consequently most application's own coding styles) use all-lowercase names for functions and types. The peculiarity lies in history: standard I/O was originally written as macros. Not only FILE but all of the methods in the library were implemented as a set of macros. The style at the time, which remains common to this day, is to give macros all-caps names. As the C language progressed and standard I/O was ratified as an official part, most of the methods were reimplemented as proper functions and FILE became a typedef. But the uppercase remains.

In standard I/O parlance, an open file is called a *stream*. Streams may be opened for reading (*input streams*), writing (*output streams*), or both (*input/output streams*).

Opening Files

Files are opened for reading or writing via fopen():

```
#include <stdio.h>

FILE * fopen (const char *path, const char *mode);
```

This function opens the file path with the behavior given by mode and associates a new stream with it.

Modes

The mode argument describes how to open the given file. It is one of the following strings:

r

Open the file for reading. The stream is positioned at the start of the file.

r+

Open the file for both reading and writing. The stream is positioned at the start of the file.

w

Open the file for writing. If the file exists, it is truncated to zero length. If the file does not exist, it is created. The stream is positioned at the start of the file.

w+

Open the file for both reading and writing. If the file exists, it is truncated to zero length. If the file does not exist, it is created. The stream is positioned at the start of the file.

a

Open the file for writing in append mode. The file is created if it does not exist. The stream is positioned at the end of the file. All writes will append to the file.

a+

Open the file for both reading and writing in append mode. The file is created if it does not exist. The stream is positioned at the end of the file. All writes will append to the file.

The given mode may also contain the character b, although this value is always ignored on Linux. Some operating systems treat text and binary files differently, and the b mode instructs the file to be opened in binary mode. Linux, as with all POSIX-conforming systems, treats text and binary files identically.

Upon success, fopen() returns a valid FILE pointer. On failure, it returns NULL and sets errno appropriately.

For example, the following code opens /etc/manifest for reading and associates it with stream:

```
FILE *stream;

stream = fopen ("/etc/manifest", "r");
if (!stream)
        /* error */
```

Opening a Stream via File Descriptor

The function fdopen() converts an already open file descriptor (fd) to a stream:

```
#include <stdio.h>

FILE * fdopen (int fd, const char *mode);
```

The possible modes are the same as for fopen() and must be compatible with the modes originally used to open the file descriptor. The modes w and w+ may be specified, but they will not cause truncation. The stream is positioned at the file position associated with the file descriptor.

Once a file descriptor is converted to a stream, I/O should no longer be directly performed on the file descriptor. It is, however, legal to do so. Note that the file descriptor is not duplicated, but is merely associated with a new stream. Closing the stream will close the file descriptor as well.

On success, `fdopen()` returns a valid file pointer; on failure, it returns `NULL` and sets `errno` appropriately.

For example, the following code opens the file */home/kidd/map.txt* via the `open()` system call and then uses the backing file descriptor to create an associated stream:

```
FILE *stream;
int fd;

fd = open ("/home/kidd/map.txt", O_RDONLY);
if (fd == -1)
        /* error */

stream = fdopen (fd, "r");
if (!stream)
        /* error */
```

Closing Streams

The `fclose()` function closes a given stream:

```
#include <stdio.h>

int fclose (FILE *stream);
```

Any buffered and not-yet-written data is first flushed. On success, `fclose()` returns 0. On failure, it returns `EOF` and sets `errno` appropriately.

Closing All Streams

The `fcloseall()` function closes all streams associated with the current process, including standard in, standard out, and standard error:

```
#define _GNU_SOURCE

#include <stdio.h>

int fcloseall (void);
```

Before closing, all streams are flushed. The function always returns 0; it is Linux-specific.

Reading from a Stream

Now that we know how to open and close streams, let's look at doing something useful: first reading from, and then writing to, them.

The standard C library implements multiple functions for reading from an open stream, ranging from the common to the esoteric. This section will look at three of the most popular approaches to reading: reading one character at a time, reading an entire line at a time, and reading binary data. To read from a stream, it must have been opened as an input stream with the appropriate mode; that is, any valid mode except w or a.

Reading a Character at a Time

Often, the ideal I/O pattern is simply reading one character at a time. The function fgetc() is used to read a single character from a stream:

```
#include <stdio.h>

int fgetc (FILE *stream);
```

This function reads the next character from stream and returns it as an unsigned char cast to an int. The casting is done to have a sufficient range for notification of end-of-file or error: EOF is returned in such conditions. The return value of fgetc() must be stored in an int. Storing it in a char is a common but dangerous mistake, as you'll lose the ability to detect errors.

The following example reads a single character from stream, checks for errors, and then prints the result as a char:

```
int c;

c = fgetc (stream);
if (c == EOF)
        /* error */
else
        printf ("c=%c\n", (char) c);
```

The stream pointed at by stream must be open for reading.

Putting the character back

Standard I/O provides a function for pushing a character back onto a stream, allowing you to "peek" at the stream and return the character if it turns out that you don't want it:

```
#include <stdio.h>

int ungetc (int c, FILE *stream);
```

Each call pushes back c, cast to an unsigned char, onto stream. On success, c is returned; on failure, EOF is returned. A subsequent read from stream will return c. If multiple characters are pushed back, they are returned in the reverse order, *last in/first out* like a stack—that is, the more recently pushed character is returned first. The C standard dictates that only one pushback is guaranteed to succeed without intervening read requests. Some implementations, in turn, allow only a single pushback; Linux allows an infinite number of pushbacks, so long as memory is available. One pushback, of course, always succeeds.

If you make an intervening call to a seeking function (see "Seeking a Stream" on page 80) after calling ungetc() but before issuing a read request, it will cause all pushed-back characters to be discarded. This is true among threads in a single process, as threads share the buffer.

Reading an Entire Line

The function fgets() reads a string from a given stream:

```
#include <stdio.h>

char * fgets (char *str, int size, FILE *stream);
```

This function reads up to *one less* than size bytes from stream and stores the results in str. A null character (\0) is stored in the buffer after the last byte read in. Reading stops after an EOF or a newline character is reached. If a newline is read, the \n is stored in str.

On success, str is returned; on failure, NULL is returned.

For example:

```
char buf[LINE_MAX];

if (!fgets (buf, LINE_MAX, stream))
        /* error */
```

POSIX defines LINE_MAX in <limits.h>: it is the maximum size of input line that POSIX line-manipulating interfaces can handle. Linux's C library has no such limitation—lines may be of any size—but there is no way to communicate that with the LINE_MAX definition. Portable programs can use LINE_MAX to remain safe; it is set relatively high on Linux. Linux-specific programs need not worry about limits on the sizes of lines.

Reading arbitrary strings

Often, the line-based reading of fgets() is useful. Nearly as often, it is annoying. Sometimes, developers want to use a delimiter other than the newline. Other times, developers do not want a delimiter at all—and rarely do developers want the delimiter stored in the buffer! In retrospect, the decision to store the newline in the returned buffer rarely appears correct.

It is not hard to write an fgets() replacement that uses fgetc(). For example, this snippet reads the n − 1 bytes from stream into str, and then appends a \0 character:

```
char *s;
int c;

s = str;
while (--n > 0 && (c = fgetc (stream)) != EOF)
```

```
        *s++ = c;
    *s = '\0';
```

The snippet can be expanded to also stop reading at a delimiter, given by the integer d (which cannot be the null character in this example):

```
char *s;
int c = 0;

s = str;
while (--n > 0 && (c = fgetc (stream)) != EOF && (*s++ = c) != d)
        ;

if (c == d)
        *--s = '\0';
else
        *s = '\0';
```

Setting d to \n would provide behavior similar to fgets(), minus storing the newline in the buffer.

Depending on the implementation of fgets(), this variant is probably slower, as it issues repeated function calls to fgetc(). This is not the same problem exhibited by our original *dd* example, however! Although this snippet incurs additional function call overhead, it does not incur the system call overhead and unaligned I/O penalty burdened on *dd* with bs=1. The latter are much larger problems.

Reading Binary Data

For some applications, reading individual characters or lines is insufficient. Sometimes, developers want to read and write complex binary data, such as C structures. For this, the standard I/O library provides fread():

```
#include <stdio.h>

size_t fread (void *buf, size_t size, size_t nr, FILE *stream);
```

A call to fread() will read up to nr elements of data, each of size bytes, from stream into the buffer pointed at by buf. The file pointer is advanced by the number of bytes read.

The number of elements read (not the number of bytes read!) is returned. The function indicates failure or EOF via a return value less than nr. Unfortunately, it is impossible to know which of the two conditions occurred without using ferror() and feof() (see "Errors and End-of-File" on page 83).

Because of differences in variable sizes, alignment, padding, and byte order, binary data written with one application may not be readable by a different application, or even by the same application on a different machine.

Issues of Alignment

All machine architectures have *data alignment* requirements. Programmers tend to think of memory as simply an array of bytes. Our processors, however, do not read and write from memory in byte-sized chunks. Instead, processors access memory with a specific granularity, such as 2, 4, 8, or 16 bytes. Since each process's address space starts at address 0, processes must initiate access from an address that is an integer multiple of the granularity.

Consequently, C variables must be stored at and accessed from aligned addresses. In general, variables are *naturally aligned*, which refers to the alignment that corresponds to the size of the C data type. For example, a 32-bit integer is aligned on a 4-byte boundary. In other words, on most architectures, an int is be stored at a memory address that is evenly divisible by four.

Accessing misaligned data has various penalties, which depend on the machine architecture. Some processors can access misaligned data, but with a performance penalty. Other processors cannot access misaligned data at all, and attempting to do so causes a hardware exception. Worse, some processors silently drop the low-order bits in order to force the address to be aligned, almost certainly resulting in unintended behavior.

Normally, the compiler naturally aligns all data, and alignment is not a visible issue to the programmer. Dealing with structures, performing memory management by hand, saving binary data to disk, and communicating over a network may bring alignment issues to the forefront. System programmers, therefore, ought to be well versed in these issues.

Chapter 9 addresses alignment in greater depth.

The simplest example of fread() is reading a single element of linear bytes from a given stream:

```
char buf[64];
size_t nr;

nr = fread (buf, sizeof(buf), 1, stream);
if (nr == 0)
        /* error */
```

We will look at examples that are more complicated when we study the write counterpart to fread(), fwrite().

Writing to a Stream

As with reading, the standard C library defines several functions for writing to an open stream. This section will look at three of the most popular approaches to writing: writing a single character, writing a string of characters, and writing binary data. Such varied writing approaches are ideally suited to buffered I/O. To write to a stream, it must have been opened as an output stream with the appropriate mode, that is, any valid mode except r.

Writing a Single Character

The counterpart of fgetc() is fputc():

```
#include <stdio.h>

int fputc (int c, FILE *stream);
```

The fputc() function writes the byte specified by c (cast to an unsigned char) to the stream pointed at by stream. Upon successful completion, the function returns c. Otherwise, it returns EOF, and errno is set appropriately.

Use is simple:

```
if (fputc ('p', stream) == EOF)
        /* error */
```

This example writes the character p to stream, which must be open for writing.

Writing a String of Characters

The function fputs() is used to write an entire string to a given stream:

```
#include <stdio.h>

int fputs (const char *str, FILE *stream);
```

A call to fputs() writes all of the null-terminated string pointed at by str to the stream pointed at by stream. On success, fputs() returns a nonnegative number. On failure, it returns EOF.

The following example opens the file for writing in append mode, writes the given string to the associated stream, and then closes the stream:

```
FILE *stream;

stream = fopen ("journal.txt", "a");
if (!stream)
        /* error */

if (fputs ("The ship is made of wood.\n", stream) == EOF)
        /* error */

if (fclose (stream) == EOF)
        /* error */
```

Writing Binary Data

Individual characters and lines will not cut it when programs need to write complex data. To directly store binary data such as C variables, standard I/O provides `fwrite()`:

```
#include <stdio.h>

size_t fwrite (void *buf,
               size_t size,
               size_t nr,
               FILE *stream);
```

A call to `fwrite()` will write to `stream` up to `nr` elements, each `size` bytes in length, from the data pointed at by `buf`. The file pointer will be advanced by the total number of bytes written.

The number of elements (not the number of bytes!) successfully written will be returned. A return value less than `nr` denotes error.

Sample Program Using Buffered I/O

Now let's look at an example—a complete program, in fact—that integrates many of the interfaces we have covered thus far in this chapter. This program first defines `struct pirate` and then declares two variables of that type. The program initializes one of the variables and subsequently writes it out to disk via an output stream to the file *data*. Via a different stream, the program reads the data back in from *data* directly to the other instance of `struct pirate`. Finally, the program writes the contents of the structure to standard out:

```
#include <stdio.h>

int main (void)
{
        FILE *in, *out;
        struct pirate {
                char            name[100]; /* real name */
                unsigned long   booty;      /* in pounds sterling */
                unsigned int    beard_len; /* in inches */
        } p, blackbeard = { "Edward Teach", 950, 48 };

        out = fopen ("data", "w");
        if (!out) {
                perror ("fopen");
                return 1;
        }

        if (!fwrite (&blackbeard, sizeof (struct pirate), 1, out)) {
                perror ("fwrite");
                return 1;
```

```
        }

        if (fclose (out)) {
                perror ("fclose");
                return 1;
        }

        in = fopen ("data", "r");
        if (!in) {
                perror ("fopen");
                return 1;
        }

        if (!fread (&p, sizeof (struct pirate), 1, in)) {
                perror ("fread");
                return 1;
        }

        if (fclose (in)) {
                perror ("fclose");
                return 1;
        }

        printf ("name=\"%s\" booty=%lu beard_len=%u\n",
                p.name, p.booty, p.beard_len);

        return 0;
}
```

The output is, of course, the original values:

```
name="Edward Teach" booty=950 beard_len=48
```

Again, it's important to bear in mind that because of differences in variable sizes, alignment, and so on, binary data written with one application may not be readable by other applications. That is, a different application—or even the same application on a different machine—may not be able to correctly read back the data written with fwrite(). In our example, consider the ramifications if the size of unsigned long changed, or if the amount of padding varied. These things are guaranteed to remain constant only on a particular machine type with a particular ABI.

Seeking a Stream

Often, it is useful to manipulate the current stream position. Perhaps the application is reading a complex record-based file and needs to jump around. Alternatively, perhaps the stream needs to be reset to position zero. Whatever the case, standard I/O provides a family of interfaces equivalent in functionality to the system call lseek() (discussed in Chapter 2). The fseek() function, the most common of the standard I/O seeking interfaces, manipulates the file position of stream in accordance with offset and whence:

```
#include <stdio.h>

int fseek (FILE *stream, long offset, int whence);
```

If whence is set to SEEK_SET, the file position is set to offset. If whence is set to SEEK_CUR, the file position is set to the current position plus offset. If whence is set to SEEK_END, the file position is set to the end of the file plus offset.

Upon successful completion, fseek() returns 0, clears the EOF indicator, and undoes the effects (if any) of ungetc(). On error, it returns –1, and errno is set appropriately. The most common errors are invalid stream (EBADF) and invalid whence argument (EINVAL).

Alternatively, standard I/O provides fsetpos():

```
#include <stdio.h>

int fsetpos (FILE *stream, fpos_t *pos);
```

This function sets the stream position of stream to pos. It works the same as fseek() with a whence argument of SEEK_SET. On success, it returns 0. Otherwise, it returns –1, and errno is set as appropriate. This function (along with its counterpart fgetpos(), which we will cover shortly) is provided solely for other (non-Unix) platforms that have complex types representing the stream position. On those platforms, this function is the only way to set the stream position to an arbitrary value, as the C long type is presumably insufficient. Linux-specific applications need not use this interface, although they may, if they want to be portable to all possible platforms.

Standard I/O also provides rewind(), as a shortcut:

```
#include <stdio.h>

void rewind (FILE *stream);
```

The invocation:

```
rewind (stream);
```

resets the position back to the start of the stream. It is equivalent to:

```
fseek (stream, 0, SEEK_SET);
```

except that it also clears the error indicator.

Note that rewind() has no return value and thus cannot directly communicate error conditions. Callers wishing to ascertain the existence of an error should clear errno before invocation, and check to see whether the variable is nonzero afterward. For example:

```
errno = 0;
rewind (stream);
if (errno)
        /* error */
```

Obtaining the Current Stream Position

Unlike lseek(), fseek() does not return the updated position. A separate interface is provided for this purpose. The ftell() function returns the current stream position of stream:

```
#include <stdio.h>

long ftell (FILE *stream);
```

On error, it returns −1 and errno is set appropriately.

Alternatively, standard I/O provides fgetpos():

```
#include <stdioh.h>

int fgetpos (FILE *stream, fpos_t *pos);
```

Upon success, fgetpos() returns 0, and places the current stream position of stream in pos. On failure, it returns −1 and sets errno appropriately. Like fsetpos(), fget pos() is provided solely for non-Unix platforms with complex file position types.

Flushing a Stream

The standard I/O library provides an interface for writing out the user buffer to the kernel, ensuring that all data written to a stream is flushed via write(). The fflush() function provides this functionality:

```
#include <stdio.h>

int fflush (FILE *stream);
```

On invocation, any unwritten data in the stream pointed to by stream is flushed to the kernel. If stream is NULL, *all* open input streams in the process are flushed. On success, fflush() returns 0. On failure, it returns EOF, and errno is set appropriately.

To understand the effect of fflush(), you have to understand the difference between the buffer maintained by the C library and the kernel's own buffering. All of the calls described in this chapter work with a buffer that is maintained by the C library, which resides in user space, not kernel space. That is where the performance improvement comes in—you are staying in user space and therefore running user code, not issuing system calls. A system call is issued only when the disk or some other medium has to be accessed.

`fflush()` merely writes the user-buffered data out to the kernel buffer. The effect is the same as if user buffering was not employed and `write()` was used directly. It does not guarantee that the data is physically committed to any medium—for that need, use something like `fsync()` (see "Synchronized I/O" on page 40). For situations where you are concerned with ensuring that your data is commited to the backing store, you will want to call `fflush()`, followed immediately by `fsync()`: that is, first ensure that the user buffer is written out to the kernel and then ensure that the kernel's buffer is written out to disk.

Errors and End-of-File

Some of the standard I/O interfaces, such as `fread()`, communicate failures back to the caller poorly, as they provide no mechanism for differentiating between error and end-of-file. With these calls, and on other occasions, it can be useful to check the status of a given stream to determine whether it has encountered an error or reached the end of a file. Standard I/O provides two interfaces to this end. The function `ferror()` tests whether the error indicator is set on `stream`:

```
#include <stdio.h>

int ferror (FILE *stream);
```

The error indicator is set by other standard I/O interfaces in response to an error condition. The function returns a nonzero value if the indicator is set, and 0 otherwise.

The function `feof()` tests whether the EOF indicator is set on `stream`:

```
#include <stdio.h>

int feof (FILE *stream);
```

The EOF indicator is set by other standard I/O interfaces when the end of a file is reached. This function returns a nonzero value if the indicator is set, and 0 otherwise.

The `clearerr()` function clears the error and the EOF indicators for `stream`:

```
#include <stdio.h>

void clearerr (FILE *stream);
```

It has no return value, and cannot fail (there is no way to know whether an invalid stream was provided). You should make a call to `clearerr()` only after checking the error and EOF indicators, as they will be discarded irretrievably afterward. For example:

```
/* 'f' is a valid stream */

if (ferror (f))
        printf ("Error on f!\n");
```

```
if (feof (f))
        printf ("EOF on f!\n");

clearerr (f);
```

Obtaining the Associated File Descriptor

Sometimes it is advantageous to obtain the file descriptor backing a given stream. For example, it might be useful to perform a system call on a stream, via its file descriptor, when an associated standard I/O function does not exist. To obtain the file descriptor backing a stream, use `fileno()`:

```
#include <stdio.h>

int fileno (FILE *stream);
```

Upon success, `fileno()` returns the file descriptor associated with `stream`. On failure, it returns –1. This can only happen when the given stream is invalid, in which case, the function sets `errno` to `EBADF`.

Intermixing standard I/O calls with system calls is not normally advised. Programmers must exercise caution when using `fileno()` to ensure their file descriptor—based actions do not conflict with the user buffering. Particularly, a good practice is to flush the stream before manipulating the backing file descriptor. You should almost never intermix file descriptor and stream-based I/O operations.

Controlling the Buffering

Standard I/O implements three types of user buffering and provides developers with an interface for controlling the type and size of the buffer. The different types of user buffering serve different purposes and are ideal for different situations.

Unbuffered
> No user buffering is performed. Data is submitted directly to the kernel. As this disables user buffering, negating any benefit, this option is not commonly used, with a lone exception: standard error, by default, is unbuffered.

Line-buffered
> Buffering is performed on a per-line basis. With each newline character, the buffer is submitted to the kernel. Line buffering makes sense for streams being output to the screen, since messages printed to the screen are delimited with newlines. Consequently, this is the default buffering used for streams connected to terminals, such as standard out.

Block-buffered

Buffering is performed on a per-block basis, where a block is a fixed number of bytes. This is the type of buffering discussed at the beginning of this chapter and it is ideal for files. By default, all streams associated with files are block-buffered. Standard I/O uses the term *full buffering* for block buffering.

Most of the time, the default buffering type is correct and optimal. However, standard I/O does provide an interface for controlling the type of buffering employed:

```
#include <stdio.h>

int setvbuf (FILE *stream, char *buf, int mode, size_t size);
```

The setvbuf() function sets the buffering type of stream to mode, which must be one of the following:

_IONBF
    Unbuffered

_IOLBF
    Line-buffered

_IOFBF
    Block-buffered

Except with _IONBF, in which case buf and size are ignored, buf may point to a buffer of size bytes that standard I/O will use as the buffer for the given stream. If buf is NULL, a buffer of the size you specify is allocated automatically by *glibc*.

The setvbuf() function must be called after opening the stream but before any other operations have been performed on it. It returns 0 on success, and a nonzero value otherwise.

The supplied buffer, if any, must exist when the stream is closed. A common mistake is to declare the buffer as an automatic variable in a scope that ends before the stream is closed. Particularly, be careful not to provide a buffer local to main() and then fail to explicitly close the streams. For example, the following is a bug:

```
#include <stdio.h>

int main (void)
{
        char buf[BUFSIZ];

        /* set stdin to block-buffered with a BUFSIZ buffer */
        setvbuf (stdout, buf, _IOFBF, BUFSIZ);
        printf ("Arrr!\n");

        return 0;
```

```
                    /* 'buf' exits scope and is freed, but stdout isn't closed until later */
    }
```

This class of bug can be prevented by explicitly closing the stream before exiting the scope or by making buf a global variable.

Generally, developers need not mess with the buffering on a stream. With the exception of standard error, terminals are line-buffered, and that makes sense. Files are block-buffered, and that, too, makes sense. The default buffer size for block buffering is BUFSIZ, defined in <stdio.h>, and it is usually an optimal choice (a large multiple of a typical block size).

Thread Safety

Threads are the units of execution within a process. Most processes have a single thread. Processes, however, can boast multiple threads, each executing their own code. We call such processes *multithreaded*. One way to conceptualize a multithreaded process is as multiple processes that share an address space. Without explicit coordination, threads can run at any time, interleaving in any way. On a multiprocessor system, two or more threads in the same process may even run concurrently. Threads can overwrite shared data unless care is taken to synchronize access to the data (a practice called *locking*) or make it *thread-local* (a practice called *thread confinement*).

Operating systems that support threads provide locking mechanisms (programming constructs that ensure mutual exclusion) to ensure that threads do not stomp on each other's feet. Standard I/O uses these mechanisms, ensuring that multiple threads in a single process may issue concurrent standard I/O calls—even against the same stream! —without the concurrent operations trampling on each other. Still, they are not always adequate. For example, sometimes you want to lock a group of calls, enlarging the *critical region* (the chunk of code that runs without interference from another thread) from one I/O operation to several. In other situations, you may want to eliminate locking altogether to improve efficiency.[1] In this section, we will discuss how to do both.

The standard I/O functions are inherently *thread-safe*. Internally, they associate a lock, a lock count, and an owning thread with each open stream. Any given thread must acquire the lock and become the owning thread before issuing any I/O requests. Two or more threads operating on the same stream cannot interleave standard I/O operations, and thus, within the context of single function calls, standard I/O operations are atomic.

---

1. Normally, eliminating locking will lead to an assortment of problems. But some programs might implement their thread safety strategy to delegate all I/O to a single thread, a form of thread confinement. In that case, there is no need for the overhead of locking.

Of course, in practice, many applications require greater atomicity than at the level of individual function calls. For example, imagine multiple threads in a single process issuing write requests. As the standard I/O functions are thread-safe, the individual writes will not interleave and result in garbled output. That is, even if two threads each issue a write request at the same time, locking will ensure that one write request completes before the other. But what if the process wants to issue several write requests in a row, all without the risk of another thread's write requests interleaving not just the individual request, but the set of requests as a whole? To allow for this, standard I/O provides a family of functions for individually manipulating the lock associated with a stream.

Manual File Locking

The function flockfile() waits until stream is no longer locked, bumps the lock count, and then acquires the lock, becoming the owning thread of the stream, and returns:

```
#include <stdio.h>

void flockfile (FILE *stream);
```

The function funlockfile() decrements the lock count associated with stream:

```
#include <stdio.h>

void funlockfile (FILE *stream);
```

If the lock count reaches zero, the current thread relinquishes ownership of the stream. Another thread is now able to acquire the lock.

These calls can nest. That is, a single thread can issue multiple flockfile() calls, and the stream will not unlock until the process issues a corresponding number of funlock file() calls.

The ftrylockfile() function is a nonblocking version of flockfile():

```
#include <stdio.h>

int ftrylockfile (FILE *stream);
```

If stream is currently locked, ftrylockfile() does nothing and immediately returns a nonzero value. If stream is not currently locked, it acquires the lock, bumps the lock count, becomes the owning thread of stream, and returns 0.

Let's consider an example. Let's say we want to write out several lines to a file, ensuring that the lines are written out without interleaving write operations from other threads:

```
flockfile (stream);

fputs ("List of treasure:\n", stream);
fputs ("    (1) 500 gold coins\n", stream);
```

```
        fputs ("    (2) Wonderfully ornate dishware\n", stream);

    funlockfile (stream);
```

Although the individual `fputs()` operations could never race with other I/O—for example, we would never end up with anything interleaving with "List of treasure"—another standard I/O operation from another thread to this same stream could interleave between two `fputs()` calls. Ideally, an application is designed such that multiple threads are not submitting I/O to the same stream. If your application does need to do so, however, and you need an atomic region greater than a single function, `flockfile()` and friends can save the day.

Unlocked Stream Operations

There is a second reason for performing manual locking on streams. With the finergrained and more precise control of locking that only the application programmer can provide, it might be possible to minimize the overhead of locking and to improve performance. To this end, Linux provides a family of functions, cousins to the usual standard I/O interfaces, that do not perform any locking whatsoever. They are, in effect, the unlocked counterparts to standard I/O:

```
#define _GNU_SOURCE

#include <stdio.h>

int fgetc_unlocked (FILE *stream);
char *fgets_unlocked (char *str, int size, FILE *stream);
size_t fread_unlocked (void *buf, size_t size, size_t nr,
                       FILE *stream);
int fputc_unlocked (int c, FILE *stream);
int fputs_unlocked (const char *str, FILE *stream);
size_t fwrite_unlocked (void *buf, size_t size, size_t nr,
                        FILE *stream);
int fflush_unlocked (FILE *stream);
int feof_unlocked (FILE *stream);
int ferror_unlocked (FILE *stream);
int fileno_unlocked (FILE *stream);
void clearerr_unlocked (FILE *stream);
```

These functions all behave identically to their locked cousins, except that they do not check for or acquire the lock associated with the given `stream`. If locking is required, it is the responsibility of the programmer to ensure that the lock is manually acquired and released.

Relegating I/O

There is a sizable performance win from using the unlocked standard I/O functions. Moreover, there's a nontrivial amount of code simplicity in not having to worry about locking complex operations with `flockfile()`. When designing your application, consider relegating all I/O to a single thread (or all I/O to a pool of threads, where each stream is mapped to exactly one thread in the pool).

Although POSIX does define some unlocked variants of the standard I/O functions, none of the above functions are defined by POSIX. They are all Linux-specific, although various other Unix systems support a subset.

We'll discuss threads thoroughly in Chapter 7.

Critiques of Standard I/O

As widely used as standard I/O is, some experts point to flaws in it. Some of the functions, such as `fgets()`, are occasionally inadequate and ill-designed. Other functions, such as `gets()`, are so horrendous that they have been all but evicted from the standards.

The biggest complaint with standard I/O is the performance impact from the double copy. When reading data, standard I/O issues a `read()` system call to the kernel, copying the data from the kernel to the standard I/O buffer. When an application then issues a read request via standard I/O using, say, `fgetc()`, the data is copied again, this time from the standard I/O buffer to the supplied buffer. Write requests work in the opposite fashion: the data is copied once from the supplied buffer to the standard I/O buffer and then later from the standard I/O buffer to the kernel via `write()`.

An alternative implementation could avoid the double copy by having each read request return a pointer into the standard I/O buffer. The data could then be read directly, inside of the standard I/O buffer, without ever needing an extraneous copy. In the event that the application did want the data in its own local buffer—perhaps to write to it—it could always perform the copy manually. This implementation would provide a "free" interface, allowing applications to signal when they are done with a given chunk of the read buffer.

Writes would be a bit more complicated, but the double copy could still be avoided. When issuing a write request, the implementation would record the pointer. Ultimately, when ready to flush the data to the kernel, the implementation could walk its list of stored pointers, writing out the data. This could be done using scatter-gather I/O, via `writev()`, and thus incur only a single system call. (We will discuss scatter-gather I/O in the next chapter.)

Highly optimal user-buffering libraries exist, solving the double copy problem with implementations similar to what we've just discussed. Alternatively, some developers choose to implement their own user-buffering solutions. But despite these alternatives, standard I/O remains popular.

Conclusion

Standard I/O is a user-buffering library provided as part of the standard C library. Modulo a few flaws, it is a powerful and very popular solution. Many C programmers, in fact, know nothing but standard I/O. Certainly, for terminal I/O, where line-based buffering is ideal, standard I/O is the only game in town. You don't often use `write()` to print to standard out!

Standard I/O—and user buffering in general, for that matter—makes sense when any of the following are true:

- You could conceivably issue many system calls, and you want to minimize the overhead by combining many calls into few.
- Performance is crucial, and you want to ensure that all I/O occurs in block-sized chunks on block-aligned boundaries.
- Your access patterns are character- or line-based, and you want interfaces to make such access easy without issuing extraneous system calls.
- You prefer a higher-level interface to the low-level Linux system calls.

The most flexibility, however, exists when you work directly with the Linux system calls. In the next chapter, we will look at advanced forms of I/O and the associated system calls.

## CHAPTER 4

Advanced File I/O

In Chapter 2, we looked at the basic I/O system calls in Linux. These calls form not only the basis of file I/O, but also the foundation of virtually all communication on Linux. In Chapter 3, we looked at how user-space buffering is often needed on top of the basic I/O system calls, and we studied a specific user-space buffering solution, C's standard I/O library. In this chapter, we'll look at the advanced I/O system calls that Linux provides:

Scatter/gather I/O
> Allows a single call to read from or write data to many buffers at once; useful for bunching together fields of different data structures to form one I/O transaction.

Epoll
> Improves on the `poll()` and `select()` system calls described in Chapter 2; useful when hundreds of file descriptors need to be polled from a single thread.

Memory-mapped I/O
> Maps a file into memory, allowing file I/O to occur via simple memory manipulation; useful for certain patterns of I/O.

File advice
> Allows a process to provide hints to the kernel on the process's intended uses for a file; can result in improved I/O performance.

Asynchronous I/O
> Allows a process to issue I/O requests without waiting for them to complete; useful for juggling heavy I/O workloads without the use of threads.

The chapter will conclude with a discussion of performance considerations and the kernel's I/O subsystems.

Scatter/Gather I/O

Scatter/gather I/O is a method of input and output where a single system call writes to a vector of buffers from a single data stream, or, alternatively, reads into a vector of buffers from a single data stream. This type of I/O is so named because the data is *scattered into* or *gathered from* the given vector of buffers. An alternative name for this approach to input and output is *vectored I/O*. In comparison, the standard read and write system calls that we covered in Chapter 2 provide *linear I/O*.

Scatter/gather I/O provides several advantages over linear I/O methods:

More natural coding pattern
> If your data is naturally segmented—say, the fields of a predefined structure—vectored I/O allows for intuitive manipulation.

Efficiency
> A single vectored I/O operation can replace multiple linear I/O operations.

Performance
> In addition to a reduction in the number of issued system calls, a vectored I/O implementation can provide improved performance over a linear I/O implementation via internal optimizations.

Atomicity
> In contrast with multiple linear I/O operations, a process can execute a single vectored I/O operation with no risk of interleaving I/O from another process.

readv() and writev()

POSIX 1003.1-2001 defines, and Linux implements, a pair of system calls that implement scatter/gather I/O. The Linux implementation satisfies all of the goals listed in the previous section.

The readv() function reads count segments from the file descriptor fd into the buffers described by iov:

```
#include <sys/uio.h>

ssize_t readv (int fd,
               const struct iovec *iov,
               int count);
```

The writev() function writes at most count segments from the buffers described by iov into the file descriptor fd:

```
#include <sys/uio.h>

ssize_t writev (int fd,
                const struct iovec *iov,
                int count);
```

The readv() and writev() functions behave the same as read() and write(), respectively, except that multiple buffers are read from or written to.

Each iovec structure describes an independent disjoint buffer, which is called a *segment*:

```
#include <sys/uio.h>

struct iovec {
        void *iov_base;    /* pointer to start of buffer */
        size_t iov_len;    /* size of buffer in bytes */
};
```

A set of segments is called a *vector*. Each segment in the vector describes the address and length of a buffer in memory to or from which data should be written or read. The readv() function fills each buffer of iov_len bytes completely before proceeding to the next buffer. The writev() function always writes out all full iov_len bytes before proceeding to the next buffer. Both functions always operate on the segments in order, starting with iov[0], then iov[1], and so on, through iov[count-1].

Return values

On success, readv() and writev() return the number of bytes read or written, respectively. This number should be the sum of all count iov_len values. On error, the system calls return −1 and set errno as appropriate. These system calls can experience any of the errors of the read() and write() system calls, and will, upon receiving such errors, set the same errno codes. In addition, the standards define two other error situations.

First, because the return type is an ssize_t, if the sum of all count iov_len values is greater than SSIZE_MAX, no data will be transferred, −1 will be returned, and errno will be set to EINVAL.

Second, POSIX dictates that count must be larger than zero and less than or equal to IOV_MAX, which is defined in <limits.h>. In Linux, IOV_MAX is currently 1024. If count is 0, the system calls return 0.[1] If count is greater than IOV_MAX, no data is transferred, the calls return −1, and errno is set to EINVAL.

---

1. Note that other Unix systems may set errno to EINVAL if count is 0. This is explicitly allowed by the standards, which say that EINVAL may be set if that value is 0 or that the system can handle the zero case in some other (nonerror) way.

Optimizing the Count

During a vectored I/O operation, the Linux kernel must allocate internal data structures to represent each segment. Normally, this allocation occurs dynamically, based on the size of count. As an optimization, however, the Linux kernel creates a small array of segments on the stack that it uses if count is sufficiently small, negating the need to dynamically allocate the segments and thereby providing a small boost in performance. This threshold is currently eight, so if count is less than or equal to 8, the vectored I/O operation occurs in a very memory-efficient manner off of the process's kernel stack.

Most likely, you won't have a choice about how many segments you need to transfer at once in a given vectored I/O operation. If you are flexible, however, and are debating over a small value, choosing a value of eight or less definitely improves efficiency.

writev() example

Let's consider a simple example that writes out a vector of three segments, each containing a string of a different size. This self-contained program is complete enough to demonstrate writev(), yet simple enough to serve as a useful code snippet:

```
#include <stdio.h>
#include <sys/types.h>
#include <sys/stat.h>
#include <fcntl.h>
#include <string.h>
#include <sys/uio.h>

int main ()
{
        struct iovec iov[3];
        ssize_t nr;
        int fd, i;

        char *buf[] = {
                "The term buccaneer comes from the word boucan.\n",
                "A boucan is a wooden frame used for cooking meat.\n",
                "Buccaneer is the West Indies name for a pirate.\n" };

        fd = open ("buccaneer.txt", O_WRONLY | O_CREAT | O_TRUNC);
        if (fd == -1) {
                perror ("open");
                return 1;
        }

        /* fill out three iovec structures */
        for (i = 0; i < 3; i++) {
                iov[i].iov_base = buf[i];
```

```
                iov[i].iov_len = strlen(buf[i]) + 1;
        }
        /* with a single call, write them all out */
        nr = writev (fd, iov, 3);
        if (nr == -1) {
                perror ("writev");
                return 1;
        }
        printf ("wrote %d bytes\n", nr);

        if (close (fd)) {
                perror ("close");
                return 1;
        }

        return 0;
}
```

Running the program produces the desired result:

```
$ ./writev
wrote 148 bytes
```

As does reading the file:

```
$ cat buccaneer.txt
The term buccaneer comes from the word boucan.
A boucan is a wooden frame used for cooking meat.
Buccaneer is the West Indies name for a pirate.
```

readv() example

Now, let's consider an example program that uses the readv() system call to read from the previously generated text file using vectored I/O. This self-contained example is likewise simple yet complete:

```
#include <stdio.h>
#include <sys/types.h>
#include <sys/stat.h>
#include <fcntl.h>
#include <sys/uio.h>

int main ()
{
        char foo[48], bar[51], baz[49];
        struct iovec iov[3];
        ssize_t nr;
        int fd, i;

        fd = open ("buccaneer.txt", O_RDONLY);
        if (fd == -1) {
                perror ("open");
                return 1;
```

```
        }

        /* set up our iovec structures */
        iov[0].iov_base = foo;
        iov[0].iov_len = sizeof (foo);
        iov[1].iov_base = bar;
        iov[1].iov_len = sizeof (bar);
        iov[2].iov_base = baz;
        iov[2].iov_len = sizeof (baz);

        /* read into the structures with a single call */
        nr = readv (fd, iov, 3);
        if (nr == -1) {
                perror ("readv");
                return 1;
        }

        for (i = 0; i < 3; i++)
                printf ("%d: %s", i, (char *) iov[i].iov_base);

        if (close (fd)) {
                perror ("close");
                return 1;
        }

        return 0;
}
```

Running this program after running the previous program produces the following
results:

```
$ ./readv
0: The term buccaneer comes from the word boucan.
1: A boucan is a wooden frame used for cooking meat.
2: Buccaneer is the West Indies name for a pirate.
```

Implementation

A naïve implementation of readv() and writev() could be implemented in user space
as a simple loop, something similar to the following:

```
#include <unistd.h>
#include <sys/uio.h>

ssize_t naive_writev (int fd, const struct iovec *iov, int count)
{
        ssize_t ret = 0;
        int i;

        for (i = 0; i < count; i++) {
                ssize_t nr;

                errno = 0;
```

```
                nr = write (fd, iov[i].iov_base, iov[i].iov_len);
                if (nr == -1) {
                        if (errno == EINTR)
                                continue;
                        ret = -1;
                        break;
                }
                ret += nr;
        }

        return ret;
}
```

Thankfully, this is *not* the Linux implementation: Linux implements readv() and writev() as system calls and internally performs scatter/gather I/O. In fact, all I/O inside the Linux kernel is vectored; read() and write() are implemented as vectored I/O with a vector of only one segment.

Event Poll

Recognizing the limitations of both poll() and select(), the 2.6 Linux kernel[2] introduced the *event poll* (epoll) facility. While more complex than the two earlier interfaces, epoll solves the fundamental performance problem shared by both of them and adds several new features.

Both poll() and select() (discussed in Chapter 2) require the full list of file descriptors to watch on each invocation. The kernel must then walk the list of each file descriptor to be monitored. When this list grows large—it may contain hundreds or even thousands of file descriptors—walking the list on each invocation becomes a scalability bottleneck.

Epoll circumvents this problem by decoupling the monitor registration from the actual monitoring. One system call initializes an epoll context, another adds monitored file descriptors to or removes them from the context, and a third performs the actual event wait.

Creating a New Epoll Instance

An epoll context is created via epoll_create1():

```
#include <sys/epoll.h>

int epoll_create1 (int flags);
```

---

2. Epoll was introduced in the 2.5.44 development kernel and the interface was finalized as of 2.5.66. It is Linux-specific.

```
/* deprecated. use epoll_create1() in new code. */
int epoll_create (int size);
```

A successful call to `epoll_create1()` instantiates a new epoll instance and returns a file descriptor associated with the instance. This file descriptor has no relationship to a real file; it is just a handle to be used with subsequent calls using the epoll facility. The `flags` parameter allows the modification of epoll behavior. Currently, only `EPOLL_CLOEXEC` is a valid flag. It enables close-on-exec behavior.

On error, the call returns –1 and sets `errno` to one of the following:

EINVAL
: Invalid `flags` parameter.

EMFILE
: The user has reached their limit on the total number of open files.

ENFILE
: The system has reached its limit on the total number of open files.

ENOMEM
: Insufficient memory was available to complete the operation.

`epoll_create()` is a deprecated, older variant of `epoll_create1()`. It does not accept any flags. Instead, it takes a `size` argument, which is unused. `size` used to provide a hint about the number of file descriptors to be watched; nowadays the kernel dynamically sizes the required data structures and this parameter just needs to be greater than zero. If it is not, `EINVAL` is returned. New applications should only use this variant if they need to target systems running before `epoll_create1()` was introduced in Linux kernel 2.6.27 and *glibc* 2.9.

A typical call is:

```
int epfd;

epfd = epoll_create1 (0);
if (epfd < 0)
        perror ("epoll_create1");
```

The file descriptor returned from `epoll_create1()` should be destroyed via a call to `close()` after polling is finished.

Controlling Epoll

The `epoll_ctl()` system call can be used to add file descriptors to and remove file descriptors from a given epoll context:

```
#include <sys/epoll.h>

int epoll_ctl (int epfd,
```

```
        int op,
        int fd,
        struct epoll_event *event);
```

The header <sys/epoll.h> defines the epoll_event structure as:

```
struct epoll_event {
        __u32 events;   /* events */
        union {
                void *ptr;
                int fd;
                __u32 u32;
                __u64 u64;
        } data;
};
```

A successful call to epoll_ctl() controls the epoll instance associated with the file descriptor epfd. The parameter op specifies the operation to be taken against the file associated with fd. The event parameter further describes the behavior of the operation.

Here are valid values for the op parameter:

EPOLL_CTL_ADD
    Add a monitor on the file associated with the file descriptor fd to the epoll instance associated with epfd, per the events defined in event.

EPOLL_CTL_DEL
    Remove a monitor on the file associated with the file descriptor fd from the epoll instance associated with epfd.

EPOLL_CTL_MOD
    Modify an existing monitor of fd with the updated events specified by event.

The events field in the epoll_event structure lists which events to monitor on the given file descriptor. Multiple events can be bitwise-ORed together. Here are valid values:

EPOLLERR
    An error condition occurred on the file. This event is always monitored, even if it's not specified.

EPOLLET
    Enables edge-triggered behavior for the monitor of the file (see "Edge- Versus Level-Triggered Events" on page 103). The default behavior is level-triggered.

EPOLLHUP
    A hangup occurred on the file. This event is always monitored, even if it's not specified.

EPOLLIN
    The file is available to be read from without blocking.

EPOLLONESHOT
>   After an event is generated and read, the file is automatically no longer monitored. A new event mask must be specified via EPOLL_CTL_MOD to reenable the watch.

EPOLLOUT
>   The file is available to be written to without blocking.

EPOLLPRI
>   There is urgent out-of-band data available to read.

The data field inside the event_poll structure is for the user's private use. The contents are returned to the user upon receipt of the requested event. The common practice is to set event.data.fd to fd, which makes it easy to look up which file descriptor caused the event.

Upon success, epoll_ctl() returns 0. On failure, the call returns −1 and sets errno to one of the following values:

EBADF
>   epfd is not a valid epoll instance, or fd is not a valid file descriptor.

EEXIST
>   op was EPOLL_CTL_ADD, but fd is already associated with epfd.

EINVAL
>   epfd is not an epoll instance, epfd is the same as fd, or op is invalid.

ENOENT
>   op was EPOLL_CTL_MOD, or EPOLL_CTL_DEL, but fd is not associated with epfd.

ENOMEM
>   There was insufficient memory to process the request.

EPERM
>   fd does not support epoll.

As an example, to add a new watch on the file associated with fd to the epoll instance epfd, you would write:

```
struct epoll_event event;
int ret;

event.data.fd = fd; /* return the fd to us later (from epoll_wait) */
event.events = EPOLLIN | EPOLLOUT;

ret = epoll_ctl (epfd, EPOLL_CTL_ADD, fd, &event);
if (ret)
        perror ("epoll_ctl");
```

To modify an existing event on the file associated with `fd` on the epoll instance `epfd`, you would write:

```
struct epoll_event event;
int ret;

event.data.fd = fd; /* return the fd to us later */
event.events = EPOLLIN;

ret = epoll_ctl (epfd, EPOLL_CTL_MOD, fd, &event);
if (ret)
        perror ("epoll_ctl");
```

Conversely, to remove an existing event on the file associated with `fd` from the epoll instance `epfd`, you would write:

```
struct epoll_event event;
int ret;

ret = epoll_ctl (epfd, EPOLL_CTL_DEL, fd, &event);
if (ret)
        perror ("epoll_ctl");
```

Note that the `event` parameter can be `NULL` when `op` is `EPOLL_CTL_DEL`, as there is no event mask to provide. Kernel versions before 2.6.9, however, erroneously check for this parameter to be non-`NULL`. For portability to these older kernels, you should pass in a valid non-`NULL` pointer; it will not be touched. Kernel 2.6.9 fixed this bug.

Waiting for Events with Epoll

The system call `epoll_wait()` waits for events on the file descriptors associated with the given epoll instance:

```
#include <sys/epoll.h>

int epoll_wait (int epfd,
                struct epoll_event *events,
                int maxevents,
                int timeout);
```

A call to `epoll_wait()` waits up to `timeout` milliseconds for events on the files associated with the epoll instance `epfd`. Upon success, `events` points to memory containing `epoll_event` structures describing each event—such as file ready to be written to or read from—up to a maximum of `maxevents` events. The return value is the number of events, or –1 on error, in which case `errno` is set to one of the following:

EBADF
> epfd is not a valid file descriptor.

EFAULT
> The process does not have write access to the memory pointed at by events.

EINTR
> The system call was interrupted by a signal before it could complete or the timeout expired.

EINVAL
> epfd is not a valid epoll instance, or maxevents is equal to or less than 0.

If timeout is 0, the call returns immediately, even if no events are available, in which case the call will return 0. If the timeout is −1, the call will not return until an event is available.

When the call returns, the events field of the epoll_event structure describes the events that occurred. The data field contains whatever the user set it to before invocation of epoll_ctl().

A full epoll_wait() example looks like this:

```
#define MAX_EVENTS      64

struct epoll_event *events;
int nr_events, i, epfd;

events = malloc (sizeof (struct epoll_event) * MAX_EVENTS);
if (!events) {
        perror ("malloc");
        return 1;
}

nr_events = epoll_wait (epfd, events, MAX_EVENTS, -1);
if (nr_events < 0) {
        perror ("epoll_wait");
        free (events);
        return 1;
}

for (i = 0; i < nr_events; i++) {
        printf ("event=%ld on fd=%d\n",
                events[i].events,
                events[i].data.fd);
```

```
        /*
         * We now can, per events[i].events, operate on
         * events[i].data.fd without blocking.
         */
    }

    free (events);
```

We will cover the functions `malloc()` and `free()` in Chapter 9.

Edge- Versus Level-Triggered Events

If the `EPOLLET` value is set in the `events` field of the `event` parameter passed to `epoll_ctl()`, the watch on `fd` is *edge-triggered*, as opposed to *level-triggered*.

Consider the following events between a producer and a consumer communicating over a Unix pipe:

1. The producer writes 1 KB of data onto a pipe.
2. The consumer performs an `epoll_wait()` on the pipe, waiting for the pipe to contain data and thus be readable.

With a level-triggered watch, the call to `epoll_wait()` in step 2 will return immediately, showing that the pipe is ready to read. With an edge-triggered watch, this call will not return until after step 1 occurs. That is, even if the pipe is readable at the invocation of `epoll_wait()`, the call will not return until the data is written onto the pipe.

Level-triggered is the default behavior. It is how `poll()` and `select()` behave, and it is what most developers expect. Edge-triggered behavior requires a different approach to programming, commonly utilizing nonblocking I/O, and careful checking for `EAGAIN`.

Edge Triggered

The terminology "edge-triggered" is borrowed from electrical engineering. A level-triggered interrupt is issued whenever a line is asserted. An edge-triggered interrupt is caused only during the rising or falling edge of the change in assertion. Level-triggered interrupts are useful when the state of the event (the asserted line) is of interest. Edge-triggered interrupts are useful when the event itself (the line being asserted) is of interest.

Assume you have a file descriptor from which you are reading. With level-triggered epoll behavior, you'll receive a notification so long as the file descriptor is ready for reading. It is the *level* of the line that causes notification. With edge-triggered, you'll receive the notification but once, when the data first becomes readable: it is the *edge*, or the change, that causes notification.

Mapping Files into Memory

As an alternative to standard file I/O, the kernel provides an interface that allows an application to map a file into memory, meaning that there is a one-to-one correspondence between a memory address and a word in the file. The programmer can then access the file directly through memory, identically to any other chunk of memory-resident data—it is even possible to allow writes to the memory region to transparently map back to the file on disk.

POSIX.1 standardizes—and Linux implements—the mmap() system call for mapping objects into memory. This section will discuss mmap() as it pertains to mapping files into memory to perform I/O; in Chapter 9, we will visit other applications of mmap().

mmap()

A call to mmap() asks the kernel to map len bytes of the object represented by the file descriptor fd, starting at offset bytes into the file, into memory. If addr is included, it indicates a preference to use that starting address in memory. The access permissions are dictated by prot, and additional behavior can be given by flags:

```
#include <sys/mman.h>

void * mmap (void *addr,
             size_t len,
             int prot,
             int flags,
             int fd,
             off_t offset);
```

The addr parameter offers a suggestion to the kernel of where best to map the file. It is only a hint; most users pass 0. The call returns the actual address in memory where the mapping begins.

The prot parameter describes the desired memory protection of the mapping. It may be either PROT_NONE, in which case the pages in this mapping may not be accessed (rarely useful!), or a bitwise OR of one or more of the following flags:

PROT_READ
   The pages may be read.

PROT_WRITE
   The pages may be written.

PROT_EXEC
   The pages may be executed.

The desired memory protection must not conflict with the open mode of the file. For example, if the program opens the file read-only, `prot` must not specify `PROT_WRITE`.

Protection Flags, Architectures, and Security

While POSIX defines three protection bits (read, write, and execute), some architectures support only a subset of these. It is common, for example, for a processor to not differentiate between the actions of reading and executing. In that case, the processor may have only a single "read" flag. On those systems, `PROT_READ` implies `PROT_EXEC`. Until recently, the x86 architecture was one such system.

Of course, relying on such behavior is not portable. Portable programs should always set `PROT_EXEC` if they intend to execute code in the mapping.

The reverse situation is one reason for the prevalence of buffer overflow attacks: even if a given mapping does not specify execution permission, the processor may allow execution anyway.

Recent x86 processors have introduced the *NX* (no-execute) bit, which allows for readable, but not executable, mappings. On these newer systems, `PROT_READ` no longer implies `PROT_EXEC`.

The `flags` argument describes the type of mapping and some elements of its behavior. It is a bitwise OR of the following values:

MAP_FIXED

Instructs `mmap()` to treat `addr` as a requirement, not a hint. If the kernel is unable to place the mapping at the given address, the call fails. If the address and length parameters overlap an existing mapping, the overlapped pages are discarded and replaced by the new mapping. As this option requires intimate knowledge of the process address space, it is nonportable, and its use is discouraged.

MAP_PRIVATE

States that the mapping is not shared. The file is mapped copy-on-write, and any changes made in memory by this process are not reflected in the actual file, or in the mappings of other processes.[3]

MAP_SHARED

Shares the mapping with all other processes that map this same file. Writing into the mapping is equivalent to writing to the file. Reads from the mapping will reflect the writes of other processes.

---

3. Copy-on-write is a concept related to process creation and is described in "Copy-on-write" on page 146.

Either MAP_SHARED or MAP_PRIVATE must be specified, but not both. Other, more advanced flags are discussed in Chapter 9.

When you map a file descriptor, the file's reference count is incremented. Therefore, you can close the file descriptor after mapping the file, and your process will still have access to it. The corresponding decrement of the file's reference count will occur when you unmap the file, or when the process terminates.

As an example, the following snippet maps the file backed by fd, beginning with its first byte, and extending for len bytes, into a read-only mapping:

```
void *p;

p = mmap (0, len, PROT_READ, MAP_SHARED, fd, 0);
if (p == MAP_FAILED)
        perror ("mmap");
```

Figure 4-1 shows the effects of parameters supplied with mmap() on the mapping between a file and a process's address space.

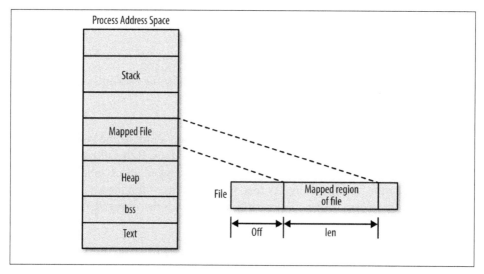

Figure 4-1. Mapping a file into a process's address space

The page size

The *page* is the unit of granularity for the memory management unit (MMU). Consequently it is the smallest unit of memory that can have distinct permissions and behavior. The page is the building block of memory mappings, which in turn are the building blocks of the process address space.

The mmap() system call operates on pages. Both the addr and offset parameters must be aligned on a page-sized boundary. That is, they must be integer multiples of the page size.

Mappings are, therefore, integer multiples of pages. If the len parameter provided by the caller is not aligned on a page boundary—perhaps because the underlying file's size is not a multiple of the page size—the mapping is rounded up to the next full page. The bytes inside this added memory, between the last valid byte and the end of the mapping, are zero-filled. Any read from that region will return zeros. Any writes to that memory will not affect the backing file, even if it is mapped as MAP_SHARED. Only the original len bytes are ever written back to the file.

The standard POSIX method of obtaining the page size is with sysconf(), which can retrieve a variety of system-specific information:

```
#include <unistd.h>

long sysconf (int name);
```

A call to sysconf() returns the value of the configuration item name, or −1 if name is invalid. On error, the call sets errno to EINVAL. Because −1 may be a valid value for some items (e.g., limits, where −1 means no limit), it may be wise to clear errno before invocation and check its value after.

POSIX defines _SC_PAGESIZE (and a synonym, _SC_PAGE_SIZE) to be the size of a page, in bytes. Therefore, obtaining the page size at runtime is simple:

```
long page_size = sysconf (_SC_PAGESIZE);
```

Linux also provides the getpagesize() function:

```
#include <unistd.h>

int getpagesize (void);
```

A call to getpagesize() will likewise return the size of a page, in bytes. Usage is even simpler than sysconf():

```
int page_size = getpagesize ();
```

Not all Unix systems support this function; it was dropped from the 1003.1-2001 revision of the POSIX standard. It is included here for completeness.

The page size is also statically stored in the macro PAGE_SIZE, which is defined in <sys/user.h>. Thus, a third way to retrieve the page size is:

```
int page_size = PAGE_SIZE;
```

Unlike the first two options, however, this approach retrieves the system page size at compile time and not runtime. Some architectures support multiple machine types with different page sizes, and some machine types even support multiple page sizes themselves! A single binary should be able to run on all machine types in a given architecture—that is, you should be able to build it once and run it everywhere. Hardcoding the page size would nullify that possibility. Consequently, you should determine the page size at runtime. Because addr and offset are usually 0, this requirement is not overly difficult to meet.

Moreover, future kernel versions will likely not export this macro to user space. We cover it in this chapter due to its frequent presence in Unix code, but you should not use it in your own programs. The sysconf() approach is your best bet for portability and future compatibility.

Return values and error codes

On success, a call to mmap() returns the location of the mapping. On failure, the call returns MAP_FAILED and sets errno appropriately. A call to mmap() never returns 0.

Possible errno values include:

EACCES
    The given file descriptor is not a regular file, or the mode with which it was opened conflicts with prot or flags.

EAGAIN
    The file has been locked via a file lock.

EBADF
    The given file descriptor is not valid.

EINVAL
    One or more of the parameters addr, len, or off are invalid.

ENFILE
    The system-wide limit on open files has been reached.

ENODEV
    The filesystem on which the file to map resides does not support memory mapping.

ENOMEM
    The process does not have enough memory.

EOVERFLOW
    The result of addr+len exceeds the size of the address space.

EPERM
    PROT_EXEC was given, but the filesystem is mounted noexec.

Associated signals

Two signals are associated with mapped regions:

SIGBUS

This signal is generated when a process attempts to access a region of a mapping that is no longer valid—for example, because the file was truncated after it was mapped.

SIGSEGV

This signal is generated when a process attempts to write to a region that is mapped read-only.

munmap()

Linux provides the munmap() system call for removing a mapping created with mmap():

```
#include <sys/mman.h>

int munmap (void *addr, size_t len);
```

A call to munmap() removes any mappings that contain pages located anywhere in the process address space starting at addr, which must be page-aligned, and continuing for len bytes. Once the mapping has been removed, the previously associated memory region is no longer valid, and further access attempts result in a SIGSEGV signal.

Normally, munmap() is passed the return value and the len parameter from a previous invocation of mmap().

On success, munmap() returns 0; on failure, it returns −1, and errno is set appropriately. The only standard errno value is EINVAL, which specifies that one or more parameters were invalid.

As an example, the following snippet unmaps any memory regions with pages contained in the interval [addr,addr+len]:

```
if (munmap (addr, len) == -1)
        perror ("munmap");
```

Mapping Example

Let's consider a simple example program that uses mmap() to print a file chosen by the user to standard out:

```
#include <stdio.h>
#include <sys/types.h>
#include <sys/stat.h>
#include <fcntl.h>
#include <unistd.h>
#include <sys/mman.h>
```

```c
int main (int argc, char *argv[])
{
        struct stat sb;
        off_t len;
        char *p;
        int fd;

        if (argc < 2) {
                fprintf (stderr, "usage: %s <file>\n", argv[0]);
                return 1;
        }

        fd = open (argv[1], O_RDONLY);
        if (fd == -1) {
                perror ("open");
                return 1;
        }

        if (fstat (fd, &sb) == -1) {
                perror ("fstat");
                return 1;
        }

        if (!S_ISREG (sb.st_mode)) {
                fprintf (stderr, "%s is not a file\n", argv[1]);
                return 1;
        }

        p = mmap (0, sb.st_size, PROT_READ, MAP_SHARED, fd, 0);
        if (p == MAP_FAILED) {
                perror ("mmap");
                return 1;
        }

        if (close (fd) == -1) {
                perror ("close");
                return 1;
        }

        for (len = 0; len < sb.st_size; len++)
                putchar (p[len]);

        if (munmap (p, sb.st_size) == -1) {
                perror ("munmap");
                return 1;
        }

        return 0;
}
```

The only unfamiliar system call in this example should be fstat(), which we will cover in Chapter 8. All you need to know at this point is that fstat() returns information about a given file. The S_ISREG() macro can check some of this information so that we can ensure that the given file is a regular file (as opposed to a device file or a directory) before we map it. The behavior of nonregular files when mapped depends on the backing device. Some device files are mmap-able; other nonregular files are not mmap-able and will set errno to EACCES.

The rest of the example should be straightforward. The program is passed a filename as an argument. It opens the file, ensures it is a regular file, maps it, closes it, prints the file byte-by-byte to standard out, and then unmaps the file from memory.

Advantages of mmap()

Manipulating files via mmap() has a handful of advantages over the standard read() and write() system calls. Among them are:

- Reading from and writing to a memory-mapped file avoids the extraneous copy that occurs when using the read() or write() system calls, where the data must be copied to and from a user-space buffer.

- Aside from any potential page faults, reading from and writing to a memory-mapped file does not incur any system call or context switch overhead. It is as simple as accessing memory.

- When multiple processes map the same object into memory, the data is shared among all the processes. Read-only and shared writable mappings are shared in their entirety; private writable mappings have their not-yet-COW (copy-on-write) pages shared.

- Seeking around the mapping involves trivial pointer manipulations. There is no need for the lseek() system call.

For these reasons, mmap() is a smart choice for many applications.

Disadvantages of mmap()

There are a few points to keep in mind when using mmap():

- Memory mappings are always an integer number of pages in size. Thus, the difference between the size of the backing file and an integer number of pages is "wasted" as slack space. For small files, a significant percentage of the mapping may be wasted. For example, with 4 KB pages, a 7-byte mapping wastes 4,089 bytes.

- The memory mappings must fit into the process's address space. With a 32-bit address space, a large number of various-sized mappings can result in fragmentation of the address space, making it hard to find large free contiguous regions. This problem, of course, is much less apparent with a 64-bit address space.

- There is overhead in creating and maintaining the memory mappings and associated data structures inside the kernel. This overhead is generally obviated by the elimination of the double copy mentioned in the previous section, particularly for larger and frequently accessed files.

For these reasons, the benefits of mmap() are most greatly realized when the mapped file is large (and thus any wasted space is a small percentage of the total mapping), or when the total size of the mapped file is evenly divisible by the page size (and thus there is no wasted space).

Resizing a Mapping

Linux provides the mremap() system call for expanding or shrinking the size of a given mapping. This function is Linux-specific:

```
#define _GNU_SOURCE

#include <sys/mman.h>

void * mremap (void *addr, size_t old_size,
               size_t new_size, unsigned long flags);
```

A call to mremap() expands or shrinks mapping in the region [addr,addr+old_size) to the new size new_size. The kernel can potentially move the mapping at the same time, depending on the availability of space in the process's address space and the value of flags.

> The opening [in [addr,addr+old_size) indicates that the region starts with (and includes) the low address, whereas the closing) indicates that the region stops just before (does not include) the high address. This convention is known as *interval notation*.

The flags parameter can be either 0 or MREMAP_MAYMOVE, which specifies that the kernel is free to move the mapping if needed to perform the requested resizing. A large resizing is more likely to succeed if the kernel can move the mapping.

Return values and error codes

On success, mremap() returns a pointer to the newly resized memory mapping. On failure, it returns MAP_FAILED and sets errno to one of the following:

EAGAIN

   The memory region is locked and cannot be resized.

EFAULT

   Some pages in the given range are not valid pages in the process's address space, or
   there was a problem remapping the given pages.

EINVAL

   An argument was invalid.

ENOMEM

   The given range cannot be expanded without moving (and MREMAP_MAYMOVE was
   not given), or there is not enough free space in the process's address space.

Libraries such as *glibc* often use mremap() to implement an efficient realloc(), which
is an interface for resizing a block of memory originally obtained via malloc(). For
example:

```
void * realloc (void *addr, size_t len)
{
        size_t old_size = look_up_mapping_size (addr);
        void *p;

        p = mremap (addr, old_size, len, MREMAP_MAYMOVE);
        if (p == MAP_FAILED)
                return NULL;
        return p;
}
```

This would work only if all malloc() allocations were unique anonymous mappings;
nonetheless, it stands as a useful example of the performance gains to be had. The
example assumes the libc provides a look_up_mapping_size() function.

The GNU C library does use mmap() and family for performing some memory allocations. We will look at that topic in depth in Chapter 9.

Changing the Protection of a Mapping

POSIX defines the mprotect() interface to allow programs to change the permissions
of existing regions of memory:

```
#include <sys/mman.h>

int mprotect (const void *addr,
              size_t len,
              int prot);
```

A call to mprotect() will change the protection mode for the memory pages contained
in [addr,addr+len), where addr is page-aligned. The prot parameter accepts the same

values as the prot given to mmap(): PROT_NONE, PROT_READ, PROT_WRITE, and PROT_EXEC. These values are not additive; if a region of memory is readable and prot is set to only PROT_WRITE, the call will make the region only writable.

On some systems, mprotect() may operate only on memory mappings previously created via mmap(). On Linux, mprotect() can operate on any region of memory.

Return values and error codes

On success, mprotect() returns 0. On failure, it returns –1, and sets errno to one of the following:

EACCES
> The memory cannot be given the permissions requested by prot. This can happen, for example, if you attempt to set the mapping of a file opened read-only to writable.

EINVAL
> The parameter addr is invalid or not page-aligned.

ENOMEM
> Insufficient kernel memory is available to satisfy the request, or one or more pages in the given memory region are not a valid part of the process's address space.

Synchronizing a File with a Mapping

POSIX provides a memory-mapped equivalent of the fsync() system call that we discussed in Chapter 2:

```
#include <sys/mman.h>

int msync (void *addr, size_t len, int flags);
```

A call to msync() flushes back to disk any changes made to a file mapped via mmap(), synchronizing the mapped file with the mapping. Specifically, the file or subset of a file associated with the mapping starting at memory address addr and continuing for len bytes is synchronized to disk. The addr argument must be page-aligned; it is generally the return value from a previous mmap() invocation.

Without invocation of msync(), there is no guarantee that a dirty mapping will be written back to disk until the file is unmapped. This is different from the behavior of write(), where a buffer is dirtied as part of the writing process and queued for writeback to disk. When writing into a memory mapping, the process directly modifies the file's pages in the kernel's page cache without kernel involvement. The kernel may not synchronize the page cache and the disk anytime soon.

The flags parameter controls the behavior of the synchronizing operation. It is a bitwise OR of the following values:

MS_SYNC

Specifies that synchronization should occur synchronously. The `msync()` call will not return until all pages are written back to disk.

MS_ASYNC

Specifies that synchronization should occur asynchronously. The update is scheduled, but the `msync()` call returns immediately without waiting for the writes to take place.

MS_INVALIDATE

Specifies that all other cached copies of the mapping be invalidated. Any future access to any mappings of this file will reflect the newly synchronized on-disk contents.

One of MS_ASYNC or MS_SYNC must be specified, but not both.

Usage is simple:

```
if (msync (addr, len, MS_ASYNC) == -1)
        perror ("msync");
```

This example asynchronously synchronizes (say that 10 times fast) to disk the file mapped in the region [`addr,addr+len`].

Return values and error codes

On success, `msync()` returns 0. On failure, the call returns −1 and sets `errno` appropriately. The following are valid `errno` values:

EINVAL

The `flags` parameter has both MS_SYNC and MS_ASYNC set, a bit other than one of the three valid flags is set, or `addr` is not page-aligned.

ENOMEM

The given memory region (or part of it) is not mapped. Note that Linux will return ENOMEM, as POSIX dictates, when asked to synchronize a region that is only partly unmapped, but it will still synchronize any valid mappings in the region.

Before version 2.4.19 of the Linux kernel, `msync()` returned EFAULT in place of ENOMEM.

Giving Advice on a Mapping

Linux provides a system call named `madvise()` to let processes give the kernel advice and hints on how they intend to use a mapping. The kernel can then optimize its behavior to take advantage of the mapping's intended use. While the Linux kernel dynamically tunes its behavior and generally provides optimal performance without explicit advice, providing such advice can ensure the desired caching and readahead behavior for some workloads.

A call to `madvise()` advises the kernel on how to behave with respect to the pages in the memory map starting at `addr`, and extending for `len` bytes:

```
#include <sys/mman.h>

int madvise (void *addr,
             size_t len,
             int advice);
```

If `len` is 0, the kernel will apply the advice to the entire mapping that starts at `addr`. The parameter `advice` delineates the advice, which can be one of:

MADV_NORMAL

> The application has no specific advice to give on this range of memory. It should be treated as normal.

MADV_RANDOM

> The application intends to access the pages in the specified range in a random (nonsequential) order.

MADV_SEQUENTIAL

> The application intends to access the pages in the specified range sequentially, from lower to higher addresses.

MADV_WILLNEED

> The application intends to access the pages in the specified range in the near future.

MADV_DONTNEED

> The application does not intend to access the pages in the specified range in the near future.

The actual behavior modifications that the kernel takes in response to this advice are implementation-specific: POSIX dictates only the meaning of the advice, not any potential consequences. The Linux kernel from 2.6 onward behaves as follows in response to the `advice` values:

MADV_NORMAL

> The kernel behaves as usual, performing a moderate amount of readahead.

MADV_RANDOM

> The kernel disables readahead, reading only the minimal amount of data on each physical read operation.

MADV_SEQUENTIAL

> The kernel performs aggressive readahead.

MADV_WILLNEED

> The kernel initiates readahead, reading the given pages into memory.

MADV_DONTNEED

The kernel frees any resources associated with the given pages and discards any dirty and not-yet-synchronized pages. Subsequent accesses to the mapped data will cause the data to be paged in from the backing file or (for anonymous mappings) zero-fill the requested pages.

MADV_DONTFORK

Do not copy these pages into the child process across a fork. This flag, available only in Linux kernel 2.6.16 and later, is needed when managing DMA pages and rarely otherwise.

MADV_DOFORK+

Undo the behavior of MADV_DONTFORK.

Typical usage is:

```
int ret;

ret = madvise (addr, len, MADV_SEQUENTIAL);
if (ret < 0)
        perror ("madvise");
```

This call instructs the kernel that the process intends to access the memory region [addr,addr+len) sequentially.

Readahead

When the Linux kernel reads files off the disk, it performs an optimization known as *readahead*: when a request is made for a given chunk of a file, the kernel also reads the following chunk of the file. If a request is subsequently made for that chunk—as is the case when reading a file sequentially—the kernel can return the requested data immediately. Because disks have track buffers (basically, hard disks perform their own readahead internally), and because files are generally laid out sequentially on disk, this optimization is low cost.

Some readahead is usually advantageous, but optimal results depend on the question of how much readahead to perform. A sequentially accessed file may benefit from a larger readahead window, while a randomly accessed file may find readahead to be worthless overhead.

As discussed in "Kernel Internals" on page 62, the kernel dynamically tunes the size of the readahead window in response to the hit rate inside that window. More hits imply that a larger window would be advantageous; fewer hits suggest a smaller window. The madvise() system call allows applications to influence the window size right off the bat.

Return values and error codes

On success, madvise() returns 0. On failure, it returns −1, and errno is set appropriately. The following are valid errors:

EAGAIN
> An internal kernel resource (probably memory) was unavailable. The process can try again.

EBADF
> The region exists but does not map a file.

EINVAL
> The parameter len is negative, addr is not page-aligned, the advice parameter is invalid, or the pages were locked or shared with MADV_DONTNEED.

EIO
> An internal I/O error occurred with MADV_WILLNEED.

ENOMEM
> The given region is not a valid mapping in this process's address space, or MADV_WILLNEED was given, but there is insufficient memory to page in the given regions.

Advice for Normal File I/O

In the previous subsection, we looked at providing advice on memory mappings. In this section, we will look at providing advice to the kernel on normal file I/O. Linux provides two interfaces for such advice giving: posix_fadvise() and readahead().

The posix_fadvise() System Call

The first advice interface, as its name alludes, is standardized by POSIX 1003.1-2003:

```
#include <fcntl.h>

int posix_fadvise (int fd,
                   off_t offset,
                   off_t len,
                   int advice);
```

A call to posix_fadvise() provides the kernel with the hint advice on the file descriptor fd in the interval [offset,offset+len). If len is 0, the advice will apply to the range [offset,length of file]. Common usage is to specify 0 for len and offset, applying the advice to the entire file.

The available advice options are similar to those for madvise(). Exactly one of the following should be provided for advice:

POSIX_FADV_NORMAL

The application has no specific advice to give on this range of the file. It should be treated as normal.

POSIX_FADV_RANDOM

The application intends to access the data in the specified range in a random (non-sequential) order.

POSIX_FADV_SEQUENTIAL

The application intends to access the data in the specified range sequentially, from lower to higher addresses.

POSIX_FADV_WILLNEED

The application intends to access the data in the specified range in the near future.

POSIX_FADV_NOREUSE

The application intends to access the data in the specified range in the near future, but only once.

POSIX_FADV_DONTNEED

The application does not intend to access the pages in the specified range in the near future.

As with madvise(), the actual response to the given advice is implementation-specific —even different versions of the Linux kernel may react dissimilarly. The following are the current responses:

POSIX_FADV_NORMAL

The kernel behaves as usual, performing a moderate amount of readahead.

POSIX_FADV_RANDOM

The kernel disables readahead, reading only the minimal amount of data on each physical read operation.

POSIX_FADV_SEQUENTIAL

The kernel performs aggressive readahead, doubling the size of the readahead window.

POSIX_FADV_WILLNEED

The kernel initiates readahead to begin reading into memory the given pages.

POSIX_FADV_NOREUSE

Currently, the behavior is the same as for POSIX_FADV_WILLNEED; future kernels may perform an additional optimization to exploit the "use once" behavior. This hint does not have an madvise() complement.

POSIX_FADV_DONTNEED
> The kernel evicts any cached data in the given range from the page cache. Note that this hint, unlike the others, is different in behavior from its madvise() counterpart.

As an example, the following snippet instructs the kernel that the entire file represented by the file descriptor fd will be accessed in a random, nonsequential manner:

```
int ret;

ret = posix_fadvise (fd, 0, 0, POSIX_FADV_RANDOM);
if (ret == -1)
        perror ("posix_fadvise");
```

Return values and error codes

On success, posix_fadvise() returns 0. On failure, −1 is returned, and errno is set to one of the following values:

EBADF
> The given file descriptor is invalid.

EINVAL
> The given advice is invalid, the given file descriptor refers to a pipe, or the specified advice cannot be applied to the given file.

The readahead() System Call

The posix_fadvise() system call is new to the 2.6 Linux kernel. The readahead() system call was previously available to provide behavior identical to the POSIX_FADV_WILLNEED hint. Unlike posix_fadvise(), readahead() is a Linux-specific interface:

```
#define _GNU_SOURCE

#include <fcntl.h>

ssize_t readahead (int fd,
                   off64_t offset,
                   size_t count);
```

A call to readahead() populates the page cache with the region [offset,offset +count) from the file descriptor fd.

Return values and error codes

On success, readahead() returns 0. On failure, it returns −1, and errno is set to one of the following values:

EBADF
> The given file descriptor is invalid or not open for reading.

EINVAL
> The given file descriptor does not map to a file that supports readahead.

Advice Is Cheap

A handful of common application workloads can readily benefit from a little well-intentioned advice to the kernel. Such advice can go a long way toward mitigating the burden of I/O. With hard disks being so slow, and modern processors being so fast, every little bit helps, and good advice can go a long way.

Before reading a chunk of a file, a process can provide the POSIX_FADV_WILLNEED hint to instruct the kernel to read the file into the page cache. The I/O will occur asynchronously in the background. When the application ultimately accesses the file, the operation can complete without generating blocking I/O.

Conversely, after reading or writing a lot of data—say, while continuously streaming video to disk—a process can provide the POSIX_FADV_DONTNEED hint to instruct the kernel to evict the given chunk of the file from the page cache. A large streaming operation can continually fill the page cache. If the application never intends to access the data again, this means the page cache will be filled with superfluous data, at the expense of potentially more useful data. Thus, it makes sense for a streaming video application to periodically request that streamed data be evicted from the cache.

A process that intends to read in an entire file can provide the POSIX_FADV_SEQUENTIAL hint, instructing the kernel to perform aggressive readahead. Conversely, a process that knows it is going to access a file randomly, seeking to and fro, can provide the POSIX_FADV_RANDOM hint, instructing the kernel that readahead will be nothing but worthless overhead.

Synchronized, Synchronous, and Asynchronous Operations

Unix systems use the terms synchronized, nonsynchronized, synchronous, and asynchronous freely, without much regard to the fact that they are confusing—in English, the differences between "synchronous" and "synchronized" do not amount to much!

A *synchronous* write operation does not return until the written data is—at least—stored in the kernel's buffer cache. A synchronous read operation does not return until the read data is stored in the user-space buffer provided by the application. On the other side of the coin, an *asynchronous* write operation may return before the data even leaves user space; an asynchronous read operation may return before the read data is available. That is, the operations may not actually take place when requested, but only be queued for later. Of course, in this case, some mechanism must exist for determining when the operation has actually completed and with what level of success.

A *synchronized* operation is more restrictive and safer than a merely synchronous operation. A synchronized write operation flushes the data to disk, ensuring that the on-disk data is always synchronized vis-à-vis the corresponding kernel buffers. A synchronized read operation always returns the most up-to-date copy of the data, presumably from the disk.

In sum, the terms synchronous and asynchronous refer to whether I/O operations wait for some event (e.g., storage of the data) before returning. The terms synchronized and nonsynchronized, meanwhile, specify exactly *what* event must occur (e.g., writing the data to disk).

Normally, Unix write operations are synchronous and nonsynchronized; read operations are synchronous and synchronized.[4] For write operations, every combination of these characteristics is possible, as Table 4-1 illustrates.

Table 4-1. Synchronicity of write operations

	Synchronized	Nonsynchronized
Synchronous	Write operations do not return until the data is flushed to disk. This is the behavior if O_SYNC is specified during file open.	Write operations do not return until the data is stored in kernel buffers. This is the usual behavior.
Asynchronous	Write operations return as soon as the request is queued. Once the write operation ultimately executes, the data is guaranteed to be on disk.	Write operations return as soon as the request is queued. Once the write operation ultimately executes, the data is guaranteed to at least be stored in kernel buffers.

Read operations are always synchronized, as reading stale data makes little sense. Such operations can be either synchronous or asynchronous, however, as illustrated in Table 4-2.

Table 4-2. Synchronicity of read operations

	Synchronized
Synchronous	Read operations do not return until the data, which is up-to-date, is stored in the provided buffer (this is the usual behavior).
Asynchronous	Read operations return as soon as the request is queued, but when the read operation ultimately executes, the data returned is up-to-date.

In Chapter 2, we discussed how to make writes synchronized (via the O_SYNC flag) and how to ensure that all I/O is synchronized as of a given point (via fsync() and friends). Now, let's look at what it takes to make reads and writes asynchronous.

---

4. Read operations are technically also nonsynchronized, like write operations, but the kernel ensures that the page cache contains up-to-date data. That is, the page cache's data is always identical to or newer than the data on disk. In this manner, the behavior in practice is always synchronized. There is little argument for behaving any other way.

Asynchronous I/O

Performing asynchronous I/O requires kernel support at the very lowest layers. POSIX 1003.1-2003 defines the *aio* interfaces, which Linux fortunately implements. The *aio* library provides a family of functions for submitting asynchronous I/O and receiving notification upon its completion:

```
#include <aio.h>

/* asynchronous I/O control block */
struct aiocb {
        int aio_fildes;                 /* file descriptor */
        int aio_lio_opcode;             /* operation to perform */
        int aio_reqprio;                /* request priority offset */
        volatile void *aio_buf;         /* pointer to buffer */
        size_t aio_nbytes;              /* length of operation */
        struct sigevent aio_sigevent;   /* signal number and value */

        /* internal, private members follow... */
};

int aio_read (struct aiocb *aiocbp);
int aio_write (struct aiocb *aiocbp);
int aio_error (const struct aiocb *aiocbp);
int aio_return (struct aiocb *aiocbp);
int aio_cancel (int fd, struct aiocb *aiocbp);
int aio_fsync (int op, struct aiocb *aiocbp);
int aio_suspend (const struct aiocb * const cblist[],
                 int n,
                 const struct timespec *timeout);
```

I/O Schedulers and I/O Performance

In a modern system, the relative performance gap between disks and the rest of the system is quite large—and widening. The worst component of disk performance is the process of moving the read/write head from one part of the disk to another, an operation known as a *seek*. In a world where many operations are measured in a handful of processor cycles (which might take all of a third of a nanosecond each), a single disk seek can average over 8 milliseconds—still a small number, to be sure, but *25 million times longer than a single processor cycle*!

Given the disparity in performance between disk drives and the rest of the system, it would be incredibly crude and inefficient to send I/O requests to the disk in the order in which they are issued. Therefore, modern operating system kernels implement *I/O schedulers*, which work to minimize the number and size of disk seeks by manipulating the order in which I/O requests are serviced and the times at which they are serviced. I/O schedulers work hard to lessen the performance penalties associated with disk access.

Disk Addressing

To understand the role of an I/O scheduler, some background information is necessary. Hard disks address their data using the familiar geometry-based addressing of cylinders, heads, and sectors, or *CHS addressing*. A hard drive is composed of multiple *platters*, each consisting of a single disk, spindle, and read/write head. You can think of each platter as a CD (or record), and the set of platters in a disk as a stack of CDs. Each platter is divided into ring-like *tracks*, like on a CD. Each track is then divided into an integer number of *sectors*.

To locate a specific unit of data on a disk, the drive's logic requires three pieces of information: the cylinder, head, and sector values. The cylinder value specifies the track on which the data resides. If you lay the platters on top of one another, a given track forms a cylinder through each platter. In other words, a cylinder is represented by a track at the same distance from the center on each disk. The head value identifies the exact read/write head (and thus the exact platter) in question. The search is now narrowed down to a single track on a single platter. The disk then uses the sector value to identify an exact sector on the track. The search is now complete: the hard disk knows what platter, what track, and what sector to look in for the data. It can position the read/write head of the correct platter over the correct track and read from or write to the requisite sector.

Thankfully, modern hard disks do not force computers to communicate with their disks in terms of cylinders, heads, and sectors. Instead, contemporary hard drives map a unique *block number* (also called *physical blocks* or *device blocks*) over each cylinder/head/sector triplet—effectively, a block maps to a specific sector. Modern operating systems can then address hard drives using these block numbers—a process known as *logical block addressing* (LBA)—and the hard drive internally translates the block number into the correct CHS address.[5] Although nothing guarantees it, the block-to-CHS mapping tends to be sequential: logical block n tends to be physically adjacent on disk to logical block n + 1. This sequential mapping is important, as we shall soon see.

Filesystems, meanwhile, exist only in software. They operate on their own units, known as *logical blocks* (sometimes called *filesystem blocks*, or, confusingly, just *blocks*). The logical block size must be an integer multiple of the physical block size. In other words, a filesystem's logical blocks map to one or more of a disk's physical blocks.

The Life of an I/O Scheduler

I/O schedulers perform two basic operations: merging and sorting. *Merging* is the process of taking two or more adjacent I/O requests and combining them into a single

---

5. Limits on the absolute size of this block number are largely responsible for the various limits on total drive sizes over the years.

---

request. Consider two requests, one to read from disk block 5, and another to read from disk blocks 6 through 7. These requests can be merged into a single request to read from disk blocks 5 through 7. The total amount of I/O might be the same, but the number of I/O operations is reduced by half.

Sorting, the more important of the two operations, is the process of arranging pending I/O requests in ascending block order. For example, given I/O operations to blocks 52, 109, and 7, the I/O scheduler would sort these requests into the ordering 7, 52, and 109. If a request was then issued to block 81, it would be inserted between the requests to blocks 52 and 109. The I/O scheduler would then dispatch the requests to the disk in the order that they exist in the queue: 7, then 52, then 81, and finally 109.

In this manner, the disk head's movements are minimized. Instead of potentially haphazard movements—here to there and back, seeking all over the disk—the disk head moves in a smooth, linear fashion. Because seeks are the most expensive part of disk I/O, performance is improved.

Helping Out Reads

Each read request must return up-to-date data. Thus, if the requested data is not in the page cache, the reading process must block until the data can be read from disk—a potentially lengthy operation. We call this performance impact *read latency*.

A typical application might initiate several read I/O requests in a short period. Because each request is individually synchronized, the later requests are *dependent* on the earlier ones' completion. Consider reading every file in a directory. The application opens the first file, reads a chunk of it, waits for data, reads another chunk, and so on, until the entire file is read. Then the application starts again, on the next file. The requests become serialized: a subsequent request cannot be issued until the current request completes.

This is in stark contrast to write requests, which (in their default, nonsynchronized state) need not initiate any disk I/O until some time in the future. Thus, from the perspective of a user-space application, write requests *stream*, unencumbered by the performance of the disk. This streaming behavior only compounds the problem for reads: as writes stream, they can hog the kernel and disk's attention. This phenomenon is known as the *writes-starving-reads* problem.

If an I/O scheduler *always* sorted new requests by the order of insertion, it would be possible to starve requests to far-off blocks indefinitely. Consider our previous example. If new requests were continually issued to blocks in, say, the 50s, the request to block 109 would never be serviced. Because read latency is critical, this behavior would greatly hurt system performance. Thus, I/O schedulers employ a mechanism to prevent starvation.

A simple approach—such as the one taken by the 2.4 Linux kernel's I/O scheduler, the *Linus Elevator*[6]—is to simply stop insertion-sorting if there is a sufficiently old request in the queue. This trades overall performance for per-request fairness and, in the case of reads, improves latency. The problem is that this heuristic is a bit too simplistic. Recognizing this, the 2.6 Linux kernel witnessed the demise of the Linus Elevator and unveiled several new I/O schedulers in its place.

The Deadline I/O Scheduler

The Deadline I/O Scheduler was introduced to solve the problems with the 2.4 I/O scheduler and traditional elevator algorithms in general. The Linus Elevator maintains a sorted list of pending I/O requests. The I/O request at the head of the queue is the next one to be serviced. The Deadline I/O Scheduler keeps this queue but kicks things up a notch by introducing two additional queues: the *read FIFO queue* and the *write FIFO queue*. The items in each of these queues are sorted by submission time (effectively, the first in is the first out). The read FIFO queue, as its name suggests, contains only read requests. The write FIFO queue, likewise, contains only write requests. Each request in the FIFO queues is assigned an expiration value. The read FIFO queue has an expiration time of 500 milliseconds. The write FIFO queue has an expiration time of 5 seconds.

When a new I/O request is submitted, it is insertion-sorted into the standard queue and placed at the tail of its respective (read or write) FIFO queue. Normally, the hard drive is sent I/O requests from the head of the standard sorted queue. This maximizes global throughput by minimizing seeks, as the normal queue is sorted by block number (as with the Linus Elevator).

When the item at the head of one of the FIFO queues grows older than the expiration value associated with its queue, however, the I/O scheduler stops dispatching I/O requests from the standard queue and begins servicing requests from that queue—the request at the head of the FIFO queue is serviced, plus a couple of extras for good measure. The I/O scheduler needs to check and handle only the requests at the head of the queue, as those are the oldest requests.

In this manner, the Deadline I/O Scheduler can enforce a soft deadline on I/O requests. Although it makes no promise that an I/O request will be serviced before its expiration time, the I/O scheduler generally services requests near their expiration times. Thus, the Deadline I/O Scheduler continues to provide good global throughput without starving any one request for an unacceptably long time. Because read requests are given shorter expiration times, the writes-starving-reads problem is minimized.

---

6. Yes, the man has an I/O scheduler named after him. I/O schedulers are sometimes called elevator algorithms because they solve a problem similar to that of keeping an elevator running smoothly.

The Anticipatory I/O Scheduler

The Deadline I/O Scheduler's behavior is good, but not perfect. Recall our discussion on read dependency. With the Deadline I/O Scheduler, the first read request in a series of reads is serviced in short order, at or before its expiration time, and the I/O scheduler then returns to servicing I/O requests from the sorted queue—so far, so good. But what if the application then swoops in and hits us with another read request? Eventually its expiration time will also approach, and the I/O scheduler will submit it to the disk, which will seek over to promptly handle the request, then seek back to continue handling requests from the sorted queue. This seeking back and forth can continue for some time because many applications exhibit this behavior. While latency is kept to a minimum, global throughput is not very good because the read requests keep coming in, and the disk has to keep seeking back and forth to handle them. Performance would be improved if the disk just took a break to wait for another read and did not move away to service the sorted queue again. But, unfortunately, by the time the application is scheduled and submits its next dependent read request, the I/O scheduler has already shifted gears.

The problem again stems from those darn dependent reads. Each new read request is issued only when the previous one is returned, but by the time the application receives the read data, is scheduled to run, and submits its next read request, the I/O scheduler has moved on and begun servicing other requests. This results in a wasted pair of seeks for each read: the disk seeks to the read, services it, and then seeks back. If only there was some way for the I/O scheduler to know—to anticipate—that another read would soon be submitted to the same part of the disk, instead of seeking back and forth, it could wait in anticipation of the next read. Saving those awful seeks certainly would be worth a few milliseconds of waiting.

This is exactly how the Anticipatory I/O Scheduler operates. It began life as the Deadline I/O Scheduler but was gifted with the addition of an anticipation mechanism. When a read request is submitted, the Anticipatory I/O Scheduler services it within its deadline, as usual. Unlike the Deadline I/O Scheduler, however, the Anticipatory I/O Scheduler then sits and waits, doing nothing, for up to 6 milliseconds. Chances are good that the application will issue another read to the same part of the filesystem during those six milliseconds. If so, that request is serviced immediately, and the Anticipatory I/O Scheduler waits some more. If 6 milliseconds go by without a read request, the Anticipatory I/O Scheduler decides it has guessed wrong and returns to whatever it was doing before (i.e., servicing the standard sorted queue). If even a moderate number of requests are anticipated correctly, a great deal of time—two expensive seeks' worth at each go—is saved. Because most reads are dependent, the anticipation pays off much of the time.

The CFQ I/O Scheduler

The Completely Fair Queuing (CFQ) I/O Scheduler works to achieve similar goals, albeit via a different approach.[7] With CFQ, each process is assigned its own queue, and each queue is assigned a timeslice. The I/O scheduler visits each queue in a round-robin fashion, servicing requests from the queue until the queue's timeslice is exhausted, or until no more requests remain. In the latter case, the CFQ I/O Scheduler will then sit idle for a brief period—by default, 10 ms—waiting for a new request on the queue. If the anticipation pays off, the I/O scheduler avoids seeking. If not, the waiting was in vain, and the scheduler moves on to the next process's queue.

Within each process's queue, synchronized requests (such as reads) are given priority over nonsynchronized requests. In this manner, CFQ favors reads and prevents the writes-starving-reads problem. Due to the per-process queue setup, the CFQ I/O Scheduler is fair to all processes while still providing good global performance.

The CFQ I/O Scheduler is well suited to most workloads, and makes an excellent first choice.

The Noop I/O Scheduler

The Noop I/O Scheduler is the most basic of the available schedulers. It performs no sorting whatsoever, only basic merging. It is used for specialized devices that do not require (or that perform) their own request sorting.

Solid-State Drives

Solid-state drives (SSDs) such as flash drives grow more popular each year. Whole classes of devices, such as mobile phones and tablets, have no rotational storage devices; everything is flash. SSDs such as flash drives have significantly lower seek times than classic hard drives, as there is no rotational cost to finding a given block of data. Instead, SSDs are referenced not unlike random-access memory: while it can be more efficient to read large chunks of contiguous data in one fell swoop, there isn't a penalty for accessing data elsewhere on the drive.

Consequently, the benefits of sorting I/O requests are significantly smaller (if not zero) for solid-state drives and the utility of I/O schedulers is less for such devices. Many systems thus use the Noop I/O Scheduler for solid-state storage, as it provides merging (which is beneficial) but not sorting. Systems, however, that wish to optimize for interactive performance prefer the fairness of the CFQ I/O Scheduler, even for SSDs.

---

7. The following text discusses the CFQ I/O Scheduler as it is currently implemented. Previous incarnations did not use timeslices or the anticipation heuristic, but operated in a similar fashion.

Selecting and Configuring Your I/O Scheduler

The default I/O scheduler is selectable at boot time via the *iosched* kernel command-line parameter. Valid options are *as*, *cfq*, *deadline*, and *noop*. The I/O scheduler is also runtime-selectable on a per-device basis via */sys/block/[device]/queue/scheduler*, where `device` is the block device in question. Reading this file returns the current I/O scheduler; writing one of the valid options to this file sets the I/O scheduler. For example, to set the device *hda* to the CFQ I/O Scheduler, one would do the following:

```
# echo cfq > /sys/block/hda/queue/scheduler
```

The directory */sys/block/[device]/queue/iosched* contains files that allow the administrator to retrieve and set tunable values related to the I/O scheduler. The exact options depend on the current I/O scheduler. Changing any of these settings requires root privileges.

A good programmer writes programs that are agnostic to the underlying I/O subsystem. Nonetheless, knowledge of this subsystem can surely help one write optimal code.

Optimzing I/O Performance

665.180bBecause disk I/O is so slow relative to the performance of other components in the system, yet I/O is such an important aspect of modern computing, maximizing I/O performance is crucial.

Minimizing I/O operations (by coalescing many smaller operations into fewer larger operations), performing block-size-aligned I/O, or using user buffering (see Chapter 3) are important tools in the system programmer's kit. Similarly, taking advantage of advanced I/O techniques, such as vectored I/O, positional I/O (see Chapter 2), and asynchronous I/O, are important patterns to consider when system programming.

The most demanding mission-critical and I/O-intense applications, however, can employ additional tricks to maximize performance. Although the Linux kernel, as discussed previously, utilizes advanced I/O schedulers to minimize dreaded disk seeks, user-space applications can work toward the same end, in a similar fashion, to further improve performance.

Scheduling I/O in user space

I/O-intensive applications that issue a large number of I/O requests and need to extract every ounce of performance can sort and merge their pending I/O requests, performing the same duties as the Linux I/O scheduler.[8]

---

8. One should apply the techniques discussed here only to I/O-intensive, mission-critical applications. Sorting the I/O requests—assuming there is even anything to sort—of applications that do not issue many such requests is silly and unneeded.

Why perform the same work twice, if you know the I/O scheduler will sort requests block-wise, minimizing seeks and allowing the disk head to move in a smooth, linear fashion? Consider an application that submits a large number of unsorted I/O requests. These requests arrive in the I/O scheduler's queue in a generally random order. The I/O scheduler does its job, sorting and merging the requests before sending them out to the disk—but the requests start hitting the disk while the application is still generating I/O and submitting requests. The I/O scheduler is able to sort only a subset of requests at a time.

Therefore, if an application is generating many requests—particularly if they are for data all over the disk—it can benefit from sorting the requests before submitting them, ensuring they reach the I/O scheduler in the desired order.

A user-space application is not bestowed with access to the same information as the kernel, however. At the lowest levels inside the I/O scheduler, requests are already specified in terms of physical disk blocks. Sorting them is trivial. But, in user space, requests are specified in terms of files and offsets. User-space applications must probe for information and make educated guesses about the layout of the filesystem.

Given the goal of determining the most seek-friendly ordering given a list of I/O requests to specific files, user-space applications have a couple of options. They can sort based on:

- The full path
- The inode number
- The physical disk block of the file

Each of these options involves a trade-off. Let's look at each briefly.

Sorting by path

Sorting by the pathname is the easiest, yet least effective, way of approximating a block-wise sort. Due to the layout algorithms used by most filesystems, the files in each directory—and thus the directories sharing a parent directory—tend to be adjacent on disk. The probability that files in the same directory were created around the same time only amplifies this characteristic.

Sorting by path, therefore, roughly approximates the physical locations of files on the disk. It is certainly true that two files in the same directory have a better chance of being located near each other than two files in radically different parts of the filesystem. The downside of this approach is that it fails to take into account fragmentation: the more fragmented the filesystem, the less useful is sorting by path. Even ignoring fragmentation, a path-wise sort only approximates the actual block-wise ordering. On the upside, a path-wise sort is at least somewhat applicable to all filesystems. No matter the approach to file layout, temporal locality suggests a path-wise sort will be at least mildly accurate. It is also an easy sort to perform.

Sorting by inode

Inodes are Unix constructs that contain the metadata associated with individual files. While a file's data may consume multiple physical disk blocks, each file has exactly one inode, which contains information such as the file's size, permissions, owner, and so on. We will discuss inodes in depth in Chapter 8. For now, you need to know two facts: that every file has an inode associated with it and that the inodes are assigned unique numbers.

Sorting by inode is better than sorting by path, assuming that the relation:

```
file i's inode number < file j's inode number
```

implies, *in general*, that:

```
physical blocks of file i < physical blocks of file j
```

This is certainly true for Unix-style filesystems such as *ext3* and *ext4*. Anything is possible for filesystems that do not employ actual inodes, but the inode number (whatever it may map to) is still a good first-order approximation.

Obtaining the inode number is done via the `stat()` system call, also discussed in Chapter 8. Given the inode associated with the file involved in each I/O request, the requests can be sorted in ascending order by inode number.

Here is a simple program that prints out the inode number of a given file:

```c
#include <stdio.h>
#include <stdlib.h>
#include <fcntl.h>
#include <sys/types.h>
#include <sys/stat.h>

/*
 * get_inode - returns the inode of the file associated
 * with the given file descriptor, or -1 on failure
 */
int get_inode (int fd)
{
        struct stat buf;
        int ret;

        ret = fstat (fd, &buf);
        if (ret < 0) {
                perror ("fstat");
                return -1;
        }

        return buf.st_ino;
```

```
        }

        int main (int argc, char *argv[])
        {
                int fd, inode;

                if (argc < 2) {
                        fprintf (stderr, "usage: %s <file>\n", argv[0]);
                        return 1;
                }

                fd = open (argv[1], O_RDONLY);
                if (fd < 0) {
                        perror ("open");
                        return 1;
                }

                inode = get_inode (fd);
                printf ("%d\n", inode);

                return 0;
        }
```

The get_inode() function is easily adaptable for use in your programs.

Sorting by inode number has a few upsides: the inode number is easy to obtain, is easy to sort on, and is a good approximation of the physical file layout. The major downsides are that fragmentation degrades the approximation, that the approximation is just a guess, and that the approximation is less accurate for non-Unix filesystems. Nonetheless, this is the most commonly used method for scheduling I/O requests in user space.

Sorting by physical block

The best approach to designing your own elevator algorithm, of course, is to sort by physical disk block. As discussed earlier, each file is broken up into logical blocks, which are the smallest allocation units of a filesystem. The size of a logical block is filesystem-dependent; each logical block maps to a single physical block. We can thus find the number of logical blocks in a file, determine what physical blocks they map to, and sort based on that.

The kernel provides a method for obtaining the physical disk block from the logical block number of a file. This is done via the ioctl() system call, discussed in Chapter 8, with the FIBMAP command:

```
ret = ioctl (fd, FIBMAP, &block);
if (ret < 0)
        perror ("ioctl");
```

Here, fd is the file descriptor of the file in question, and block is the logical block whose physical block we want to determine. On successful return, block is replaced with the physical block number. The logical blocks passed in are zero-indexed and file-relative. That is, if a file is made up of eight logical blocks, valid values are 0 through 7.

Finding the logical-to-physical-block mapping is thus a two-step process. First, we must determine the number of blocks in a given file. This is done via the `stat()` system call. Second, for each logical block, we must issue an `ioctl()` request to find the corresponding physical block.

Here is a sample program to do just that for a file passed in on the command line:

```
#include <stdio.h>
#include <stdlib.h>
#include <fcntl.h>
#include <sys/types.h>
#include <sys/stat.h>
#include <sys/ioctl.h>
#include <linux/fs.h>

/*
 * get_block - for the file associated with the given fd, returns
 * the physical block mapping to logical_block
 */
int get_block (int fd, int logical_block)
{
        int ret;

        ret = ioctl (fd, FIBMAP, &logical_block);
        if (ret < 0) {
                perror ("ioctl");
                return -1;
        }

        return logical_block;
}

/*
 * get_nr_blocks - returns the number of logical blocks
 * consumed by the file associated with fd
 */
int get_nr_blocks (int fd)
{
        struct stat buf;
        int ret;

        ret = fstat (fd, &buf);
        if (ret < 0) {
                perror ("fstat");
                return -1;
        }
        return buf.st_blocks;
}
```

```c
/*
 * print_blocks - for each logical block consumed by the file
 * associated with fd, prints to standard out the tuple
 * "(logical block, physical block)"
 */
void print_blocks (int fd)
{
        int nr_blocks, i;

        nr_blocks = get_nr_blocks (fd);
        if (nr_blocks < 0) {
                fprintf (stderr, "get_nr_blocks failed!\n");
                return;
        }

        if (nr_blocks == 0) {
                printf ("no allocated blocks\n");
                return;
        } else if (nr_blocks == 1)
                printf ("1 block\n\n");
        else
                printf ("%d blocks\n\n", nr_blocks);

        for (i = 0; i < nr_blocks; i++) {
                int phys_block;

                phys_block = get_block (fd, i);
                if (phys_block < 0) {
                        fprintf (stderr, "get_block failed!\n");
                        return;
                }
                if (!phys_block)
                        continue;

                printf ("(%u, %u) ", i, phys_block);
        }

        putchar ('\n');
}

int main (int argc, char *argv[])
{
        int fd;

        if (argc < 2) {
                fprintf (stderr, "usage: %s <file>\n", argv[0]);
                return 1;
        }

        fd = open (argv[1], O_RDONLY);
        if (fd < 0) {
                perror ("open");
```

```
            return 1;
    }

    print_blocks (fd);

    return 0;
}
```

Because files tend to be contiguous, and it would be difficult (at best) to sort our I/O requests on a per-logical-block basis, it makes sense to sort based on the location of just the first logical block of a given file. Consequently, `get_nr_blocks()` is not needed, and our applications can sort based on the return value from:

```
get_block (fd, 0);
```

The downside of `FIBMAP` is that it requires the `CAP_SYS_RAWIO` capability—effectively, root privileges. Consequently, nonroot applications cannot make use of this approach. Further, while the `FIBMAP` command is standardized, its actual implementation is left up to the filesystems. While common systems such as *ext2* and *ext3* support it, a more esoteric beast may not. The `ioctl()` call will return `EINVAL` if `FIBMAP` is not supported.

Among the pros of this approach, however, is that it returns the *actual* physical disk block at which a file resides, which is exactly what you want to sort on. Even if you sort all I/O to a single file based on the location of just one block (the kernel's I/O scheduler sorts each individual request on a block-wise basis), this approach comes very close to the optimal ordering. The root requirement, however, is a bit of a nonstarter for many.

Conclusion

Over the course of the last three chapters, we have touched on all aspects of file I/O in Linux. In Chapter 2, we looked at the basics of Linux file I/O—really, the basis of Unix programming—with system calls such as `read()`, `write()`, `open()`, and `close()`. In Chapter 3, we discussed user-space buffering and the standard C library's implementation thereof. In this chapter, we discussed various facets of advanced I/O, from the more-powerful-but-more-complex I/O system calls to optimization techniques and the dreaded performance-sucking disk seek.

In the next two chapters, we will look at process management: creating, destroying, and managing processes. Onward!

## CHAPTER 5

Process Management

As discussed in Chapter 1, processes are, after files, the most fundamental abstraction in a Unix system. As object code in execution—active, alive, running programs—processes are more than just assembly language; they consist of data, resources, state, and a virtualized computer.

In this chapter, we will look at the fundamentals of the process, from creation to termination. The basics have remained relatively unchanged since the earliest days of Unix. It is here, in the subject of process management, that the longevity and forward thinking of Unix's original design shines brightest. Unix took an interesting path, one seldom traveled, separating the creation of a new process from the act of loading a new binary image. Although the two tasks are performed in tandem much of the time, the division has allowed a great deal of freedom for experimentation and evolution for each of the tasks. This road less traveled has survived to this day, and while most operating systems offer a single system call to start up a new program, Unix requires two: a fork and an exec. But before we cover those system calls, let's look more closely at the process itself.

Programs, Processes, and Threads

A *binary* is compiled, executable code lying dormant on a storage medium such as a disk. Colloquially, we may also use the term *program*; large and significant binaries we might call *applications*. */bin/ls* and */usr/bin/X11* are both binaries.

A *process* is a running program. A process includes the binary image, loaded into memory, but also much more: an instance of virtualized memory, kernel resources such as open files, a security context such as an associated user, and one or more threads. A *thread* is the unit of activity inside of a process. Each thread has its own virtualized processor, which includes a stack, processor state such as registers, and an instruction pointer.

In a single threaded process, the process is the thread. There is one instance of virtualized memory and one virtualized processor. In a multithreaded process, there are multiple threads. As the virtualization of memory is associated with the process, the threads all share the same memory address space.

The Process ID

733.510bEach process is represented by a unique identifier, the *process ID* (frequently shortened to *pid*). The pid is guaranteed to be unique at any *single point in time*. That is, while at time t+0 there can be only one process with the pid 770 (if any process at all exists with such a value), there is no guarantee that at time t+1 a different process won't exist with pid 770. Essentially, however, most programs presume that the kernel does not readily reissue process identifiers—an assumption that, as you will see shortly, is fairly safe. And, of course, from the view of a process, *its* pid never changes.

The *idle process*, which is the process that the kernel "runs" when there are no other runnable processes, has the pid 0. The first process that the kernel executes after booting the system, called the *init process*, has the pid 1. Normally, the init process on Linux is the *init* program. We use the term "init" to refer to both the initial process that the kernel runs, and the specific program used for that purpose.

Unless the user explicitly tells the kernel what process to run (through the *init* kernel command-line parameter), the kernel has to identify a suitable init process on its own— a rare example where the kernel dictates policy. The Linux kernel tries four executables, in the following order:

1. */sbin/init*: The preferred and most likely location for the init process.
2. */etc/init*: Another likely location for the init process.
3. */bin/init*: A fallback location for the init process.
4. */bin/sh*: The location of the Bourne shell, which the kernel tries to run if it fails to find an init process.

The first of these processes that exists is executed as the init process. If all four processes fail to execute, the Linux kernel halts the system with a panic.

After the handoff from the kernel, the init process handles the remainder of the boot process. Typically, this includes initializing the system, starting various services, and launching a login program.

Process ID Allocation

By default, the kernel imposes a maximum process ID value of 32768. This is for compatibility with older Unix systems, which used signed 16-bit types for process IDs.

System administrators can set the value higher via */proc/sys/kernel/pid_max*, trading a larger pid space for reduced compatibility.

The kernel allocates process IDs to processes in a strictly linear fashion. If pid 17 is the highest number currently allocated, pid 18 will be allocated next, even if the process last assigned pid 17 is no longer running when the new process starts. The kernel does not reuse process ID values until it wraps around from the top—that is, earlier values will not be reused until the value in */proc/sys/kernel/pid_max* is allocated. Therefore, while Linux makes no guarantee of the uniqueness of process IDs over a long period, its allocation behavior does provide at least short-term comfort in the stability and uniqueness of pid values.

The Process Hierarchy

The process that spawns a new process is known as the *parent*; the new process is known as the *child*. Every process is spawned from another process (except, of course, the init process). Therefore, every child has a parent. This relationship is recorded in each process's *parent process ID* (ppid), which is the pid of the child's parent.

Each process is owned by a *user* and a *group*. This ownership is used to control access rights to resources. To the kernel, users and groups are mere integer values. Through the files */etc/passwd* and */etc/group*, these integers are mapped to the human-readable names with which Unix users are familiar, such as the user *root* or the group *wheel* (generally speaking, the Linux kernel has no interest in human-readable strings, and prefers to identify objects with integers). Each child process inherits its parent's user and group ownership.

Each process is also part of a *process group*, which simply expresses its relationship to other processes and should not be confused with the aforementioned user/group concept. Children normally belong to the same process groups as their parents. In addition, when a shell starts up a pipeline (e.g., when a user enters *ls | less*), all the commands in the pipeline go into the same process group. The notion of a process group makes it easy to send signals to or get information on an entire pipeline, as well as all children of the processes in the pipeline. From the perspective of a user, a process group is closely related to a *job*.

pid_t

Programmatically, the process ID is represented by the `pid_t` type, which is defined in the header file `<sys/types.h>`. The exact backing C type is architecture-specific and not defined by any C standard. On Linux, however, `pid_t` is generally a typedef to the C `int` type.

Obtaining the Process ID and Parent Process ID

The `getpid()` system call returns the process ID of the invoking process:

```
#include <sys/types.h>
#include <unistd.h>

pid_t getpid (void);
```

The `getppid()` system call returns the process ID of the invoking process's parent:

```
#include <sys/types.h>
#include <unistd.h>

pid_t getppid (void);
```

Neither call will return an error. Consequently, usage is trivial:

```
printf ("My pid=%jd\n", (intmax_t) getpid ());
printf ("Parent's pid=%jd\n", (intmax_t) getppid ());
```

Here, we typecast the return value to `intmax_t`, which is a C/C++ type guaranteed to be capable of storing any signed integer value on the system. In other words, it is as large or larger than all other signed integer types. Coupled with a `printf()` modifier (`%j`), this approach lets us safely print integers represented by a typedef. Prior to `intmax_t` there was no portable way to do this (if your system lacks `intmax_t`, you can assume `pid_t` is an `int`, which is true on most Unix systems).

Running a New Process

In Unix, the act of loading into memory and executing a program image is separate from the act of creating a new process. One system call loads a binary program into memory, replacing the previous contents of the address space, and begins execution of the new program. This is called *executing* a new program, and the functionality is provided by the *exec* family of calls.

A different system call is used to create a new process, which initially is a near-duplicate of its parent process. Often, the new process immediately executes a new program. The act of creating a new process is called *forking*, and this functionality is provided by the `fork()` system call. Two acts—first a fork to create a new process, and then an exec to load a new binary into that process—are thus required to execute a new program in a new process. We will cover the exec calls first, then `fork()`.

The Exec Family of Calls

There is no single exec function; instead, there is a family of exec functions built on a single system call. Let's first look at the simplest of these calls, `execl()`:

```
#include <unistd.h>

int execl (const char *path,
           const char *arg,
           ...);
```

A call to `execl()` replaces the current process image with a new one by loading into memory the program pointed at by `path`. The parameter `arg` is the first argument to this program. The ellipsis signifies a variable number of arguments—the `execl()` function is *variadic*, which means that additional arguments may optionally follow, one by one. The list of arguments must be `NULL`-terminated.

For example, the following code replaces the currently executing program with */bin/vi*:

```
int ret;

ret = execl ("/bin/vi", "vi", NULL);
if (ret == -1)
        perror ("execl");
```

Note that we follow the Unix convention and pass "vi" as the program's first argument. The shell puts the last component of the path, the "vi," into the first argument when it forks/execs processes, so a program can examine its first argument, `argv[0]`, to discover the name of its binary image. In many cases, several system utilities that appear as different names to the user are in fact a single program with hard links for their multiple names. The program uses the first argument to determine its behavior.

As another example, if you wanted to edit the file */home/kidd/hooks.txt*, you could execute the following code:

```
int ret;

ret = execl ("/bin/vi", "vi", "/home/kidd/hooks.txt", NULL);
if (ret == -1)
        perror ("execl");
```

Normally, `execl()` does not return. A successful invocation ends by jumping to the entry point of the new program, and the just-executed code no longer exists in the process's address space. On error, however, `execl()` returns –1 and sets `errno` to indicate the problem. We will look at the possible `errno` values later in this section.

A successful `execl()` call changes not only the address space and process image, but certain other attributes of the process:

- Any pending signals are lost.
- Any signals that the process is catching (see Chapter 10) are returned to their default behavior, as the signal handlers no longer exist in the process's address space.
- Any memory locks (see Chapter 9) are dropped.

- Most thread attributes are returned to the default values.

- Most process statistics are reset.

- Anything related to the process's memory address space, including any mapped files, is cleared.

- Anything that exists solely in user space, including features of the C library, such as `atexit()` behavior, is cleared.

Some properties of the process, however, do *not* change. For example, the pid, parent pid, priority, and owning user and group all remain the same.

Normally, open files are inherited across an exec. This means the newly executed program has full access to all of the files open in the original process, assuming it knows the file descriptor values. However, this is often not the desired behavior. The usual practice is to close files before the exec, although it is also possible to instruct the kernel to do so automatically via `fcntl()`.

The rest of the family

In addition to `execl()`, there are five other members of the exec family:

```
#include <unistd.h>

int execlp (const char *file,
            const char *arg,
            ...);

int execle (const char *path,
            const char *arg,
            ...,
            char * const envp[]);

int execv (const char *path, char *const argv[]);

int execvp (const char *file, char *const argv[]);

int execve (const char *filename,
            char *const argv[],
            char *const envp[]);
```

The mnemonics are simple. The l and v delineate whether the arguments are provided via a *list* or an array (*vector*). The p denotes that the user's full *path* is searched for the given file. Commands using the p variants can specify just a filename, so long as it is located in the user's path. Finally, the e notes that a new environment is also supplied for the new process. Curiously, although there is no technical reason for the omission, the exec family contains no member that both searches the path and takes a new environment. This is probably because the p variants were implemented for use by shells, and shell-executed processes generally inherit their environments from the shell.

The following snippet uses execvp() to execute *vi*, as we did previously, relying on the fact that *vi* is in the user's path:

```
int ret;

ret = execvp ("vi", "vi", "/home/kidd/hooks.txt", NULL);
if (ret == -1)
        perror ("execvp");
```

Security Risk with execlp() and execvp()

Set-group-ID and set-user-ID programs—processes that run as the group or user of their binary's owner and not the group or user of their invoker, respectively—should never invoke the shell or operations that in turn invoke the shell. Doing so opens a security hole as the invoking user may set environment variables to manipulate the behavior of the shell. The most common form of this attack is *path injection*, in which the attacker sets the PATH variable to cause the process to execlp() a binary of the attacker's choosing, effectively allowing the attacker to run any program with the credentials of the set-group-ID or set-user-ID program.

The members of the exec family that accept an array work about the same, except that an array is constructed and passed in instead of a list. The use of an array allows the arguments to be determined at runtime. As with the variadic list of arguments, the array must be NULL-terminated.

The following snippet uses execv() to execute *vi*, as we did previously:

```
const char *args[] = { "vi", "/home/kidd/hooks.txt", NULL };
int ret;

ret = execv ("/bin/vi", args);
if (ret == -1)
        perror ("execvp");
```

In Linux, only one member of the exec family is a system call. The rest are wrappers in the C library around the system call. Because variadic system calls would be difficult to implement and because the concept of the user's path exists solely in user space, the only option for the lone system call is execve(). The system call prototype is identical to the user call.

Error values

On success, the exec system calls do not return. On failure, the calls return −1 and set errno to one of the following values:

E2BIG

The total number of bytes in the provided arguments list (`arg`) or environment (`envp`) is too large.

EACCES

The process lacks search permission for a component in `path`; `path` is not a regular file; the target file is not marked executable; or the filesystem on which `path` or `file` resides is mounted `noexec`.

EFAULT

A given pointer is invalid.

EIO

A low-level I/O error occurred (this is bad).

EISDIR

The final component in `path`, or the interpreter, is a directory.

ELOOP

The system encountered too many symbolic links in resolving `path`.

EMFILE

The invoking process has reached its limit on open files.

ENFILE

The system-wide limit on open files has been reached.

ENOENT

The target of `path` or `file` does not exist, or a needed shared library does not exist.

ENOEXEC

The target of `path` or `file` is an invalid binary or is intended for a different machine architecture.

ENOMEM

There is insufficient kernel memory available to execute a new program.

ENOTDIR

A nonfinal component in `path` is not a directory.

EPERM

The filesystem on which `path` or `file` resides is mounted `nosuid`, the user is not root, and `path` or `file` has the suid or sgid bit set.

ETXTBSY

The target of `path` or `file` is open for writing by another process.

The fork() System Call

A new process running the same image as the current one can be created via the fork() system call:

```
#include <sys/types.h>
#include <unistd.h>

pid_t fork (void);
```

A successful call to fork() creates a new process, identical in almost all aspects to the invoking process. Both processes continue to run, returning from fork() as if nothing special had happened.

The new process is called the "child" of the original process, which in turn is called the "parent." In the child, a successful invocation of fork() returns 0. In the parent, fork() returns the pid of the child. The child and the parent process are identical in nearly every facet, except for a few necessary differences:

- The pid of the child is, of course, newly allocated and different from that of the parent.
- The child's parent pid is set to the pid of its parent process.
- Resource statistics are reset to zero in the child.
- Any pending signals are cleared and not inherited by the child (see Chapter 10).
- Any acquired file locks are not inherited by the child.

On error, a child process is not created, fork() returns −1, and errno is set appropriately. There are two possible errno values, with three possible meanings:

EAGAIN
: The kernel failed to allocate certain resources, such as a new pid, or the RLIMIT_NPROC resource limit (rlimit) has been reached (see Chapter 6).

ENOMEM
: Insufficient kernel memory was available to complete the request.

Use is simple:

```
pid_t pid;

pid = fork ();
if (pid > 0)
        printf ("I am the parent of pid=%d!\n", pid);
else if (!pid)
        printf ("I am the child!\n");
else if (pid == -1)
        perror ("fork");
```

The most common usage of fork() is to create a new process in which a new binary image is then loaded—think a shell running a new program for the user or a process spawning a helper program. First the process forks a new process, and then the child executes a new binary image. This "fork plus exec" combination is frequent and simple. The following example spawns a new process running the binary */bin/windlass*:

```
pid_t pid;

pid = fork ();
if (pid == -1)
        perror ("fork");

/* the child ... */
if (!pid) {
        const char *args[] = { "windlass", NULL };
        int ret;

        ret = execv ("/bin/windlass", args);
        if (ret == -1) {
                perror ("execv");
                exit (EXIT_FAILURE);
        }
}
```

The parent process continues running with no change, other than that it now has a new child. The call to execv() changes the child to running the */bin/windlass* program.

Copy-on-write

In early Unix systems, forking was simple, even naïve. Upon invocation, the kernel created copies of all internal data structures, duplicated the process's page table entries, and then performed a page-by-page copy of the parent's address space into the child's new address space. Unfortunately, this page-by-page copy is time-consuming.

Modern Unix systems have superior behavior. Instead of a wholesale copy of the parent's address space, modern Unix systems such as Linux employ *copy-on-write* (COW) pages.

Copy-on-write is a lazy optimization strategy designed to mitigate the overhead of duplicating resources. The premise is simple: if multiple consumers request read access to their own copies of a resource, duplicate copies of the resource need not be made. Instead, each consumer can be handed a pointer to the same resource. So long as no consumer attempts to modify its "copy" of the resource, the illusion of exclusive access to the resource remains, and the overhead of a copy is avoided. If a consumer does attempt to modify its copy of the resource, at that point, the resource is transparently duplicated, and the copy is given to the modifying consumer. The consumer, never the wiser, can then modify its copy of the resource while the other consumers continue to share the original, unchanged version. Hence the name: the *copy* occurs only *on write*.

The primary benefit is that if a consumer never modifies its copy of the resource, a copy is never needed. The general advantage of lazy algorithms—that they defer expensive actions until the last possible moment—also applies.

In the specific example of virtual memory, copy-on-write is implemented on a per-page basis. Thus, so long as a process does not modify all of its address space, a copy of the entire address space is not required. At the completion of a fork, the parent and child believe that they each have a unique address space, while in fact they are sharing the parent's original pages—which in turn may be shared with other parent or child processes, and so on!

The kernel implementation is simple. The pages are marked as read-only and as copy-on-write in the kernel's page-related data structures. If either process attempts to modify a page, a page fault occurs. The kernel then handles the page fault by transparently making a copy of the page; at this point, the page's copy-on-write attribute is cleared, and it is no longer shared. Because modern machine architectures provide hardware-level support for copy-on-write in their memory management units (MMUs), this dance is simple and easy to implement.

Copy-on-write has yet a bigger benefit in the case of forking. Because a large percentage of forks are followed by an exec, copying the parent's address space into the child's address space is often a complete waste of time: if the child summarily executes a new binary image, its previous address space is wiped out. Copy-on-write optimizes for this case.

vfork()

Before the arrival of copy-on-write pages, Unix designers were concerned with the wasteful address-space copy during a fork that is immediately followed by an exec. BSD developers therefore unveiled the vfork() system call in 3.0BSD:

```
#include <sys/types.h>
#include <unistd.h>

pid_t vfork (void);
```

A successful invocation of vfork() has the same behavior as fork(), except that the child process must immediately issue a successful call to one of the exec functions or exit by calling _exit() (discussed in the next section). The vfork() system call avoids the address space and page table copies by suspending the parent process until the child terminates or executes a new binary image. In the interim, the parent and the child share —without copy-on-write semantics—their address space and page table entries. In fact, the only work done during a vfork() is the duplication of internal kernel data structures. Consequently, the child must not modify any memory in the address space.

The vfork() system call is a relic and should never have been implemented on Linux, although it should be noted that even with copy-on-write, vfork() is faster than fork()

because the page table entries need not be copied.[1] Nonetheless, the advent of copy-on-write pages weakens any argument for an alternative to fork(). Indeed, until the 2.2.0 Linux kernel, vfork() was simply a wrapper around fork(). As the requirements for vfork() are weaker than the requirements for fork(), such a vfork() implementation is feasible.

Strictly speaking, no vfork() implementation is bug-free. Consider the situation if the exec call were to fail: the parent would be suspended indefinitely while the child figured out what to do or until it exited. Programs should prefer straight fork().

Terminating a Process

POSIX and C89 both define a standard function for terminating the current process:

```
#include <stdlib.h>

void exit (int status);
```

A call to exit() performs some basic shutdown steps, then instructs the kernel to terminate the process. This function has no way of returning an error—in fact, it never returns at all. Therefore, it does not make sense for any instructions to follow the exit() call.

The status parameter is used to denote the process's exit status. Other programs—as well as the user at the shell—can check this value. Specifically, status & 0377 is returned to the parent. We will look at retrieving the return value later in this chapter.

EXIT_SUCCESS and EXIT_FAILURE are defined as portable ways to represent success and failure. On Linux, 0 typically represents success; a nonzero value, such as 1 or –1, corresponds to failure.

Consequently, a successful exit is as simple as this one-liner:

```
exit (EXIT_SUCCESS);
```

Before terminating the process, the C library performs the following shutdown steps, in order:

1. Call any functions registered with atexit() or on_exit(), in the reverse order of their registration. (We will discuss these functions later in this chapter.)
2. Flush all open standard I/O streams (see Chapter 3).

---

1. Although not currently part of the Linux kernel, a patch implementing copy-on-write shared page table entries has been floated on the Linux Kernel Mailing List (*lkml*). Should it be merged, there would be absolutely no benefit to using vfork().

3. Remove any temporary files created with the `tmpfile()` function.

These steps finish all the work the process needs to do in user space, so `exit()` invokes the system call `_exit()` to let the kernel handle the rest of the termination process:

```
#include <unistd.h>

void _exit (int status);
```

When a process exits, the kernel cleans up all of the resources that it created on the process's behalf that are no longer in use. This includes, but is not limited to, allocated memory, open files, and System V semaphores. After cleanup, the kernel destroys the process and notifies the parent of its child's demise.

Applications can call `_exit()` directly, but such a move seldom makes sense: most applications need to do some of the cleanup provided by a full exit, such as flushing the *stdout* stream. Note, however, that `vfork()` users should call `_exit()`, and not `exit()`, after a fork.

In a redundant stroke of redundancy, the ISO C99 standard added the `_Exit()` function, which has identical behavior to `_exit()`:

```
#include <stdlib.h>

void _Exit (int status);
```

Other Ways to Terminate

The classic way to end a program is not via an explicit system call, but by simply "falling off the end" of the program. In the case of C or C++, this happens when the `main()` function returns. The "falling off the end" approach, however, still invokes a system call: the compiler simply inserts an implicit call to `exit()` after its own shutdown code. It is good coding practice to explicitly return an exit status, either via `exit()`, or by returning a value from `main()`. The shell uses the exit value for evaluating the success or failure of commands. Note that a successful return is `exit(0)`, or a return from `main()` of 0.

A process can also terminate if it is sent a signal whose default action is to terminate the process. Such signals include `SIGTERM` and `SIGKILL` (see Chapter 10).

A final way to end a program's execution is by incurring the wrath of the kernel. The kernel can kill a process for executing an illegal instruction, causing a segmentation violation, running out of memory, consuming more resources that allowed, and so on.

atexit()

POSIX 1003.1-2001 defines, and Linux implements, the `atexit()` library call, used to register functions to be invoked upon process termination:

```
#include <stdlib.h>

int atexit (void (*function)(void));
```

A successful invocation of `atexit()` registers the given function to run during normal
process termination, that is, when a process is terminated via either `exit()` or a return
from `main()`. If a process invokes an exec function, the list of registered functions is
cleared (as the functions no longer exist in the new process's address space). If a process
terminates via a signal, the registered functions are not called.

The given function takes no parameters, and returns no value. A prototype has the form:

```
void my_function (void);
```

Functions are invoked in the reverse order that they are registered. That is, the functions
are stored in a stack, and the last in is the first out (LIFO). Registered functions must
not call `exit()` lest they begin an endless recursion. If a function needs to end the
termination process early, it should call `_exit()`. Such behavior is not recommended,
however, as a potentially important shutdown function may then not run.

The POSIX standard requires that `atexit()` support at least `ATEXIT_MAX` registered
functions and that this value be at least 32. The exact maximum may be obtained via
`sysconf()` and the value of `_SC_ATEXIT_MAX`:

```
long atexit_max;

atexit_max = sysconf (_SC_ATEXIT_MAX);
printf ("atexit_max=%ld\n", atexit_max);
```

On success, `atexit()` returns 0. On error, it returns −1.

Here's a simple example:

```
#include <stdio.h>
#include <stdlib.h>

void out (void)
{
        printf ("atexit() succeeded!\n");
}

int main (void)
{
        if (atexit (out))
                fprintf(stderr, "atexit() failed!\n");

        return 0;
}
```

on_exit()

SunOS 4 defined its own equivalent to atexit( ), and Linux's *glibc* supports it:

```
#include <stdlib.h>

int on_exit (void (*function)(int, void *), void *arg);
```

This function works the same as atexit( ), but the registered function's prototype is different:

```
void my_function (int status, void *arg);
```

The status argument is the value passed to exit( ) or returned from main( ). The arg argument is the second parameter passed to on_exit( ). Care must be taken to ensure that the memory pointed at by arg is valid when the function is ultimately invoked.

The latest version of Solaris no longer supports this function. You should use the standards-compliant atexit( ) instead.

SIGCHLD

When a process terminates, the kernel sends the signal SIGCHLD to the parent. By default, this signal is ignored, and no action is taken by the parent. Processes can elect to handle this signal, however, via the signal( ) or sigaction( ) system calls. These calls, and the rest of the wonderful world of signals, are covered in Chapter 10.

The SIGCHLD signal may be generated and dispatched at any time, as a child's termination is asynchronous with respect to its parent. But often, the parent wants to learn more about its child's termination or even explicitly wait for the event's occurrence. This is possible with the system calls discussed next.

Waiting for Terminated Child Processes

Receiving notification via a signal is nice, but many parents want to obtain more information when one of their child processes terminates—for example, the child's return value.

If a child process were to entirely disappear when terminated, as one might expect, no remnants would remain for the parent to investigate. Consequently, the original designers of Unix decided that when a child dies before its parent, the kernel should put the child into a special process state. A process in this state is known as a *zombie*. Only a minimal skeleton of what was once the process—some basic kernel data structures containing potentially useful data—is retained. A process in this state waits for its parent to inquire about its status (a procedure known as *waiting on* the zombie process). Only after the parent obtains the information preserved about the terminated child does the process formally exit and cease to exist even as a zombie.

The Linux kernel provides several interfaces for obtaining information about terminated children. The simplest such interface, defined by POSIX, is wait():

```
#include <sys/types.h>
#include <sys/wait.h>

pid_t wait (int *status);
```

A call to wait() returns the pid of a terminated child or –1 on error. If no child has terminated, the call blocks until a child terminates. If a child has already terminated, the call returns immediately. Consequently, a call to wait() in response to news of a child's demise—say, upon receipt of a SIGCHLD—will always return without blocking.

On error, there are two possible errno values:

ECHILD
    The calling process does not have any children.

EINTR
    A signal was received while waiting, and the call returned early.

If not NULL, the status pointer contains additional information about the child. Because POSIX allows implementations to define the bits in status as they see fit, the standard provides a family of macros for interpreting the parameter:

```
#include <sys/wait.h>

int WIFEXITED (status);
int WIFSIGNALED (status);
int WIFSTOPPED (status);
int WIFCONTINUED (status);

int WEXITSTATUS (status);
int WTERMSIG (status);
int WSTOPSIG (status);
int WCOREDUMP (status);
```

Either of the first two macros may return true (a nonzero value), depending on how the process terminated. The first, WIFEXITED, returns true if the process terminated normally—that is, if the process called _exit(). In this case, the macro WEXITSTATUS provides the low-order eight bits that were passed to _exit().

WIFSIGNALED returns true if a signal caused the process's termination (see Chapter 10 for further discussion on signals). In this case, WTERMSIG returns the number of the signal that caused the termination, and WCOREDUMP returns true if the process dumped core in response to receipt of the signal. WCOREDUMP is not defined by POSIX, although many Unix systems, Linux included, support it.

WIFSTOPPED and WIFCONTINUED return true if the process was stopped or continued, respectively, and is currently being traced via the ptrace() system call. These conditions are generally applicable only when implementing a debugger, although when used with `waitpid()` (see the following subsection), they are used to implement job control, too. Normally, `wait()` is used only to communicate information about a process's termination. If `WIFSTOPPED` is true, `WSTOPSIG` provides the number of the signal that stopped the process. `WIFCONTINUED` is not defined by POSIX, although future standards define it for `waitpid()`. As of the 2.6.10 Linux kernel, Linux provides this macro for `wait()`, too.

Let's look at an example program that uses `wait()` to figure out what happened to its child:

```c
#include <unistd.h>
#include <stdio.h>
#include <sys/types.h>
#include <sys/wait.h>

int main (void)
{
        int status;
        pid_t pid;

        if (!fork ())
                return 1;

        pid = wait (&status);
        if (pid == -1)
                perror ("wait");

        printf ("pid=%d\n", pid);

        if (WIFEXITED (status))
                printf ("Normal termination with exit status=%d\n",
                        WEXITSTATUS (status));

        if (WIFSIGNALED (status))
                printf ("Killed by signal=%d%s\n",
                        WTERMSIG (status),
                        WCOREDUMP (status) ? " (dumped core)" : "");

        if (WIFSTOPPED (status))
                printf ("Stopped by signal=%d\n",
                        WSTOPSIG (status));

        if (WIFCONTINUED (status))
                printf ("Continued\n");

        return 0;
}
```

This program forks a child, which immediately exits. The parent process then executes the `wait()` system call to determine the status of its child. The process prints the child's pid, and how it died. Because in this case the child terminated by returning from main(), we know that we will see output similar to the following:

```
$ ./wait
pid=8529
Normal termination with exit status=1
```

If, instead of having the child return, we have it call abort(),[2] which sends itself the SIGABRT signal, we will instead see something resembling the following:

```
$ ./wait
pid=8678
Killed by signal=6
```

Waiting for a Specific Process

Observing the behavior of child processes is important. Often, however, a process has multiple children, and does not wish to wait for all of them, but rather for a specific child process. One solution would be to make multiple invocations of wait(), each time noting the return value. This is cumbersome, though—what if you later wanted to check the status of a different terminated process? The parent would have to save all of the wait() output in case it needed it later.

If you know the pid of the process you want to wait for, you can use the waitpid() system call:

```
#include <sys/types.h>
#include <sys/wait.h>

pid_t waitpid (pid_t pid, int *status, int options);
```

The waitpid() call is a more powerful version of wait(). Its additional parameters allow for fine-tuning.

The pid parameter specifies exactly which process or processes to wait for. Its values fall into four camps:

< -1

Wait for any child process whose process group ID is equal to the absolute value of this value. For example, passing –500 waits for any process in process group 500.

-1

Wait for any child process. This is the same behavior as wait().

2. Defined in the header <stdlib.h>.

0
> Wait for any child process that belongs to the same process group as the calling process.

> 0
> Wait for any child process whose pid is exactly the value provided. For example, passing 500 waits for the child process with pid 500.

The `status` parameter works identically to the sole parameter to `wait()` and can be operated on using the macros discussed previously.

The `options` parameter is a binary OR of zero or more of the following options:

WNOHANG
> Do not block, but return immediately if no matching child process has already terminated (or stopped or continued).

WUNTRACED
> If set, the `WIFSTOPPED` bit in the returned status parameter is set, even if the calling process is not tracing the child process. This flag allows for the implementation of more general job control, as in a shell.

WCONTINUED
> If set, the `WIFCONTINUED` bit in the returned status parameter is set even if the calling process is not tracing the child process. As with `WUNTRACED`, this flag is useful for implementing a shell.

On success, `waitpid()` returns the pid of the process whose state has changed. If WNOHANG is specified, and the specified child or children have not yet changed state, `waitpid()` returns 0. On error, the call returns −1, and `errno` is set to one of three values:

ECHILD
> The process or processes specified by the `pid` argument do not exist or are not children of the calling process.

EINTR
> The `WNOHANG` option was not specified, and a signal was received while waiting.

EINVAL
> The `options` argument is invalid.

As an example, assume your program wants to grab the return value of the specific child with pid 1742 but return immediately if the child has not yet terminated. You might code up something similar to the following:

```
int status;
pid_t pid;

pid = waitpid (1742, &status, WNOHANG);
```

```
if (pid == -1)
        perror ("waitpid");
else {
        printf ("pid=%d\n", pid);

        if (WIFEXITED (status))
                printf ("Normal termination with exit status=%d\n",
                        WEXITSTATUS (status));

        if (WIFSIGNALED (status))
                printf ("Killed by signal=%d%s\n",
                        WTERMSIG (status),
                        WCOREDUMP (status) ? " (dumped core)" : "");
}
```

As a final example, note the following usage of wait():

```
wait (&status);
```

This is identical to the following usage of waitpid():

```
waitpid (-1, &status, 0);
```

Even More Waiting Versatility

753.400bFor applications that require even greater versatility in their waiting-for-children functionality, the XSI extension to POSIX defines, and Linux provides, waitid():

```
#include <sys/wait.h>

int waitid (idtype_t idtype,
            id_t id,
            siginfo_t *infop,
            int options);
```

As with wait() and waitpid(), waitid() is used to wait for and obtain information about the status change (termination, stopping, continuing) of a child process. It provides even more options, but it offers them with the trade-off of greater complexity.

Like waitpid(), waitid() allows the developer to specify what to wait for. However, waitid() accomplishes this task with not one, but two parameters. The idtype and id arguments specify which children to wait for, accomplishing the same goal as the sole pid argument in waitpid(). idtype may be one of the following values:

P_PID
    Wait for a child whose pid matches id.

P_GID
    Wait for a child whose process group ID matches id.

P_ALL

> Wait for any child; `id` is ignored.

The `id` argument is the rarely seen `id_t` type, which is a type representing a generic identification number. It is employed in case future implementations add a new `id` type value and supposedly offers greater insurance that the predefined type will be able to hold the newly created identifier. The type is guaranteed to be sufficiently large to hold any `pid_t`. On Linux, developers may use it as if it were a `pid_t`. For example, you may directly provide `pid_t` values or numeric constants for an `id_t`. Pedantic programmers, however, are free to typecast.

The `options` parameter is a binary OR of one or more of the following values:

WEXITED

> The call will wait for children (as determined by `id` and `idtype`) that have terminated.

WSTOPPED

> The call will wait for children that have stopped execution in response to receipt of a signal.

WCONTINUED

> The call will wait for children that have continued execution in response to receipt of a signal.

WNOHANG

> The call will never block, but will return immediately if no matching child process has already terminated (or stopped, or continued).

WNOWAIT

> The call will not remove the matching process from the zombie state. The process may be waited upon in the future.

Upon successfully waiting for a child, `waitid()` fills in the `infop` parameter, which must point to a valid `siginfo_t` type. The exact layout of the `siginfo_t` structure is implementation-specific,[3] but a handful of fields are valid after a call to `waitid()`. That is, a successful invocation will ensure that the following fields are filled in:

si_pid

> The child's pid.

si_uid

> The child's uid.

---

3. Indeed, the `siginfo_t` structure is very complicated on Linux. For its definition, see */usr/include/bits/siginfo.h*. We will study this structure in more detail in Chapter 10.

si_code

Set to one of CLD_EXITED, CLD_KILLED, CLD_STOPPED, or CLD_CONTINUED in response to the child terminating, dying via signal, stopping via signal, or continuing via signal, respectively.

si_signo

Set to SIGCHLD.

si_status

If si_code is CLD_EXITED, this field is the exit code of the child process. Otherwise, this field is the number of the signal delivered to the child that caused the state change.

On success, waitid() returns 0. On error, waitid() returns −1, and errno is set to one of the following values:

ECHLD

The process or processes delineated by id and idtype do not exist.

EINTR

WNOHANG was not set in options, and a signal interrupted execution.

EINVAL

The options argument or the combination of the id and idtype arguments is invalid.

The waitid() function provides additional, useful semantics not found in wait() and waitpid(). In particular, the information retrievable from the siginfo_t structure may prove quite valuable. If such information is not needed, however, it may make more sense to stick to the simpler functions, which are supported on a wider range of systems and thus are portable to more non-Linux systems.

BSD Wants to Play: wait3() and wait4()

While waitpid() derives from AT&T's System V Release 4, BSD takes its own route and provides two other functions used to wait for a child to change state:

```
#include <sys/types.h>
#include <sys/time.h>
#include <sys/resource.h>
#include <sys/wait.h>

pid_t wait3 (int *status,
             int options,
             struct rusage *rusage);

pid_t wait4 (pid_t pid,
             int *status,
```

```
        int options,
        struct rusage *rusage);
```

The 3 and 4 come from the fact that these two functions are three- and four-parameter versions, respectively, of `wait()`. Berkeley reserved its creative facilities for other endeavors, apparently.

The functions work similarly to `waitpid()`, with the exception of the `rusage` argument. The following `wait3()` invocation:

```
pid = wait3 (status, options, NULL);
```

is equivalent to the following `waitpid()` call:

```
pid = waitpid (-1, status, options);
```

While the following `wait4()` invocation:

```
pid = wait4 (pid, status, options, NULL);
```

is equivalent to this `waitpid()` call:

```
pid = waitpid (pid, status, options);
```

That is, `wait3()` waits for any child to change state, and `wait4()` waits for the specific child identified by the `pid` parameter to change state. The `options` argument behaves the same as with `waitpid()`.

As mentioned earlier, the big difference between these calls and `waitpid()` is the `rusage` parameter. If it is non-`NULL`, the function fills out the pointer at `rusage` with information about the child. This structure provides information about the child's resource usage:

```
#include <sys/resource.h>

struct rusage {
        struct timeval ru_utime; /* user time consumed */
        struct timeval ru_stime; /* system time consumed */
        long ru_maxrss;    /* maximum resident set size */
        long ru_ixrss;     /* shared memory size */
        long ru_idrss;     /* unshared data size */
        long ru_isrss;     /* unshared stack size */
        long ru_minflt;    /* page reclaims */
        long ru_majflt;    /* page faults */
        long ru_nswap;     /* swap operations */
        long ru_inblock;   /* block input operations */
        long ru_oublock;   /* block output operations */
        long ru_msgsnd;    /* messages sent */
        long ru_msgrcv;    /* messages received */
        long ru_nsignals;  /* signals received */
        long ru_nvcsw;     /* voluntary context switches */
        long ru_nivcsw;    /* involuntary context switches */
};
```

I will address resource usage further in the next chapter.

On success, these functions return the pid of the process that changed state. On failure, they return –1 and set `errno` to one of the same error values returned by `waitpid()`.

Because `wait3()` and `wait4()` are not POSIX-defined,[4] it is advisable to use them only when resource-usage information is critical. Despite the lack of POSIX standardization, however, nearly every Unix system supports these two calls.

Launching and Waiting for a New Process

Both ANSI C and POSIX define an interface that couples spawning a new process and waiting for its termination—think of it as synchronous process creation. If a process is spawning a child only to immediately wait for its termination, it makes sense to use this interface:

```
#define _XOPEN_SOURCE     /* if we want WEXITSTATUS, etc. */
#include <stdlib.h>

int system (const char *command);
```

The `system()` function is so named because the synchronous process invocation is called *shelling out to the system*. It is common to use `system()` to run a simple utility or shell script, often with the explicit goal of simply obtaining its return value.

A call to `system()` invokes the command provided by the `command` parameter, including any additional arguments. The `command` parameter is suffixed to the arguments */bin/sh -c*. In this sense, the parameter is passed wholesale to the shell.

On success, the return value is the return status of the command as provided by `wait()`. Consequently, the exit code of the executed command is obtained via `WEXIT STATUS`. If invoking */bin/sh* itself failed, the value given by `WEXITSTATUS` is the same as that returned by `exit(127)`. Because it is also possible for the invoked command to return 127, there is no surefire method to check whether the shell itself returned that error. On error, the call returns –1.

If `command` is `NULL`, `system()` returns a nonzero value if the shell */bin/sh* is available, and 0 otherwise.

During execution of the command, `SIGCHLD` is blocked, and `SIGINT` and `SIGQUIT` are ignored. Ignoring `SIGINT` and `SIGQUIT` has several implications, particularly if `system()` is invoked inside a loop. If calling `system()` from within a loop, you should ensure that the program properly checks the exit status of the child. For example:

---

4. `wait3()` was included in the original Single UNIX Specification, but it has since been removed.

```
do {
        int ret;

        ret = system ("pidof rudderd");
        if (WIFSIGNALED (ret) &&
            (WTERMSIG (ret) == SIGINT ||
             WTERMSIG (ret) == SIGQUIT))
                break; /* or otherwise handle */
} while (1);
```

Implementing system() using fork(), a function from the exec family, and wait pid() is a useful exercise. You should attempt this yourself, as it ties together many of the concepts of this chapter. In the spirit of completeness, however, here is a sample implementation:

```
/*
 * my_system - synchronously spawns and waits for the command
 * "/bin/sh -c <cmd>".
 *
 * Returns -1 on error of any sort, or the exit code from the
 * launched process. Does not block or ignore any signals.
 */
int my_system (const char *cmd)
{
        int status;
        pid_t pid;

        pid = fork ();
        if (pid == -1)
                return -1;
        else if (pid == 0) {
                const char *argv[4];

                argv[0] = "sh";
                argv[1] = "-c";
                argv[2] = cmd;
                argv[3] = NULL;
                execv ("/bin/sh", argv);

                exit (-1);
        }

        if (waitpid (pid, &status, 0) == -1)
                return -1;
        else if (WIFEXITED (status))
                return WEXITSTATUS (status);

        return -1;
}
```

Note that this example does not block or disable any signals, unlike the official system(). This behavior may be better or worse, depending on your program's situation, but leaving at least SIGINT unblocked is often smart because it allows the invoked command to be interrupted in the way a user normally expects. A better implementation could add additional pointers as parameters that, when non-NULL, signify errors currently differentiable from each other. For example, one might add fork_failed and shell_failed.

Security Risks with system()

The system() system call suffers the same security issues as execlp() and execvp() (see previous discussion). You should never invoke system() from a set-group-ID or set-user-ID program as an attacker may manipulate environment variables (most commonly PATH) to gain escalated privileges. Our handwritten system() replacement, as it uses the shell, is also vulnerable.

To avoid this attack vector, set-group-ID and set-user-ID programs should invoke the desired external binary manually via fork() and execl() without use of the shell. Not invoking an external binary at all is an even better practice!

Zombies

As discussed earlier, a process that has terminated but has not yet been waited upon by its parent is called a "zombie." Zombie processes continue to consume system resources, although only a small percentage—enough to maintain a mere skeleton of what they once were. These resources remain so that parent processes that want to check up on the status of their children can obtain information relating to the life and termination of those processes. Once the parent does so, the kernel cleans up the process for good and the zombie ceases to exist.

However, anyone who has used Unix for a good while is sure to have seen zombie processes sitting around. These processes, often called *ghosts*, have irresponsible parents. If your application forks a child process, it is your application's responsibility (unless it is short-lived, as you will see shortly) to wait on the child, even if it will merely discard the information gleaned. Otherwise, all of your process's children will become ghosts and live on, crowding the system's process listing and generating disgust at your application's sloppy implementation.

What happens, however, if the parent process dies before the child, or if it dies before it has a chance to wait on its zombie children? Whenever a process terminates, the Linux kernel walks a list of its children and *reparents* all of them to the init process (the process with a pid value of 1). This guarantees that no process is ever without an immediate parent. The init process, in turn, periodically waits on all of its children, ensuring that none remain zombies for too long—no ghosts! Thus, if a parent dies before its children or does not wait on its children before exiting, the child processes are eventually reparented to init and waited upon, allowing them to fully exit. Although doing so is still considered good practice, this safeguard means that short-lived processes need not worry excessively about waiting on all of their children.

Users and Groups

As mentioned earlier in this chapter and discussed in Chapter 1, processes are associated with users and groups. The user and group identifiers are numeric values represented by the C types uid_t and gid_t, respectively. The mapping between numeric values and human-readable names—as in the root user having the uid 0—is performed in user space using the files */etc/passwd* and */etc/group*. The kernel deals only with the numeric values.

In a Linux system, a process's user and group IDs dictate the operations that the process may undertake. Processes must therefore run under the appropriate users and groups. Many processes run as the root user. However, best practices in software development encourage the doctrine of *least-privileged* rights, meaning that a process should execute with the minimum level of rights possible. This requirement is dynamic: if a process requires root privileges to perform an operation early in its life but does not require these extensive privileges thereafter, it should drop root privileges as soon as possible. To this end, many processes—particularly those that need root privileges to carry out certain operations—often manipulate their user or group IDs.

Before we can look at how this is accomplished, we need to cover the complexities of user and group IDs.

Real, Effective, and Saved User and Group IDs

 The following discussion focuses on user IDs, but the text applies equally to group IDs.

There are, in fact, not one, but four user IDs associated with a process: the real, effective, saved, and filesystem user IDs. The *real user ID* is the uid of the user who originally ran the process. It is set to the real user ID of the process's parent, and does not change during an exec call. Normally, the login process sets the real user ID of the user's login shell to that of the user, and all of the user's processes continue to carry this user ID. The superuser (root) may change the real user ID to any value, but no other user can change this value.

The *effective user ID* is the user ID that the process is currently wielding. Permission verifications normally check against this value. Initially, this ID is equal to the real user ID, because when a process forks, the effective user ID of the parent is inherited by the child. Furthermore, when the process issues an exec call, the effective user is usually unchanged. But it is during the exec call that the key difference between real and effective IDs emerges: by executing a *setuid* (*suid*) binary, the process can change its effective user ID. To be exact, the effective user ID is set to the user ID of the owner of the program file. For instance, because the */usr/bin/passwd* file is a setuid file and root is its owner, when a normal user's shell spawns a process to exec this file, the process takes on the effective user ID of root regardless of who the executing user is.

Nonprivileged users may set the effective user ID to the real or the saved user ID, as you'll see momentarily. The superuser may set the effective user ID to any value.

The *saved user ID* is the process's original effective user ID. When a process forks, the child inherits the saved user ID of its parent. Upon an exec call, however, the kernel sets the saved user ID to the effective user ID, thereby making a record of the effective user ID at the time of the exec. Nonprivileged users may not change the saved user ID; the superuser can change it to the same value as the real user ID.

What is the point of all these values? The effective user ID is the value that matters: it's the user ID that is checked in the course of validating a process's credentials. The real user ID and saved user ID act as surrogates or potential user ID values that nonroot processes are allowed to switch to and from. The real user ID is the effective user ID belonging to the user actually running the program, and the saved user ID is the effective user ID from before a suid binary caused a change during exec.

Changing the Real or Saved User or Group ID

The user and group IDs are set via two system calls:

```
#include <sys/types.h>
#include <unistd.h>

int setuid (uid_t uid);
int setgid (gid_t gid);
```

A call to setuid() sets the effective user ID of the current process. If the current effective user ID of the process is 0 (root), the real and saved user IDs are also set. The root user may provide any value for uid, thereby setting all three of the user ID values to uid. A nonroot user is allowed only to provide the real or saved user ID for uid. In other words, a nonroot user can only set the effective user ID to one of those values.

On success, setuid() returns 0. On error, the call returns –1, and errno is set to one of the following values:

EAGAIN
    uid is different from the real user ID, and setting the real user ID to uid will put the user over its RLIM_NPROC rlimit (which specifies the number of processes that a user may own).

EPERM

The user is not root, and uid is neither the effective nor the saved user ID.

The preceding discussion also applies to groups—simply replace setuid() with setgid() and uid with gid.

Changing the Effective User or Group ID

Linux provides two POSIX-mandated functions for setting the effective user and group IDs of the currently executing process:

```
#include <sys/types.h>
#include <unistd.h>

int seteuid (uid_t euid);
int setegid (gid_t egid);
```

A call to seteuid() sets the effective user ID to euid. Root may provide any value for euid. Nonroot users may set the effective user ID only to the real or saved user ID. On success, seteuid() returns 0. On failure, it returns –1 and sets errno to EPERM, which signifies that the current process is not owned by root, and that euid is equal to neither the real nor the saved user ID.

Note that in the nonroot case, seteuid() and setuid() behave the same. It is thus standard practice and a good idea to always use seteuid() unless your process tends to run as root, in which case setuid() makes more sense.

The preceding discussion also applies to groups—simply replace seteuid() with setegid(), and euid with egid.

Changing the User and Group IDs, BSD Style

BSD settled on its own interfaces for setting the user and group IDs. Linux provides these interfaces for compatibility:

```
#include <sys/types.h>
#include <unistd.h>

int setreuid (uid_t ruid, uid_t euid);
int setregid (gid_t rgid, gid_t egid);
```

A call to setreuid() sets the real and effective user IDs of a process to ruid and euid, respectively. Specifying a value of –1 for either parameter leaves the associated user ID unchanged. Nonroot processes are only allowed to set the effective user ID to the real or saved user ID and the real user ID to the effective user ID. If the real user ID is changed, or if the effective user ID is changed to a value not equal to the previous real user ID value, the saved user ID is changed to the new effective user ID. At least, that's how Linux and most other Unix systems react to such changes; the behavior is left undefined by POSIX.

On success, `setreuid()` returns 0. On failure, it returns –1 and sets `errno` to `EPERM`, which signifies that the current process is not owned by root, and that `euid` is equal to neither the real nor the saved user ID or that `ruid` is not equal to the effective user ID.

The preceding discussion also applies to groups—simply replace `setreuid()` with `setregid()`, `ruid` with `rgid`, and `euid` with `egid`.

Changing the User and Group IDs, HP-UX Style

You may feel the situation is quickly becoming parody, but HP-UX, Hewlett-Packard's Unix system, has also introduced its own mechanisms for setting a process's user and group IDs. Linux follows along and provides these interfaces, which are useful if you want to maintain portability to HP-UX:

```
#define _GNU_SOURCE
#include <unistd.h>

int setresuid (uid_t ruid, uid_t euid, uid_t suid);
int setresgid (gid_t rgid, gid_t egid, gid_t sgid);
```

A call to `setresuid()` sets the real, effective, and saved user IDs to `ruid`, `euid`, and `suid`, respectively. Specifying a value of –1 for any of the parameters leaves its value unchanged.

The root user may set any user ID to any value. Nonroot users may set any user ID to the current real, effective, or saved user ID. On success, `setuid()` returns 0. On error, the call returns –1, and `errno` is set to one of the following values:

EAGAIN
> `uid` does not match the real user ID, and setting the real user ID to `uid` will put the user over its `RLIM_NPROC` rlimit (which specifies the number of processes that a user may own).

EPERM
> The user is not root and attempted to set new values for the real, effective, or saved user ID that did not match one of the current real, effective, or saved user IDs.

The preceding discussion also applies to groups—simply replace `setresuid()` with `setresgid()`, `ruid` with `rgid`, `euid` with `egid`, and `suid` with `sgid`.

Preferred User/Group ID Manipulations

Nonroot processes should use `seteuid()` to change their effective user IDs. Root processes should use `setuid()` if they wish to change all three user IDs and `seteuid()` if they wish to temporarily change just the effective user ID. These functions are simple and behave in accordance with POSIX, properly taking into account saved user IDs.

Despite providing additional functionality, the BSD and HP-UX style functions do not allow for any useful changes that `setuid()` and `seteuid()` do not.

Support for Saved User IDs

The existence of the saved user and group IDs is mandated by IEEE Std 1003.1-2001 (POSIX 2001), and Linux has supported these IDs since the early days of the 1.1.38 kernel. Programs written only for Linux may rest assured of the existence of the saved user IDs. Programs written for older Unix systems should check for the macro `_POSIX_SAVED_IDS` before making any references to a saved user or group ID.

In the absence of saved user and group IDs, the preceding discussions are still valid; just ignore any parts of the rules that mention the saved user or group ID.

Obtaining the User and Group IDs

These two system calls return the real user and group IDs, respectively:

```
#include <unistd.h>
#include <sys/types.h>

uid_t getuid (void);
gid_t getgid (void);
```

They cannot fail. Likewise, these two system calls return the effective user and group IDs, respectively:

```
#include <unistd.h>
#include <sys/types.h>

uid_t geteuid (void);
gid_t getegid (void);
```

These two system calls cannot fail, either.

Sessions and Process Groups

Each process is a member of a *process group*, which is a collection of one or more processes generally associated with each other for the purposes of *job control*. The primary attribute of a process group is that signals may be sent to all processes in the group: a single action can terminate, stop, or continue all processes in the same process group.

Each process group is identified by a *process group ID* (*pgid*) and has a *process group leader*. The process group ID is equal to the pid of the process group leader. Process groups exist so long as they have one remaining member. Even if the process group leader terminates, the process group continues to exist.

When a new user first logs into a machine, the login process creates a new *session* that consists of a single process, the user's *login shell*. The login shell functions as the *session leader*. The pid of the session leader is used as the *session ID*. A session is a collection of one or more process groups. Sessions arrange a logged-in user's activities and associate that user with a *controlling terminal*, which is a specific tty device that handles the user's terminal I/O. Consequently, sessions are largely the business of shells. In fact, nothing else really cares about them.

While process groups provide a mechanism to address signals to all of their members, making job control and other shell functions easy, sessions exist to consolidate logins around controlling terminals. Process groups in a session are divided into a single *foreground process group* and zero or more *background process groups*. When a user exits a terminal, a SIGQUIT is sent to all processes in the foreground process group. When a network disconnect is detected by a terminal, a SIGHUP is sent to all processes in the foreground process group. When the user enters the interrupt key (generally Ctrl-C), a SIGINT is sent to all processes in the foreground process group. Thus, sessions make managing terminals and logins easier for shells.

As a review, say a user logs into the system and her login shell, *bash*, has the pid 1700. The user's *bash* instance is now the sole member and leader of a new process group, with the process group ID 1700. This process group is inside a new session with the session ID 1700, and *bash* is the sole member and the leader of this session. New commands that the user runs in the shell run in new process groups within session 1700. One of these process groups—the one connected directly to the user and in control of the terminal—is the *foreground process group*. All the other process groups are *background process groups*.

On a given system, there are many sessions: one for each user login session and others for processes not tied to user login sessions, such as daemons. Daemons tend to create their own sessions to avoid the issues of association with other sessions that may exit.

Each of these sessions contains one or more process groups, and each process group contains at least one process. Process groups that contain more than one process are generally implementing job control.

A command on the shell such as this one:

```
$ cat ship-inventory.txt | grep booty | sort
```

results in one process group containing three processes. This way, the shell can signal all three processes in one fell swoop. Because the user has typed this command on the console without a trailing ampersand, we can also say that this process group is in the foreground. Figure 5-1 illustrates the relationship between sessions, process groups, processes, and controlling terminals.

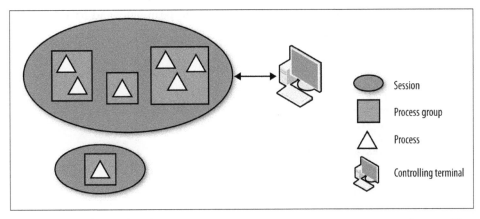

Figure 5-1. Relationship between sessions, process groups, processes, and controlling terminals

Linux provides several interfaces for setting and retrieving the session and process group associated with a given process. These are primarily of use for shells, but can also be useful to processes such as daemons that want to get out of the business of sessions and process groups altogether.

Session System Calls

Shells create new sessions on login. They do so via a special system call, which makes creating a new session easy:

```
#include <unistd.h>

pid_t setsid (void);
```

A call to `setsid()` creates a new session, assuming that the process is not already a process group leader. The calling process is made the session leader and sole member of the new session, which has no controlling tty. The call also creates a new process group inside the session and makes the calling process the process group leader and sole member. The new session's and process group's IDs are set to the calling process's `pid`.

In other words, `setsid()` creates a new process group inside of a new session and makes the invoking process the leader of both. This is useful for daemons, which do not want to be members of existing sessions or to have controlling terminals, and for shells, which want to create a new session for each user upon login.

On success, `setsid( )` returns the session ID of the newly created session. On error, the call returns –1. The only possible `errno` code is EPERM, which indicates that the process is currently a process group leader. The easiest way to ensure that any given process is not a process group leader is to fork, have the parent terminate, and have the child perform the `setsid( )`. For example:

```
pid_t pid;

pid = fork ();
if (pid == -1) {
        perror ("fork");
        return -1;
} else if (pid != 0)
        exit (EXIT_SUCCESS);

if (setsid () == -1) {
        perror ("setsid");
        return -1;
}
```

Obtaining the current session ID, while less useful, is also possible:

```
#define _XOPEN_SOURCE 500
#include <unistd.h>

pid_t getsid (pid_t pid);
```

A call to `getsid( )` returns the session ID of the process identified by `pid`. If the `pid` argument is 0, the call returns the session ID of the calling process. On error, the call returns –1. The only possible `errno` value is ESRCH, indicating that `pid` does not correspond to a valid process. Note that other Unix systems may also set `errno` to EPERM, indicating that `pid` and the invoking process do not belong to the same session; Linux does not return this error and happily returns the session ID of any process.

Usage of `getsid( )` is uncommon and is primarily for diagnostic purposes:

```
pid_t sid;

sid = getsid (0);
if (sid == -1)
        perror ("getsid"); /* should not be possible */
else
        printf ("My session id=%d\n", sid);
```

Process Group System Calls

A call to `setpgid( )` sets the process group ID of the process identified by `pid` to `pgid`:

```
#define _XOPEN_SOURCE 500
#include <unistd.h>
```

```
int setpgid (pid_t pid, pid_t pgid);
```

The current process is used if the pid argument is 0. If pgid is 0, the process ID of the process identified by pid is used as the process group ID.

On success, setpgid() returns 0. Success is contingent on several conditions:

- The process identified by pid must be the calling process, or a child of the calling process that has not issued an exec call and is in the same session as the calling process.
- The process identified by pid must not be a session leader.
- If pgid already exists, it must be in the same session as the calling process.
- pgid must be nonnegative.

On error, the call returns −1 and sets errno to one of the following error codes:

EACCES
: The process identified by pid is a child of the calling process that has already invoked exec.

EINVAL
: pgid is less than 0.

EPERM
: The process identified by pid is a session leader or is in a different session from the calling process. Alternatively, an attempt was made to move a process into a process group inside a different session.

ESRCH
: pid is not the current process, 0, or a child of the current process.

As with sessions, obtaining a process's process group ID is possible, although less useful:

```
#define _XOPEN_SOURCE 500
#include <unistd.h>

pid_t getpgid (pid_t pid);
```

A call to getpgid() returns the process group ID of the process identified by pid. If pid is 0, the process group ID of the current process is used. On error, it returns −1 and sets errno to ESRCH, the only possible value, indicating that pid is an invalid process identifier.

As with getsid(), usage is largely for diagnostic purposes:

```
pid_t pgid;
```

```
pgid = getpgid (0);
if (pgid == -1)
        perror ("getpgid"); /* should not be possible */
else
        printf ("My process group id=%d\n", pgid);
```

Obsolete Process Group Functions

Linux supports two older interfaces from BSD for manipulating or obtaining the process group ID. As they are less useful than the previously discussed system calls, new programs should use them only when portability is stringently required. setpgrp() can be used to set the process group ID:

```
#include <unistd.h>

int setpgrp (void);
```

This invocation:

```
if (setpgrp () == -1)
        perror ("setpgrp");
```

is identical to the following invocation:

```
if (setpgid (0,0) == -1)
        perror ("setpgid");
```

Both attempt to assign the current process to the process group with the same number as the current process's pid, returning 0 on success, and –1 on failure. All of the errno values of setpgid() are applicable to setpgrp(), except ERSCH.

Similarly, a call to getpgrp() can be used to retrieve the process group ID:

```
#include <unistd.h>

pid_t getpgrp (void);
```

This invocation:

```
pid_t pgid = getpgrp ();
```

is identical to:

```
pid_t pgid = getpgid (0);
```

Both return the process group ID of the calling process. The function getpgid() cannot fail.

Daemons

A *daemon* is a process that runs in the background, not connecting to any controlling terminal. Daemons are normally started at boot time, are run as root or some other special user (such as *apache* or *postfix*), and handle system-level tasks. As a convention, the name of a daemon often ends in *d* (as in *crond* and *sshd*), but this is not required or even universal.

 The name derives from *Maxwell's demon*, an 1867 thought experiment by the physicist James Maxwell. Daemons are also supernatural beings in Greek mythology, existing somewhere between humans and the gods and gifted with powers and divine knowledge. Unlike Judeo-Christian demons, the Greek daemon need not be evil. Indeed, the daemons of mythology were often aides to the gods, performing tasks that the denizens of Mount Olympus found themselves unwilling to do—much as Unix daemons perform tasks that foreground users would rather avoid.

A daemon has two general requirements: it must run as a child of init and it must not be connected to a terminal.

In general, a program performs the following steps to become a daemon:

1. Call `fork()`. This creates a new process, which will become the daemon.

2. In the parent, call `exit()`. This ensures that the original parent (the daemon's grandparent) is satisfied that its child terminated, that the daemon's parent is no longer running, and that the daemon is not a process group leader. This last point is a requirement for the successful completion of the next step.

3. Call `setsid()`, giving the daemon a new process group and session, both of which have it as leader. This also ensures that the process has no associated controlling terminal (as the process just created a new session and will not assign one).

4. Change the working directory to the root directory via `chdir()`. This is done because the inherited working directory can be anywhere on the filesystem. Daemons tend to run for the duration of the system's uptime, and you don't want to keep some random directory open and thus prevent an administrator from unmounting the filesystem containing that directory.

5. Close all file descriptors. You do not want to inherit open file descriptors, and, unaware, hold them open.

6. Open file descriptors 0, 1, and 2 (standard in, standard out, and standard error) and redirect them to */dev/null*.

Following these rules, here is a program that daemonizes itself:

```
#include <sys/types.h>
#include <sys/stat.h>
#include <stdlib.h>
#include <stdio.h>
```

```
#include <fcntl.h>
#include <unistd.h>
#include <linux/fs.h>

int main (void)
{
        pid_t pid;
        int i;

        /* create new process */
        pid = fork ();
        if (pid == -1)
                return -1;
        else if (pid != 0)
                exit (EXIT_SUCCESS);

        /* create new session and process group */
        if (setsid () == -1)
                return -1;

        /* set the working directory to the root directory */
        if (chdir ("/") == -1)
                return -1;

        /* close all open files--NR_OPEN is overkill, but works */
        for (i = 0; i < NR_OPEN; i++)
                close (i);

        /* redirect fd's 0,1,2 to /dev/null */
        open ("/dev/null", O_RDWR);      /* stdin */
        dup (0);                         /* stdout */
        dup (0);                         /* stderror */

        /* do its daemon thing... */

        return 0;
}
```

Most Unix systems provide a daemon() function in their C library that automates these steps, turning the cumbersome into the simple:

```
#include <unistd.h>

int daemon (int nochdir, int noclose);
```

If nochdir is nonzero, the daemon will not change its working directory to the root directory. If noclose is nonzero, the daemon will not close all open file descriptors. These options are useful if the parent process already set up these aspects of the dae-monizing procedure. Normally, though, one passes 0 for both of these parameters.

On success, the call returns 0. On failure, the call returns –1, and errno is set to a valid error code from fork() or setsid().

Conclusion

In this chapter, we covered the fundamentals of Unix process management, from process creation to process termination. In the next chapter, we will cover more advanced process management interfaces, including interfaces for changing the scheduling behavior of processes.

## CHAPTER 6

Advanced Process Management

Chapter 5 explained what a process is and what parts of the system it encompasses, along with system calls to create, control, and destroy it. This chapter builds on those concepts, beginning with a discussion of the Linux process scheduler and its scheduling algorithm, and then presenting advanced process management interfaces. These system calls manipulate the scheduling behavior of a process, influencing the scheduler's behavior in pursuit of an application or user-dictated goal.

Process Scheduling

The *process scheduler* is the kernel subsystem that divides the finite resource of processor time among a system's processes. In other words, the process scheduler (or simply the *scheduler*) is the component of a kernel that selects which process to run next. In deciding which processes can run and when, the scheduler is responsible for maximizing processor usage while simultaneously providing the illusion that multiple processes are executing concurrently and seamlessly.

In this chapter, we will talk a lot about *runnable* processes. A runnable process is one that is not blocked; a *blocked process* is one that is sleeping, waiting for I/O from the kernel. Processes that interact with users, read and write files heavily, or respond to network events tend to spend a lot of time blocked while they wait for resources to become available, and they are not runnable during those periods. Given only one runnable process, the job of a process scheduler is trivial: run that process! A scheduler proves its worth, however, when there are more runnable processes than processors. In such a situation, some processes will run while others must wait their turn. Deciding which processes run, when, and for how long is the process scheduler's fundamental responsibility.

An operating system on a single-processor machine is *multitasking* if it can interleave the execution of multiple processes, providing the illusion that more than one process is running at the same time. On multiprocessor machines, a multitasking operating system allows processes to actually run in parallel, on different processors. A nonmultitasking operating system, such as DOS, can run only one application at a time.

Multitasking operating systems come in two variants: *cooperative* and *preemptive*. Linux implements the latter form of multitasking, where the scheduler decides when one process is to stop running and a different process is to resume. We call the act of suspending a running process in lieu of another one *preemption*. The length of time a process is allowed to run before the scheduler preempts it is known as the process's *timeslice*, so called because the scheduler allocates the process a "slice" of the processor's time.

In cooperative multitasking, conversely, a process does not stop running until it voluntarily decides to do so. Voluntarily suspending itself is called *yielding*. Ideally, processes yield often, but the operating system is unable to enforce this behavior. A rude or broken program can run long enough to break the illusion of multitasking, or even indefinitely so as to bring down the entire system. Due to the shortcomings of this approach, modern operating systems are almost universally preemptively multitasked; Linux is no exception.

Linux's process scheduler has changed over the years. The current process scheduler, available since Linux kernel version 2.6.23, is called the *Completely Fair Scheduler* (*CFS*). The name derives from the scheduler's adoption of *fair queuing*, a scheduling algorithm that attempts to enforce fair access to a resource among contending consumers. CFS is drastically unlike any other Unix process scheduler, including its predecessor, the *O(1) process scheduler*. We will further discuss CFS in "The Completely Fair Scheduler" on page 180.

Timeslices

The timeslice that the process scheduler allots to each process is an important variable in the overall behavior and performance of a system. If timeslices are too large, processes must wait a long time in between executions, minimizing the appearance of concurrent execution. The user may become frustrated at the perceptible delay. Conversely, if the timeslices are too small, a significant proportion of the system's time is spent switching from one application to another, and benefits such as temporal locality are lost.

Consequently, determining an ideal timeslice is not easy. Some operating systems give processes large timeslices, hoping to maximize system throughput and overall performance. Other operating systems give processes very small timeslices, hoping to provide a system with excellent interactive performance. As we will see, CFS answers the "what size timeslice" question in a very odd way: by abolishing timeslices.

I/O- Versus Processor-Bound Processes

Processes that continually consume all of their available timeslices are considered *processor-bound*. Such processes are hungry for CPU time and will consume all that the scheduler gives them. The simplest example is an infinite loop:

```
// 100% processor-bound
while (1)
    ;
```

Other, less extreme examples include scientific computations, mathematical calculations, and image processing.

On the other hand, processes that spend more time blocked waiting for some resource than executing are considered *I/O-bound*. I/O-bound processes are often issuing and waiting for file or network I/O, blocking on keyboard input, or waiting for the user to move the mouse. Examples of I/O-bound applications include file utilities that do very little except issue system calls asking the kernel to perform I/O, such as *cp* or *mv*, and many GUI applications, which spend a great deal of time waiting for user input.

Processor- and I/O-bound applications differ in the type of scheduler behavior from which they most benefit. Processor-bound applications crave the largest timeslices possible, allowing them to maximize cache hit rates (via temporal locality) and get their jobs done as quickly as possible. In contrast, I/O-bound processes do not necessarily need large timeslices because they typically run for only very short periods before issuing I/O requests and blocking on some kernel resource. I/O-bound processes, however, do benefit from prioritized attention from the scheduler. The quicker such an application can restart after blocking and dispatch more I/O requests, the better it can utilize the system's hardware. Further, if the application was waiting for user input, the faster it is scheduled, the greater the user's perception of seamless execution will be.

Juggling the needs of processor- and I/O-bound processes is not easy. In reality, most applications are some mix of I/O- and processor-bound. Audio/video encoding/decoding is a good example of a type of application that defies categorization. Many games are also quite mixed. It is not always possible to identify the proclivity of a given application, and, at any point in time, a given process may behave in one way only to behave in another way later.

Preemptive Scheduling

In traditional Unix process scheduling, all runnable processes are assigned a timeslice. When a process exhausts its timeslice, the kernel suspends it and begins running a different process. If there are no runnable processes on the system, the kernel takes the set of processes with exhausted timeslices, replenishes their timeslices, and begins running them again. And so the process repeats, with processes continually entering and exiting the runnable process list as they are created or terminate, block on I/O, or wake up from sleep. In this fashion, all processes eventually get to run, even if there are higher-priority processes on the system—the lower-priority processes just have to wait for the higher-priority processes to exhaust their timeslices or block. This behavior formulates an important but tacit rule of Unix scheduling: all processes must make forward progress.

The Completely Fair Scheduler

The Completely Fair Scheduler (CFS) is a significant departure from traditional Unix process schedulers. In most Unix systems, including Linux before CFS's introduction, there were two fundamental per-process variables in process scheduling: priority and timeslice. As discussed in the previous section, in traditional process schedulers, processes are assigned a timeslice that represents the "slice" of the processor allotted to that process. Processes may run until they exhaust that timeslice. Similarly, processes are assigned a priority. The process scheduler runs higher-priority processes before lower-priority ones. The algorithm is very simple and worked very well for early time-sharing Unix systems. It performs less admirably on systems requiring good interactive performance and fairness, such as today's modern desktops and mobile devices.

CFS introduces a quite different algorithm called *fair scheduling* that eliminates timeslices as the unit of allotting access to the processor. Instead of timeslices, CFS assigns each process a *proportion* of the processor's time. The algorithm is simple: CFS starts by assigning N processes each $1/N$ of the processor's time. CFS then adjusts this allotment by weighting each process's proportion by its nice value. Processes with the default nice value of zero have a weight of one, so their proportion is unchanged. Processes with a smaller nice value (higher priority) receive a larger weight, increasing their fraction of the processor, while process's with a larger nice value (lower priority) receive a smaller weight, decreasing their fraction of the processor.

CFS now has a weighted proportion of processor time assigned to each process. To determine the actual length of time each process runs, CFS needs to divide the proportions into a fixed period. That period is called the *target latency*, as it represents the scheduling latency of the system. To understand the target latency, let's assume it is set to 20 milliseconds and that there are two runnable processes of the same priority. Thus, each process has the same weight and is assigned the same proportion of the processor, 10 milliseconds. Thus, CFS will run one process for 10 milliseconds, then the other for 10 milliseconds, and then repeat. If there are 5 runnable processes on the system, CFS will run each for 4 milliseconds.

So far, so good. But what if we have, say, 200 processes? With a target latency of 20 milliseconds, CFS would run each of those processes for only 100 microseconds. Due to the cost of context switching from one process to another, known as *switching costs*, and the reduced temporal locality, the system's overall throughput would suffer. To deal with this situation, CFS introduces a second key variable, the minimum granularity.

The *minimum granularity* is a floor on the length of time any process is run. All processes, regardless of their allotted proportion of the processor, will run for at least the minimum granularity (or until they block). This helps ensure that switching costs do not consume an unacceptably large amount of the system's total time at the expense of honoring the target latency. That is, when the minimum granularity kicks in, fairness is violated. With typical values for the target latency and minimum granularity, in the common case of a reasonable number of runnable processes, the minimum granularity is not applied, the target latency is met, and fairness is maintained.

By assigning proportions of the processor and not fixed timeslices, CFS is able to enforce fairness: each process gets its *fair share* of the processor. Moreover, CFS is able to enforce a configurable scheduling latency, as the *target latency* is user-settable. On traditional Unix schedulers, processes run for fixed timeslices known *a priori*, but the scheduling latency (how often they run) is unknown. On CFS, processes run for proportions and with a latency that is known *a priori*, but the timeslice is dynamic, a function of the number of runnable processes on the system. It is a markedly different way of handling process scheduling, solving many of the problems around interactive and I/O-bound processes that has plagued traditional process schedulers.

Yielding the Processor

Although Linux is a preemptively multitasked operating system, it also provides a system call that allows processes to explicitly yield execution and instruct the scheduler to select a new process for execution:

```
#include <sched.h>

int sched_yield (void);
```

A call to `sched_yield()` results in suspension of the currently running process, after which the process scheduler selects a new process to run, in the same manner as if the kernel had itself preempted the currently running process in favor of executing a new process. Note that if no other runnable process exists, which is often the case, the yielding process will immediately resume execution. Because of this uncertainty, coupled with the general belief that there are generally better choices, use of this system call is not common.

On success, the call returns 0; on failure, it returns –1 and sets `errno` to the appropriate error code. On Linux—and, more than likely, most other Unix systems—`sched_yield()` cannot fail and thus always returns 0. A thorough programmer may still check the return value, however:

```
if (sched_yield ())
        perror ("sched_yield");
```

Legitimate Uses

In practice, there are few legitimate uses of `sched_yield()` on a proper preemptive multitasking system such as Linux. The kernel is fully capable of making the optimal and most efficient scheduling decisions—certainly, the kernel is better equipped than an individual application to decide what to preempt and when. This is precisely why operating systems ditched cooperative multitasking in favor of preemptive multitasking.

Why, then, does POSIX dictate a "reschedule me" system call at all? The answer lies in applications having to wait for external events, which may be caused by the user, a hardware component, or another process. For instance, if one process needs to wait for another, "just yield the processor until the other process is done" is a first-pass solution. As an example, the implementation of a naïve consumer in a consumer/producer pair might be similar to the following:

```
/* the consumer... */
do {
        while (producer_not_ready ())
                sched_yield ());
        process_data ();
} while (!time_to_quit ());
```

Thankfully, Unix programmers do not tend to write code such as this. Unix programs are normally event-driven and tend to utilize some sort of blockable mechanism (such as a pipe) between the consumer and the producer in lieu of `sched_yield()`. In this case, the consumer reads from the pipe, blocking as necessary until data is available. The producer, in turn, writes to the pipe as fresh data becomes available. This removes the responsibility for coordination from the user-space process, who just busy-loops, to the kernel, who can optimally manage the situation by putting the processes to sleep and waking them up only as needed. In general, Unix programs should aim toward event-driven solutions that rely on blockable file descriptors.

Until recently, one situation vexingly required `sched_yield()`: user-space thread locking. When a thread attempted to acquire a lock that another thread already held, the new thread would yield the processor until the lock became available. Without kernel support for user-space locks, this approach was the simplest and most efficient. Thankfully, the modern Linux thread implementation (the Native POSIX Threading Library, or NPTL) ushered in an optimal solution using *futexes*, which provide kernel support for efficient user-space locks.

One other use for `sched_yield()` is "playing nicely": a processor-intensive program can call `sched_yield()` periodically, attempting to minimize its impact on the system. While noble in pursuit, this strategy has two flaws. First, the kernel is able to make global scheduling decisions much better than an individual process and consequently the responsibility for ensuring smooth system operation should lie with the process scheduler, not the processes. Second, mitigating the overhead of a processor-intensive application with respect to other applications is the responsibility of the user, not of individual applications. The user can convey her relative preferences for application performance via the *nice* shell command, which we will discuss later in this chapter.

Process Priorities

 The discussion in this section pertains to normal, non-real-time processes. Real-time processes require different scheduling criteria and a separate priority system. We will discuss real-time computing later in this chapter.

Linux does not schedule processes willy-nilly. Instead, processes are assigned *priorities* that affect how long they run: recall that the proportion of processor allotted to a process is weighted by its nice value. Unix has historically called these priorities *nice values* because the idea behind them was to "be nice" to other processes on the system by lowering a process's priority, allowing other processes to consume more of the system's processor time.

Legal nice values range from −20 to 19 inclusive, with a default value of 0. Somewhat confusingly, the lower a process's nice value, the higher its priority and the larger its timeslice; conversely, the higher the value, the lower the process's priority and the smaller its timeslice. Increasing a process's nice value is therefore "nice" to the rest of the system. The numerical inversion is rather confusing. When we say a process has a "high priority" we mean that it can run for longer than lower-priority processes, but such a process will have a lower nice value.

nice()

Linux provides several system calls for retrieving and setting a process's nice value. The simplest is `nice()`:

```
#include <unistd.h>

int nice (int inc);
```

A successful call to `nice()` increments a process's nice value by `inc` and returns the newly updated value. Only a process with the `CAP_SYS_NICE` capability (effectively, processes owned by root) may provide a negative value for `inc`, decreasing its nice value and thereby increasing its priority. Consequently, nonroot processes may only lower their priorities (by increasing their nice values).

On error, nice() returns –1. However, because nice() returns the new nice value, –1 is also a successful return value. To differentiate between success and failure, you can zero out errno before invocation and subsequently check its value. For example:

```
int ret;

errno = 0;
ret = nice (10);      /* increase our nice by 10 */
if (ret == -1 && errno != 0)
        perror ("nice");
else
        printf ("nice value is now %d\n", ret);
```

Linux returns only a single error code: EPERM, signifying that the invoking process attempted to increase its priority (via a negative inc value), but it does not possess the CAP_SYS_NICE capability. Other systems also return EINVAL when inc would place the nice value out of the range of valid values, but Linux does not. Instead, Linux silently rounds invalid inc values up or down to the value at the limit of the allowable range, as needed.

Passing 0 for inc is an easy way to obtain the current nice value:

```
printf ("nice value is currently %d\n", nice (0));
```

Often, a process wants to set an absolute nice value rather than a relative increment. This can be done with code like the following:

```
int ret, val;

/* get current nice value */
val = nice (0);

/* we want a nice value of 10 */
val = 10 - val;
errno = 0;
ret = nice (val);
if (ret == -1 && errno != 0)
        perror ("nice");
else
        printf ("nice value is now %d\n", ret);
```

getpriority() and setpriority()

A preferable solution is to use the getpriority() and setpriority() system calls, which allow more control but are more complex in operation:

```
#include <sys/time.h>
#include <sys/resource.h>

int getpriority (int which, int who);
int setpriority (int which, int who, int prio);
```

These calls operate on the process, process group, or user, as specified by which and who. The value of which must be one of PRIO_PROCESS, PRIO_PGRP, or PRIO_USER, in which case who specifies a process ID, process group ID, or user ID, respectively. If who is 0, the call operates on the current process ID, process group ID, or user ID, respectively.

A call to getpriority() returns the highest priority (lowest numerical nice value) of any of the specified processes. A call to setpriority() sets the priority of all specified processes to prio. As with nice(), only a process possessing CAP_SYS_NICE may raise a process's priority (lower the numerical nice value). Further, only a process with this capability can raise or lower the priority of a process not owned by the invoking user.

Like nice(), getpriority() returns −1 on error. As this is also a successful return value, programmers should clear errno before invocation if they want to handle error conditions. Calls to setpriority() have no such problem; setpriority() always returns 0 on success and −1 on error.

The following code returns the current process's priority:

```
int ret;

ret = getpriority (PRIO_PROCESS, 0);
printf ("nice value is %d\n", ret);
```

The following code sets the priority of all processes in the current process group to 10:

```
int ret;

ret = setpriority (PRIO_PGRP, 0, 10);
if (ret == -1)
        perror ("setpriority");
```

On error, both functions set errno to one of the following values:

EACCES
  The process attempted to raise the specified process's priority but does not possess CAP_SYS_NICE (setpriority() only).

EINVAL
  The value specified by which was not one of PRIO_PROCESS, PRIO_PGRP, or PRIO_USER.

EPERM
  The effective user ID of the matched process does not match the effective user ID of the running process, and the running process does not possess CAP_SYS_NICE (setpriority() only).

ESRCH
  No process was found matching the criteria provided by which and who.

I/O Priorities

In addition to a scheduling priority, Linux allows processes to specify an *I/O priority*. This value affects the relative priority of the processes' I/O requests. The kernel's I/O scheduler (discussed in Chapter 4) services requests originating from processes with higher I/O priorities before requests from processes with lower I/O priorities.

By default, I/O schedulers use a process's nice value to determine the I/O priority. Ergo, setting the nice value automatically changes the I/O priority. However, the Linux kernel additionally provides two system calls for explicitly setting and retrieving the I/O priority independently of the nice value:

```
int ioprio_get (int which, int who)
int ioprio_set (int which, int who, int ioprio)
```

Unfortunately, *glibc* does not provide a user-space interface to these system calls. Without *glibc* support, usage is cumbersome at best. Further, when and if *glibc* support arrives, the interfaces may differ from the system calls. Until such support is available, there are two portable ways to manipulate a process's I/O priority: via the nice value or a utility such as *ionice*, part of the *util-linux* package.[1]

Not all I/O schedulers support I/O priorities. Specifically, the Completely Fair Queuing (CFQ) I/O Scheduler supports them; currently, the other standard schedulers do not. If the current I/O scheduler does not support I/O priorities, they are silently ignored.

Processor Affinity

Linux supports multiple processors in a single system. Aside from the boot process, the bulk of the work of supporting multiple processors rests on the process scheduler. On a multiprocessing machine, the process scheduler must decide which processes run on each CPU.

Two challenges derive from this responsibility: the scheduler must work toward fully utilizing all of the system's processors because it is inefficient for one CPU to sit idle while a process is waiting to run. However, once a process has been scheduled on one CPU, the process scheduler should aim to schedule it on the same CPU in the future. This is beneficial because *migrating* a process from one processor to another has costs.

The largest of these costs are related to the *cache effects* of migration. Due to the design of modern SMP systems, most of the caches associated with each processor are separate and distinct. That is, the data in one processor's cache is not in another's. Therefore, if a process moves to a new CPU and writes new data into memory, the data in the old CPU's cache can become stale. Relying on that cache would now cause corruption. To

---

1. The *util-linux* package is located at kernel.org (*http://www.kernel.org/pub/linux/utils/util-linux*). It is licensed under the GNU General Public License v2.

---

prevent this, caches *invalidate* each other's data whenever they cache a new chunk of memory. Consequently, a given piece of data is strictly in only one processor's cache at any given moment (assuming the data is cached at all). When a process moves from one processor to another, there are thus two associated costs: cached data is no longer accessible to the process that moved, and data in the original processor's cache must be invalidated. Because of these costs, process schedulers attempt to keep a process on a specific CPU for as long as possible.

The process scheduler's two goals, of course, are potentially conflicting. If one processor has a significantly larger process load than another—or, worse, if one processor is busy while another is idle—it makes sense to reschedule some processes on the less-busy CPU. Deciding when to move processes in response to such imbalances, called *load balancing*, is of great importance to the performance of SMP machines.

Processor affinity refers to the likelihood of a process to be scheduled consistently on the same processor. The term *soft affinity* refers to the scheduler's natural propensity to continue scheduling a process on the same processor. As we've discussed, this is a worthwhile trait. The Linux scheduler attempts to schedule the same processes on the same processors for as long as possible, migrating a process from one CPU to another only in situations of extreme load imbalance. This allows the scheduler to minimize the cache effects of migration but still ensure that all processors in a system are evenly loaded.

Sometimes, however, the user or an application wants to enforce a process-to-processor bond. This is often because the process is strongly cache-sensitive and desires to remain on the same processor. Bonding a process to a particular processor and having the kernel enforce the relationship is called setting a *hard affinity*.

sched_getaffinity() and sched_setaffinity()

Processes inherit the CPU affinities of their parents and, by default, processes may run on any CPU. Linux provides two system calls for retrieving and setting a process's hard affinity:

```
#define _GNU_SOURCE

#include <sched.h>

typedef struct cpu_set_t;

size_t CPU_SETSIZE;

void CPU_SET (unsigned long cpu, cpu_set_t *set);
void CPU_CLR (unsigned long cpu, cpu_set_t *set);
int CPU_ISSET (unsigned long cpu, cpu_set_t *set);
void CPU_ZERO (cpu_set_t *set);
```

```
int sched_setaffinity (pid_t pid, size_t setsize,
                       const cpu_set_t *set);

int sched_getaffinity (pid_t pid, size_t setsize,
                       cpu_set_t *set);
```

A call to sched_getaffinity() retrieves the CPU affinity of the process pid and stores it in the special cpu_set_t type, which is accessed via special macros. If pid is 0, the call retrieves the current process's affinity. The setsize parameter is the size of the cpu_set_t type, which may be used by *glibc* for compatibility with future changes in the size of this type. On success, sched_getaffinity() returns 0; on failure, it returns −1, and errno is set. Here's an example:

```
cpu_set_t set;
int ret, i;

CPU_ZERO (&set);
ret = sched_getaffinity (0, sizeof (cpu_set_t), &set);
if (ret == -1)
        perror ("sched_getaffinity");

for (i = 0; i < CPU_SETSIZE; i++) {
        int cpu;

        cpu = CPU_ISSET (i, &set);
        printf ("cpu=%i is %s\n", i,
                cpu ? "set" : "unset");
}
```

Before invocation, we use CPU_ZERO to "zero out" all of the bits in the set. We then iterate from 0 to CPU_SETSIZE over the set. Note that CPU_SETSIZE is, confusingly, not the size of the set: you should *never* pass it for setsize. Instead, it represents the number of processors that could potentially be represented by a set. Because the current implementation represents each processor with a single bit, CPU_SETSIZE is much larger than sizeof(cpu_set_t). We use CPU_ISSET to check whether a given processor in the system, i, is bound or unbound to this process. The macro returns 0 if the processor is unbound and a nonzero value if bound.

Only processors physically on the system are set. Thus, running this snippet on a system with two processors will yield:

```
cpu=0 is set
cpu=1 is set
cpu=2 is unset
cpu=3 is unset
...
cpu=1023 is unset
```

As the output shows, CPU_SETSIZE (which is zero-based) is currently 1,024.

We are concerned only with CPUs #0 and #1 because they are the only physical processors on this system. Perhaps we want to ensure that our process runs only on CPU #0, and never on #1. This code does just that:

```
cpu_set_t set;
int ret, i;

CPU_ZERO (&set);        /* clear all CPUs */
CPU_SET (0, &set);      /* allow CPU #0 */
CPU_CLR (1, &set);      /* disallow CPU #1 */
ret = sched_setaffinity (0, sizeof (cpu_set_t), &set);
if (ret == -1)
        perror ("sched_setaffinity");

for (i = 0; i < CPU_SETSIZE; i++) {
        int cpu;

        cpu = CPU_ISSET (i, &set);
        printf ("cpu=%i is %s\n", i,
                cpu ? "set" : "unset");
}
```

We start, as always, by zeroing out the set with CPU_ZERO. We then set CPU #0 with CPU_SET and unset (clear) CPU #1 with CPU_CLR. The CPU_CLR operation is redundant as we just zeroed out the whole set, but it is provided for completeness.

Running this on the same two-processor system will result in slightly different output than before:

```
cpu=0 is set
cpu=1 is unset
cpu=2 is unset
...
cpu=1023 is unset
```

Now, CPU #1 is unset. This process will run only on CPU #0, no matter what!

Four errno values are possible:

EFAULT
    The provided pointer was outside of the process's address space or otherwise invalid.

EINVAL
    In this case, there were no processors physically on the system enabled in set (sched_setaffinity() only), or setsize is smaller than the size of the kernel's internal data structure that represents sets of processors.

EPERM

The process associated with `pid` is not owned by the current effective user ID of the calling process, and the process does not possess `CAP_SYS_NICE`.

ESRCH

No process associated with `pid` was found.

Real-Time Systems

In computing, the term *real-time* is often the source of some confusion and misunderstanding. A system is "real-time" if it is subject to *operational deadlines*: minimum and mandatory times between stimuli and responses. A familiar real-time system is the *anti-lock braking system* (ABS) found on nearly all modern automobiles. In this system, when the brake is pressed, a computer regulates the brake pressure, often applying and releasing maximum brake pressure many times a second. This prevents the wheels from "locking up," which can reduce stopping power or even send the car into an uncontrolled skid. In such a system, the operational deadlines are how fast the system must respond to a "locked" wheel condition and how quickly the system can apply brake pressure.

Most modern operating systems, Linux included, provide some level of real-time support.

Hard Versus Soft Real-Time Systems

Real-time systems come in two varieties: hard and soft. A *hard real-time system* requires absolute adherence to operational deadlines. Exceeding the deadlines constitutes failure and is a major bug. A *soft real-time system*, on the other hand, does not consider overrunning a deadline to be a critical failure.

Hard real-time applications are easy to identify: some examples are anti-lock braking systems, military weapons systems, medical devices, and signal processing. Soft real-time applications are not always so easy to identify. One obvious member of that group is video-processing applications: users notice a drop in quality if their deadlines are missed, but a few lost frames can be tolerated.

Many other applications have timing constraints that, if not met, result in a detriment to the user experience. Multimedia applications, games, and networking programs come to mind. What about a text editor, however? If the program cannot respond quickly enough to keypresses, the experience is poor, and the user may grow angry or frustrated. Is this a soft real-time application? Certainly, when the developers were writing the application, they realized that they needed to respond to keypresses in a timely manner. But does this count as an operational deadline? The line defining soft real-time applications is anything but clear.

Contrary to common belief, a real-time system is not necessarily fast. Indeed, given comparable hardware, a real-time system is probably slower than a non-real-time system—due to, if nothing else, the increase in overhead required to support real-time processes. Likewise, the division between hard and soft real-time systems is independent of the size of the operational deadlines. A nuclear reactor will overheat if the SCRAM system does not lower the control rods within several seconds of detecting excessive neutron flux. This is a hard real-time system with a lengthy (as far as computers are concerned) operational deadline. Conversely, a video player might skip a frame or stutter the sound if the application cannot refill the playback buffer within 100 ms. This is a soft real-time system with a demanding operational deadline.

Latency, Jitter, and Deadlines

Latency refers to the period from the occurrence of the stimulus until the execution of the response. If latency is less than or equal to the operational deadline, the system is operating correctly. In many hard real-time systems, the operational deadline and the latency are equal—the system handles stimuli in fixed intervals, at exact times. In soft real-time systems, the required response is less exact, and latency exhibits some amount of variance—the aim is simply for the response to occur within the deadline.

It is often hard to measure latency because its calculation requires knowing the time when the stimulus occurred. The ability to timestamp the stimulus, however, begs the ability to respond to it. Therefore, many attempts at instrumenting latency do no such thing; instead, they measure the variation in timing between responses. The variation in timing between successive events is *jitter*, not latency.

For example, consider a stimulus that occurs every 10 milliseconds. To measure the performance of our system, we might timestamp our responses to ensure that they occur every 10 milliseconds. The deviation from this target is not latency, however—it is jitter. What we are measuring is the variance in successive responses. Without knowing when the stimulus occurred, we do not know the actual difference in time between stimulus and response. Even knowing that the stimulus occurs every 10 ms, we do not know when the *first* occurrence was. Perhaps surprisingly, many attempts at measuring latency make this mistake and report jitter, not latency. To be sure, jitter is a useful metric, and such instrumentation is probably quite useful. Nevertheless, we must call a duck a duck!

Hard real-time systems often exhibit very low jitter because they respond to stimuli after—not *within*—an exact amount of time. Such systems aim for a jitter of zero and a latency equal to the operational delay. If the latency exceeds the delay, the system fails.

Soft real-time systems are more susceptible to jitter. In these systems, the response time is ideally within the operational delay—often much sooner, sometimes not. Jitter, therefore, is often an excellent surrogate for latency as a performance metric.

Linux's Real-Time Support

Linux provides applications with soft real-time support via a family of system calls defined by IEEE Std 1003.1b-1993 (often shortened to POSIX 1993 or POSIX.1b).

Technically speaking, the POSIX standard does not dictate whether the provided real-time support is soft or hard. In fact, all the POSIX standard really does is describe several scheduling policies that respect priorities. What sorts of timing constraints the operating system enforces on these policies is up to the OS designers.

Over the years, the Linux kernel has gained better and better real-time support, providing lower and lower latency and more consistent jitter, without compromising system performance. Much of this is because improving latency helps many classes of application, such as desktop and I/O-bound processes, and not just real-time applications. The improvements are also attributable to the success of Linux in embedded and real-time systems.

Unfortunately, many of the embedded and real-time modifications that have been made to the Linux kernel exist only in custom Linux solutions outside of the mainstream official kernel. Some of these modifications provide further reductions in latency and even hard real-time behavior. The following sections discuss only the official kernel interfaces and the behavior of the mainstream kernel. Luckily, most real-time modifications continue to utilize the POSIX interfaces. Ergo, the subsequent discussion is also relevant on modified systems.

Linux Scheduling Policies and Priorities

The behavior of the Linux scheduler with respect to a process depends on the process's *scheduling policy*, also called the *scheduling class.* In addition to the normal default policy, Linux provides two real-time scheduling policies. A preprocessor macro from the header <sched.h> represents each policy: the macros are SCHED_FIFO, SCHED_RR, and SCHED_OTHER.

Every process possesses a *static priority*, unrelated to the nice value. For normal applications, this priority is always 0. For the real-time processes, it ranges from 1 to 99, inclusive. The Linux scheduler always selects the highest-priority process to run (i.e., the one with the largest numerical static priority value). If a process is running with a static priority of 50, and a process with a priority of 51 becomes runnable, the scheduler will immediately preempt the running process and switch to the newly runnable process. Conversely, if a process is running with a priority of 50, and a process with a priority of 49 becomes runnable, the scheduler will not run it until the priority-50 process blocks, becoming unrunnable. Because normal processes have a priority of 0, any real-time process that is runnable will always preempt a normal process and run.

The first in, first out policy

The *first in, first out (FIFO) class* is a very simple real-time policy without timeslices. A FIFO-classed process will continue running so long as no higher-priority process becomes runnable. The FIFO class is represented by the macro `SCHED_FIFO`.

As the policy lacks timeslices, its rules of operation are rather simple:

- A runnable FIFO-classed process will always run if it is the highest-priority process on the system. Particularly, once a FIFO-classed process becomes runnable, it will immediately preempt a normal process.

- A FIFO-classed process will continue running until it blocks or calls `sched_yield()`, or until a higher-priority process becomes runnable.

- When a FIFO-classed process blocks, the scheduler removes it from the list of runnable processes. When it again becomes runnable, it is inserted at the end of the list of processes at its priority. Thus, it will not run until any other processes of higher *or equal* priority cease execution.

- When a FIFO-classed process calls `sched_yield()`, the scheduler moves it to the end of the list of processes at its priority. Thus, it will not run until any other equal-priority processes cease execution. If the invoking process is the only process at its priority, `sched_yield()` will have no effect.

- When a higher-priority process preempts a FIFO-classed process, the FIFO-classed process remains at the same location in the list of processes for its given priority. Thus, once the higher-priority process ceases execution, the preempted FIFO-classed process will continue executing.

- When a process joins the FIFO class, or when a process's static priority changes, it is put at the head of the list of processes for its given priority. Consequently, a newly prioritized FIFO-classed process can preempt an executing process of the same priority.

Essentially, we can say that FIFO-classed processes always run for as long as they want, so long as they are the highest-priority processes on the system. The interesting rules pertain to what happens among FIFO-classed processes with the same priority.

The round-robin policy

The *round-robin (RR) class* is identical to the FIFO class, except that it imposes additional rules in the case of processes with the same priority. The macro `SCHED_RR` represents this class.

The scheduler assigns each RR-classed process a timeslice. When an RR-classed process exhausts its timeslice, the scheduler moves it to the end of the list of processes at its priority. In this manner, RR-classed processes of a given priority are scheduled round-robin amongst themselves. If there is only one process at a given priority, the RR class is identical to the FIFO class. In such a case, when its timeslice expires, the process simply resumes execution.

We can think of an RR-classed process as identical to a FIFO-classed process, except that it additionally ceases execution when it exhausts its timeslice, at which time it moves to the end of the list of runnable processes at its priority.

Deciding whether to use SCHED_FIFO or SCHED_RR is entirely a question of intra-priority behavior. The RR class's timeslices are relevant only among processes of the same priority. FIFO-classed processes will continue running unabated; RR-classed processes will schedule amongst themselves at a given priority. In neither case will a lower-priority process ever run if a higher-priority process exists.

The normal policy

SCHED_OTHER represents the standard scheduling policy, the default nonreal-time class. All normal-classed processes have a static priority of 0. Consequently, any runnable FIFO- or RR-classed process will preempt a running normal-classed process.

The scheduler uses the nice value, discussed earlier, to prioritize processes within the normal class. The nice value has no bearing on the static priority, which remains 0.

The batch scheduling policy

SCHED_BATCH is the *batch* or *idle scheduling policy*. Its behavior is somewhat the antithesis of the real-time policies: processes in this class run only when there are no other runnable processes on the system, even if the other processes have exhausted their timeslices. This is different from the behavior of processes with the largest nice values (i.e., the lowest-priority processes) in that eventually such processes will run, as the higher-priority processes exhaust their timeslices.

Setting the Linux scheduling policy

Processes can manipulate the Linux scheduling policy via sched_getscheduler() and sched_setscheduler():

```
#include <sched.h>

struct sched_param {
        /* ... */
        int sched_priority;
        /* ... */
};

int sched_getscheduler (pid_t pid);

int sched_setscheduler (pid_t pid,
```

```
                       int policy,
                       const struct sched_param *sp);
```

A successful call to sched_getscheduler() returns the scheduling policy of the process represented by pid. If pid is 0, the call returns the invoking process's scheduling policy. An integer defined in <sched.h> represents the scheduling policy: the first in, first out policy is SCHED_FIFO; the round-robin policy is SCHED_RR; and the normal policy is SCHED_OTHER. On error, the call returns −1 (which is never a valid scheduling policy), and errno is set as appropriate.

Usage is simple:

```
int policy;

/* get our scheduling policy */
policy = sched_getscheduler (0);

switch (policy) {
case SCHED_OTHER:
        printf ("Policy is normal\n");
        break;
case SCHED_RR:
        printf ("Policy is round-robin\n");
        break;
case SCHED_FIFO:
        printf ("Policy is first-in, first-out\n");
        break;
case -1:
        perror ("sched_getscheduler");
        break;
default:
        fprintf (stderr, "Unknown policy!\n");
}
```

A call to sched_setscheduler() sets the scheduling policy of the process represented by pid to policy. Any parameters associated with the policy are set via sp. If pid is 0, the invoking process's policy and parameters are set. On success, the call returns 0. On failure, the call returns −1, and errno is set as appropriate.

The valid fields inside the sched_param structure depend on the scheduling policies supported by the operating system. The SCHED_RR and SCHED_FIFO policies require one field, sched_priority, which represents the static priority. SCHED_OTHER does not use any field, while scheduling policies supported in the future may use new fields. Portable and legal programs must therefore not make assumptions about the layout of the structure.

Setting a process's scheduling policy and parameters is easy:

```
struct sched_param sp = { .sched_priority = 1 };
int ret;

ret = sched_setscheduler (0, SCHED_RR, &sp);
if (ret == -1) {
        perror ("sched_setscheduler");
        return 1;
}
```

This snippet sets the invoking process's scheduling policy to round-robin with a static priority of 1. We presume that 1 is a valid priority—technically, it need not be. We will discuss how to find the valid priority range for a given policy in an upcoming section.

Setting a scheduling policy other than SCHED_OTHER requires the CAP_SYS_NICE capability. Consequently, the root user typically runs real-time processes. Since the 2.6.12 kernel, the RLIMIT_RTPRIO resource limit allows nonroot users to set real-time policies up to a certain priority ceiling.

On error, four errno values are possible:

EFAULT
> The pointer sp points to an invalid or inaccessible region of memory.

EINVAL
> The scheduling policy denoted by policy is invalid, or a value set in sp does not make sense for the given policy (sched_setscheduler() only).

EPERM
> The invoking process does not have the necessary capabilities.

ESRCH
> The value pid does not denote a running process.

Setting Scheduling Parameters

The POSIX-defined sched_getparam() and sched_setparam() interfaces retrieve and set the parameters associated with a scheduling policy that has already been set:

```
#include <sched.h>

struct sched_param {
        /* ... */
        int sched_priority;
        /* ... */
};

int sched_getparam (pid_t pid, struct sched_param *sp);

int sched_setparam (pid_t pid, const struct sched_param *sp);
```

The `sched_getscheduler()` interface returns only the scheduling policy, not any associated parameters. A call to `sched_getparam()` returns via `sp` the scheduling parameters associated with `pid`:

```
struct sched_param sp;
int ret;

ret = sched_getparam (0, &sp);
if (ret == -1) {
        perror ("sched_getparam");
        return 1;
}

printf ("Our priority is %d\n", sp.sched_priority);
```

If `pid` is 0, the call returns the parameters of the invoking process. On success, the call returns 0. On failure, it returns −1 and sets `errno` as appropriate.

Because `sched_setscheduler()` also sets any associated scheduling parameters, `sched_setparam()` is useful only to later modify the parameters:

```
struct sched_param sp;
int ret;

sp.sched_priority = 1;
ret = sched_setparam (0, &sp);
if (ret == -1) {
        perror ("sched_setparam");
        return 1;
}
```

On success, the scheduling parameters of `pid` are set according to `sp`, and the call returns 0. On failure, the call returns −1, and `errno` is set as appropriate.

If we ran the two preceding snippets in reverse order, we would see the following output:

```
Our priority is 1
```

This example again assumes that 1 is a valid priority. It is, but portable applications should make sure. We'll look at how to check the range of valid priorities momentarily.

Error codes

On error, four `errno` values are possible:

EFAULT
    The pointer `sp` points to an invalid or inaccessible region of memory.

EINVAL
    A value set in `sp` does not make sense for the given policy (`sched_getparam()` only).

EPERM

The invoking process does not have the necessary capabilities.

ESRCH

The value pid does not denote a running process.

Determining the range of valid priorities

Our previous examples have passed hardcoded priority values into the scheduling system calls. POSIX makes no guarantees about what scheduling priorities exist on a given system, except to say that there must be at least 32 priorities between the minimum and maximum values. As mentioned earlier in "Linux Scheduling Policies and Priorities" on page 192, Linux implements a range of 1 to 99 inclusive for the two real-time scheduling policies. A clean, portable program normally implements its own range of priority values and maps them onto the operating system's range. For instance, if you want to run processes at four different real-time priority levels, you dynamically determine the range of priorities and choose four values.

Linux provides two system calls for retrieving the range of valid priority values. One returns the minimum value and the other returns the maximum:

```
#include <sched.h>

int sched_get_priority_min (int policy);

int sched_get_priority_max (int policy);
```

On success, the call `sched_get_priority_min()` returns the minimum, and the call `sched_get_priority_max()` returns the maximum valid priority associated with the scheduling policy denoted by policy. Upon failure, the calls both return –1. The only possible error is if policy is invalid, in which case errno is set to EINVAL.

Usage is simple:

```
int min, max;

min = sched_get_priority_min (SCHED_RR);
if (min == -1) {
        perror ("sched_get_priority_min");
        return 1;
}

max = sched_get_priority_max (SCHED_RR);
if (max == -1) {
        perror ("sched_get_priority_max");
        return 1;
}

printf ("SCHED_RR priority range is %d - %d\n", min, max);
```

On a standard Linux system, this snippet yields the following:

```
SCHED_RR priority range is 1 - 99
```

As discussed previously, numerically larger priority values denote higher priorities. To set a process to the highest priority for its scheduling policy, you can do the following:

```c
/*
 * set_highest_priority - set the associated pid's scheduling
 * priority to the highest value allowed by its current
 * scheduling policy. If pid is zero, sets the current
 * process's priority.
 *
 * Returns zero on success.
 */
int set_highest_priority (pid_t pid)
{
        struct sched_param sp;
        int policy, max, ret;

        policy = sched_getscheduler (pid);
        if (policy == -1)
                return -1;

        max = sched_get_priority_max (policy);
        if (max == -1)
                return -1;

        memset (&sp, 0, sizeof (struct sched_param));
        sp.sched_priority = max;
        ret = sched_setparam (pid, &sp);

        return ret;
}
```

Programs typically retrieve the system's minimum or maximum value and then use increments of 1 (such as max-1, max-2, etc.) to assign priorities as desired.

sched_rr_get_interval()

As discussed earlier, SCHED_RR processes behave the same as SCHED_FIFO processes, except that the scheduler assigns these processes timeslices. When a SCHED_RR process exhausts its timeslice, the scheduler moves the process to the end of the run list for its current priority. In this manner, all SCHED_RR processes of the same priority are executed in a round-robin rotation. Higher-priority processes (and SCHED_FIFO processes of the same or higher priority) will always preempt a running SCHED_RR process, regardless of whether it has any of its timeslice remaining.

POSIX defines an interface for retrieving the length of a given process's timeslice:

```
#include <sched.h>

struct timespec {
        time_t  tv_sec;     /* seconds */
        long    tv_nsec;    /* nanoseconds */
};

int sched_rr_get_interval (pid_t pid, struct timespec *tp);
```

A successful call to the awfully named `sched_rr_get_interval()` saves in the `time
spec` structure pointed at by `tp` the duration of the timeslice allotted to `pid` and returns
0. On failure, the call returns –1, and `errno` is set as appropriate.

According to POSIX, this function is required to work only with SCHED_RR processes.
On Linux, however, it can retrieve the length of any process's timeslice. Portable applications should assume that the function works only with round-robin processes; Linux-
specific programs may exploit the call as needed. Here's an example:

```
struct timespec tp;
int ret;

/* get the current task's timeslice length */
ret = sched_rr_get_interval (0, &tp);
if (ret == -1) {
        perror ("sched_rr_get_interval");
        return 1;
}

/* convert the seconds and nanoseconds to milliseconds */
printf ("Our time quantum is %.2lf milliseconds\n",
        (tp.tv_sec * 1000.0f) + (tp.tv_nsec / 1000000.0f));
```

If the process is running in the FIFO class, `tv_sec` and `tv_nsec` are both 0, denoting
infinity.

Error codes

On error, three `errno` values are possible:

EFAULT
     The memory pointed at by the pointer `tp` is invalid or inaccessible.

EINVAL
     The value `pid` is invalid (for example, it is negative).

ESRCH
     The value `pid` is valid but refers to a nonexistent process.

Precautions with Real-Time Processes

Because of the nature of real-time processes, developers should exercise caution when developing and debugging such programs. If a real-time program goes off the deep end, the system can become unresponsive. Any CPU-bound loop in a real-time program—that is, any chunk of code that does not block—will continue running ad infinitum so long as no higher-priority real-time processes become runnable.

Consequently, designing real-time programs requires care and attention. Such programs reign supreme and can easily bring down the entire system. Some tips and precautions:

- Keep in mind that any CPU-bound loop will run until completion, without interruption, if there is no higher-priority real-time process on the system. If the loop is infinite, the system will become unresponsive.

- Because real-time processes run at the expense of everything else on the system, special attention must be paid to their design. Take care not to starve the rest of the system of processor time.

- Be very careful with busy waiting. If a real-time process busy-waits for a resource held by a lower-priority process, the real-time process will busy-wait forever.

- While developing a real-time process, keep a terminal open, running as a real-time process with a higher priority than the process in development. In an emergency, the terminal will remain responsive and allow you to kill the runaway real-time process. (As the terminal remains idle, waiting for keyboard input, it will not interfere with the other real-time process until you need it.)

- The *chrt* utility, part of the *util-linux* package of tools, makes it easy to retrieve and set the real-time attributes of other processes. This tool makes it easy to launch arbitrary programs in a real-time scheduling class, such as the aforementioned terminal, or change the real-time priorities of existing applications.

Determinism

Real-time processes are big on determinism. In real-time computing, an action is *deterministic* if, given the same input, it always produces the same result in the same amount of time. Modern computers are the very definition of something that is not deterministic: multiple levels of caches (which incur hits or misses without predictability), multiple processors, paging, swapping, and multitasking wreak havoc on any estimate of how long a given action will take. Sure, we have reached a point where just about every action (modulo hard drive access) is "incredibly fast," but simultaneously, modern systems have also made it hard to pinpoint exactly how long a given operation will take.

Real-time applications often try to limit unpredictability in general and worst-case delays specifically. The following sections discuss two methods that are used to this end.

Prefaulting data and locking memory

Picture this: the hardware interrupt from the custom incoming intercontinental ballistic missile (ICBM) monitor hits, and the device's driver quickly copies data from the hardware into the kernel. The driver notes that a process is asleep, blocked on the hardware's device node, waiting for data. The driver tells the kernel to wake up the process. The kernel, noting that this process is running with a real-time scheduling policy and a high priority, immediately preempts the currently running process and shifts into overdrive, determined to schedule the real-time process immediately. The scheduler switches to running the real-time process, and context-switches into its address space. The process is now running. The whole ordeal took 0.3 ms, well within the 1 ms worst-case acceptable latency period.

Now, in user space, the real-time process notes the incoming ICBM and begins processing its trajectory. With the ballistics calculated, the real-time process initiates the deployment of an anti-ballistic missile system. Only another 0.1 ms have passed—quick enough to deploy the anti-ballistic missile (ABM) response and save lives. But—oh no! —the ABM code has been swapped to disk. A page fault occurs, the processor switches back to kernel mode, and the kernel initiates hard disk I/O to retrieve the swapped-out data. The scheduler puts the process to sleep until the page fault is serviced. Several seconds elapse. It is too late.

Clearly, paging and swapping introduce quite undeterministic behavior that can wreak havoc on a real-time process. To prevent this catastrophe, a real-time application will often "lock" or "hardwire" all of the pages in its address space into physical memory, prefaulting them into memory and preventing them from being swapped out. Once the pages are locked into memory, the kernel will never swap them out to disk. Any accesses of the pages will not cause page faults. Most real-time applications lock some or all of their pages into physical memory.

Linux provides interfaces for both prefaulting and locking data. Chapter 4 discussed interfaces for prefaulting data into physical memory. Chapter 9 will discuss interfaces for locking data into physical memory.

CPU affinity and real-time processes

A second concern of real-time applications is multitasking. Although the Linux kernel is preemptive, its scheduler is not always able to immediately reschedule one process in favor of another. Sometimes, the currently running process is executing inside of a critical region in the kernel, and the scheduler cannot preempt it until it exits that region. If the process that is waiting to run is real-time, this delay may be unacceptable, quickly overrunning the operational deadline.

Ergo, multitasking introduces indeterminism similar in nature to the unpredictability associated with paging. The solution with respect to multitasking is the same: eliminate it. Of course, chances are you cannot simply abolish all other processes. If that were possible in your environment, you probably would not need Linux to begin with—a simple custom operating system would suffice. If, however, your system has multiple processors, you can dedicate one or more of those processors to your real-time process or processes. In effect, you can shield the real-time processes from multitasking.

We discussed system calls for manipulating a process's CPU affinity earlier in this chapter. A potential optimization for real-time applications is to reserve one processor for each real-time process and let all other processes time-share on the remaining processor(s).

The simplest way to achieve this is to modify Linux's *init* program, *SysVinit*,[2] to do something similar to the following before it begins the boot process:

```
cpu_set_t set;
int ret;

CPU_ZERO (&set);          /* clear all CPUs */
ret = sched_getaffinity (0, sizeof (cpu_set_t), &set);
if (ret == -1) {
        perror ("sched_getaffinity");
        return 1;
}

CPU_CLR (1, &set);        /* forbid CPU #1 */
ret = sched_setaffinity (0, sizeof (cpu_set_t), &set);
if (ret == -1) {
        perror ("sched_setaffinity");
        return 1;
}
```

This snippet grabs init's current set of allowed processors, which we expect is all of them. It then removes one processor, CPU #1, from the set and updates the list of allowed processors.

Because the set of allowed processors is inherited from parent to child, and init is the super-parent of all processes, all of the system's processes will run with this set of allowed processors. Consequently, no processes will ever run on CPU #1.

Next, modify your real-time process to run only on CPU #1:

```
cpu_set_t set;
int ret;
```

2. The *SysVinit* source is located at *http://freecode.com/projects/sysvinit*. It is licensed under the GNU General Public License v2.

```
CPU_ZERO (&set);        /* clear all CPUs */
CPU_SET (1, &set);      /* allow CPU #1 */
ret = sched_setaffinity (0, sizeof (cpu_set_t), &set);
if (ret == -1) {
        perror ("sched_setaffinity");
        return 1;
}
```

The result is that your real-time process runs only on CPU #1 and all other processes run on the other processors.

Resource Limits

The Linux kernel imposes several *resource limits* on processes. These resource limits place hard ceilings on the amount of kernel resources that a process can consume—that is, the number of open files, pages of memory, pending signals, and so on. The limits are strictly enforced; the kernel will not allow an action that places a process's resource consumption over a hard limit. For example, if opening a file would cause a process to have more open files than allowed by the applicable resource limit, the open() invocation will fail.[3]

Linux provides two system calls for manipulating resource limits. POSIX standardized both interfaces, but Linux supports several limits in addition to those dictated by the standard. Limits can be checked with getrlimit() and set with setrlimit():

```
#include <sys/time.h>
#include <sys/resource.h>

struct rlimit {
        rlim_t rlim_cur;  /* soft limit */
        rlim_t rlim_max;  /* hard limit */
};

int getrlimit (int resource, struct rlimit *rlim);
int setrlimit (int resource, const struct rlimit *rlim);
```

Integer constants, such as RLIMIT_CPU, represent the resources. The rlimit structure represents the actual limits. The structure defines two ceilings: a *soft limit* and a *hard limit*. The kernel enforces soft resource limits on processes, but a process may freely change its soft limit to any value from 0 up to and including the hard limit. A process without the CAP_SYS_RESOURCE capability (i.e., any nonroot process) can only lower its hard limit. An unprivileged process can never raise its hard limit, not even to a previously higher value; lowering the hard limit is irreversible. A privileged process can set the hard limit to any valid value.

---

3. In which case the call will set errno to EMFILE, indicating that the process hit the resource limit on the maximum number of open files. Chapter 2 discusses the open() system call.

What the limits actually represent depends on the resource in question. If `resource` is `RLIMIT_FSIZE`, for example, the limit represents the maximum size of a file that a process can create, in bytes. In this case, if `rlim_cur` is 1,024, a process cannot create or extend a file to a size greater than one kilobyte.

All of the resource limits have two special values: 0 and infinity. The former disables use of the resource altogether. For example, if `RLIMIT_CORE` is 0, the kernel will never create a core file. Conversely, the latter removes any limit on the resource. The kernel denotes infinity by the special value `RLIM_INFINITY`, which happens to be –1 (this can cause some confusion, as –1 is also the return value indicating error). If `RLIMIT_CORE` is infinity, the kernel will create core files of any size.

The function `getrlimit()` places the current hard and soft limits on the resource denoted by `resource` in the structure pointed at by `rlim`. On success, the call returns 0. On failure, the call returns –1 and sets `errno` as appropriate.

Correspondingly, the function `setrlimit()` sets the hard and soft limits associated with `resource` to the values pointed at by `rlim`. On success, the call returns 0, and the kernel updates the resource limits as requested. On failure, the call returns –1 and sets `errno` as appropriate.

The Limits

Linux currently provides 16 resource limits:

`RLIMIT_AS`
> Limits the maximum size of a process's address space, in bytes. Attempts to increase the size of the address space past this limit (via calls such as `mmap()` and `brk()`) will fail and return `ENOMEM`. If the process's stack, which automatically grows as needed, expands beyond this limit, the kernel sends the process the `SIGSEGV` signal. This limit is usually `RLIM_INFINITY`.

`RLIMIT_CORE`
> Dictates the maximum size of core files, in bytes. If nonzero, core files larger than this limit are truncated to the maximum size. If 0, core files are never created.

`RLIMIT_CPU`
> Dictates the maximum CPU time that a process can consume, in seconds. If a process runs for longer than this limit, the kernel sends it a `SIGXCPU` signal, which processes may catch and handle. Portable programs should terminate on receipt of this signal, as POSIX leaves undefined what action the kernel may take next. Some systems may terminate the process if it continues to run. Linux, however, allows the process to continue executing and continues sending `SIGXCPU` signals at one second intervals. Once the process reaches the hard limit, it is sent a `SIGKILL` and terminated.

RLIMIT_DATA

Controls the maximum size of a process's data segment and heap, in bytes. Attempts to enlarge the data segment beyond this limit via brk( ) will fail and return ENOMEM.

RLIMIT_FSIZE

Specifies the maximum file size that a process may create, in bytes. If a process expands a file beyond this size, the kernel sends the process a SIGXFSZ signal. By default, this signal terminates the process. A process may, however, elect to catch and handle this signal, in which case the offending system call fails and returns EFBIG.

RLIMIT_LOCKS

Controls the maximum number of file locks that a process may hold (see Chapter 8 for a discussion of file locks). Once this limit is reached, further attempts to acquire additional file locks should fail and return ENOLCK. Linux kernel 2.4.25, however, removed this functionality. In current kernels, this limit is settable, but has no effect.

RLIMIT_MEMLOCK

Specifies the maximum number of bytes of memory that a process without the CAP_SYS_IPC capability (effectively, a nonroot process) can lock into memory via mlock( ), mlockall( ), or shmctl( ). If this limit is exceeded, these calls fail, and return EPERM. In practice, the effective limit is rounded down to an integer multiple of pages. Processes possessing CAP_SYS_IPC can lock any number of pages into memory, and this limit has no effect. Before kernel 2.6.9, this limit was the maximum that a process with CAP_SYS_IPC could lock into memory, and unprivileged processes could not lock any pages whatsoever. This limit is not part of POSIX; BSD introduced it.

RLIMIT_MSGQUEUE

Specifies the maximum number of bytes that a user may allocate for POSIX message queues. If a newly created message queue would exceed this limit, mq_open( ) fails and returns ENOMEM. This limit is not part of POSIX; it was added in kernel 2.6.8 and is Linux-specific.

RLIMIT_NICE

Specifies the maximum value to which a process can lower its nice value (raise its priority). As discussed earlier in this chapter, normally processes can only raise their nice values (lower their priorities). This limit allows the administrator to impose a maximum level (nice value floor) to which processes may legally raise their priorities. Because nice values may be negative, the kernel interprets the value as 20 - rlim_cur. Thus, if this limit is set to 40, a process can lower its nice value to the minimum value of −20 (the highest priority). Kernel 2.6.12 introduced this limit.

RLIMIT_NOFILE

Specifies one greater than the maximum number of file descriptors that a process may hold open. Attempts to surpass this limit result in failure and the applicable system call returning EMFILE. This limit is also specifiable as RLIMIT_OFILE, which is BSD's name for it.

RLIMIT_NPROC

Specifies the maximum number of processes that the user may have running on the system at any given moment. Attempts to surpass this limit result in failure and fork() will return EAGAIN. This limit is not part of POSIX; it was introduced by BSD.

RLIMIT_RSS

Specifies the maximum number of pages that a process may have resident in memory (known as the resident set size, or RSS). Only early 2.4 kernels enforced this limit. Current kernels allow the setting of this limit, but it is not enforced. This limit is not part of POSIX; BSD introduced it.

RLIMIT_RTTIME

Specifies a limit (in microseconds) on CPU time that a real-time process may consume without issuing a blocking system call. Once the process makes a blocking system call, the CPU time is reset to zero. This prevents a runaway real-time process from taking down the system. It was added in Linux kernel version 2.6.25 and is Linux-specific.

RLIMIT_RTPRIO

Specifies the maximum real-time priority level a process without the CAP_SYS_NICE capability (effectively, nonroot processes) may request. Normally, unprivileged processes may not request any real-time scheduling class. It was added in kernel 2.6.12 and is Linux-specific.

RLIMIT_SIGPENDING

Specifies the maximum number of signals (standard and real-time) that may be queued for this user. Attempts to queue additional signals fail, and system calls such as sigqueue() return EAGAIN. Note that it is always possible, regardless of this limit, to queue one instance of a not-yet-queued signal. Therefore, it is always possible to deliver to the process a SIGKILL or SIGTERM. This limit is not part of POSIX; it is Linux-specific.

RLIMIT_STACK

Denotes the maximum size of a process's stack, in bytes. Surpassing this limit results in the delivery of a SIGSEGV.

The kernel manages the resource limits on a per-process basis. A child process inherits its limits from its parent during fork; limits are maintained across exec.

Default limits

The default limits available to your process depend on three variables: the initial soft limit, the initial hard limit, and your system administrator. The kernel dictates the initial hard and soft limits; Table 6-1 lists them. The kernel sets these limits on the init process, and because children inherit the limits of their parents, all subsequent processes inherit the soft and hard limits of init.

Table 6-1. Default soft and hard resource limits

Resource limit	Soft limit	Hard limit
RLIMIT_AS	RLIM_INFINITY	RLIM_INFINITY
RLIMIT_CORE	0	RLIM_INFINITY
RLIMIT_CPU	RLIM_INFINITY	RLIM_INFINITY
RLIMIT_DATA	RLIM_INFINITY	RLIM_INFINITY
RLIMIT_FSIZE	RLIM_INFINITY	RLIM_INFINITY
RLIMIT_LOCKS	RLIM_INFINITY	RLIM_INFINITY
RLIMIT_MEMLOCK	8 pages	8 pages
RLIMIT_MSGQUEUE	800 KB	800 KB
RLIMIT_NICE	0	0
RLIMIT_NOFILE	1024	1024
RLIMIT_NPROC	0 (implies no limit)	0 (implies no limit)
RLIMIT_RSS	RLIM_INFINITY	RLIM_INFINITY
RLIMIT_RTPRIO	0	0
RLIMIT_SIGPENDING	0	0
RLIMIT_STACK	8 MB	RLIM_INFINITY

Two things can change these default limits:

- Any process is free to increase a soft limit to any value from 0 to the hard limit, or to decrease a hard limit. Children will inherit these updated limits during a fork.

- A privileged process is free to set a hard limit to any value. Children will inherit these updated limits during a fork.

It is unlikely that a root process in a regular process's lineage will change any hard limits. Consequently, the first item is a much more likely source of limit changes than the second. Indeed, the actual limits presented to a process are generally set by the user's shell, which the system administrator can set up to provide various limits. In the Bourne-again shell (*bash*), for example, the administrator accomplishes this via the *ulimit* command. Note that the administrator need not lower values; he can also raise soft limits to the hard limits, providing users with saner defaults. This is often done with RLIMIT_STACK, which is set to RLIM_INFINITY on many systems.

Setting and Retrieving Limits

With the explanations of the various resource limits behind us, let's look at retrieving and setting limits. Retrieving a resource limit is quite simple:

```
struct rlimit rlim;
int ret;

/* get the limit on core sizes */
ret = getrlimit (RLIMIT_CORE, &rlim);
if (ret == -1) {
        perror ("getrlimit");
        return 1;
}

printf ("RLIMIT_CORE limits: soft=%ld hard=%ld\n",
        rlim.rlim_cur, rlim.rlim_max);
```

Compiling this snippet in a larger program and running it yields the following:

```
RLIMIT_CORE limits: soft=0 hard=-1
```

We have a soft limit of 0 and a hard limit of infinity (-1 denotes RLIM_INFINITY). Therefore, we can set a new soft limit of any size. This example sets the maximum core size to 32 MB:

```
struct rlimit rlim;
int ret;

rlim.rlim_cur = 32 * 1024 * 1024; /* 32 MB */
rlim.rlim_max = RLIM_INFINITY;    /* leave it alone */
ret = setrlimit (RLIMIT_CORE, &rlim);
if (ret == -1) {
        perror ("setrlimit");
        return 1;
}
```

Error codes

On error, three errno codes are possible:

EFAULT
> The memory pointed at by rlim is invalid or inaccessible.

EINVAL
> The value denoted by resource is invalid, or rlim.rlim_cur is greater than rlim.rlim_max (setrlimit() only).

EPERM
> The caller did not possess CAP_SYS_RESOURCE but tried to raise the hard limit.

## CHAPTER 7

Threading

Threading is the creation and management of multiple units of execution within a single process. Threading is a significant source of programming error, through the introduction of data races and deadlocks. The topic of threading can—and indeed does—fill whole books. Those works tend to focus on the myriad interfaces in a particular threading library. While we will cover the basics of the Linux threading API, the goal of this chapter is to go meta: How does threading fit into the system programmer's overall toolkit? Why use threads—and, more importantly, why not? What design patterns help us conceptualize and build threading applications? And, finally, what are data races and how can we prevent them?

Binaries, Processes, and Threads

Binaries are dormant programs residing on a storage medium, compiled to a format accessible by a given operating system and machine architecture, ready to execute but not yet in motion. *Processes* are the operating system abstraction representing those binaries in action: the loaded binary, virtualized memory, kernel resources such as open files, an associated user, and so on. *Threads* are the unit of execution within a process: a virtualized processor, a stack, and program state. Put another way, processes are running binaries and threads are the smallest unit of execution schedulable by an operating system's process scheduler.

A process *contains* one or more threads. If a process contains but one thread, there is only a single unit of execution in the process and only one thing going on at a time. We call such processes *single threaded*. They are the classic Unix process. If a process contains more than one thread, then there is more than one thing going on at once. We call such processes *multithreaded*.

Modern operating systems provide two fundamental virtualized abstractions to userspace: virtual memory and a virtualized processor. Together, they give the illusion to each running process that it alone consumes the machine's resources. Virtualized memory affords each process a unique view of memory that seamlessly maps back to physical RAM or on-disk storage (via paging). The system's RAM may in actuality contain the data of 100 different running processes, but each process sees virtual memory all of its own. A virtualized processor lets processes act as if they alone run on the system, with the operating system hiding the fact that multiple processes are multitasking across (perhaps) multiple processors.

Virtualized memory is associated with the process and not the thread. Thus, each process has a unique view of memory, but all of the threads in a given process *share* that memory. Conversely, a virtualized processor is associated with threads and not processes. Each thread is an independently schedulable entity, allowing a single process to "do" more than one thing at a time. Many programmers combine the two illusions of virtualized memory and virtualized processor, but threads require you to separate them. Threads have the illusion, as processes do, of having a processor (or several) all to themselves. Threads, unlike processes, do not have the illusion of having memory all to themselves—all the threads within a process share the entirety of their memory address space.

Multithreading

What is the point of threads? We obviously need processes, since they are the abstraction of a running program. But why decouple the unit of execution and introduce threads? There are six primary benefits to multithreading:

Programming abstraction

Dividing up work and assigning each division to a unit of execution (a thread) is a natural approach to many problems. Design patterns that utilize this approach include the thread-per-connection and thread pool patterns. Programmers find these patterns useful and intuitive. Some, however, view threads as an anti-pattern. The inimitable Alan Cox summed this up well with the quote, "threads are for people who can't program state machines." That is, there is in theory no programming problem that is solvable with threads that isn't solvable with a state machine.

Parallelism

In machines with multiple processors, threads provide an efficient way to achieve *true parallelism*. As each thread receives its own virtualized processor and is an independently schedulable entity, multiple threads may run on multiple processors at the same time, improving a system's throughput. To the extent that threads are used to achieve parallelism—that is, there are no more threads than processors—the "threads are for people who can't program state machines" maxim does not apply.

Improving responsiveness

Even on a uniprocessor machine, multithreading can improve a process's responsiveness. In a single-threaded process, a long-running operation can prevent an application from responding to user input, making it appear as if the application has froze. With multithreading, such operations may be delegated to worker threads, allowing at least one thread to remain responsive to user input and perform UI operations.

Blocking I/O

This is related to the previous item. Without threads, blocking I/O halts the entire process. This can be detrimental to both throughput and latency. In a multithreaded process, individual threads may block, waiting on I/O, while other threads continue to make forward progress. Asynchronous and nonblocking I/O are alternative solutions to threads for this issue.

Context switching

The cost of switching from one thread to a different thread within the same process is significantly cheaper than process-to-process context switching.

Memory savings

Threads provide an efficient way to share memory yet utilize multiple units of execution. In this manner they are an alternative to multiple processes.

For these reasons, threading is a relatively common feature of operating systems and their applications. On some systems, such as Android, nearly every process on the system sports multiple threads. A decade or two ago, "threads are for people who can't program state machines" was quite often true, as most of the benefits of threads were realizable through other means, such as nonblocking I/O and, yes, state machines. Today, the number of processors in even the smallest of machines—even mobile devices have multiple processors—and technologies such as multicore and simultaneous multithreading (SMT) necessitate threads as a tool to maximize throughput in system programming. Now it is unimaginable to find a high-performance web service *not* running with many threads on many cores.

Context Switching: Processes Versus Threads

One of the performance wins from threading comes from the inexpensive cost of context switching from thread-to-thread within the same process (*intraprocess switching*). On any system, the cost of intraprocess switching is less than the cost of interprocess switching; the former is always a subset of the latter. This cost gap is particularly large on systems other than Linux, where processes are costly abstractions. Hence many systems call threads "lightweight processes."

On Linux, the cost of interprocess switching is not high, but intraprocess switching is near zero: approximately the cost of entering and exiting the kernel. Processes aren't expensive, but threads are cheaper still.

Machine architectures impose costs to process switching that threads do not bear, as process switching involves swapping out one virtual address space for another. On x86, for example, the translation lookaside buffer (TLB), which is a cache mapping virtual to physical memory addresses, must be flushed when swapping out the virtual address space. In certain workloads, TLB misses are incredibly detrimental to system performance. As an extreme example, on some ARM machines, the entirety of the CPU cache must be flushed! Threads do not bear these costs, as thread-to-thread switching does not swap out the virtual address space.

Costs of Multithreading

Despite these benefits, multithreading is not without cost. Indeed, some of the scariest, most nefarious bugs in the history of programming have been caused by threading. Designing, writing, understanding, and—most treacherous of all—debugging multithreading programs is significantly more difficult than with a single-threaded process.

The source of consternation with threads is also their raison d'être: multiple virtualized processors but only one instance of virtualized memory. Put another way, a multithreaded process has multiple things going on at once (*concurrency*) yet all those things share the same memory. Inevitably, the threads in a process are going to share resources— say, the need to read from or write to the same data. Understanding how your program works thus changes from understanding the simple sequential execution of instructions to conceptualizing multiple threads, executing independently, with timing and ordering that can be unpredictable yet absolutely essential to correct operation. Failing to *synchronize* threads can lead to corrupt output, incorrect execution, and program crash. Because understanding and debugging multithreaded programs is so difficult, it is imperative that your threading model and synchronization strategy be part of your system's design from day one.

Alternatives to Multithreading

Depending on your goals with multithreading, there are alternatives. For example, the latency and I/O benefits to threading are attainable via a combination of multiplexed I/O (see "Multiplexed I/O" on page 51), nonblocking I/O ("Nonblocking Reads" on page 35), and asynchronous I/O ("Asynchronous I/O" on page 123). These techniques allow processes to issue I/O operations that do not block the process. If true parallelism is your goal, *N* processes can achieve the same processor utilization as *N* threads, albeit at some cost of increased resource consumption and context switching overhead. Conversely, if memory savings is your goal, Linux provides tools to share memory in a more limited manner than threads.

Contemporary system programmers tend to not find these alternatives compelling. Asynchronous I/O, for example, is often infuriating. And even if you can mitigate the cost of multiple processes via shared memory and other shared resources, the context switching overhead is not going anywhere. Thus, threads are common not just in system programming, but across the stack: from the kernel up through to GUI applications. With the increasing prevalence of multiple cores, the use of threads will only increase.

Threading Models

There are several approaches to implementing threads on a system, with varying degrees of functionality provided by the kernel and user space. The simplest model is realized when the kernel provides native support for threads, and each of those kernel threads translates directly to the user-space concept of a thread. Such a model is called *1:1 threading*, as there is a one-to-one relationship between what the kernel provides and what the user consumes. This model is also known as *kernel-level threading*, as the kernel is the core of the system's threading model.

Threading in Linux, which we will discuss in "Linux Threading Implementations" on page 226, is *1:1*. The Linux kernel implements threads simply as processes that share resources. The threading library creates a new thread via the `clone()` system call and the returned "process" is directly managed as the user-space concept of a thread. That is, on Linux, what user space calls a thread is pretty much what the kernel calls a thread, too.

User-Level Threading

The complete opposite model is *N:1 threading*, also called *user-level threading*. Contra kernel-level threading, in this model user space is the key to the system's threading support, as it implements the concept of a thread. A process with *N* threads will map to a single kernel process—hence *N:1*. This model requires little or no kernel support but significant user-space code, including a user-space scheduler to manage the threads and a mechanism to catch and handle I/O in a nonblocking fashion. The benefit of user-level threads is that context switches are nearly free, as the application itself can decide what thread to run and when, without involving the kernel. The downside is that, as there is only a single kernel entity backing the *N* threads, this model cannot utilize multiple processors and thus is unable to provide true parallelism. On modern hardware, this is a significant downside, particularly given that the benefit of reduced-cost context switching is of marginal value on Linux, which sports cheap context switching.

While there are user-level threading libraries for Linux, most libraries provide *1:1* threading, which is what we will discuss later in this chapter.

Hybrid Threading

What if we combine kernel- and user-level threading? Is it possible to achieve the true parallelism of the *1:1* model with the free context switches of the *N:1* model? Indeed it is, if you are willing to accept quite a bit of complexity. *N:M threading*, also known as *hybrid threading*, attempts to achieve the best of both worlds: the kernel provides a native thread concept, while user space also implements user threads. User space, perhaps in conjunction with the kernel, then decides how to map *N* user threads onto *M* kernel threads, where *N>=M*.

Approaches differ by implementation, but the typical strategy is to not back most of the user threads with a kernel thread. A process might contain hundreds of user threads but only a small number of kernel threads, with that small number a function of processors (with at least one kernel thread for each processor enabling the full utilization of the system) and blocking I/O. As you might imagine, this model is rather complex to implement. Given Linux's cheap context switches, most system developers do not feel this approach worthwhile and the *1:1* model remains popular for Linux.

 Scheduler Activations is a solution that provides kernel support for user-level threads, enabling more performant execution of *N:M* threading. It began as an academic paper out of the University of Washington and was later adopted by both FreeBSD and NetBSD, becoming the core of their threading implementation. Scheduler Activations allow user-space control of and insight into the kernel's process scheduling, which makes the hybrid model more efficient and fixes several issues that can crop up in an implementation unassisted by the kernel.

Both FreeBSD and NetBSD have abandoned Scheduler Activations in preference for simpler *1:1* threading. You can view this as both a rejection of the complexity of the *N:M* model and a response to the ubiquity of the x86 architecture, which allows for relatively efficient context switches.

Coroutines and Fibers

Coroutines and *fibers* provide a unit of execution even lighter in weight than the thread (with the former being their name when they are a programming language construct, and the latter when they are a system construct). They are, like user-level threads, user-space phenomena but unlike user-level threads, there is little or no user-space support for their scheduling and execution. Instead, they are cooperatively scheduled, requiring an explicit *yield* in one to move to another. Coroutines and fibers are only subtly different from subroutines (normal C/C++ functions). Indeed, you can look at subroutines as a special case of coroutines. Coroutines and fibers are more about control of program flow than concurrency.

Linux does not natively support coroutines or fibers, again likely due to its already-fast context switch speed obviating the need for a construct with superior performance to the kernel thread. The Go programming language provides language-level support for coroutine-like constructs in Linux, called *Go-routines*. Coroutines enable differing programming paradigms and I/O models and, although beyond the scope of this book, are worth consideration.

Threading Patterns

The first and most important step in building a threaded application is deciding on a threading pattern, which will also be the processing and I/O model for your application. There are a myriad of abstractions and implementation details to settle on, but the two core programming patterns, of which you must pick one, are *thread-per-connection* and *event-driven*.

Thread-per-Connection

Thread-per-connection is a programming pattern in which a unit of work is assigned to one thread, and that thread is assigned at most one unit of work, for the duration of the unit of work's execution. The unit of work is however you break down your application's work: a request, a connection, etc. For this discussion, we'll say "connection" as that is the common terminology in describing this pattern.

Another way of describing this pattern is "run until completion." A thread grabs a connection or a request and processes it until done, at which time the thread is available to process another request anew. This has interesting implications for I/O and, indeed, I/O is one of the large differences between this and the event-driven pattern. In thread-per-connection, blocking I/O—indeed, any I/O—is permissible as the connection "owns" the thread. Blocking a thread can stall only the connection causing the blocking. In this manner, the thread-per-connection pattern uses the kernel to handle the scheduling of work and the management of I/O.

In this pattern, the number of threads is an implementation detail. We've discussed thread-per-connection thus far as if there is always a thread for every unit of work. That can be true, but most implementations like to put a bound on the number of threads they create. When the number of in-flight connections (and thus the number of threads) reaches a limit, connections are either queued or rejected until the number of in-flight connections drops below the limit.

Note there is nothing about this pattern that requires threading. Indeed, replace "thread" with "process" and you are describing the old-school Unix server. Apache's standard "fork" model, for example, follows this pattern. This is also the typical pattern for I/O in Java, although preferences are changing.

Event-Driven Threading

The event-driven pattern is a rejoinder to the thread-per-connection pattern. Consider the web server. In terms of computing power, modern hardware is capable of handling significant numbers of requests at once. In the thread-per-connection pattern, that is a lot of threads. Threads have fixed costs, most notably requiring both a kernel and user-space stack. These fixed costs place scalability limits on the number of threads in a given process, particularly on 32-bit systems. (The arguments against thread-per-connection are less relevant to 64-bit systems, but sufficiently valid that event-driven is still considered a superior choice even for 64-bit systems.) Systems might have the computing resources to handle several thousand in-flight connections, yet hit scalability limits in running that many concurrent threads.

In seeking an alternative, system designers noticed that most of the threads are doing a lot of waiting: reading files, waiting for databases to return results, issuing remote procedure calls. Indeed, recall our discussion from "Multithreading" on page 212: using more threads than you have processors on the system does not provide any benefits to parallelism. Instead, such uses of threads reflect a programming abstraction, an ease of programming that can be replicated through a more formal flow of control model.

These observations begot *event-driven threading*. Since so much of many thread-per-connection workloads is simply waiting, let's decouple that waiting from threads. Instead, issue all I/O asynchronously (see "Asynchronous I/O" on page 123) and use multiplexed I/O (see "Multiplexed I/O" on page 51) to manage the flow of control in the server. In this model, request processing is converted into a series of asynchronous I/O requests and associated callbacks. These callbacks can be waited on via multiplexed I/O; the process of doing so is called an *event loop*. When the I/O requests are returned, the event loop hands the callback off to a waiting thread.

As with the thread-per-connection pattern, nothing about the event-driven pattern need be threaded. Indeed, the event loop could simply be the fall-through when a single-threaded process is done executing a callback. Threads need only be added to provide true parallelism. In this model, there is no reason to have more threads than processors.

Patterns ebb and flow in popularity, but the event-driven pattern is currently the preferred approach to designing a multithreaded server. Several popular alternatives to Apache, for example, have developed over the last few years, all of which are event-driven. In designing your threaded system software, I suggest you first consider the event-driven pattern: asynchronous I/O, callbacks, an event loop, and a small thread pool with just a thread per processor.

Concurrency, Parallelism, and Races

Threads create two related but distinct phenomena: concurrency and parallelism. Both are bittersweet, touching on the costs of threading as well as its benefits. *Concurrency*

---

is the ability of two or more threads to execute in overlapping time periods. *Parallelism* is the ability to execute two or more threads simultaneously. Concurrency can occur without parallelism: for example, multitasking on a single processor system. Parallelism (sometimes emphasized as *true parallelism*) is a specific form of concurrency requiring multiple processors (or a single processor capable of multiple engines of execution, such as a GPU). With concurrency, multiple threads make forward progress, but not necessarily simultaneously. With parallelism, threads literally execute in parallel, allowing multithreaded programs to utilize multiple processors.

Concurrency is a programming pattern, a way of approaching problems. Parallelism is a hardware feature, achievable through concurrency. Both are useful.

Race Conditions

It is concurrency that introduces most of the hardships of threading. By enabling overlapping execution, threads can execute in an unpredictable order with respect to each other. At times, this is fine. But what if threads need to share a resource? Accessing even something as simple as a word of memory becomes a "race," where program behavior differs depending on which thread "gets there first."

Formally, a *race condition* is a situation in which the unsynchronized access of a shared resource by two or more threads leads to erroneous program behavior.[1] The shared resource can be anything: the system's hardware, a kernel resource, or data in memory. The latter is the most common form and is called a *data race*. The window in which a race can occur—the region of code which should be synchronized—is called a *critical region*. Races are eliminated by *synchronizing* threads' access to critical regions. Before diving into methods of synchronization, let's discuss a couple example race conditions.

Real-world races

Imagine an automated teller machine (ATM), also called an automated banking machine (ABM) or a cash machine. Usage is simple: you walk up, swipe your card, enter your PIN, and enter a withdrawal amount. You then collect your money. Somewhere in there, the bank needs to verify that you actually have the funds in your account and, if so, deduct the amount of withdrawal. The algorithm looks something like this:

1. Does the account hold at least X units of currency?

2. If so, deduct X from the account's balance and disburse X to the user.

3. If not, return error.

---

1. A *benign race* occurs when unsynchronized access leads to unpredictable but not erroneous program behavior. Occasionally programmers decide not to synchronize shared data that isn't critical, such as statistical counters, in pursuit of performance. I recommend always synchronizing shared data.

The code in C might look something like this:

```c
int withdraw (struct account *account, int amount)
{
        const int balance = account->balance;
        if (balance < amount)
                return -1;
        account->balance = balance - amount;

        disburse_money (amount);

        return 0;
}
```

There's a disastrous race in here if concurrent execution is possible. Imagine if the bank is executing this function twice, concurrently. Perhaps the customer is withdrawing funds at the same moment the bank is processing an online bill payment or assessing an egregious fee. What if the funds checks both happen at about the same time, before the account balance is updated and the money is dispersed? Both disbursements can happen, even if the account's balance is insufficient to handle both! For example, if there were $500 in the account and two withdraw requests came in for $200 and $400, they could both succeed, even though that would leave the account $100 in the red, which isn't something the code as written was intended to permit.

In fact, there is a second race in this function. Consider the store of the updated balance into the account structure. The two withdrawals can also race on updating the balance. Using our previous example, we'd end up with either $300 or $100 stored as the balance. Not only did this bank allow withdrawals to execute that should not, but it gifted this lucky customer with up to an extra $400.

Indeed, nearly every line of this function is inside a critical region. For this bank to survive as a viable business, it needs to synchronize access to the withdraw() function, ensuring that even if it is executed concurrently by two or more threads, the entire function is executed as one atomic unit: the bank needs to load the account balance, check for available funds, and debit the balance in one indivisible transaction.

Before we look at how this bank can do that, let's consider an example that shows just how fundamental race conditions are. This bank withdrawal example was rather high level: indeed, we didn't even need to show the example code. A bank executive can understand that if you allow accountants to credit and debit accounts concurrently, the math can get screwed up. But race conditions exist at the most fundamental of levels, too.

Consider this very simple line of C code:

```c
x++; // x is an integer
```

This is the *post-increment* operator and we all know what it does: it takes the current value of x, increments it by one, and stores that new value back in x, with the value of the expression being the updated x. How this compiles to machine code depends, of course, on the architecture, but we can imagine it might look something like this:

```
load x into register
add 1 to register
store register in x
```

Yes, even x++ is a racy operation. Imagine two threads executing x++ concurrently with x=5. Here is a desirable outcome:

Time	Thread 1	Thread 2
1	load x into register (5)	
2	add 1 to register (6)	
3	store register in x (6)	
4		load x into register (6)
5		add 1 to register (7)
6		store register in x (7)

This, too, is desirable:

Time	Thread 1	Thread 2
1		load x into register (5)
2		add 1 to register (6)
3		store register in x (6)
4	load x into register (6)	
5	add 1 to register (7)	
6	store register in x (7)	

We are lucky if that is the outcome. Nothing prevents this:

Time	Thread 1	Thread 2
1	load x into register (5)	
2	add 1 to register (6)	
3		load x into register (5)
4	store register in x (6)	
5		add 1 to register (6)
6		store register in x (6)

Many other combinations can also lead to unintended results. These examples exhibit concurrency but not parallelism. With parallelism, the threads can execute at the same time, adding even more combinations of peril:

Time	Thread 1	Thread 2
1	load x into register (5)	load x into register (5)
2	add 1 to register (6)	add 1 to register (6)
3	store register in x (6)	store register in x (6)

You get the picture. Even something as simple as adding one to a variable—a single line of C or C++—is fraught with races once we have multiple threads executing concurrently. We don't even need parallelism. A single processor machine can—and probably will—suffer these races. Race conditions are among the largest sources of programmer frustration and program bugs. Let's look at how programmers handle them.

Synchronization

The fundamental source of races is that critical regions are a window during which correct program behavior requires that threads do not interleave execution. To prevent race conditions, then, the programmer needs to synchronize access to that window, ensuring *mutually exclusive* access to the critical region.

In computer science, we say that an operation (or set of operations) is *atomic* if it is indivisible, unable to be interleaved with other operations. To the rest of the system, an atomic operation (or operations) appears to occur *instantaneously*. And that's the problem with critical regions: they are not indivisible, they don't occur instantaneously, they aren't atomic.

Mutexes

There are many techniques for making critical regions atomic, from solutions for single instructions up through large blocks of code. The most common technique is the *lock*, a mechanism for ensuring mutual exclusion within a critical region, rendering it atomic. Because locks enforce mutual exclusion, they are known in Pthreads (and elsewhere) as *mutexes*.[2]

A lock works similarly to its real-world namesake: imagine that a room is a critical region. Without a lock, people (threads) can come and go from the room (critical region) as they please. Specifically, there can be more than one person in the room at a time. So we put a door on the room and a lock on the door. We distribute but a single key to that door. When a person (a thread) comes to the door, they find the key sitting outside. They use the key to open the door, they go inside, and then they lock the door from the inside. No one else may enter. They can then go about their business in the room without interruption. No one else may occupy the room concurrently; it is a mutually exclusive

---

2. Which in turn are also known as *binary semaphores*.

---

resource. When the person is done with the room, they unlock the door and exit, leaving the key outside. The next person may then enter, lock the door behind them, and repeat.

A lock in the threading context works much the same. The programmer defines the lock and makes sure to acquire it before entering the critical region. The lock implementation ensures that only one thread can "hold" the lock at once. If it is in use by another thread, a new thread must wait for it before continuing. When done with a critical region, you release the lock, letting a waiting thread (if any) acquire the lock and proceed.

Recall from "Race Conditions" on page 219 our bank withdrawal example. Let's look at how a mutex would prevent the disastrous (at least for the bank) race condition we studied. We will discuss the actual mutex operations provided by Pthreads later (see "Pthread Mutexes" on page 235), but for now let's assume we have the functions lock() and unlock() to acquire and release, respectively, a mutex.

```
int withdraw (struct account *account, int amount)
{
        lock ();
        const int balance = account->balance;
        if (balance < amount) {
                unlock ();
                return -1;
        }
        account->balance = balance - amount;
        unlock ();

        disburse_money (amount);

        return 0;
}
```

We are locking only the part of the function that can race: the reading of the account balance, the sufficient funds check, and the updating of the account balance. Once the program knows it has a valid transaction and has updated the account balance, it can drop the lock and thus disburse the funds without enforcing mutual exclusion. The smaller you make the critical region, the better, as locks prevent concurrency and thus negate the benefits of threading.

Note there is nothing magic about locks. Nothing physically enforces the mutual exclusion. Locks are akin to a *gentlemen's agreement*. All threads must acquire the right locks in the right places. Nothing prevents a thread from not acquiring a necessary lock except conscientious programming.

Lock Data, Not Code

One of the most important programming patterns in multithreaded programming is *lock data, not code*. Although we have framed the discussion about race conditions around critical regions, a good programmer does not view code as the object of locking. You never say, "this lock protects this function." Instead, a good programmer associates data with locks. Shared data has an associated lock and accessing that data always requires that the associated lock be held.

What's the difference? When you associate locks with code, the locking semantics are harder to understand. Over time, the relationship between the lock and the data can grow unclear, and programmers may introduce new uses of the data without the appropriate lock. By associating locks with data, you help keep that mapping clear.

Deadlocks

The cruel irony of threads is the chain of desires begetting pain, which prompt solutions that only beget more pain. We want threads for concurrency, but that concurrency introduces race conditions. So we introduce mutexes, but those mutexes introduce a new source of programming bug: the deadlock.

A *deadlock* is a situation in which two threads are waiting for the other to finish, and thus neither does. In the case of mutexes, a deadlock occurs where two threads are each waiting for a different mutex, which the other thread holds. A degenerate case is when a single thread is blocked, waiting for a mutex that it already holds. Debugging deadlocks is often tricky, as your program needn't crash. Instead, it simply stops making forward progress, as ever more of your threads wait for a day that will never come.

Multithreading Mishaps on Mars

There are many real-life tales of threading woes, but one of the more intriguing is that of Mars Pathfinder, which in July of 1997 had successfully arrived on the Martian surface, only to find its mission of analyzing Martian climate and geology interrupted by frequent system resets.

Mars Pathfinder was powered by a real-time, highly threaded, embedded kernel (not Linux). The kernel provided preemptive scheduling of threads. Like Linux, real-time threads have priorities, and a thread of a given priority would always run before lower priority threads. There were, among many other threads, three that are pertinent to this bug: a low-priority thread to gather meteorological data, a medium-priority thread to communicate with Earth, and a high-priority thread to manage storage throughout the rover. As seen earlier in this chapter (see "Race Conditions" on page 219), synchronization is critical to preventing data races, and thus the threads managed concurrency

---

via mutexes. Notably, a mutex synchronized the low-priority meteorological thread (which was generating data) against the high-priority storage thread (which was managing that data).

The meteorological thread ran infrequently, polling the various sensors on the spacecraft. The thread would then acquire the mutex, write the meteorological data to the storage subsystem, and finally release the mutex. The storage thread ran more often, responding to system events. Before managing the storage subsystem, it too would acquire the mutex. If it were unavailable, it would sleep until the meteorological thread released it.

So far, so good. Occasionally, however, the communication thread would wake up and run while the meteorological thread was holding and the storage thread was waiting for the mutex. As the communication thread was a higher priority than the meteorological thread, the former ran at the expense of the latter. Unfortunately, the communication thread was a long-running task: Mars is far away! Thus, for the entirety of the communication thread's operation, the meteorological thread was not run. This seems by design, as dictated by the given priorities. But the meteorological thread held a resource (the mutex) that the storage thread wanted. Consequently, a lower priority thread (communication) was indirectly running at the expense of a higher priority thread (storage). The system would eventually notice the storage thread wasn't making forward progress, determine there must be an issue, and perform a system reset. This is a classic example of a class of bugs known as *priority inversion*.

The fix is a technique known as *priority inheritance*, where the process holding a resource inherits the priority of the highest priority process waiting for that resource. In this case, the lower priority meteorological thread would have inherited the higher priority of the storage thread for the duration it held the mutex. This would have prevented the communication thread from preempting the meteorological thread, allowing the quick release of the mutex and scheduling of the storage thread. If you don't find this a cautionary tale, stick to single-threaded programming!

Deadlock avoidance

Avoiding deadlocks is important, and the only consistent, safe way to do so is by designing locking into your multithreaded program from day one. It is important to associate mutexes with data, not code, and have a clear hierarchy of data (and thus mutexes). For example, a simple form of deadlock is known as the *ABBA deadlock* or the *deadly embrace*. This occurs when one thread acquires mutex A followed by mutex B, while another thread acquires mutex B followed by A (hence *ABBA*). With the right timing, both threads can successfully acquire their first mutex: Thread 1 holds A and Thread 2 holds B. When they then go to acquire the other mutex, they find it taken by the other thread, and each block, waiting for the mutex's release. Because each thread that holds a mutex is also waiting for a mutex, neither is ever released, and the threads deadlock.

Fixing this requires clear rules: Mutex *A* must always be acquired before *B*. As the complexity of your program, and thus of its synchronization, grows, it only becomes more difficult to enforce these rules. Start early and design things cleanly.

Pthreads

The Linux kernel provides only the underlying primitives that enable threading, such as the clone() system call. The bulk of any threading library is in user space. Many large software projects define their own threading library: Android, Apache, GNOME, and Mozilla all provide their own threading library, for example, and languages such as C++11 and Java provide standard library support for threads. Nonetheless, POSIX standardized a threading library with IEEE Std 1003.1c-1995, also known as POSIX 1995 or POSIX.1c. Developers call this standard *POSIX threads* or, for short, *Pthreads*. Pthreads remains the predominant threading solution for both C and C++ on Unix systems.

Linux Threading Implementations

Pthreads, as a standard, is just a bunch of words on a page. In Linux, the implementation of that standard is provided by *glibc*, Linux's C library. Over time, *glibc* has provided two different implementations of Pthreads: LinuxThreads and NPTL.

LinuxThreads is Linux's original Pthread implementation, providing *1:1* threading. It was first included in *glibc* with version 2.0, although it was available as an external library prior. LinuxThreads was designed for a kernel that provided very little support for threading: other than the clone() system call to create a new thread, LinuxThreads implemented POSIX threading using existing Unix interfaces. For example, LinuxThreads handles thread-to-thread communication using signals (see Chapter 10). Due to the lack of kernel support for Pthreads, LinuxThreads required a "manager" thread to coordinate activity, scaled poorly to large numbers of threads, and was imperfect in its conformance to the POSIX standard.

Native POSIX Thread Library (NPTL) superseded LinuxThreads and remains the standard Linux Pthread implementation. It was introduced in Linux 2.6 and *glibc* 2.3. Like LinuxThreads, NPTL provides *1:1* threading based around the clone() system call and the kernel's model that threads are just like any other process, except they share certain resources. Unlike LinuxThreads, NPTL capitalizes on additional kernel interfaces new to the 2.6 kernel, including the futex() system call for thread synchronization, the exit_group() system call for terminating all the threads in a process, and kernel support for thread-local storage (TLS). NPTL resolves LinuxThreads' nonconformance issues and vastly improves threading scalability, allowing for the creation of thousands of threads in a single process without slowdown.

NGPT

A competitor and early alternative to NPTL was *Next Generation POSIX Threads* (*NGPT*). Like NPTL, NGPT attempted to overcome the limitations of LinuxThreads and improve scalability. Unlike NPTL and LinuxThreads, however, NGPT implemented *N:M* threading. As is often the case in Linux, the simpler solution won out and NGPT is but a sidebar in history.

Although LinuxThreads-based systems are growing a bit long in the tooth, they can still be found. As NPTL is such a significant improvement over LinuxThreads, strongly consider upgrading such systems to NPTL (as if you needed another reason to not use such an ancient system) or, failing that, sticking to single-threaded programming.

The Pthread API

The Pthread API defines everything needed—albeit at a rather low level—to build a multithreaded program. Providing over 100 interfaces, the Pthread API is large. Due to its size and ungainliness, Pthreads is not without detractors. Nonetheless, it is *the* core threading library on Unix systems and is worth learning even if you use a different threading solution, as most are built on top of Pthreads.

The Pthread API is defined in `<pthread.h>`. Every function in the API is prefixed by `pthread_`. For example, the function to create a thread is called `pthread_create()` (we will study it soon, in "Creating Threads" on page 228). Pthread functions may be broken into two large groupings:

Thread management
    Functions to create, destroy, join, and detach threads. We will cover all of these in this chapter.

Synchronization
    Functions to manage the synchronization of threads, including mutexes, condition variables, and barriers. We will cover mutexes in this chapter.

Linking Pthreads

Although Pthreads is provided by *glibc*, it is in a separate library, *libpthread*, and thus requires explicit linkage. With *gcc*, this is automated by the *-pthread* flag, which ensures the proper library is linked into your executable:

```
gcc -Wall -Werror -pthread beard.c -o beard
```

If you build and link your binary with multiple invocations to *gcc* you'll want to provide `-pthread` to all of them: the flag also effects the preprocessor, by setting certain preprocessor defines that control thread safety.

Creating Threads

When your program is first run and executes the main() function, it is single threaded. Indeed, other than the compiler enabling some thread safety options and the linker linking in the Pthreads library, your process isn't any different from any other. From this initial thread, sometimes called the *default* or *master thread*, you must create one or more additional threads to become multithreaded.

Pthreads provides a single function to define and launch a new thread, pthread_create():

```
#include <pthread.h>

int pthread_create (pthread_t *thread,
                    const pthread_attr_t *attr,
                    void *(*start_routine) (void *),
                    void *arg);
```

Upon successful invocation, a new thread is created and begins executing the function provided by start_routine, passed the sole argument arg. The function will store the thread ID, used to represent the new thread, in the pthread_t pointed at by thread, if it is not NULL (we will discuss thread IDs in the next section, "Thread IDs" on page 229).

The pthread_attr_t object pointed at by attr is used to change the default *thread attributes* of the newly created thread. Most invocations of pthread_create() pass NULL for attr, receiving the default attributes. Thread attributes let programs change many aspects of threads, such as their stack size, schedulizing parameters, and initial detached state. A full discussion of thread attributes is outside the scope of this chapter; the Pthread *man pages* are a good resource.

The start_routine must have the following signature:

```
void * start_thread (void *arg);
```

Thus, the thread begins life by executing a function that accepts a void pointer as its sole argument and returns a void pointer as its return value. Similar to fork(), the new thread inherits most attributes, capabilities, and state from its parent. Unlike fork(), threads *share* the resources of their parent instead of receiving a copy. The most notable shared resource is, of course, the process address space, but threads also share (in lieu of receiving copies of) signal handlers and open files.

Code using this function should pass -pthread to *gcc*. That is true for all the Pthread functions and I won't mention it again.

On error, pthread_create() returns a nonzero error code directly (without the use of errno) and the contents of thread are undefined. Likely errors include:

EAGAIN

    The invoking process lacks sufficient resources to create a new thread. Usually this is caused by the process hitting either a per-user or system-wide thread limit.

EINVAL

    The `pthread_attr_t` object pointed at by `attr` contains invalid attributes.

EPERM

    The `pthread_attr_t` object pointed at by `attr` contains attributes for which the invoking process does not have permission to instill.

Example usage:

```
pthread_t tread;
int ret;

ret = pthread_create (&thread, NULL, start_routine, NULL);
if (!ret) {
        errno = ret;
        perror("pthread_create");
        return -1;
}

/* a new thread is created and running start_routine concurrently ... */
```

We'll look at a full-program example once we build up a few more techniques.

Thread IDs

The *thread ID* (*TID*) is the thread analogue to the process ID (PID). While the PID is assigned by the Linux kernel, the TID is just assigned in the Pthread library.[3] It is an opaque type represented by `pthread_t`, and POSIX does not require it to be an arithmetic type. As we've seen, the TID of a new thread is provided via the `thread` argument in a successful call to `pthread_create()`. A thread can obtain its TID at runtime via the `pthread_self()` function:

```
#include <pthread.h>

pthread_t pthread_self (void);
```

Usage is simple, because the function cannot fail:

```
const pthread_t me = pthread_self ();
```

---

3. To the Linux kernel, threads are just processes that happen to share resources, so the kernel references each thread via a unique PID, just like any other process. User-space programs can obtain this PID via the `get tid()` system call, but only occasionally is this value useful. Programmers should use the Pthread ID concept to reference their threads.

Comparing thread IDs

Because the Pthread standard does not require `pthread_t` to be an arithmetic type, there is no guarantee that the equality operator will work. Consequently, to compare thread IDs, the Pthread library needs to provide a special interface:

```
#include <pthread.h>

int pthread_equal (pthread_t t1, pthread_t t2);
```

If the provided thread IDs are equal, `pthread_equal()` returns a nonzero value. If the provided thread IDs aren't equal, it returns 0; it cannot fail. Here's a simple example:

```
int ret;

ret = pthread_equal(thing1, thing2);
if (ret != 0)
        printf("The TIDs are equal!\n");
else
        printf("The TIDs are unequal!\n");
```

Terminating Threads

The counterpart to thread creation is thread termination. Thread termination is similar to process termination, except that when a thread terminates, the rest of the threads in the process continue executing. In some threading patterns, such as *thread-per-connection* (see "Thread-per-Connection" on page 217), threads are frequently created and destroyed.

Threads may terminate under several circumstances, all of which have analogues to process termination:

- If a thread returns from its start routine, it terminates. This is akin to "falling off the end" of `main()`.
- If a thread invokes the `pthread_exit()` function (discussed subsequently), it terminates. This is akin to calling `exit()`.
- If the thread is canceled by another thread via the `pthread_cancel()` function, it terminates. This is akin to being sent the `SIGKILL` signal via `kill()`.

These three examples kill only the thread in question. *All* of the threads in a process are killed, and thus the entire process is killed, in the following circumstances:

- The process returns from its `main()` function.
- The process terminates via `exit()`.
- The process executes a new binary image via `execve()`.

Signals can kill a process or an individual thread, depending on how they're issued. Pthreads make signal handling rather complicated; it is best to minimize the use of signals in multithreaded programs. See Chapter 10 for a full treatment of signals.

Terminating yourself

The easiest way for a thread to terminate itself is to "fall off the end" of its start routine. Often you want to terminate a thread deep in a function call stack, far from your start routine. For those cases, Pthreads provides `pthread_exit()`, the thread equivalent of `exit()`:

```
#include <pthread.h>

void pthread_exit (void *retval);
```

Upon invocation, the calling thread is terminated. `retval` is provided to any thread waiting on the terminating thread's death (see "Joining and Detaching Threads" on page 233), again similar to `exit()`. There is no chance of error.

Usage:

```
/* Goodbye, cruel world! */
pthread_exit (NULL);
```

Terminating others

Pthreads calls the termination of threads by other threads *cancellation*. It provides the `pthread_cancel()` function to do so:

```
#include <pthread.h>

int pthread_cancel (pthread_t thread);
```

A successful call to `pthread_cancel()` sends a cancellation request to the thread represented by the thread ID `thread`. Whether and when a thread is cancellable depends on its *cancellation state* and *cancellation type*, respectively. On success, `pthread_cancel()` returns zero. Note that success is only demonstrative of successfully processing the cancellation request. The actual termination occurs asynchronously. On error, `pthread_cancel()` returns ESRCH, indicating that `thread` was invalid.

If and when a thread is cancellable is a bit complicated. A thread's cancellation state is either *enabled* or *disabled*. The default for new threads is enabled. If a thread has disabled cancellation, the request is queued until it is enabled. Otherwise, the cancellation type dictates when cancellation occurs. Threads can change their state via `pthread_set cancelstate()`:

```
#include <pthread.h>

int pthread_setcancelstate (int state, int *oldstate);
```

On success, the cancellation state of the invoking thread is set to `state` and the old state is stored in `oldstate`.[4] `state` may be PTHREAD_CANCEL_ENABLE or PTHREAD_CAN CEL_DISABLE, to enable or disable cancellation, respectively.

On error, `pthread_setcancelstate()` returns EINVAL, noting an invalid `state` value.

A thread's cancellation type is either *asynchronous* or *deferred*, with the latter being the default. With asynchronous cancellation, a thread may be killed at any point after the issuing of a cancel request. With deferred cancellation, a thread may only be killed at specific *cancellation points*, which are functions in the Pthreads or C library that represent safe points from which to terminate the caller. Asynchronous cancellation is useful only in certain situations because it can leave the process in an undefined state. For example, what if the canceled thread were in the middle of a critical region? For proper program behavior, asynchronous cancellation should be used only from threads that take care to never use shared resources and call only signal-safe functions (see "Guaranteed-Reentrant Functions" on page 349). Threads can change their type via `pthread_setcanceltype()`:

```
#include <pthread.h>

int pthread_setcanceltype (int type, int *oldtype);
```

On success, the cancellation type of the invoking thread is set to `type` and the old type is stored in `oldtype`.[5] `type` may be PTHREAD_CANCEL_ASYNCHRONOUS or PTHREAD_CANCEL_DEFERRED, to use asynchronous or deferred cancellation, respectively.

On error, `pthread_setcanceltype()` returns EINVAL, noting an invalid `type` value.

Let's consider an example of one thread terminating another. First, the to-terminate thread enables cancellation and sets the type to deferred (these are the defaults, so this acts only as an example):

```
int unused;
int ret;

ret = pthread_setcancelstate (PTHREAD_CANCEL_ENABLE, &unused);
if (ret) {
        errno = ret;
        perror ("pthread_setcancelstate");
        return -1;
}

ret = pthread_setcanceltype (PTHREAD_CANCEL_DEFERRED, &unused);
if (ret) {
```

4. Linux allows for a NULL `oldstate`, but POSIX does not. Portable programs should always pass a valid pointer here, if only to ignore it.

5. As with `pthread_setcancelstate()`, it is not portable to pass NULL for `oldtype`, although Linux allows it.

```
        errno = ret;
        perror ("pthread_setcanceltype");
        return -1;
}
```

Next, a different thread sends the cancellation request:

```
int ret;

/* `thread' is the thread ID of the to-terminate thread */
ret = pthread_cancel (thread);
if (ret) {
        errno = ret;
        perror ("pthread_cancel");
        return -1;
}
```

Joining and Detaching Threads

Given that threads can be easily created and destroyed, there must be some way to synchronize threads against the termination of other threads—the threading equivalent of wait(). Indeed, there is: the joining of threads.

Joining threads

Joining allows one thread to block while waiting for the termination of another:

```
#include <pthread.h>

int pthread_join (pthread_t thread, void **retval);
```

Upon successful invocation, the invoking thread is blocked until the thread specified by thread terminates (if thread has already terminated, pthread_join() returns immediately). Once thread terminates, the invoking thread is woken up and, if retval is not NULL, provided the return value the terminated thread passed to pthread_exit() or returned from its start routine. We then say the threads are *joined*. Joining allows threads to synchronize their execution against the lifetime of other threads. All threads in Pthreads are peers; any thread may join any other. A single thread can join many threads (in fact, as we'll see, this is often how the main thread waits for the threads it has created), but only one thread should try to join any particular thread; multiple threads should not attempt to join with any one other.

On error, pthread_join() returns one of the following nonzero error codes:

EDEADLK
    A deadlock was detected: thread is already waiting to join the caller or thread *is* the caller.

EINVAL
    The thread specified by thread is not joinable (see next section).

ESRCH

The thread specified by `thread` is invalid.

Example usage:

```
int ret;

/* join with `thread' and we don't care about its return value */
ret = pthread_join (thread, NULL);
if (ret) {
        errno = ret;
        perror ("pthread_join");
        return -1;
}
```

Detaching threads

By default, threads are created as *joinable*. Threads may, however, *detach*, rendering them no longer joinable. Because threads consume system resources until joined, just as processes consume system resources until their parent calls `wait()`, threads that you do not intend to join should be detached.

```
#include <pthread.h>

int pthread_detach (pthread_t thread);
```

On success, `pthread_detach()` detaches the thread specified by `thread` and returns zero. Results are undefined if you call `pthread_detach()` on a thread that is already detached. On error, the function returns ESRCH indicating that `thread` is invalid.

Either `pthread_join()` or `pthread_detach()` should be called *on each thread in a process* so that system resources are released when the thread terminates. (Of course, if the entire process exits, all threading resources are freed, but it remains good practice to explicitly join or detach all threads.)

A Threading Example

The following full-program example ties together the interfaces discussed thus far. It creates two threads (for a total of three), starting both threads in the same start routine, `start_thread()`. It differentiates their behavior in the start routine by providing differing arguments. It then joins both threads; if it did not, the main thread could exit before the other threads, terminating the entire process.

```
#include <stdlib.h>
#include <stdio.h>
#include <pthread.h>

void * start_thread (void *message)
{
        printf ("%s\n", (const char *) message);
```

```
        return message;
}

int main (void)
{
        pthread_t thing1, thing2;
        const char *message1 = "Thing 1";
        const char *message2 = "Thing 2";

        /* Create two threads, each with a different message. */
        pthread_create (&thing1, NULL, start_thread, (void *) message1);
        pthread_create (&thing2, NULL, start_thread, (void *) message2);

        /*
         * Wait for the threads to exit. If we didn't join here,
         * we'd risk terminating this main thread before the
         * other two threads finished.
         */
        pthread_join (thing1, NULL);
        pthread_join (thing2, NULL);

        return 0;
}
```

This is a full program. If you save it as *example.c*, you can compile it with this command:

```
gcc -Wall -O2 -pthread example.c -o example
```

and then run it like so:

```
./example
```

yielding:

```
Thing 1
Thing 2
```

or perhaps:

```
Thing 2
Thing 1
```

but never gibberish. Why no gibberish? Because `printf()` is thread-safe.

Pthread Mutexes

Recall from "Mutexes" on page 222 that the primary method of ensuring mutual exclusion is the mutex. For all their power and importance, mutexes are in fact rather easy to use.

Initializing mutexes

Mutexes are represented by the `pthread_mutex_t` object. Like most of the objects in the Pthread API, it is meant to be an opaque structure provided to the various mutex interfaces. Although you can dynamically create mutexes, most uses are static:

```
/* define and initialize a mutex named `mutex' */
pthread_mutex_t mutex = PTHREAD_MUTEX_INITIALIZER;
```

This snippet defines and initializes a mutex named `mutex`. That is all we have to do to start using it.

Locking mutexes

Locking (also called *acquiring*) a Pthreads mutex is accomplished via the `pthread_mutex_lock()` function:

```
#include <pthread.h>

int pthread_mutex_lock (pthread_mutex_t *mutex);
```

A successful call to `pthread_mutex_lock()` will block the calling thread until the mutex pointed at by `mutex` becomes available. Once available, the calling thread will wake up and this function will return zero. If the mutex is available on invocation, the function will return immediately.

On error, the function returns one of the following nonzero error codes:

EDEADLK
> The invoking thread already holds the requested mutex. This error code is not guaranteed by default; attempting to acquire an already-held mutex may result in deadlock (see "Deadlocks" on page 224).

EINVAL
> The mutex pointed at by `mutex` is invalid.

Callers tend not to check the return value, since well-formed code should not generate any errors at runtime. An example of usage is:

```
pthread_mutex_lock (&mutex);
```

Unlocking mutexes

The counterpart to locking is unlocking, or *releasing*, the mutex.

```
#include <pthread.h>

int pthread_mutex_unlock (pthread_mutex_t *mutex);
```

A successful call to `pthread_mutex_unlock()` releases the mutex pointed at by `mutex` and returns zero. The call does not block; the mutex is released immediately.

On error, the function returns a nonzero error code, including:

EINVAL

The mutex pointed at by mutex is invalid.

EPERM

The invoking process does not hold the mutex pointed at by mutex. This error code is not guaranteed; attempting to release a mutex you do not hold is a bug.

As with locking, users tend not to check the return value:

```
pthread_mutex_unlock (&mutex);
```

Scoped Locks

Resource Acquisition Is Initialization (RAII) is a C++ programming pattern—one of the most powerful patterns in the language. RAII efficiently deals with resource allocation and deallocation by tying the lifetime of the resource to the lifetime of a scoped object. While RAII was created to deal with resource cleanup after an exception is thrown, it is most powerful as a way to manage resources. For example, RAII lets you create a "scoped file" object where the file is opened when the object is created and automatically closed when the object falls out of scope. Similarly, we can create a "scoped lock" that acquires a mutex on creation and automatically releases the mutex when it falls out of scope:

```cpp
class ScopedMutex {
    public:
        ScopedMutex (pthread_mutex_t& mutex)
            :mutex_ (mutex)
        {
            pthread_mutex_lock (&mutex_);
        }

        ~ScopedMutex ()
        {
            pthread_mutex_unlock (&mutex_);
        }

    private:
        pthread_mutex_t& mutex_;
};
```

To use this, one just calls ScopedMutex m(mutex). The lock is automatically released when m falls out of scope. This makes unwinding functions and handling errors convenient and free of goto statements.

Mutex example

Let's look at a simple snippet that utilizes a mutex to ensure synchronization. Recall the banking withdraw example in "Real-world races" on page 219. Our imaginary bank suffered a serious race condition, enabling unintended behavior. Here's how we could fix the withdraw function using Pthread's mutexes:

```
static pthread_mutex_t the_mutex = PTHREAD_MUTEX_INITIALIZER;

int withdraw (struct account *account, int amount)
{
        pthread_mutex_lock (&the_mutex);
        const int balance = account->balance;
        if (balance < amount) {
                pthread_mutex_unlock (&the_mutex);
                return -1;
        }
        account->balance = balance - amount;
        pthread_mutex_unlock (&the_mutex);

        disburse_money (amount);

        return 0;
}
```

This example uses pthread_mutex_lock() to acquire a mutex and then pthread_mutex_unlock() to eventually release it. This serves to eliminate the race condition, but it introduces a single point of contention in the bank: only one customer can withdraw money at a time! That is quite a bottleneck; for a too-big-to-fail bank, that's a failure.

Thus most uses of locks avoid *global locks* and instead associate locks with specific instances of data structures. This is called *fine-grained locking*. It can make your locking semantics more complicated, particularly around deadlock avoidance, but is key in scaling to the number of cores on modern machines.

In this example, instead of defining a global the_mutex lock, we define a mutex inside of the account structure, giving each account its own lock. This works well as the data within the critical region is only the account structure. By locking only the account being debited, we allow the bank to process *other* customers' withdraws in parallel.

```
int withdraw (struct account *account, int amount)
{
        pthread_mutex_lock (&account->mutex);
        const int balance = account->balance;
        if (balance < amount) {
                pthread_mutex_unlock (&account->mutex);
                return -1;
        }
        account->balance = balance - amount;
        pthread_mutex_unlock (&account->mutex);

        disburse_money (amount);

        return 0;
}
```

Further Study

A single chapter cannot hope to do justice to the POSIX threading API, which, if we are being kind, is a full-featured and powerful library with myriad interfaces to learn. (If we are feeling grouchy, we might say that POSIX threads are overly complicated and cumbersome.) Many large-scale system applications define their own threading interfaces, as mechanisms such as thread pools and work queues are a more relevant level of abstraction in system software than what POSIX provides. In that case, the background on threading in this chapter is a perfect introduction to your in-house solution.

If you do require a deeper dive into Pthreads, I recommend the further reading in Appendix B. The relevant man pages are also particularly helpful.

## CHAPTER 8

File and Directory Management

In Chapters 2, 3, and 4, we covered a multitude of approaches to file I/O. In this chapter, we'll revisit files, this time focusing not on reading from or writing to them, but rather on manipulating and managing them and their metadata.

Files and Their Metadata

As discussed in Chapter 1, each file is referenced by an *inode*, which is addressed by a filesystem-unique numerical value known as an *inode number*. An inode is both a physical object located on the disk of a Unix-style filesystem and a conceptual entity represented by a data structure in the Linux kernel. The inode stores the *metadata* associated with a file, such as the file's access permissions, last access timestamp, owner, group, and size, as well as the location of the file's data.[1]

You can obtain the inode number for a file using the *-i* flag to the *ls* command:

```
$ ls -i
1689459 Kconfig     1689461 main.c      1680144 process.c  1689464 swsusp.c
1680137 Makefile    1680141 pm.c        1680145 smp.c       1680149 user.c
1680138 console.c   1689462 power.h     1689463 snapshot.c
1689460 disk.c      1680143 poweroff.c  1680147 swap.c
```

This output shows that, for example, *disk.c* has an inode number of 1689460. On this particular filesystem, no other file will have this inode number. On a different filesystem, however, we can make no such guarantees.

The Stat Family

Unix provides a family of functions for obtaining the metadata of a file:

---

1. Interestingly, the one thing not in an inode is the file's name! That's stored in the *directory entry*.

```
#include <sys/types.h>
#include <sys/stat.h>
#include <unistd.h>

int stat (const char *path, struct stat *buf);
int fstat (int fd, struct stat *buf);
int lstat (const char *path, struct stat *buf);
```

Each of these functions returns information about a file. stat() returns information about the file denoted by the path path, while fstat() returns information about the file represented by the file descriptor fd. lstat() is identical to stat(), except that in the case of a symbolic link, lstat() returns information about the link itself and not the target file.

Each of these functions stores information in a stat structure, which is provided by the user. The stat structure is defined in <bits/stat.h>, which is included from <sys/stat.h>:

```
struct stat {
        dev_t st_dev;        /* ID of device containing file */
        ino_t st_ino;        /* inode number */
        mode_t st_mode;      /* permissions */
        nlink_t st_nlink;    /* number of hard links */
        uid_t st_uid;        /* user ID of owner */
        gid_t st_gid;        /* group ID of owner */
        dev_t st_rdev;       /* device ID (if special file) */
        off_t st_size;       /* total size in bytes */
        blksize_t st_blksize; /* blocksize for filesystem I/O */
        blkcnt_t st_blocks;  /* number of blocks allocated */
        time_t st_atime;     /* last access time */
        time_t st_mtime;     /* last modification time */
        time_t st_ctime;     /* last status change time */
};
```

In more detail, the fields are as follows:

- The st_dev field describes the device node on which the file resides (we will cover device nodes later in this chapter). If the file is not backed by a device—for example, if it resides on an NFS volume—this value is 0.

- The st_ino field provides the file's inode number.

- The st_mode field provides the file's mode bytes, which describe the file type (such as a regular file or a directory) and the access permissions (such as world-readable). Chapters 1 and 2 covered mode bytes and permissions.

- The st_nlink field provides the number of hard links pointing at the file. Every file on a filesystem has at least one hard link.

- The st_uid field provides the user ID of the user who owns the file.

- The st_gid field provides the group ID of the group who owns the file.

- If the file is a device node, the st_rdev field describes the device that this file represents.

- The st_size field provides the size of the file, in bytes.

- The st_blksize field describes the preferred block size for efficient file I/O. This value (or an integer multiple of it) is the optimal block size for user-buffered I/O (see Chapter 3).

- The st_blocks field provides the number of filesystem blocks allocated to the file. This value multiplied by the block size will be smaller than the value provided by st_size if the file has holes (that is, if the file is a sparse file).

- The st_atime field contains the last *file access time*. This is the most recent time at which the file was accessed (for example, by read() or execle()).

- The st_mtime field contains the last *file modification time*—that is, the last time the file was written to.

- The st_ctime field contains the last *file change time*. The field contains the last time that the file's metadata (for example, its owner or permissions) was changed. This is often misunderstood to be the file creation time, which is not preserved on Linux or other Unix-style systems.

On success, all three calls return 0 and store the file's metadata in the provided stat structure. On error, they return −1 and set errno to one of the following:

EACCES
> The invoking process lacks search permission for one of the directory components of path (stat() and lstat() only).

EBADF
> fd is invalid (fstat() only).

EFAULT
> path or buf is an invalid pointer.

ELOOP
> path contains too many symbolic links (stat() and lstat() only).

ENAMETOOLONG
> path is too long (stat() and lstat() only).

ENOENT
> A component in path does not exist (stat() and lstat() only).

ENOMEM

There is insufficient memory available to complete the request.

ENOTDIR

A component in path is not a directory (stat() and lstat() only).

The following program uses stat() to retrieve the size of a file provided on the command line:

```
#include <sys/types.h>
#include <sys/stat.h>
#include <unistd.h>
#include <stdio.h>

int main (int argc, char *argv[])
{
        struct stat sb;
        int ret;

        if (argc < 2) {
                fprintf (stderr,
                        "usage: %s <file>\n", argv[0]);
                return 1;
        }

        ret = stat (argv[1], &sb);
        if (ret) {
                perror ("stat");
                return 1;
        }

        printf ("%s is %ld bytes\n",
                argv[1], sb.st_size);

        return 0;
}
```

Here is the result of running the program on its own source file:

```
$ ./stat stat.c
stat.c is 392 bytes
```

This program, in turn, reports the file type (such as symbolic link or block device node) of the file given by the first argument to the program:

```
#include <sys/types.h>
#include <sys/stat.h>
#include <unistd.h>
#include <stdio.h>

int main (int argc, char *argv[])
{
        struct stat sb;
```

```
        int ret;

        if (argc < 2) {
                fprintf (stderr,
                            "usage: %s <file>\n", argv[0]);
                return 1;
        }

        ret = stat (argv[1], &sb);
        if (ret) {
                perror ("stat");
                return 1;
        }

        printf ("File type: ");
        switch (sb.st_mode & S_IFMT) {
        case S_IFBLK:
                printf("block device node\n");
                break;
        case S_IFCHR:
                printf("character device node\n");
                break;
        case S_IFDIR:
                printf("directory\n");
                break;
        case S_IFIFO:
                printf("FIFO\n");
                break;
        case S_IFLNK:
                printf("symbolic link\n");
                break;
        case S_IFREG:
                printf("regular file\n");
                break;
        case S_IFSOCK:
                printf("socket\n");
                break;
        default:
                printf("unknown\n");
                break;
        }

        return 0;
}
```

Finally, this snippet uses `fstat()` to check whether an already opened file is on a physical (as opposed to a network) device:

```
/*
 * is_on_physical_device - returns a positive
 * integer if 'fd' resides on a physical device,
 * 0 if the file resides on a nonphysical or
 * virtual device (e.g., on an NFS mount), and
 * -1 on error.
 */
int is_on_physical_device (int fd)
{
        struct stat sb;
        int ret;

        ret = fstat (fd, &sb);
        if (ret) {
                perror ("fstat");
                return -1;
        }

        return gnu_dev_major (sb.st_dev);
}
```

Permissions

While the stat calls can be used to obtain the permission values for a given file, two other system calls set those values:

```
#include <sys/types.h>
#include <sys/stat.h>

int chmod (const char *path, mode_t mode);
int fchmod (int fd, mode_t mode);
```

Both chmod( ) and fchmod( ) set a file's permissions to mode. With chmod( ), path denotes the relative or absolute pathname of the file to modify. For fchmod( ), the file is given by the file descriptor fd.

The legal values for mode, represented by the opaque mode_t integer type, are the same as those returned by the st_mode field in the stat structure. Although the values are simple integers, their meanings are specific to each Unix implementation. Consequently, POSIX defines a set of constants that represent the various permissions (see "Permissions of New Files" on page 29 in Chapter 2 for full details). These constants can be binary-ORed together to form the legal values for mode. For example, (S_IRUSR | S_IRGRP) sets the file's permissions as both owner- and group-readable.

To change a file's permissions, the effective ID of the process calling chmod( ) or fchmod( ) must match the owner of the file, or the process must have the CAP_FOWNER capability.

On success, both calls return 0. On failure, both calls return -1 and set errno to one of the following error values:

EACCES

The invoking process lacked search permission for a component in `path` (`chmod()` only).

EBADF

The file descriptor `fd` is invalid (`fchmod()` only).

EFAULT

`path` is an invalid pointer (`chmod()` only).

EIO

An internal I/O error occurred on the filesystem. This is a very bad error to encounter; it could indicate a corrupt disk or filesystem.

ELOOP

The kernel encountered too many symbolic links while resolving `path` (`chmod()` only).

ENAMETOOLONG

`path` is too long (`chmod()` only).

ENOENT

`path` does not exist (`chmod()` only).

ENOMEM

There is insufficient memory available to complete the request.

ENOTDIR

A component in `path` is not a directory (`chmod()` only).

EPERM

The effective ID of the invoking process does not match the owner of the file, and the process lacks the `CAP_FOWNER` capability.

EROFS

The file resides on a read-only filesystem.

This code snippet sets the file *map.png* to owner-readable and -writable:

```
int ret;

/*
 * Set 'map.png' in the current directory to
 * owner-readable and -writable. This is the
 * same as 'chmod 600 ./map.png'.
 */
ret = chmod ("./map.png", S_IRUSR | S_IWUSR);
if (ret)
        perror ("chmod");
```

This code snippet does the same thing, assuming that fd represents the open file *map.png*:

```
int ret;

/*
 * Set the file behind 'fd' to owner-readable
 * and -writable.
 */
ret = fchmod (fd, S_IRUSR | S_IWUSR);
if (ret)
        perror ("fchmod");
```

Both chmod() and fchmod() are available on all modern Unix systems. POSIX requires the former and makes the latter optional.

Ownership

In the stat structure, the st_uid and st_gid fields provide the file's owner and group, respectively. Three system calls allow a user to change those two values:

```
#include <sys/types.h>
#include <unistd.h>

int chown (const char *path, uid_t owner, gid_t group);
int lchown (const char *path, uid_t owner, gid_t group);
int fchown (int fd, uid_t owner, gid_t group);
```

chown() and lchown() set the ownership of the file specified by the path path. They have the same effect, unless the file is a symbolic link: the former follows symbolic links and changes the ownership of the link target rather than the link itself, while lchown() does not follow symbolic links and therefore changes the ownership of the symbolic link file instead. fchown() sets the ownership of the file represented by the fd file descriptor.

On success, all three calls set the file's owner to owner, set the file's group to group, and return 0. If either the owner or the group field is –1, that value is not set. Only a process with the CAP_CHOWN capability (usually a root process) may change the owner of a file. The owner of a file can change the file's group to any group to which the user is a member; processes with CAP_CHOWN can change the file's group to any value.

On failure, the calls return –1, and set errno to one of the following values:

EACCES

> The invoking process lacks search permission for a component in path (chown() and lchown() only).

EBADF

> fd is invalid (fchown() only).

EFAULT

    `path` is invalid (`chown()` and `lchown()` only).

EIO

    There was an internal I/O error (this is bad).

ELOOP

    The kernel encountered too many symbolic links in resolving `path` (`chown()` and `lchown()` only).

ENAMETOOLONG

    `path` is too long (`chown()` and `lchown()` only).

ENOENT

    The file does not exist.

ENOMEM

    There is insufficient memory available to complete the request.

ENOTDIR

    A component in `path` is not a directory (`chown()` and `lchown()` only).

EPERM

    The invoking process lacked the necessary rights to change the owner or the group as requested.

EROFS

    The filesystem is read-only.

This code snippet changes the group of the file *manifest.txt* in the current working directory to *officers*. For this to succeed, the invoking user either must possess the `CAP_CHOWN` capability or must be *kidd* and in the *officers* group:

```
struct group *gr;
int ret;
/*
 * getgrnam() returns information on a group
 * given its name.
 */
gr = getgrnam ("officers");
if (!gr) {
        /* likely an invalid group */
        perror ("getgrnam");
        return 1;
}

/* set manifest.txt's group to 'officers' */
ret = chown("manifest.txt", -1, gr->gr_gid);
if (ret)
        perror ("chown");
```

Before invocation, the file's group is *crew*:

```
$ ls -l
-rw-r--r-- 1 kidd  crew  13274 May 23 09:20 manifest.txt
```

After invocation, the file is for the sole privilege of the officers:

```
$ ls -l
-rw-r--r-- 1 kidd  officers 13274 May 23 09:20 manifest.txt
```

The file's owner, *kidd*, is not changed because the code snippet passed –1 for uid.

This function sets the file represented by fd to root ownership and group:

```
/*
 * make_root_owner - changes the owner and group of the file
 * given by 'fd' to root. Returns 0 on success and -1 on
 * failure.
 */
int make_root_owner (int fd)
{
        int ret;

        /* 0 is both the gid and the uid for root */
        ret = fchown (fd, 0, 0);
        if (ret)
                perror ("fchown");

        return ret;
}
```

The invoking process must have the CAP_CHOWN capability. As is par for the course with capabilities, this generally means that it must be owned by root.

Extended Attributes

Extended attributes, also called *xattrs*, provide a mechanism for associating key/value pairs with files. In this chapter, we have already discussed all sorts of key/value metadata associated with files: the file's size, owner, last modification timestamp, and so on. Extended attributes allow existing filesystems to support new features that weren't anticipated in their original designs, such as mandatory access controls for security. What makes extended attributes interesting is that user-space applications may arbitrarily create, read from, and write to the key/value pairs.

Extended attributes are *filesystem-agnostic*, in the sense that applications use a standard interface for manipulating them; the interface is not specific to any filesystem. Applications can thus use extended attributes without concern for what filesystem the files reside on or how the filesystem internally stores the keys and values. Still, the implementation of extended attributes is very filesystem-specific. Different filesystems store extended attributes in quite different ways, but the kernel hides these differences, abstracting them away behind the extended attribute interface.

The *ext4* filesystem, for example, stores a file's extended attributes in empty space in the file's inode.[2] This feature makes reading extended attributes very fast. Because the filesystem block containing the inode is read off the disk and into memory whenever an application accesses a file, the extended attributes are "automatically" read into memory and can be accessed without any additional overhead.

Other filesystems, such as *FAT* and *minixfs*, do not support extended attributes at all. These filesystems return ENOTSUP when extended attribute operations are invoked on their files.

Keys and values

A unique *key* identifies each extended attribute. Keys must be valid UTF-8. They take the form *namespace.attribute*. Every key must be fully qualified; that is, it must begin with a valid namespace, followed by a period. An example of a valid key name is *user.mime_type*; this key is in the *user* namespace with the attribute name *mime_type*.

Old and New Ways for a Filesystem to Store MIME Types

GUI file managers, such as GNOME's, behave differently for files of varying types: they offer unique icons, different default click behavior, special lists of operations to perform, and so on. To accomplish this, the file manager has to know the format of each file. To determine the format, systems such as Windows simply look at the file's extension. For reasons of both tradition and security, however, Unix systems tend to inspect the file and interpret its type. This process is called *MIME type sniffing*.

Some file managers generate this information on the fly; others generate the information once and then cache it. Those that cache the information tend to put it in a custom database. The file manager must work to keep this database in sync with the files, which can change without the file manager's knowledge. A better approach is to jettison the custom database and store such metadata in extended attributes: these are easier to maintain, faster to access, and readily accessible by any application.

A key is either *defined* or *undefined*. If a key is defined, its value may be empty or nonempty. That is, there is a difference between an undefined key and a defined key with no assigned value. As we shall see, this means a special interface is required for removing keys as assigning them an empty value is insufficient.

---

2. Until the inode runs out of space, of course. Then *ext4* stores extended attributes in additional filesystem blocks.

The value associated with a key, if nonempty, may be any arbitrary array of bytes. Because the value is not necessarily a string, it need not be null-terminated, although null-termination certainly makes sense if you choose to store a C string as a key's value. Since the values are not guaranteed to be null-terminated, all operations on extended attributes require the size of the value. When reading an attribute, the kernel provides the size; when writing an attribute, you must provide the size.

Linux does not enforce any limits on the number of keys, the length of a key, the size of a value, or the total space that can be consumed by all of the keys and values associated with a file. Filesystems, however, have practical limits. These limits are usually manifested as constraints on the total size of all of the keys and values associated with a given file.

With *ext3*, for example, all extended attributes for a given file must fit within the slack space in the file's inode and up to one additional filesystem block. (Older versions of *ext3* were limited to the one filesystem block, without the in-inode storage.) This equates to a practical limit of about 1 KB to 8 KB per file, depending on the size of the filesystem's blocks. *XFS*, in contrast, has no practical limits. Even with *ext3*, these limits are usually not an issue, as most keys and values are short text strings. Nonetheless, keep them in mind—think twice before storing the entire revision control history of a project in a file's extended attributes!

Extended attribute namespaces

The namespaces associated with extended attributes are more than just organizational tools. The kernel enforces different access policies depending on the namespace.

Linux currently defines four extended attribute namespaces and may define more in the future. The current four are as follows:

system
> The *system* namespace is used to implement kernel features that utilize extended attributes, such as access control lists (ACLs). An example of an extended attribute in this namespace is `system.posix_acl_access`. Whether users can read from or write to these attributes depends on the security module in place. Assume at worst that no user (including root) can even read these attributes.

security
> The *security* namespace is used to implement security modules, such as SELinux. Whether user-space applications can access these attributes depends, again, on the security module in place. By default, all processes can read these attributes, but only processes with the `CAP_SYS_ADMIN` capability can write to them.

trusted
> The *trusted* namespace stores restricted information in user space. Only processes with the `CAP_SYS_ADMIN` capability can read from or write to these attributes.

The *user* namespace is the standard namespace for use by regular processes. The kernel controls access to this namespace via the normal file permission bits. To read the value from an existing key, a process must have read access to the given file. To create a new key or to write a value to an existing key, a process must have write access to the given file. You can assign extended attributes in the user namespace only to regular files, not to symbolic links or device files. When designing a user-space application that uses extended attributes, this is likely the namespace you want.

Extended Attribute Operations

POSIX defines four operations that applications may perform on a given file's extended attributes:

- Given a file, return a list of all of the file's assigned extended attribute keys.
- Given a file and a key, return the corresponding value.
- Given a file, a key, and a value, assign that value to the key.
- Given a file and a key, remove that extended attribute from the file.

For each operation, POSIX provides three system calls:

- A version that operates on a given pathname; if the path refers to a symbolic link, the target of the link is operated upon (the usual behavior).
- A version that operates on a given pathname; if the path refers to a symbolic link, the link itself is operated upon (the standard l variant of a system call).
- A version that operates on a file descriptor (the standard f variant).

In the following subsections, we will cover all 12 combinations.

Retrieving an extended attribute

The simplest operation is returning the value of an extended attribute from a file, given the key:

```
#include <sys/types.h>
#include <attr/xattr.h>

ssize_t getxattr (const char *path, const char *key,
                  void *value, size_t size);
ssize_t lgetxattr (const char *path, const char *key,
                   void *value, size_t size);
ssize_t fgetxattr (int fd, const char *key,
                   void *value, size_t size);
```

A successful call to getxattr() stores the extended attribute with name key from the file path in the provided buffer value, which is size bytes in length. It returns the actual size of the value.

If size is 0, the call returns the size of the value without storing it in value. Thus, passing 0 allows applications to determine the correct size for the buffer in which to store the key's value. Given this size, applications can then allocate or resize the buffer as needed.

lgetxattr() behaves the same as getxattr(), unless path is a symbolic link, in which case it returns extended attributes from the link itself rather than the target of the link. Recall from the previous section that attributes in the user namespace cannot be applied to symbolic links—thus, this call is rarely used.

fgetxattr() operates on the file descriptor fd; otherwise, it behaves the same as get xattr().

On error, all three calls return –1 and set errno to one of the following values:

EACCES
    The invoking process lacks search permission for one of the directory components of path (getxattr() and lgetxattr() only).

EBADF
    fd is invalid (fgetxattr() only).

EFAULT
    path, key, or value is an invalid pointer.

ELOOP
    path contains too many symbolic links (getxattr() and lgetxattr() only).

ENAMETOOLONG
    path is too long (getxattr() and lgetxattr() only).

ENOATTR
    The attribute key does not exist, or the process does not have access to the attribute.

ENOENT
    A component in path does not exist (getxattr() and lgetxattr() only).

ENOMEM
    There is insufficient memory available to complete the request.

ENOTDIR
    A component in path is not a directory (getxattr() and lgetxattr() only).

ENOTSUP
    The filesystem on which path or fd resides does not support extended attributes.

ERANGE

size is too small to hold the value of key. As previously discussed, the call may be reissued with size set to 0; the return value will indicate the required buffer size, and value may be resized appropriately.

Setting an extended attribute

The following three system calls set a given extended attribute:

```
#include <sys/types.h>
#include <attr/xattr.h>

int setxattr (const char *path, const char *key,
              const void *value, size_t size, int flags);
int lsetxattr (const char *path, const char *key,
               const void *value, size_t size, int flags);
int fsetxattr (int fd, const char *key,
               const void *value, size_t size, int flags);
```

A successful call to setxattr() sets the extended attribute key on the file path to value, which is size bytes in length. The flags field modifies the behavior of the call. If flags is XATTR_CREATE, the call will fail if the extended attribute already exists. If flags is XATTR_REPLACE, the call will fail if the extended attribute does not exist. The default behavior, which is performed if flags is 0, allows both creations and replacements. Regardless of the value of flags, keys other than key are unaffected.

lsetxattr() behaves the same as setxattr(), unless path is a symbolic link, in which case it sets the extended attributes on the link itself, rather than on the target of the link. Recall that attributes in the user namespace cannot be applied to symbolic links—thus, this call is also rarely used.

fsetxattr() operates on the file descriptor fd; otherwise, it behaves the same as setxattr().

On success, all three system calls return 0; on failure, the calls return –1 and set errno to one of the following:

EACCES

The invoking process lacks search permission for one of the directory components of path (setxattr() and lsetxattr() only).

EBADF

fd is invalid (fsetxattr() only).

EDQUOT

A quota limit prevents the space consumption required by the requested operation.

EEXIST

XATTR_CREATE was set in flags, and key already exists on the given file.

EFAULT

path, key, or value is an invalid pointer.

EINVAL

flags is invalid.

ELOOP

path contains too many symbolic links (setxattr() and lsetxattr() only).

ENAMETOOLONG

path is too long (setxattr() and lsetxattr() only).

ENOATTR

XATTR_REPLACE was set in flags, and key does not exist on the given file.

ENOENT

A component in path does not exist (setxattr() and lsetxattr() only).

ENOMEM

There is insufficient memory available to complete the request.

ENOSPC

There is insufficient space on the filesystem to store the extended attribute.

ENOTDIR

A component in path is not a directory (setxattr() and lsetxattr() only).

ENOTSUP

The filesystem on which path or fd resides does not support extended attributes.

Listing the extended attributes on a file

The following three system calls enumerate the set of extended attribute keys assigned to a given file:

```
#include <sys/types.h>
#include <attr/xattr.h>

ssize_t listxattr (const char *path,
                   char *list, size_t size);
ssize_t llistxattr (const char *path,
                    char *list, size_t size);
ssize_t flistxattr (int fd,
                    char *list, size_t size);
```

A successful call to `listxattr()` returns a list of the extended attribute keys associated with the file denoted by `path`. The list is stored in the buffer provided by `list`, which is `size` bytes in length. The system call returns the actual size of the list, in bytes.

Each extended attribute key returned in `list` is terminated by a null character, so a list might look like this:

```
"user.md5_sum\0user.mime_type\0system.posix_acl_default\0"
```

Thus, although each key is a traditional, null-terminated C string, you need the length of the entire list (which you can retrieve from the call's return value) to walk the list of keys. To find out how large a buffer you need to allocate, call one of the list functions with a `size` of 0; this causes the function to return the actual length of the full list of keys. As with `getxattr()`, applications may use this functionality to allocate or resize the buffer to pass for `value`.

`llistxattr()` behaves the same as `listxattr()`, unless `path` is a symbolic link, in which case the call enumerates the extended attribute keys associated with the link itself rather than with the target of the link. Recall that attributes in the user namespace cannot be applied to symbolic links—thus, this call is rarely used.

`flistxattr()` operates on the file descriptor `fd`; otherwise, it behaves the same as `listxattr()`.

On failure, all three calls return –1 and set `errno` to one of the following error codes:

EACCES
> The invoking process lacks search permission for one of the directory components of `path` (`listxattr()` and `llistxattr()` only).

EBADF
> `fd` is invalid (`flistxattr()` only).

EFAULT
> `path` or `list` is an invalid pointer.

ELOOP
> `path` contains too many symbolic links (`listxattr()` and `llistxattr()` only).

ENAMETOOLONG
> `path` is too long (`listxattr()` and `llistxattr()` only).

ENOENT
> A component in `path` does not exist (`listxattr()` and `llistxattr()` only).

ENOMEM
> There is insufficient memory available to complete the request.

ENOTDIR

A component in path is not a directory (listxattr() and llistxattr() only).

ENOTSUP

The filesystem on which path or fd resides does not support extended attributes.

ERANGE

size is nonzero and is insufficiently large to hold the complete list of keys. The application may reissue the call with size set to 0 to discover the actual size of the list. The program may then resize value and reissue the system call.

Removing an extended attribute

Finally, these three system calls remove a given key from a given file:

```
#include <sys/types.h>
#include <attr/xattr.h>

int removexattr (const char *path, const char *key);
int lremovexattr (const char *path, const char *key);
int fremovexattr (int fd, const char *key);
```

A successful call to removexattr() removes the extended attribute key from the file path. Recall that there is a difference between an undefined key and a defined key with an empty (zero-length) value.

lremovexattr() behaves the same as removexattr(), unless path is a symbolic link, in which case the call removes the extended attribute key associated with the link itself rather than with the target of the link. Recall that attributes in the user namespace cannot be applied to symbolic links—thus, this call is also rarely used.

fremovexattr() operates on the file descriptor fd; otherwise, it behaves the same as removexattr().

On success, all three system calls return 0. On failure, all three calls return –1 and set errno to one of the following:

EACCES

The invoking process lacks search permission for one of the directory components of path (removexattr() and lremovexattr() only).

EBADF

fd is invalid (fremovexattr() only).

EFAULT

path or key is an invalid pointer.

ELOOP

path contains too many symbolic links (`removexattr()` and `lremovexattr()` only).

ENAMETOOLONG

path is too long (`removexattr()` and `lremovexattr()` only).

ENOATTR

key does not exist on the given file.

ENOENT

A component in `path` does not exist (`removexattr()` and `lremovexattr()` only).

ENOMEM

There is insufficient memory available to complete the request.

ENOTDIR

A component in `path` is not a directory (`removexattr()` and `lremovexattr()` only).

ENOTSUP

The filesystem on which `path` or `fd` resides does not support extended attributes.

Directories

528.80bIn Unix, a *directory* is a simple concept: it contains a list of filenames, each of which maps to an inode number. Each name is called a *directory entry*, and each name-to-inode mapping is called a *link*. A directory's contents—what the user sees as the result of the *ls* command—are a listing of all the filenames in that directory. When the user opens a file in a given directory, the kernel looks up the filename in that directory's list to find the corresponding inode number. The kernel then passes that inode number to the filesystem, which uses it to find the physical location of the file on the device.

Directories can also contain other directories. A *subdirectory* is a directory inside of another directory. Given this definition, all directories are subdirectories of some *parent directory*, with the exception of the directory at the very root of the filesystem tree, /. Not surprisingly, this directory is called the *root directory* (not to be confused with the root user's home directory, */root*).

A *pathname* consists of a filename along with one or more of its parent directories. An *absolute pathname* is a pathname that begins with the root directory—for example, */usr/bin/sextant*. A *relative pathname* is a pathname that does not begin with the root directory, such as *bin/sextant*. For such a pathname to be useful, the operating system must know the directory to which the path is relative. The current working directory (discussed in the next section) is used as the starting point.

File and directory names can contain any character except /, which delineates directories in a pathname, and *null*, which terminates the pathname. That said, it is standard practice to constrain the characters in pathnames to valid printable characters under the current locale, or even just ASCII. Since neither the kernel nor the C library enforces this practice, however, it is up to applications to enforce the use of only valid printable characters.

Older Unix systems limited filenames to 14 characters. Today, all modern Unix filesystems allow at least 255 bytes for each filename.[3] Many filesystems under Linux allow even longer filenames.[4]

Every directory contains two special directories, . and .. (called *dot* and *dot-dot*). The dot directory is a reference to the directory itself. The dot-dot directory is a reference to the directory's parent directory. For example, */home/kidd/gold/..* is the same directory as */home/kidd*. The root directory's dot and dot-dot directories point to itself—that is, /, /., and /.. are all the same directory. Technically speaking, therefore, one could say that even the root directory is a subdirectory—in this case, of itself.

The Current Working Directory

Every process has a current directory, which it initially inherits from its parent process. That directory is known as the process's *current working directory* (cwd). The current working directory is the starting point from which the kernel resolves relative pathnames. For example, if a process's current working directory is */home/blackbeard*, and that process tries to open *parrot.jpg*, the kernel will attempt to open */home/blackbeard/parrot.jpg*. Conversely, if the process tries to open */usr/bin/mast*, the kernel will indeed open */usr/bin/mast*. The current working directory has no impact on absolute pathnames (that is, pathnames that start with a slash).

A process can both obtain and change its current working directory.

Obtaining the current working directory

The preferred method for obtaining the current working directory is the getcwd() system call, which POSIX standardized:

```
#include <unistd.h>

char * getcwd (char *buf, size_t size);
```

---

3. Note that this limit is 255 *bytes*, not 255 *characters*. Multibyte characters obviously consume more than 1 of these 255 bytes.

4. Of course, older filesystems that Linux provides for backward compatibility, such as FAT, still carry their own limitations. In the case of FAT, this limitation is eight characters, followed by a dot, followed by three characters. Yes, enforcing the dot as a special character inside of the filesystem is silly.

A successful call to getcwd() copies the current working directory as an absolute path-name into the buffer pointed at by buf, which is of length size bytes and returns a pointer to buf. On failure, the call returns NULL and sets errno to one of the following values:

EFAULT

buf is an invalid pointer.

EINVAL

size is 0, but buf is not NULL.

ENOENT

The current working directory is no longer valid. This can happen if the current working directory has been removed.

ERANGE

size is too small to hold the current working directory in buf. The application needs to allocate a larger buffer and try again.

Here's an example of using getcwd():

```
char cwd[BUF_LEN];

if (!getcwd (cwd, BUF_LEN)) {
        perror ("getcwd");
        exit (EXIT_FAILURE);
}

printf ("cwd = %s\n", cwd);
```

POSIX dictates that the behavior of getcwd() is undefined if buf is NULL. Linux's C library, in this case, will allocate a buffer of length size bytes, and store the current working directory there. If size is 0, the C library will allocate a buffer sufficiently large to store the current working directory. It is then the application's responsibility to free the buffer, via free(), when it's done with it. Because this behavior is Linux-specific, applications that value portability or a strict adherence to POSIX should not rely on this functionality. This feature, however, does make usage very simple! Here's an example:

```
char *cwd;

cwd = getcwd (NULL, 0);
if (!cwd) {
        perror ("getcwd");
        exit (EXIT_FAILURE);
}

printf ("cwd = %s\n", cwd);

free (cwd);
```

Linux's C library also provides a `get_current_dir_name()` function, which has the same behavior as `getcwd()` when passed a `NULL buf` and a `size` of 0:

```
#define _GNU_SOURCE
#include <unistd.h>

char * get_current_dir_name (void);
```

Thus, this snippet behaves the same as the previous one:

```
char *cwd;

cwd = get_current_dir_name ();
if (!cwd) {
        perror ("get_current_dir_name");
        exit (EXIT_FAILURE);
}

printf ("cwd = %s\n", cwd);

free (cwd);
```

Older BSD systems favored the `getwd()` call, which Linux provides for backward compatibility:

```
#define _XOPEN_SOURCE_EXTENDED /* or _BSD_SOURCE */
#include <unistd.h>

char * getwd (char *buf);
```

A call to `getwd()` copies the current working directory into buf, which must be at least `PATH_MAX` bytes in length. The call returns buf on success and `NULL` on failure. For example:

```
char cwd[PATH_MAX];

if (!getwd (cwd)) {
        perror ("getwd");
        exit (EXIT_FAILURE);
}

printf ("cwd = %s\n", cwd);
```

For reasons of both portability and security, applications should not use `getwd()`; `getcwd()` is preferred.

Changing the current working directory

When a user first logs into her system, the login process sets her current working directory to her home directory, as specified in /etc/passwd. Sometimes, however, a process wants to change its current working directory. For example, a shell may want to do this when the user types *cd*.

Linux provides two system calls for changing the current working directory: one that accepts the pathname of a directory and another that accepts a file descriptor representing an open directory.

```
#include <unistd.h>

int chdir (const char *path);
int fchdir (int fd);
```

A call to chdir() changes the current working directory to the pathname specified by path, which can be an absolute or a relative pathname. Similarly, a call to fchdir() changes the current working directory to the pathname represented by the file descriptor fd, which must be opened against a directory. On success, both calls return 0. On failure, both calls return −1.

On failure, chdir() also sets errno to one of the following values:

EACCES
>   The invoking process lacks search permission for one of the directory components of path.

EFAULT
>   path is not a valid pointer.

EIO
>   An internal I/O error occurred.

ELOOP
>   The kernel encountered too many symbolic links while resolving path.

ENAMETOOLONG
>   path is too long.

ENOENT
>   The directory pointed at by path does not exist.

ENOMEM
>   There is insufficient memory available to complete the request.

ENOTDIR
>   One or more of the components in path is not a directory.

fchdir() sets errno to one of the following values:

EACCES
>   The invoking process lacks search permission for the directory referenced by fd (i.e., the execute bit is not set). This happens if the top-level directory is readable but not executable; open() succeeds, but fchdir() will not.

EBADF

fd is not an open file descriptor.

Depending on the filesystem, other error values are valid for either call.

These system calls affect only the currently running process. There is no mechanism in Unix for changing the current working directory of a different process. Therefore, the *cd* command found in shells cannot be a separate process (like most commands) that simply executes chdir() on the first command-line argument and then exits. Instead, *cd* must be a special built-in command that causes the shell itself to call chdir(), changing its own current working directory.

The most common use of getcwd() is to save the current working directory so that the process can return to it later. For example:

```
char *swd;
int ret;

/* save the current working directory */
swd = getcwd (NULL, 0);
if (!swd) {
        perror ("getcwd");
        exit (EXIT_FAILURE);
}

/* change to a different directory */
ret = chdir (some_other_dir);
if (ret) {
        perror ("chdir");
        exit (EXIT_FAILURE);
}

/* do some other work in the new directory... */

/* return to the saved directory */
ret = chdir (swd);
if (ret) {
        perror ("chdir");
        exit (EXIT_FAILURE);
}

free (swd);
```

It's better, however, to open() the current directory and then fchdir() to it later. This approach is faster because the kernel does not store the pathname of the current working directory in memory; it stores only the inode. Consequently, whenever the user calls getcwd(), the kernel must generate the pathname by walking the directory structure. Conversely, opening the current working directory is cheaper because the kernel already has its inode available and the human-readable pathname is not needed to open a file. The following snippet uses this approach:

```
int swd_fd;

swd_fd = open (".", O_RDONLY);
if (swd_fd == -1) {
        perror ("open");
        exit (EXIT_FAILURE);
}

/* change to a different directory */
ret = chdir (some_other_dir);
if (ret) {
        perror ("chdir");
        exit (EXIT_FAILURE);
}

/* do some other work in the new directory... */

/* return to the saved directory */
ret = fchdir (swd_fd);
if (ret) {
        perror ("fchdir");
        exit (EXIT_FAILURE);
}

/* close the directory's fd */
ret = close (swd_fd);
if (ret) {
        perror ("close");
        exit (EXIT_FAILURE);
}
```

This is how shells implement the caching of the previous directory (for example, with *cd - * in *bash*).

A process that does not care about its current working directory—such as a daemon—generally sets it to / with the call chdir("/"). An application that interfaces with a user and his data, such as a word processor, generally sets its current working directory to the user's home directory or to a special documents directory. Because current working directories are relevant only in the context of relative pathnames, the current working directory is of most utility to command-line utilities that the user invokes from the shell.

Creating Directories

Linux provides a single system call, standardized by POSIX, for creating new directories:

```
#include <sys/stat.h>
#include <sys/types.h>

int mkdir (const char *path, mode_t mode);
```

A successful call to mkdir() creates the directory path, which may be relative or absolute, with the permission bits mode (as modified by the current umask), and returns 0.

The current umask modifies the mode argument in the usual way, plus any operating-system-specific mode bits. In Linux, the permission bits of the newly created directory are (mode & ~umask & 01777). In other words, the umask for the process imposes restrictions that the mkdir() call cannot override. If the new directory's parent directory has the set group ID (*sgid*) bit set, or if the filesystem is mounted with BSD group semantics, the new directory will inherit the group affiliation from its parent. Otherwise, the effective group ID of the process will apply to the new directory.

On failure, mkdir() returns –1 and sets errno to one of the following values:

EACCES
> The parent directory is not writable by the current process, or one or more components of path are not searchable.

EEXIST
> path already exists (and not necessarily as a directory).

EFAULT
> path is an invalid pointer.

ELOOP
> The kernel encountered too many symbolic links while resolving path.

ENAMETOOLONG
> path is too long.

ENOENT
> A component in path does not exist or is a dangling symbolic link.

ENOMEM
> There is insufficient kernel memory to complete the request.

ENOSPC
> The device containing path is out of space, or the user's disk quota is over the limit.

ENOTDIR
> One or more of the components in path is not a directory.

EPERM
> The filesystem containing path does not support the creation of directories.

EROFS
> The filesystem containing path is mounted read-only.

Removing Directories

As the counterpart to mkdir(), the POSIX-standardized rmdir() removes a directory from the filesystem hierarchy:

```
#include <unistd.h>

int rmdir (const char *path);
```

On success, rmdir() removes path from the filesystem and returns 0. The directory specified by path must be empty, aside from the dot and dot-dot directories. There is no system call that implements the equivalent of a recursive delete, as with *rm -r*. Such a tool must manually perform a depth-first traversal of the filesystem, removing all files and directories starting with the leaves, and moving back up the filesystem; rmdir() can be used at each stage to remove a directory once its files have been removed.

On failure, rmdir() returns –1 and sets errno to one of the following values:

EACCES
Write access to the parent directory of path is not allowed, or one of the component directories of path is not searchable.

EBUSY
path is currently in use by the system and cannot be removed. In Linux, this can happen only if path is a mount point or a root directory (root directories need not be mount points, thanks to chroot()!).

EFAULT
path is not a valid pointer.

EINVAL
path has the dot directory as its final component.

ELOOP
The kernel encountered too many symbolic links while resolving path.

ENAMETOOLONG
path is too long.

ENOENT
A component in path does not exist, or is a dangling symbolic link.

ENOMEM
There is insufficient kernel memory to complete the request.

ENOTDIR
One or more of the components in path is not a directory.

ENOTEMPTY
>   `path` contains entries other than the special dot and dot-dot directories.

EPERM
>   The parent directory of `path` has the sticky bit (`S_ISVTX`) set, but the process's effective user ID is neither the user ID of said parent nor of `path` itself, and the process does not have the `CAP_FOWNER` capability. Alternatively, the filesystem containing `path` does not allow the removal of directories.

EROFS
>   The filesystem containing `path` is mounted read-only.

Usage is simple:

```
int ret;

/* remove the directory /home/barbary/maps */
ret = rmdir ("/home/barbary/maps");
if (ret)
        perror ("rmdir");
```

Reading a Directory's Contents

POSIX defines a family of functions for reading the contents of directories—that is, obtaining a list of the files that reside in a given directory. These functions are useful if you are implementing *ls* or a graphical file save dialog, if you need to operate on every file in a given directory, or if you want to search for files in a directory that match a given pattern.

To begin reading a directory's contents you need to create a *directory stream*, which is represented by a `DIR` object:

```
#include <sys/types.h>
#include <dirent.h>

DIR * opendir (const char *name);
```

A successful call to `opendir()` creates a directory stream representing the directory given by `name`.

A directory stream is little more than a file descriptor representing the open directory, some metadata, and a buffer to hold the directory's contents. Consequently, it is possible to obtain the file descriptor behind a given directory stream:

```
#define _BSD_SOURCE /* or _SVID_SOURCE */
#include <sys/types.h>
#include <dirent.h>

int dirfd (DIR *dir);
```

A successful call to dirfd() returns the file descriptor backing the directory stream dir. On error, the call returns –1. As the directory stream functions use this file descriptor internally, programs should not invoke calls that manipulate the file position. dirfd() is a BSD extension and is not standardized by POSIX; programmers wishing to proclaim their POSIX compliance should avoid it.

Reading from a directory stream

Once you have created a directory stream with opendir(), your program can begin reading entries from the directory. To do this, use readdir(), which returns entries one by one from a given DIR object:

```
#include <sys/types.h>
#include <dirent.h>

struct dirent * readdir (DIR *dir);
```

A successful call to readdir() returns the next entry in the directory represented by dir. The dirent structure represents a directory entry. Defined in <dirent.h>, on Linux, its definition is:

```
struct dirent {
        ino_t d_ino; /* inode number */
        off_t d_off; /* offset to the next dirent */
        unsigned short d_reclen; /* length of this record */
        unsigned char d_type; /* type of file */
        char d_name[256]; /* filename */
};
```

POSIX requires only the d_name field, which is the name of a single file within the directory. The other fields are optional or Linux-specific. Applications desiring portability to other systems, or conformance to POSIX should access only d_name.

Applications successively invoke readdir(), obtaining each file in the directory, until they find the file they are searching for or until the entire directory is read, at which time readdir() returns NULL.

On failure, readdir() also returns NULL. To differentiate between an error and having read all of the files, applications must set errno to 0 before each readdir() invocation and then check both the return value and errno. The only errno value set by read dir() is EBADF, signifying that dir is invalid. Thus, many applications do not bother to check for errors and assume that NULL means that no more files remain.

Closing the directory stream

To close a directory stream opened with opendir(), use closedir():

```
#include <sys/types.h>
#include <dirent.h>
```

```
int closedir (DIR *dir);
```

A successful call to `closedir()` closes the directory stream represented by `dir`, including the backing file descriptor, and returns 0. On failure, the function returns −1 and sets `errno` to `EBADF`, the only possible error code, signifying that `dir` is not an open directory stream.

The following snippet implements a function, `find_file_in_dir()`, that uses `readdir()` to search a given directory for a given filename. If the file exists in the directory, the function returns 0. Otherwise, it returns a nonzero value:

```
/*
 * find_file_in_dir - searches the directory 'path' for a
 * file named 'file'.
 *
 * Returns 0 if 'file' exists in 'path' and a nonzero
 * value otherwise.
 */
int find_file_in_dir (const char *path, const char *file)
{
        struct dirent *entry;
        int ret = 1;
        DIR *dir;

        dir = opendir (path);

        errno = 0;
        while ((entry = readdir (dir)) != NULL) {
                if (strcmp(entry->d_name, file) == 0) {
                        ret = 0;
                        break;
                }
        }

        if (errno && !entry)
                perror ("readdir");

        closedir (dir);
        return ret;
}
```

System calls for reading directory contents

The previously discussed functions for reading the contents of directories are standardized by POSIX and provided by the C library. Internally, these functions use one of two system calls, `readdir()` and `getdents()`, which are provided here for completeness:

```
#include <unistd.h>
#include <linux/types.h>
#include <linux/dirent.h>
```

```
#include <linux/unistd.h>
#include <errno.h>

/*
 * Not defined for user space: need to
 * use the _syscall3() macro to access.
 */
int readdir (unsigned int fd,
             struct dirent *dirp,
             unsigned int count);

int getdents (unsigned int fd,
              struct dirent *dirp,
              unsigned int count);
```

You do not want to use these system calls! They are obtuse and not portable. Instead, user-space applications should use the C library's `opendir()`, `readdir()`, and `close dir()` system calls.

Links

Recall from our discussion of directories that each name-to-inode mapping in a directory is called a *link*. Given this simple definition—that a link is essentially just a name in a list (a directory) that points at an inode—there would appear to be no reason why multiple links to the same inode could not exist. That is, a single inode (and thus a single file) could be referenced from, say, both */etc/customs* and */var/run/ledger*.

Indeed, this is the case, with one catch: because links map to inodes, and inode numbers are specific to a particular filesystem, */etc/customs* and */var/run/ledger* must both reside on the same filesystem. Within a single filesystem, there can be a large number of links to any given file. The only limit is in the size of the integer data type used to hold the number of links. Among various links, no one link is the "original" or the "primary" link. All of the links enjoy the same status, pointing at the same file.

We call these types of links *hard links*. Files can have 0, 1, or many links. Most files have a link count of 1—that is, they are pointed at by a single directory entry—but some files have 2 or even more links. Files with a link count of 0 have no corresponding directory entries on the filesystem. When a file's link count reaches 0, the file is marked as free, and its disk blocks are made available for reuse.[5] Such a file, however, remains on the filesystem if a process has the file open. Once no process has the file open, the file is removed.

---

5. Finding files with a link count of 0, but whose blocks are marked as allocated is a primary job of *fsck*, the filesystem checker. Such a condition can occur when a file is deleted, but remains open, and the system crashes before the file is closed. The kernel is never able to mark the filesystem blocks as free, and thus the discrepancy arises. Journaling filesystems eliminate this type of error.

The Linux kernel implements this behavior by using a link count and a usage count. The *usage count* is a tally of the number of instances where the file is open. A file is not removed from the filesystem until both the link and the usage counts hit 0.

Another type of link, the *symbolic link*, is not a filesystem mapping, but a higher-level pointer that is interpreted at runtime. Such links may span filesystems—we'll look at them shortly.

Hard Links

The link() system call, one of the original Unix system calls, and now standardized by POSIX, creates a new link for an existing file:

```
#include <unistd.h>

int link (const char *oldpath, const char *newpath);
```

A successful call to link() creates a new link under the path newpath for the existing file oldpath, and then returns 0. Upon completion, both oldpath and newpath refer to the same file—there is, in fact, no way to even tell which was the "original" link.

On failure, the call returns -1 and sets errno to one of the following:

EACCES
> The invoking process lacks search permission for a component in oldpath, or the invoking process does not have write permission for the directory containing new path.

EEXIST
> newpath already exists—link() will not overwrite an existing directory entry.

EFAULT
> oldpath or newpath is an invalid pointer.

EIO
> An internal I/O error occurred (this is bad!).

ELOOP
> Too many symbolic links were encountered in resolving oldpath or newpath.

EMLINK
> The inode pointed at by oldpath already has the maximum number of links pointing at it.

ENAMETOOLONG
> oldpath or newpath is too long.

ENOENT

A component in `oldpath` or `newpath` does not exist.

ENOMEM

There is insufficient memory available to complete the request.

ENOSPC

The device containing `newpath` has no room for the new directory entry.

ENOTDIR

A component in `oldpath` or `newpath` is not a directory.

EPERM

The filesystem containing `newpath` does not allow the creation of new hard links, or `oldpath` is a directory.

EROFS

`newpath` resides on a read-only filesystem.

EXDEV

`newpath` and `oldpath` are not on the same mounted filesystem. (Linux allows a single filesystem to be mounted in multiple places, but even in this case, hard links cannot be created across the mount points.)

This example creates a new directory entry, *pirate*, that maps to the same inode (and thus the same file) as the existing file *privateer*, both of which are in */home/kidd*:

```
int ret;

/*
 * create a new directory entry,
 * '/home/kidd/privateer', that points at
 * the same inode as '/home/kidd/pirate'
 */
ret = link ("/home/kidd/privateer", /home/kidd/pirate");
if (ret)
        perror ("link");
```

Symbolic Links

Symbolic links, also known as *symlinks* or *soft links*, are similar to hard links in that both point at files in the filesystem. The symbolic link differs, however, in that it is not merely an additional directory entry, but a special type of file altogether. This special file contains the pathname for a *different* file, called the symbolic link's *target*. At runtime, on the fly, the kernel substitutes this pathname for the symbolic link's pathname (unless using the various l versions of system calls, such as `lstat()`, which operate on the link itself, and not the target). Thus, whereas one hard link is indistinguishable from another hard link to the same file, it is easy to tell the difference between a symbolic link and its target file.

A symbolic link may be relative or absolute. It may also contain the special dot directory discussed earlier, referring to the directory in which it is located, or the dot-dot directory, referring to the parent of this directory. These sorts of "relative" symbolic links are quite common and often rather useful.

Soft links, unlike hard links, can span filesystems. They can point anywhere, in fact! Symbolic links can point at files that exist (the common practice) or at nonexistent files. The latter type of link is called a *dangling symlink*. Sometimes, dangling symlinks are unwanted—such as when the target of the link was deleted, but not the symlink—but at other times, they are intentional. Symbolic links can even point at other symbolic links. This can create loops. System calls that deal with symbolic links check for loops by maintaining a maximum traversal depth. If that depth is surpassed, they return ELOOP.

The system call for creating a symbolic link is very similar to its hard link cousin:

```
#include <unistd.h>

int symlink (const char *oldpath, const char *newpath);
```

A successful call to symlink() creates the symbolic link newpath pointing at the target oldpath, and then returns 0.

On error, symlink() returns –1 and sets errno to one of the following:

EACCES
  The invoking process lacks search permission for a component in oldpath, or the invoking process does not have write permission for the directory containing new path.

EEXIST
  newpath already exists—symink() will not overwrite an existing directory entry.

EFAULT
  oldpath or newpath is an invalid pointer.

EIO
  An internal I/O error occurred (this is bad!).

ELOOP
  Too many symbolic links were encountered in resolving oldpath or newpath.

EMLINK
  The inode pointed at by oldpath already has the maximum number of links pointing at it.

ENAMETOOLONG

oldpath or newpath is too long.

ENOENT

A component in oldpath or newpath does not exist.

ENOMEM

There is insufficient memory available to complete the request.

ENOSPC

The device containing newpath has no room for the new directory entry.

ENOTDIR

A component in oldpath or newpath is not a directory.

EPERM

The filesystem containing newpath does not allow the creation of new symbolic links.

EROFS

newpath resides on a read-only filesystem.

This snippet is the same as our previous example, but it creates */home/kidd/pirate* as a symbolic link (as opposed to a hard link) to */home/kidd/privateer*:

```
int ret;

/*
 * create a symbolic link,
 * '/home/kidd/privateer', that
 * points at '/home/kidd/pirate'
 */
ret = symlink ("/home/kidd/privateer", "/home/kidd/pirate");
if (ret)
        perror ("symlink");
```

Unlinking

The converse to linking is unlinking, the removal of pathnames from the filesystem. A single system call, unlink(), handles this task:

```
#include <unistd.h>

int unlink (const char *pathname);
```

A successful call to unlink() deletes pathname from the filesystem and returns 0. If that name was the last reference to the file, the file is deleted from the filesystem. If, however, a process has the file open, the kernel will not delete the file from the filesystem until that process closes the file. Once no process has the file open, it is deleted.

If `pathname` refers to a symbolic link, the link, not the target, is destroyed.

If `pathname` refers to another type of special file, such as a device, FIFO, or socket, the special file is removed from the filesystem, but processes that have the file open may continue to utilize it.

On error, `unlink()` returns –1 and sets `errno` to one of the following error codes:

EACCES
> The invoking process does not have write permission for the parent directory of `pathname`, or the invoking process does not have search permission for a component in `pathname`.

EFAULT
> `pathname` is an invalid pointer.

EIO
> An I/O error occurred (this is bad!).

EISDIR
> `pathname` refers to a directory.

ELOOP
> Too many symbolic links were encountered in traversing `pathname`.

ENAMETOOLONG
> `pathname` is too long.

ENOENT
> A component in `pathname` does not exist.

ENOMEM
> There is insufficient memory available to complete the request.

ENOTDIR
> A component in `pathname` is not a directory.

EPERM
> The system does not allow the unlinking of files.

EROFS
> `pathname` resides on a read-only filesystem.

`unlink()` does not remove directories. For that, applications should use `rmdir()`, which we discussed earlier (see "Removing Directories" on page 267).

To ease the wanton destruction of any type of file, the C language provides the `remove()` function:

```
#include <stdio.h>

int remove (const char *path);
```

A successful call to remove() deletes path from the filesystem and returns 0. If path is a file, remove() invokes unlink(); if path is a directory, remove() calls rmdir().

On error, remove() returns -1 and sets errno to any of the valid error codes set by unlink() and rmdir(), as applicable.

Copying and Moving Files

Two of the most basic file manipulation tasks are copying and moving files, commonly carried out via the *cp* and *mv* commands. At the filesystem level, *copying* is the act of duplicating a given file's contents under a new pathname. This differs from creating a new hard link to the file in that changes to one file will not affect the other—that is, there now exist two distinct copies of the file, under (at least) two different directory entries. *Moving*, conversely, is the act of renaming the directory entry under which a file is located. This action does not result in the creation of a second copy.

Copying

Although it is surprising to some, Unix does not include a system or library call to facilitate the copying of files and directories. Instead, utilities such as *cp* or GNOME's file manager perform these tasks manually.

In copying a file src to a file named dst, the steps are as follows:

1. Open src.
2. Open dst, creating it if it does not exist, and truncating it to zero length if it does exist.
3. Read a chunk of src into memory.
4. Write the chunk to dst.
5. Continue until all of src has been read and written to dst.
6. Close dst.
7. Close src.

If copying a directory, the individual directory and any subdirectories are created via mkdir(); each file therein is then copied individually.

Moving

Unlike for copying files, Unix does provide a system call for moving files. The ANSI C standard introduced the call for files, and POSIX standardized it for both files and directories:

```
#include <stdio.h>

int rename (const char *oldpath, const char *newpath);
```

A successful call to `rename()` renames the pathname `oldpath` to `newpath`. The file's contents and inode remain the same. Both `oldpath` and `newpath` must reside on the same filesystem;[6] if they do not, the call will fail. Utilities such as *mv* handle this case by resorting to a copy and unlink.

On success, `rename()` returns 0, and the file once referenced by `oldpath` is now referenced by `newpath`. On failure, the call returns –1, does not touch `oldpath` or `newpath`, and sets `errno` to one of the following values:

EACCES
: The invoking process lacks write permission for the parent of `oldpath` or `newpath`, search permission for a component of `oldpath` or `newpath`, or write permission for `oldpath` in the case that `oldpath` is a directory. The last case is an issue because `rename()` must update .. in `oldpath` if it is a directory.

EBUSY
: `oldpath` or `newpath` is a mount point.

EFAULT
: `oldpath` or `newpath` is an invalid pointer.

EINVAL
: `newpath` is contained within `oldpath`, and thus, renaming one to the other would make `oldpath` a subdirectory of itself.

EISDIR
: `newpath` exists and is a directory, but `oldpath` is not a directory.

ELOOP
: In resolving `oldpath` or `newpath`, too many symbolic links were encountered.

EMLINK
: `oldpath` already has the maximum number of links to itself, or `oldpath` is a directory, and `newpath` already has the maximum number of links to itself.

---

6. Although Linux allows you to mount a device at multiple points in the directory structure, you still cannot rename from one of these mount points to another, even though they are backed by the same device.

ENAMETOOLONG

oldpath or newpath is too long.

ENOENT

A component in oldpath or newpath does not exist or is a dangling symbolic link.

ENOMEM

There is insufficient kernel memory to complete the request.

ENOSPC

There is insufficient space on the device to complete the request.

ENOTDIR

A component (aside from potentially the final component) in oldpath or new path is not a directory, or oldpath is a directory, and newpath exists but is not a directory.

ENOTEMPTY

newpath is a directory and is not empty.

EPERM

At least one of the paths specified in the arguments exists, the parent directory has the sticky bit set, the invoking process's effective user ID is neither the user ID of the file, nor that of the parent, and the process is not privileged.

EROFS

The filesystem is marked read-only.

EXDEV

oldpath and newpath are not on the same filesystem.

Table 8-1 reviews the results of moving to and from different types of files.

Table 8-1. Effects of moving to and from different types of files

	Destination is a file	Destination is a directory	Destination is a link	Destination does not exist
Source is a file	The destination is overwritten by the source.	Failure with EISDIR.	The file is renamed and the destination is overwritten.	The file is renamed.
Source is a directory	Failure with ENOTDIR.	The source is renamed as the destination if the destination is empty; failure with ENOTEMPTY otherwise.	The directory is renamed, and the destination is overwritten.	The directory is renamed.
Source is a link	The link is renamed and the destination is overwritten.	Failure with EISDIR.	The link is renamed and the destination is overwritten.	The link is renamed.

	Destination is a file	Destination is a directory	Destination is a link	Destination does not exist
Source does not exist	Failure with ENOENT.	Failure with ENOENT.	Failure with ENOENT.	Failure with ENOENT.

For all of these cases, regardless of their type, if the source and destination reside on different filesystems, the call fails and returns EXDEV.

Device Nodes

Device nodes are special files that allow applications to interface with device drivers. When an application performs the usual Unix I/O—opening, closing, reading, writing, and so on—on a device node, the kernel does not handle those requests as normal file I/O. Instead, the kernel passes such requests to a device driver. The device driver handles the I/O operation and returns the results to the user. Device nodes provide device abstraction so that applications do not need to be familiar with device specifics, or even master special interfaces. Indeed, device nodes are the standard mechanism for accessing hardware on Unix systems. Network devices are the rare exception, and over the course of Unix's history, some have argued that this exception is a mistake. There is, indeed, an elegant beauty in manipulating all of a machine's hardware using read(), write(), and mmap() calls.

How does the kernel identify the device driver to which it should hand off the request? Each device node is assigned two numerical values, called a *major number* and a *minor number*. These major and minor numbers map to a specific device driver loaded into the kernel. If a device node has a major and minor number that do not correspond to a device driver in the kernel—which occasionally happens, for a variety of reasons—an open() request on the device node returns –1 with errno set to ENODEV. We say that such device nodes front nonexistent devices.

Special Device Nodes

Several device nodes are present on all Linux systems. These device nodes are part of the Linux development environment, and their presence is considered part of the Linux ABI.

The *null device* has a major number of 1 and a minor number of 3. It lives at */dev/null*. The device file should be owned by root and be readable and writable by all users. The kernel silently discards all write requests to the device. All read requests to the file return end-of-file (EOF).

The *zero device* lives at */dev/zero* and has a major of 1 and a minor of 5. Like the null device, the kernel silently discards writes to the zero device. Reading from the device returns an infinite stream of null bytes.

The *full device*, with a major of 1 and a minor of 7, lives at */dev/full*. As with the zero device, read requests return null characters (`\0`). Write requests, however, always trigger the `ENOSPC` error, signifying that the underlying device is full.

These devices have varied purposes. They are useful for testing how an application handles corner and problem cases—a full filesystem, for example. Because the null and zero devices ignore writes, they also provide a no-overhead way to throw away unwanted I/O.

The Random Number Generator

The kernel's random number generators live at */dev/random* and */dev/urandom*. They have a major number of 1 and minor numbers of 8 and 9, respectively.

The kernel's random number generator gathers noise from device drivers and other sources, and the kernel concatenates together and one-way hashes the gathered noise. The result is then stored in an *entropy pool*. The kernel keeps an estimate of the number of bits of entropy in the pool.

Reads from */dev/random* return entropy from this pool. The results are suitable for seeding random number generators, performing key generation, and other tasks that require cryptographically strong entropy.

In theory, an adversary who was able to obtain enough data from the entropy pool *and* successfully break the one-way hash could gain knowledge about the state of the rest of the entropy pool. Although such an attack is currently only a theoretical possibility—no such attacks are publicly known to have occurred—the kernel reacts to this possibility by decrementing its estimate of the amount of entropy in the pool with each read request. If the estimate reaches zero, the read will block until the system generates more entropy, and the entropy estimate is large enough to satisfy the read.

/dev/urandom does not have this property; reads from the device will succeed even if the kernel's entropy estimate is insufficient to complete the request. Since only the most secure of applications—such as the generation of keys for secure data exchange in GNU Privacy Guard—should care about cryptographically strong entropy, most applications should use */dev/urandom* and not */dev/random*. Reads to the latter can potentially block for a very long time if no I/O activity occurs that feeds the kernel's entropy pool. This is not uncommon on diskless, headless servers.

Out-of-Band Communication

The Unix file model is impressive. With only simple read and write operations, Unix abstracts nearly any conceivable act one could perform on an object. Sometimes, however, programmers need to communicate with a file outside of its primary data stream. For example, consider a serial port device. Reading from the device would read from the hardware on the far end of the serial port; writing to the device would send data to that hardware. How would a process read one of the serial port's special status pins, such as the data terminal ready (DTR) signal? Alternatively, how would a process set the parity of the serial port?

The answer is to use the ioctl() system call. ioctl(), which stands for *I/O control*, allows for *out-of-band communication*:

```
#include <sys/ioctl.h>

int ioctl (int fd, int request, ...);
```

The system call requires two parameters:

fd
> The file descriptor of a file.

request
> A special request code value, predefined and agreed upon by the kernel and the process, that denotes what operation to perform on the file referenced by fd.

It may also receive one or more untyped optional parameters (usually unsigned integers or pointers) to pass into the kernel.

The following program uses the CDROMEJECT request to eject the media tray from a CD-ROM device, which the user provides as the first argument on the program's command line. This program thus functions similarly to the standard *eject* command:

```
#include <sys/types.h>
#include <sys/stat.h>
#include <fcntl.h>
#include <sys/ioctl.h>
#include <unistd.h>
#include <linux/cdrom.h>
#include <stdio.h>

int main (int argc, char *argv[])
{
        int fd, ret;

        if (argc < 2) {
                fprintf (stderr,
                        "usage: %s <device to eject>\n",
                        argv[0]);
                return 1;
        }
        /*
         * Opens the CD-ROM device, read-only. O_NONBLOCK
         * tells the kernel that we want to open the device
         * even if there is no media present in the drive.
         */
```

```
        fd = open (argv[1], O_RDONLY | O_NONBLOCK);
        if (fd < 0) {
                perror ("open");
                return 1;
        }

        /* Send the eject command to the CD-ROM device. */
        ret = ioctl (fd, CDROMEJECT, 0);
        if (ret) {
                perror ("ioctl");
                return 1;
        }

        ret = close (fd);
        if (ret) {
                perror ("close");
                return 1;
        }

        return 0;
}
```

The CDROMEJECT request is a feature of Linux's CD-ROM device driver. When the kernel receives an ioctl() request, it finds the filesystem (in the case of real files) or device driver (in the case of device nodes) responsible for the file descriptor provided and passes on the request for handling. In this case, the CD-ROM device driver receives the request and physically ejects the drive.

Later in this chapter, we will look at an ioctl() example that uses an optional parameter to return information to the requesting process.

Monitoring File Events

Linux provides an interface, *inotify*, for monitoring files—for example, to see when they are moved, read from, written to, or deleted. Imagine that you are writing a graphical file manager, such as GNOME's file manager. If a file is copied into a directory while the file manager is displaying its contents, the file manager's view of the directory becomes inconsistent.

One solution is to continually reread the contents of the directory, detecting changes and updating the display. This imposes a periodic overhead and is far from an elegant solution. Worse, there is always a race between when a file is removed from or added to the directory, and when the file manager rereads the directory.

With inotify, the kernel can *push* the event to the application the moment it happens. As soon as a file is deleted, the kernel can notify the file manager. The file manager, in response, can immediately remove the deleted file from the graphical display of the directory.

Many other applications are also concerned with file events. Consider a backup utility or a data-indexing tool. inotify allows both of these programs to operate in real time: the moment a file is created, deleted, or written to, the tools can update the backup archive or data index.

inotify replaces *dnotify*, an earlier file-monitoring mechanism with a cumbersome signals-based interface. Applications should always favor inotify over dnotify. inotify, introduced with kernel 2.6.13, is flexible and easy to use because the same operations that programs perform on regular files work with inotify. We cover only inotify in this book.

Initializing inotify

Before a process can use inotify, the process must initialize it. The `inotify_init()` system call initializes inotify and returns a file descriptor representing the initialized instance:

```
#include <sys/inotify.h>

int inotify_init1 (int flags);
```

The `flags` parameter is usually 0, but may be a bitwise OR of the following flags:

IN_CLOEXEC
> Sets close-on-exec on the new file descriptor.

IN_NONBLOCK
> Sets O_NONBLOCK on the new file descriptor.

On error, `inotify_init1()` returns –1 and sets `errno` to one of the following codes:

EMFILE
> The per-user limit on the maximum number of inotify instances has been reached.

ENFILE
> The system-wide limit on the maximum number of file descriptors has been reached.

ENOMEM
> There is insufficient memory available to complete the request.

Let's initialize inotify so we can use it in subsequent steps:

```
int fd;

fd = inotify_init1 (0);
if (fd == -1) {
        perror ("inotify_init1");
        exit (EXIT_FAILURE);
}
```

Watches

After a process initializes inotify, it sets up *watches*. A watch, represented by a *watch descriptor*, is a standard Unix path, and an associated *watch mask*, which tells the kernel what events the process is interested in—for example, reads, writes, or both.

inotify can watch both files and directories. If watching a directory, inotify reports events that occur on the directory itself and on any of the files residing in the directory (but not on files in subdirectories of the watched directory—the watch is not recursive).

Adding a new watch

The system call `inotify_add_watch()` adds a watch for the event or events described by mask on the file or directory path to the inotify instance represented by fd:

```
#include <sys/inotify.h>

int inotify_add_watch (int fd,
                       const char *path,
                       uint32_t mask);
```

On success, the call returns a new watch descriptor. On failure, `inotify_add_watch()` returns −1 and sets errno to one of the following:

EACCES
> Read access to the file specified by path is not permitted. The invoking process must be able to read the file to add a watch to it.

EBADF
> The file descriptor fd is not a valid inotify instance.

EFAULT
> The pointer path is not valid.

EINVAL
> The watch mask, mask, contains no valid events.

ENOMEM
> There is insufficient memory available to complete the request.

ENOSPC
> The per-user limit on the total number of inotify watches has been reached.

Watch masks

The watch mask is a binary OR of one or more inotify events, which <inotify.h> defines:

IN_ACCESS
> The file was read from.

IN_MODIFY
> The file was written to.

IN_ATTRIB
> The file's metadata (for example, the owner, permissions, or extended attributes) was changed.

IN_CLOSE_WRITE
> The file was closed and had been open for writing.

IN_CLOSE_NOWRITE
> The file was closed and had not been open for writing.

IN_OPEN
> The file was opened.

IN_MOVED_FROM
> A file was moved away from the watched directory.

IN_MOVED_TO
> A file was moved into the watched directory.

IN_CREATE
> A file was created in the watched directory.

IN_DELETE
> A file was deleted from the watched directory.

IN_DELETE_SELF
> The watched object itself was deleted.

IN_MOVE_SELF
> The watched object itself was moved.

The following events are also defined, grouping two or more events into a single value:

IN_ALL_EVENTS
> All legal events.

IN_CLOSE
> All events related to closing (currently, both IN_CLOSE_WRITE and IN_CLOSE_NOW RITE).

IN_MOVE
> All move-related events (currently, both IN_MOVED_FROM and IN_MOVED_TO).

Now, we can look at adding a new watch to an existing inotify instance:

```
int wd;

wd = inotify_add_watch (fd, "/etc", IN_ACCESS | IN_MODIFY);
if (wd == -1) {
        perror ("inotify_add_watch");
        exit (EXIT_FAILURE);
}
```

This example adds a watch for all reads or writes on the directory */etc*. If any file in */etc* is written to or read from, inotify sends an event to the inotify file descriptor, fd, providing the watch descriptor wd. Let's look at how inotify represents these events.

inotify Events

The inotify_event structure, defined in <inotify.h>, represents inotify events:

```
#include <sys/inotify.h>

struct inotify_event {
        int wd;            /* watch descriptor */
        uint32_t mask;     /* mask of events */
        uint32_t cookie;   /* unique cookie */
        uint32_t len;      /* size of 'name' field */
        char name[];       /* nul-terminated name */
};
```

wd identifies the watch descriptor, as obtained by inotify_add_watch(), and mask represents the events. If wd identifies a directory and one of the watched-for events occurred on a file within that directory, name provides the filename relative to the directory. In this case, len is nonzero. Note that len is *not* the same as the string length of name; name can have more than one trailing null character that acts as padding to ensure that a subsequent inotify_event is properly aligned. Consequently, you must use len, and not strlen(), to calculate the offset of the next inotify_event structure in an array.

Zero-Length Arrays

name is an example of a zero-length array. Zero-length arrays, also known as flexible arrays, are a C99 language feature that allow the creation of arrays of variable length. They have one very powerful use: embedding arrays of variable size in structures. You can think of them as pointers whose contents are inlined at the site of the pointer itself.

Consider the example of inotify: the obvious way to hand the filename back in this structure is to have a name field such as, say, name[512]. But there is no maximum filename length across all filesystems. Any value would put a limit on inotify's utility. Moreover, most filenames are very small, so a large buffer would incur a lot of waste for most files. This situation is not uncommon; the classic solution is to make name a pointer, dynamically allocate a buffer elsewhere, and point name at it. But that won't work for a system call. A zero-length array was the perfect solution.

For example, if wd represents */home/kidd* and has a mask of IN_ACCESS, and the file */home/kidd/canon* is read from, name will equal canon, and len will be at least 6. Conversely, if we were watching */home/kidd/canon* directly with the same mask, len would be 0 and name would be zero-length—you must not touch it.

cookie is used to link together two related but disjoint events. We will address it in a subsequent section.

Reading inotify events

Obtaining inotify events is easy: you just read from the file descriptor associated with the inotify instance. inotify provides a feature known as *slurping*, which allows you to read multiple events with a single read request—as many as fit in the buffer provided to read(). Because of the variable-length name field, this is the most common way to read inotify events.

Our previous example instantiated an inotify instance, and added a watch to that instance. Now, let's read pending events:

```
char buf[BUF_LEN] __attribute__((aligned(4)));
ssize_t len, i = 0;

/* read BUF_LEN bytes' worth of events */
len = read (fd, buf, BUF_LEN);

/* loop over every read event until none remain */
while (i < len) {
        struct inotify_event *event =
                (struct inotify_event *) &buf[i];
        printf ("wd=%d mask=%d cookie=%d len=%d dir=%s\n",
                event->wd, event->mask,
                event->cookie, event->len,
                (event->mask & IN_ISDIR) ? "yes" : "no");

        /* if there is a name, print it */
        if (event->len)
                printf ("name=%s\n", event->name);
```

```
                    /* update the index to the start of the next event */
                    i += sizeof (struct inotify_event) + event->len;
    }
```

Because the inotify file descriptor acts like a regular file, programs can monitor it via select(), poll(), and epoll(). This allows processes to multiplex inotify events with other file I/O from a single thread.

Advanced inotify events

In addition to the standard events, inotify can generate other events:

IN_IGNORED
> The watch represented by wd has been removed. This can occur because the user manually removed the watch or because the watched object no longer exists. We will discuss this event in a subsequent section.

IN_ISDIR
> The affected object is a directory. (If not set, the affected object is a file.)

IN_Q_OVERFLOW
> The inotify queue overflowed. The kernel limits the size of the event queue to prevent unbounded consumption of kernel memory. Once the number of pending events reaches one less than the maximum, the kernel generates this event and appends it to the tail of the queue. No further events are generated until the queue is read from, reducing its size below the limit.

IN_UNMOUNT
> The device backing the watched object was unmounted. Thus, the object is no longer available; the kernel will remove the watch and generate the IN_IGNORED event.

Any watch can generate these events; the user need not set them explicitly.

Programmers must treat mask as a bitmask of pending events. Consequently, do *not* check for events using direct tests of equivalence:

```
/* Do NOT do this! */

if (event->mask == IN_MODIFY)
        printf ("File was written to!\n");
else if (event->mask == IN_Q_OVERFLOW)
        printf ("Oops, queue overflowed!\n");
```

Instead, perform bitwise tests:

```
if (event->mask & IN_ACCESS)
        printf ("The file was read from!\n");
if (event->mask & IN_UNMOUNTED)
        printf ("The file's backing device was unmounted!\n");
```

```
if (event->mask & IN_ISDIR)
        printf ("The file is a directory!\n");
```

Linking together move events

The IN_MOVED_FROM and IN_MOVED_TO events each represent only half of a move: the former represents the removal from a given location, while the latter represents the arrival at a new location. Therefore, to be truly useful to a program that is attempting to intelligently track files as they move around the filesystem (consider an indexer with the intention that it not reindex moved files), processes need to be able to link the two move events together.

Enter the cookie field in the inotify_event structure.

The cookie field, if nonzero, contains a unique value that links two events together. Consider a process that is watching /bin and /sbin. Assume that /bin has a watch descriptor of 7 and that /sbin has a watch descriptor of 8. If the file /bin/compass is moved to /sbin/compass, the kernel will generate two inotify events.

The first event will have wd equal to 7, mask equal to IN_MOVED_FROM, and a name of compass. The second event will have wd equal to 8, mask equal to IN_MOVED_TO, and a name of compass. In both events, cookie will be the same—say, 12.

If a file is renamed, the kernel still generates two events. wd is the same for both.

Note that if a file is moved from or to a directory that is not watched, the process will not receive one of the corresponding events. It is up to the program to notice that the second event with a matching cookie never arrives.

Advanced Watch Options

When creating a new watch, you can add one or more of the following values to mask to control the behavior of the watch:

IN_DONT_FOLLOW
    If this value is set, and if the target of path or any of its components is a symbolic link, the link is not followed and inotify_add_watch() fails.

IN_MASK_ADD
    Normally, if you call inotify_add_watch() on a file on which you have an existing watch, the watch mask is updated to reflect the newly provided mask. If this flag is set in mask, the provided events are *added* to the existing mask.

IN_ONESHOT
    If this value is set, the kernel automatically removes the watch after generating the first event against the given object. The watch is, in effect, "one shot."

IN_ONLYDIR

If this value is set, the watch is added only if the object provided is a directory. If path represents a file, not a directory, inotify_add_watch() fails.

For example, this snippet only adds the watch on */etc/init.d* if *init.d* is a directory and if neither */etc* nor */etc/init.d* is a symbolic link:

```
int wd;

/*
 * Watch '/etc/init.d' to see if it moves, but only if it is a
 * directory and no part of its path is a symbolic link.
 */
wd = inotify_add_watch (fd,
                        "/etc/init.d",
                        IN_MOVE_SELF |
                        IN_ONLYDIR |
                        IN_DONT_FOLLOW);
if (wd == -1)
        perror ("inotify_add_watch");
```

Removing an inotify Watch

As shown in this instance, you can remove a watch from an inotify instance with the system call inotify_rm_watch():

```
#include <inotify.h>

int inotify_rm_watch (int fd, uint32_t wd);
```

A successful call to inotify_rm_watch() removes the watch represented by the watch descriptor wd from the inotify instance (represented by the file descriptor) fd and returns 0.

For example:

```
int ret;

ret = inotify_rm_watch (fd, wd);
if (ret)
        perror ("inotify_rm_watch");
```

On failure, the system call returns –1 and sets errno to one of the following two options:

EBADF

fd is not a valid inotify instance.

EINVAL

wd is not a valid watch descriptor on the given inotify instance.

When removing a watch, the kernel generates the IN_IGNORED event. The kernel sends this event not only during a manual removal, but when destroying the watch as a side effect of another operation. For example, when a watched file is deleted, any watches on the file are removed. In all such cases, the kernel sends IN_IGNORED. This behavior allows applications to consolidate their handling of watch removal in a single place: the event handler for IN_IGNORED. This is useful for advanced consumers of inotify that manage complex data structures backing each inotify watch, such as GNOME's Beagle search infrastructure.

Obtaining the Size of the Event Queue

The size of the pending event queue can be obtained via the FIONREAD ioctl on the inotify instance's file descriptor. The first argument to the request receives the size of the queue in bytes, as an unsigned integer:

```
unsigned int queue_len;
int ret;

ret = ioctl (fd, FIONREAD, &queue_len);
if (ret < 0)
        perror ("ioctl");
else
        printf ("%u bytes pending in queue\n", queue_len);
```

Note that the request returns the size of the queue in bytes, and not the number of events in the queue. A program can estimate the number of events from the number of bytes, using the known size of the inotify_event structure (obtained via sizeof()) and a guess at the average size of the name field. What's more useful is that the number of bytes pending gives the process an ideal size to read.

The header <sys/ioctl.h> defines the FIONREAD constant.

Destroying an inotify Instance

Destroying an inotify instance, and any associated watches, is as simple as closing the instance's file descriptor:

```
int ret;

/* 'fd' was obtained via inotify_init() */
ret = close (fd);
if (fd == -1)
        perror ("close");
```

Of course, as with any file descriptor, the kernel automatically closes the file descriptor and cleans up the resource when the process exits.

## CHAPTER 9

Memory Management

Memory is among the most basic, but also most essential, of resources available to a process. This chapter covers the management of this resource: the allocation, manipulation, and eventual release of memory.

The verb *allocate*, which is the common term for obtaining memory, is a bit misleading, as it conjures up images of rationing a scarce resource for which demand outstrips supply. To be sure, many users would love more memory. On modern systems, however, the problem is not really one of sharing too little among too many, but of properly using and keeping track of the bounty.

In this chapter, you will learn about all of the approaches to allocating memory in various regions of a program, including each method's advantages and disadvantages. We'll also go over some ways to set and manipulate the contents of arbitrary memory regions and look at how to lock memory so it remains in RAM and your program runs no risk of having to wait for the kernel to page in data from swap space.

The Process Address Space

Linux, like any modern operating system, virtualizes its physical resource of memory. Processes do not directly address physical memory. Instead, the kernel associates each process with a unique *virtual address space*. This address space is *linear*, with addresses starting at zero, increasing contiguously to some maximum value. The address space is also *flat*: it exists in one space, directly accessible, without the need for segmentation.

Pages and Paging

Memory is composed of bits, of which (usually) eight make a byte. Bytes compose words, which in turn compose *pages*. For the purposes of memory management, the page is the most important of these: it is the smallest addressable unit of memory that the memory management unit (MMU) can manage. Thus the virtual address space is carved up into pages. The machine architecture determines the *page size*. Typical sizes include 4 KB for 32-bit systems and 8 KB for 64-bit systems.[1]

A 32-bit address space contains roughly a million 4 KB pages; a 64-bit address space with 8 KB pages contains several magnitudes more. A process cannot necessarily access all of those pages; they may not correspond to anything. Thus, pages are either valid or invalid. A *valid page* is associated with an actual page of data, either in physical memory (RAM) or on secondary storage, such as a swap partition or file on disk. An *invalid page* is not associated with anything and represents an unused, unallocated piece of the address space. Accessing an invalid page results in a segmentation violation.

If a valid page is associated with data on secondary storage, a process cannot access that page until the data is brought into physical memory. When a process attempts to access such a page, the memory management unit generates a *page fault*. The kernel then intervenes, transparently *paging in* the data from secondary storage to physical memory. Because there is considerably more virtual memory than physical memory, the kernel may have to move data out of memory to make room for the data paging in. *Paging out* is the process of moving data from physical memory to secondary storage. To minimize subsequent page ins, the kernel attempts to page out the data that is the least likely to be used in the near future.

Sharing and copy-on-write

Multiple pages of virtual memory, even in different virtual address spaces owned by different processes, may map to a single physical page. This allows different virtual address spaces to *share* the data in physical memory. For example, at any given moment there is a good chance that many processes on the system are using the standard C library. With shared memory, each of these processes may map the library into their virtual address space, but only one copy need exist in physical memory. As a more explicit example, two processes may both map into memory a large database. While both of these processes will have the database in their virtual address spaces, it will exist in RAM only once.

The shared data may be read-only, writable, or both readable and writable. When a process writes to a shared writable page, one of two things can happen. The simplest is that the kernel allows the write to occur, in which case all processes sharing the page can see the results of the write operation. Usually, allowing multiple processes to read from or write to a shared page requires some level of coordination and synchronization

---

1. Some systems support multiple page sizes. For this reason, the page size is not part of the ABI. Applications must programmatically obtain the page size at runtime. We covered doing so in Chapter 4 and will review the topic in this chapter.

---

among the processes, but at the kernel level the write "just works" and all processes sharing the data instantly see the modifications.

Alternatively, the MMU can intercept the write operation and raise an exception; the kernel, in response, will transparently create a new copy of the page for the writing process, and allow the write to continue against the new page. We call this approach *copy-on-write* (*COW*).[2] Effectively, processes are allowed read access to shared data, which saves space. But when a process wants to write to a shared page, it receives a unique copy of that page on the fly, thereby allowing the kernel to act as if the process always had its own private copy. As copy-on-write occurs on a page-by-page basis, with this technique a huge file may be efficiently shared among many processes, and the individual processes will receive unique physical pages only for those pages to which they themselves write.

Memory Regions

The kernel arranges pages into blocks that share certain properties, such as access permissions. These blocks are called *mappings*, *memory areas*, or *memory regions*. Certain types of memory regions can be found in every process:

- The *text segment* contains a process's program code, string literals, constant variables, and other read-only data. In Linux, this segment is marked read-only and is mapped in directly from the object file (the program executable or a library).

- The *stack* contains the process's execution stack, which grows and shrinks dynamically as the stack depth increases and decreases. The execution stack contains local variables and function return data. In a multithreaded process, there is one stack per thread.

- The *data segment*, or *heap*, contains a process's dynamic memory. This segment is writable and can grow or shrink in size. `malloc()` (discussed in the next section) can satisfy memory requests from this segment.

- The *bss segment*[3] contains uninitialized global variables. These variables contain special values (essentially, all zeros), per the C standard.

Linux optimizes these variables in two ways. First, because the bss segment is dedicated to uninitialized data, the linker (*ld*) does not actually store the special values in the object file. This reduces the binary's size. Second, when this segment is loaded into memory, the kernel simply maps it on a copy-on-write basis to a page of zeros, efficiently setting the variables to their default values.

---

2. Recall from Chapter 5 that `fork()` uses copy-on-write to duplicate and share the parent's address space with the child.

3. The name is historic; it comes from *block started by symbol*.

Most address spaces contain a handful of *mapped files*, such as the program executable itself, the C and other shared libraries, and data files. Take a look at */proc/self/maps*, or the output from the *pmap* program for an example of the mapped files in a process.

This chapter covers the interfaces that Linux provides to obtain and return memory, create and destroy new mappings, and everything in between.

Allocating Dynamic Memory

Memory also comes in the form of automatic and static variables, but the foundation of any memory management system is the allocation, use, and eventual return of *dynamic memory*. Dynamic memory is allocated at runtime, not compile time, in sizes that may be unknown until the moment of allocation. As a developer, you need dynamic memory when the amount of memory that you will need, or how long you might need it, varies and is not known before the program runs. For example, you might want to store in memory the contents of a file or input read in from the keyboard. Because the size of the file is unknown, and the user may type any number of keystrokes, the size of the buffer will vary, and you may need to make it dynamically larger as you read more and more data.

There is no C variable that is backed by dynamic memory. For example, C does not provide a mechanism to obtain a `struct pirate_ship` that exists in dynamic memory. Instead, C provides a mechanism for allocating dynamic memory sufficient to hold a `pirate_ship` structure. The programmer then interacts with the memory via a pointer—in this case, a `struct pirate_ship*`.

The classic C interface for obtaining dynamic memory is `malloc()`:

```
#include <stdlib.h>

void * malloc (size_t size);
```

A successful call to `malloc()` allocates `size` bytes of memory and returns a pointer to the start of the newly allocated region. The contents of the memory are undefined; do not expect the memory to be zeroed. Upon failure, `malloc()` returns NULL, and `errno` is set to ENOMEM.

Usage of `malloc()` may be rather straightforward, as in this example used to allocate a fixed number of bytes:

```
char *p;

/* give me 2 KB! */
p = malloc (2048);
```

```
    if (!p)
            perror ("malloc");
```

Or this example used to allocate a structure:

```
struct treasure_map *map;

/*
 * allocate enough memory to hold a treasure_map stucture
 * and point 'map' at it
 */
map = malloc (sizeof (struct treasure_map));
if (!map)
        perror ("malloc");
```

C automatically promotes pointers to void to any other pointer type on assignment. Thus, these examples do not need to typecast the return value of malloc() to the lvalue's type used in the assignments. The C++ programming language, however, does not perform automatic void pointer promotion. Consequently, users of C++ need to typecast malloc()'s return as follows:

```
char *name;

/* allocate 512 bytes */
name = (char *) malloc (512);
if (!name)
        perror ("malloc");
```

Some C programmers like to typecast the result of any function that returns a pointer to void, malloc() included. I argue against this practice because it will hide an error if the return value of the function ever changes to something other than a void pointer. Moreover, such a typecast also hides a bug if a function is not properly declared. While the former is not a risk with malloc(), the latter certainly is.

 Undeclared functions default to returning an int. Integer-to-pointer casts are not automatic and generate a warning. The typecast will suppress the resulting warning.

Because malloc() can return NULL, it is vitally important that developers *always* check for and handle error conditions. Many programs define and use a malloc() wrapper that prints an error message and terminates the program if malloc() returns NULL. By convention, developers call this common wrapper xmalloc():

```
/* like malloc(), but terminates on failure */
void * xmalloc (size_t size)
{
        void *p;
```

```
        p = malloc (size);
        if (!p) {
                perror ("xmalloc");
                exit (EXIT_FAILURE);
        }

        return p;
}
```

Allocating Arrays

Dynamic memory allocation may also be quite complex when the specified size is itself dynamic. One such example is the dynamic allocation of arrays, where the size of an array element may be fixed but the number of elements to allocate is dynamic. To simplify this scenario, C provides the calloc() function:

```
#include <stdlib.h>

void * calloc (size_t nr, size_t size);
```

A successful call to calloc() returns a pointer to a block of memory suitable for holding an array of nr elements, each of size bytes. Consequently, the amount of memory requested in these two calls is identical (either may end up returning more memory than requested, but never less):

```
int *x, *y;

x = malloc (50 * sizeof (int));
if (!x) {
        perror ("malloc");
        return -1;
}

y = calloc (50, sizeof (int));
if (!y) {
        perror ("calloc");
        return -1;
}
```

The behavior, however, is not identical. Unlike malloc(), which makes no such guarantees about the contents of allocated memory, calloc() zeros all bytes in the returned chunk of memory. Thus, each of the 50 elements in the array of integers y holds the value of 0, while the contents of the elements in x are undefined. Unless the program is going to immediately set all 50 values, programmers should use calloc() to ensure that the array elements are not filled with gibberish. Note that binary zero might not be the same as floating-point zero!

On the Etymology of calloc()

There remains no original documentation on the etymology of cal
loc(). Unix historians debate the origin: Does the *c* stand for *count*,
since the function accepts a count of array elements? Or perhaps it
stands for *clear*, since the function zeros out memory? Take your pick.
The debate is fierce.

In pursuit of the truth, I asked Brian Kernighan, the *K* in *K&R* and early
Unix contributor, for his recollection. Brian cautioned that he didn't
write the original function but that he believes the "*c* is for *clear*." That
is likely as authoritative a view as we will get.

Users often want to "zero out" dynamic memory, even when not dealing with arrays.
Later in this chapter, we will consider memset(), which provides an interface for setting
every byte in a chunk of memory to a given value. Letting calloc() perform the zeroing,
however, is faster because the kernel can provide memory that is already zeroed.

On failure, like malloc(), calloc() returns NULL and sets errno to ENOMEM.

Why the standards bodies never defined an "allocate and zero" function separate from
calloc() is a mystery. Developers can easily define their own interface, however:

```
/* works identically to malloc(), but memory is zeroed */
void * malloc0 (size_t size)
{
        return calloc (1, size);
}
```

Conveniently, we can combine this malloc0() with our previous xmalloc():

```
/* like malloc(), but zeros memory and terminates on failure */
void * xmalloc0 (size_t size)
{
        void *p;

        p = calloc (1, size);
        if (!p) {
                perror ("xmalloc0");
                exit (EXIT_FAILURE);
        }

        return p;
}
```

Resizing Allocations

The C language provides an interface for resizing (making larger or smaller) existing
allocations:

```
#include <stdlib.h>

void * realloc (void *ptr, size_t size);
```

A successful call to realloc() resizes the region of memory pointed at by ptr to a new size of size bytes. It returns a pointer to the newly sized memory, which may or may not be the same as ptr. When enlarging a memory region, if realloc() is unable to enlarge the existing chunk of memory by growing the chunk *in situ*, the function may allocate a new region of memory size bytes in length, copy the old region into the new one, and free the old region. On any operation, the contents of the memory region are preserved up to the minimum of the old and the new sizes. Because of the potentiality of a copy, a realloc() operation to enlarge a memory region can be a relatively costly operation.

If size is 0, the effect is the same as an invocation of free() on ptr.

If ptr is NULL, the result of the operation is the same as a fresh malloc(). If ptr is non-NULL, it must have been returned via a previous call to malloc(), calloc(), or realloc().

On failure, realloc() returns NULL and sets errno to ENOMEM. The state of the memory pointed at by ptr is unchanged.

Let's consider an example of shrinking a memory region. First, we'll use calloc() to allocate enough memory to hold a two-element array of map structures:

```
struct map *p;

/* allocate memory for two map structures */
p = calloc (2, sizeof (struct map));
if (!p) {
        perror ("calloc");
        return -1;
}

/* use p[0] and p[1]... */
```

Now, let's assume we've found one of the treasures and no longer need the second map, so we decide to resize the memory and give half of the region back to the system. This wouldn't generally be a worthwhile operation, but it might be if the map structure were very large and we were going to hold the remaining map for a long time:

```
struct map *r;

/* we now need memory for only one map */
r = realloc (p, sizeof (struct map));
if (!r) {
        /* note that 'p' is still valid! */
        perror ("realloc");
        return -1;
```

```
}

/* use 'r'... */

free (r);
```

In this example, `p[0]` is preserved after the `realloc()` call. Whatever data was there before is still there. If the call returned failure, p is untouched and thus still valid. We can continue using it, and will eventually need to free it. Conversely, if the call succeeded, we ignore p, and in lieu use r. We now have the responsibility to free r when we're done.

Freeing Dynamic Memory

Unlike automatic allocations, which are automatically reaped when the stack unwinds, dynamic allocations are permanent parts of the process's address space until they are manually freed. The programmer thus bears the responsibility of returning dynamically allocated memory to the system. (Both static and dynamic allocations, of course, disappear when the entire process exits.)

Memory allocated with `malloc()`, `calloc()`, or `realloc()` must be returned to the system when no longer in use via `free()`:

```
#include <stdlib.h>

void free (void *ptr);
```

A call to `free()` frees the memory at `ptr`. The parameter `ptr` must have been previously returned by `malloc()`, `calloc()`, or `realloc()`. That is, you cannot use `free()` to free partial chunks of memory—say, half of a chunk of memory—by passing in a pointer halfway into an allocated block. Doing so will result in undefined memory, likely manifested as a crash.

`ptr` may be `NULL`, in which case `free()` silently returns. Thus, the oft-seen practice of checking `ptr` for `NULL` before calling `free()` is redundant.

Let's look at an example:

```
void print_chars (int n, char c)
{
        int i;

        for (i = 0; i < n; i++) {
                char *s;
                int j;

                /*
                 * Allocate and zero an i+2 element array
                 * of chars. Note that 'sizeof (char)'
                 * is always 1.
                 */
```

```
                s = calloc (i + 2, 1);
                if (!s) {
                        perror ("calloc");
                        break;
                }

                for (j = 0; j < i + 1; j++)
                        s[j] = c;

                printf ("%s\n", s);

                /* Okay, all done. Hand back the memory. */
                free (s);
        }
}
```

This example allocates n arrays of chars containing successively larger numbers of elements, ranging from two elements (2 bytes) up to n + 1 elements (n + 1 bytes). Then,
for each array, the loop writes the character c into each byte except the last (leaving the
0 that is already in the last byte), prints the array as a string, and then frees the dynamically allocated memory.

Invoking print_chars() with n equal to 5 and c set to X, we get the following:

```
X
XX
XXX
XXXX
XXXXX
```

There are, of course, significantly more efficient ways of implementing this function.
The point, however, is that we can dynamically allocate and free memory even when
the size and the number of said allocations are known only at runtime.

Unix systems such as SunOS and SCO provide a variant of free()
named cfree(), which, depending on the system, behaves the same as
free() or receives three parameters, mirroring calloc(). In Linux,
free() can handle memory obtained from any of the allocation mechanisms we have discussed thus far. cfree() should never be used, except
for backward compatibility. The Linux version is the same as free().

Note what the repercussions would be if this example did not invoke free(). The program would never return the memory to the system, and, even worse, it would lose its
only reference to the memory—the pointer s—thereby making it impossible to ever
access the memory. We call this type of programming error a *memory leak*. Memory
leaks and similar dynamic memory mistakes are among the most common, and, unfortunately, the most detrimental mishaps in C programming. Because the C language

places full responsibility for managing memory on the programmer, C programmers must keep a fastidious eye on all memory allocations.

Another common C programming pitfall is *use-after-free*. This foible occurs when a block of memory is freed and then subsequently accessed. Once `free()` is called on a block of memory, a program must never again access its contents. Programmers must be particularly careful to watch for *dangling pointers*: non-`NULL` pointers that nevertheless point at invalid blocks of memory. An excellent tool to detect memory errors in your programs is *Valgrind* (*http://valgrind.org*).

Alignment

Data alignment refers to the way data is arranged in memory. A memory address A is said to be n-byte aligned when n is a power-of-2 and A is a multiple of n. Processors, memory subsystems, and other components in a system have specific alignment requirements. For example, most processors operate on words and can only access memory addresses that are word-size-aligned. Similarly, as discussed, memory management units deal only in page-size-aligned addresses.

A variable located at a memory address that is a multiple of its size is said to be *naturally aligned*. For example, a 32-bit variable is naturally aligned if it is located in memory at an address that is a multiple of 4—in other words, if the address's lowest two bits are 0. Thus, a type that is *2n* bytes in size must have an address with the *n* least-significant bits set to 0.

Rules pertaining to alignment derive from hardware and thus differ from system to system. Some machine architectures have very stringent requirements on the alignment of data. Others are more lenient. Some systems generate a catchable error. The kernel can then choose to terminate the offending process or (more likely) manually perform the unaligned access (generally through multiple aligned accesses). This incurs a performance hit and sacrifices atomicity, but at least the process isn't terminated. When writing portable code, programmers must be careful to avoid violating alignment requirements.

Allocating aligned memory

For the most part, the compiler and the C library transparently handle alignment concerns. POSIX decrees that the memory returned via `malloc()`, `calloc()`, and `real loc()` be properly aligned for use with any of the standard C types. On Linux, these functions always return memory that is aligned along an 8-byte boundary on 32-bit systems and along a 16-byte boundary on 64-bit systems.

Occasionally, programmers require dynamic memory aligned along a larger boundary, such as a page. While motivations vary, the most common is a need to properly align buffers used in direct block I/O or other software-to-hardware communication. For this purpose, POSIX 1003.1d provides a function named posix_memalign():

```
/* one or the other -- either suffices */
#define _XOPEN_SOURCE 600
#define _GNU_SOURCE

#include <stdlib.h>

int posix_memalign (void **memptr,
                    size_t alignment,
                    size_t size);
```

A successful call to posix_memalign() allocates size bytes of dynamic memory, ensuring it is aligned along a memory address that is a multiple of alignment. The parameter alignment must be a power of 2 and a multiple of the size of a void pointer. The address of the allocated memory is placed in memptr, and the call returns 0.

On failure, no memory is allocated, memptr is undefined, and the call returns one of the following error codes:

EINVAL
> The parameter alignment is not a power of 2 or is not a multiple of the size of a void pointer.

ENOMEM
> There is insufficient memory available to satisfy the requested allocation.

Note that errno is not set; the function directly returns these errors.

Memory obtained via posix_memalign() is freed via free(). Usage is simple:

```
char *buf;
int ret;

/* allocate 1 KB along a 256-byte boundary */
ret = posix_memalign (&buf, 256, 1024);
if (ret) {
        fprintf (stderr, "posix_memalign: %s\n",
                strerror (ret));
        return -1;
}

/* use 'buf'... */

free (buf);
```

Before POSIX defined posix_memalign(), BSD and SunOS provided the following interfaces, respectively:

```
#include <malloc.h>
```

```
void * valloc (size_t size);
void * memalign (size_t boundary, size_t size);
```

The function valloc() operates identically to malloc(), except that the allocated memory is aligned along a page boundary. Recall from Chapter 4 that the system's page size is easily obtained via getpagesize().

The function memalign() is similar to posix_memalign. It aligns the allocation along a boundary of boundary bytes, which must be a power of 2. In this example, both of these allocations return a block of memory sufficient to hold a ship structure, aligned along a page boundary:

```
struct ship *pirate, *hms;

pirate = valloc (sizeof (struct ship));
if (!pirate) {
        perror ("valloc");
        return -1;
}

hms = memalign (getpagesize (), sizeof (struct ship));
if (!hms) {
        perror ("memalign");
        free (pirate);
        return -1;
}

/* use 'pirate' and 'hms'... */

free (hms);
free (pirate);
```

On Linux, memory obtained via both of these functions is freeable via free(). This may not be the case on other Unix systems, some of which provide no mechanism for safely freeing memory allocated with these functions. Programs concerned with portability may have no choice but to not free memory allocated via these interfaces!

Linux programmers should use these two functions only for the purposes of portability with older systems; posix_memalign() is superior and standardized. All three of these interfaces are needed only if an alignment greater than that provided by malloc() is required.

Other alignment concerns

Alignment concerns extend beyond natural alignment of the standard types and dynamic memory allocations. For example, nonstandard and complex types have more complex requirements than the standard types. Further, alignment concerns are doubly important when assigning values between pointers of varying types and using typecasting.

Nonstandard and complex data types possess alignment requirements beyond the simple requirement of natural alignment. Four useful rules follow:

- The alignment requirement of a structure is that of its largest constituent type. For example, if a structure's largest type is a 32-bit integer that is aligned along a 4-byte boundary, the structure must be aligned along at least a 4-byte boundary as well.

- Structures also introduce the need for padding, which is used to ensure that each constituent type is properly aligned to that type's own requirement. Thus, if a char (with a probable alignment of 1 byte) finds itself followed by an int (with a probable alignment of 4 bytes), the compiler will insert 3 bytes of padding between the two types to ensure that the int lives on a 4-byte boundary. Programmers sometimes order the members of a structure—for example, by descending size—to minimize the space "wasted" by padding. The gcc option -Wpadded can aid in this endeavor, as it generates a warning whenever the compiler inserts implicit padding.

- The alignment requirement of a union is that of the largest unionized type.

- The alignment requirement of an array is that of the base type. Thus, arrays carry no requirement beyond a single instance of their type. This behavior results in the natural alignment of all members of an array.

As the compiler transparently handles most alignment requirements, it takes a bit of effort to expose potential issues. It is not unheard of, however, to encounter alignment concerns when dealing with pointers and casting.

Accessing data via a pointer recast from a lesser-aligned to a larger-aligned block of data can result in the processor loading data that is not properly aligned for the larger type. For example, in the following code snippet, the assignment of c to badnews attempts to read c as an unsigned long:

```
char greeting[] = "Ahoy Matey";
char *c = greeting[1];
unsigned long badnews = *(unsigned long *) c;
```

An unsigned long is naturally aligned along a 4- or 8-byte boundary; c is likely not aligned to that same boundary. Consequently, the load of c, when typecast, causes an alignment violation. Depending on the architecture, this can cause results ranging from as minor as a performance hit to as major as a program crash. On machine architectures that can detect but not properly handle alignment violations, the kernel sends the offending process the SIGBUS signal, which terminates the process. We will discuss signals in Chapter 10.

Examples such as this are more common than one might think. Real-world examples will not be quite so silly in appearance, but they will likely be less obvious as well.

Strict Aliasing

This typecasting example also violates strict aliasing, one of the least-understood aspects of C and C++. *Strict aliasing* is the requirement that an object is only accessed through the actual type of that object, a qualified (e.g., `const` or `volatile`) version of the actual type, a signed (or unsigned) version of the actual type, a `struct` or `union` that contains the actual type among its members, or a `char` pointer. For example, the common pattern of accessing a `uint32_t` through two `uint16_t` pointers violates strict aliasing.

Here's a succinct summary: *dereferencing a cast of a pointer from one type of variable to a different type is usually a violation of the strict aliasing rule.* If you have ever seen the *gcc* warning, "dereferencing type-punned pointer will break strict-aliasing rules," you have violated the rule. Strict aliasing has been part of C++ for a long time, but it was standardized in C only with C99. gcc, as the warning attests, enforces strict aliasing; doing so allows it to generate more optimal code.

For the curious, the actual rules are laid out in section 6.5 of the ISO C99 standard.

Managing the Data Segment

Unix systems historically have provided interfaces for directly managing the data segment. However, most programs have no direct use for these interfaces because `malloc()` and other allocation schemes are easier to use and more powerful. I'll cover these interfaces here to satisfy the curious and for the rare reader who wants to implement her own heap-based allocation mechanism:

```
#include <unistd.h>

int brk (void *end);
void * sbrk (intptr_t increment);
```

These functions derive their names from old-school Unix systems, where the heap and the stack lived in the same segment. Dynamic memory allocations in the heap grew upward from the bottom of the segment; the stack grew downward toward the heap from the top of the segment. The line of demarcation separating the two was called the *break* or the *break point*. On modern systems where the data segment lives in its own memory mapping, we continue to label the end address of the mapping the break point.

A call to `brk()` sets the break point (the end of the data segment) to the address specified by `end`. On success, it returns 0. On failure, it returns −1 and sets `errno` to `ENOMEM`.

A call to `sbrk()` increments the end of the data segment by `increment` bytes, which may be a positive or negative delta. `sbrk()` returns the revised break point. Thus, an `increment` of 0 provides the current break point:

```
printf ("The current break point is %p\n", sbrk (0));
```

Deliberately, both POSIX and the C standard define neither of these functions. Nearly all Unix systems, however, support one or both. Portable programs should stick to the standards-based interfaces.

Anonymous Memory Mappings

Memory allocation in *glibc* uses a combination of the data segment and memory mappings. The classic method of implementing `malloc()` is to divide the data segment into a series of power-of-2 partitions and satisfy allocations by returning the partition that is the closest fit to the requested size. Freeing memory is as simple as marking the partition as "free." If adjacent partitions are free, they can be coalesced into a single, larger partition. If the top of the heap is entirely free, the system can use `brk()` to lower the break point, shrinking the heap and returning memory to the kernel.

This algorithm is called a *buddy memory allocation scheme.* It has the upside of speed and simplicity but the downside of introducing two types of fragmentation. *Internal fragmentation* occurs when more memory than requested is used to satisfy an allocation. This results in inefficient use of the available memory. *External fragmentation* occurs when sufficient memory is free to satisfy a request, but it is split into two or more nonadjacent chunks. This can result in inefficient use of memory (because a larger, less suitable block may be used), or failed memory allocations (if no alternative block exists).

Moreover, this scheme allows one memory allocation to "pin" another, preventing a traditional C library from returning freed memory to the kernel. Imagine that two blocks of memory, block *A* and block *B*, are allocated. Block *A* sits right on the break point, and block *B* sits right below *A*. Even if the program frees *B*, the C library cannot adjust the break point until *A* is likewise freed. In this manner, a long-living allocation can pin all other allocations in memory.

This is not always a concern as C libraries do not strictly return memory to the system. Generally, the heap is not shrunk after each free. Instead, the `malloc()` implementation keeps freed memory around for a subsequent allocation. Only when the size of the heap is significantly larger than the amount of allocated memory does `malloc()` shrink the data segment. A large allocation, however, can prevent this shrinkage.

Consequently, for large allocations, *glibc* does not use the heap. Instead, *glibc* creates an *anonymous memory mapping* to satisfy the allocation request. Anonymous memory mappings are similar to the file-based mappings discussed in Chapter 4, except that they are not backed by any file—hence the "anonymous" moniker. Instead, an anonymous memory mapping is simply a large, zero-filled block of memory, ready for your use. Think of it as a brand new heap, solely for a single allocation. Because these mappings are located outside of the heap, they do not contribute to the data segment's fragmentation.

Allocating memory via anonymous mappings has several benefits:

- No fragmentation concerns. When the program no longer needs an anonymous memory mapping, the mapping is unmapped, and the memory is immediately returned to the system.

- Anonymous memory mappings are resizable, have adjustable permissions, and can receive advice just like normal mappings (see Chapter 4).

- Each allocation exists in a separate memory mapping. There is no need to manage the global heap.

There are also two downsides to using anonymous memory mappings rather than the heap:

- Each memory mapping is an integer multiple of the system page size in size. Ergo, allocations that are not integer multiples of pages in size result in wasted "slack" space. This slack space is more of a concern with small allocations, where the wasted space is large relative to the allocation size.

- Creating a new memory mapping incurs more overhead than satisfying allocations from the heap, which may not involve any kernel interaction whatsoever. The smaller the allocation, the more this overhead is detrimental.

Juggling the pros against the cons, *glibc*'s `malloc()` uses the data segment to satisfy small allocations and anonymous memory mappings to satisfy large allocations. The threshold is configurable (see "Advanced Memory Allocation" on page 312), and may change from one *glibc* release to another. Currently, the threshold is 128 KB: allocations smaller than or equal to 128 KB derive from the heap, whereas larger allocations derive from anonymous memory mappings.

Creating Anonymous Memory Mappings

Perhaps because you want to force the use of a memory mapping over the heap for a specific allocation, or perhaps because you are writing your own memory allocation system, you may want to manually create your own anonymous memory mapping—either way, Linux makes it easy. Recall from Chapter 4 that the system call `mmap()` creates a memory mapping and the system call `munmap()` destroys a mapping:

```
#include <sys/mman.h>

void * mmap (void *start,
```

```
                size_t length,
                int prot,
                int flags,
                int fd,
                off_t offset);

    int munmap (void *start, size_t length);
```

Creating an anonymous memory mapping is actually easier than creating a file-backed mapping, as there is no file to open and manage. The primary difference is the presence of a special flag, signifying that the mapping is anonymous.

Let's look at an example:

```
    void *p;

    p = mmap (NULL,                        /* do not care where */
            512 * 1024,                    /* 512 KB */
            PROT_READ | PROT_WRITE,        /* read/write */
            MAP_ANONYMOUS | MAP_PRIVATE,   /* anonymous, private */
            -1,                            /* fd (ignored) */
            0);                            /* offset (ignored) */

    if (p == MAP_FAILED)
            perror ("mmap");
    else
            /* 'p' points at 512 KB of anonymous memory... */
```

For most anonymous mappings, the parameters to mmap() mirror this example, with the exception, of course, of passing in whatever size (in bytes) the programmer desires. The other parameters are generally as follows:

- The first parameter, start, is set to NULL, signifying that the anonymous mapping may begin anywhere in memory that the kernel wishes. Specifying a non-NULL value here is possible, so long as it is page-aligned, but limits portability. Rarely does a program care where mappings exist in memory.

- The prot parameter usually sets both the PROT_READ and PROT_WRITE bits, making the mapping readable and writable. An empty mapping is of no use if you cannot read from and write to it. On the other hand, executing code from an anonymous mapping is rarely desired, and allowing execution opens up an attack vector.

- The flags parameter sets the MAP_ANONYMOUS bit, making this mapping anonymous, and the MAP_PRIVATE bit, making this mapping private.

- The fd and offset parameters are ignored when MAP_ANONYMOUS is set. Some older systems, however, expect a value of -1 for fd, so it is a good idea to pass that if portability is a concern.

Memory obtained via an anonymous mapping looks the same as memory obtained via the heap. One benefit to allocating from anonymous mappings is that the pages are already filled with zeros. This occurs at no cost, because the kernel maps the application's anonymous pages to a zero-filled page via copy-on-write. Thus, there is no need to memset() the returned memory. Indeed, this is one benefit to using calloc() as opposed to malloc() followed by memset(): *glibc* knows that anonymous mappings are already zeroed, and that a calloc() satisfied from a mapping does not require explicit zeroing.

The system call munmap() frees an anonymous mapping, returning the allocated memory to the kernel:

```
int ret;

/* all done with 'p', so give back the 512 KB mapping */
ret = munmap (p, 512 * 1024);
if (ret)
        perror ("munmap");
```

 For a review of mmap(), munmap(), and mappings in general, see Chapter 4.

Mapping /dev/zero

Other Unix systems, such as BSD, do not have a MAP_ANONYMOUS flag. Instead, they implement a similar solution by mapping a special device file, */dev/zero*. This device file provides identical semantics to anonymous memory. A mapping contains copy-on-write pages of all zeros; the behavior is thus the same as with anonymous memory.

Linux has always provided a */dev/zero* device and the ability to map it and obtain zero-filled memory. Indeed, before the introduction of MAP_ANONYMOUS, Linux programmers used this BSD-style approach. To provide backward compatibility with older versions of Linux, or portability to other Unix systems, developers can still map */dev/zero* in lieu of creating an anonymous mapping. The syntax is no different from mapping any other file:

```
void *p;
int fd;

/* open /dev/zero for reading and writing */
fd = open ("/dev/zero", O_RDWR);
if (fd < 0) {
        perror ("open");
        return -1;
}

/* map [0,page size) of /dev/zero */
```

```
p = mmap (NULL,                           /* do not care where */
          getpagesize (),                 /* map one page */
          PROT_READ | PROT_WRITE,         /* map read/write */
          MAP_PRIVATE,                    /* private mapping */
          fd,                             /* map /dev/zero */
          0);                             /* no offset */

if (p == MAP_FAILED) {
        perror ("mmap");
        if (close (fd))
                perror ("close");
        return -1;
}

/* close /dev/zero, no longer needed */
if (close (fd))
        perror ("close");

/* 'p' points at one page of memory, use it... */
```

Memory mapped in this manner is, of course, unmapped using `munmap()`.

This approach involves the additional system call overhead of opening and closing the device file. Thus, anonymous memory is a faster solution.

Advanced Memory Allocation

Many of the allocation operations discussed in this chapter are limited and controlled by *glibc* or kernel parameters that the programmer can change. To do so, use the `mallopt()` call:

```
#include <malloc.h>

int mallopt (int param, int value);
```

A call to `mallopt()` sets the memory-management-related parameter specified by par am to the value specified by `value`. On success, the call returns a nonzero value; on failure, it returns 0. Note that `mallopt()` does not set `errno`. It also tends to always return success, so avoid any optimism over receiving useful information from the return value.

Linux currently supports seven values for `param`, all defined in <malloc.h>:

M_CHECK_ACTION
> The value of the `MALLOC_CHECK_` environment variable (discussed in the next section).

M_MMAP_MAX
> The maximum number of mappings that the system will create to satisfy dynamic memory requests. When this limit is reached, the data segment will be used for all

allocations until one of the previously created mappings is freed. A value of 0 disables all use of anonymous mappings as a basis for dynamic memory allocations.

M_MMAP_THRESHOLD

The threshold (measured in bytes) over which an allocation request will be satisfied via an anonymous mapping instead of the data segment. Note that allocations smaller than this threshold may also be satisfied via anonymous mappings at the system's discretion. A value of 0 enables the use of anonymous mappings for all allocations, effectively disabling use of the data segment for dynamic memory allocations.

M_MXFAST

The maximum size (in bytes) of a fast bin. *Fast bins* are special chunks of memory in the heap that are never coalesced with adjacent chunks and never returned to the system, allowing for very quick allocations at the cost of increased fragmentation. A value of 0 disables all use of fast bins.

M_PERTURB

Enables memory poisoning, which aids in the detection of memory management errors. If provided a nonzero `value`, *glibc* sets all allocated bytes (except those requested via `calloc()`) to the logical compliment of the least-significant byte in `value`. This helps detect use-before-initialized errors. Moreover, *glibc* also sets all freed bytes to the least-significant byte in `value`. This helps detect use-after-free errors.

M_TOP_PAD

The amount of padding (in bytes) used when adjusting the size of the data segment. Whenever *glibc* uses `brk()` to increase the size of the data segment, it can ask for more memory than needed in the hopes of alleviating the need for an additional `brk()` call in the near future. Likewise, whenever *glibc* shrinks the size of the data segment, it can keep extra memory, giving back a little less than it would otherwise. These extra bytes are the *padding*. A value of 0 disables all use of padding.

M_TRIM_THRESHOLD

The minimum amount of free memory (in bytes) at the top of the data segment before *glibc* invokes `sbrk()` to return memory to the kernel.

The XPG standard, which loosely defines `mallopt()`, specifies three other parameters: `M_GRAIN`, `M_KEEP`, and `M_NLBLKS`. Linux defines these parameters, but setting their value has no effect. See Table 9-1 for a full listing of all valid parameters, their default values, and their ranges of accepted values.

Table 9-1. mallopt() parameters

Parameter	Origin	Default value	Valid values	Special values
M_CHECK_ACTION	Linux-specific	0	0 – 2	
M_GRAIN	XPG standard	Unsupported on Linux		
M_KEEP	XPG standard	Unsupported on Linux		
M_MMAP_MAX	Linux-specific	64 * 1024	>= 0	0 disables use of mmap()
M_MMAP_THRESHOLD	Linux-specific	128 * 1024	>= 0	0 disables use of the heap
M_MXFAST	XPG standard	64	0 - 80	0 disables fast bins
M_NLBLKS	XPG standard	Unsupported on Linux		
M_PERTURB	Linux-specific	0	0 or 1	0 disables perturbation
M_TOP_PAD	Linux-specific	0	>= 0	0 disables top padding
M_TRIM_THRESHOLD	Linux-specific	128 * 1024	>= -1	-1 disables trimming

Programs must make any invocations of mallopt() before their first call to malloc() or any other memory allocation interface. Usage is simple:

```
int ret;

/* use mmap() for all allocations over 64 KB */
ret = mallopt (M_MMAP_THRESHOLD, 64 * 1024);
if (!ret)
        fprintf (stderr, "mallopt failed!\n");
```

Fine-Tuning with malloc_usable_size() and malloc_trim()

Linux provides a couple of functions that offer low-level control of *glibc*'s memory allocation system. The first such function allows a program to ask how many usable bytes a given memory allocation contains:

```
#include <malloc.h>

size_t malloc_usable_size (void *ptr);
```

A successful call to malloc_usable_size() returns the actual allocation size of the chunk of memory pointed to by ptr. Because *glibc* may round up allocations to fit within an existing chunk or anonymous mapping, the usable space in an allocation can be larger than requested. Of course, the allocation will never be smaller than requested. Here's an example of the function's use:

```
size_t len = 21;
size_t size;
char *buf;

buf = malloc (len);
if (!buf) {
        perror ("malloc");
```

```
        return -1;
}

size = malloc_usable_size (buf);

/* we can actually use 'size' bytes of 'buf' ... */
```

The second of the two functions allows a program to force *glibc* to return all immediately freeable memory to the kernel:

```
#include <malloc.h>

int malloc_trim (size_t padding);
```

A successful call to `malloc_trim()` shrinks the data segment as much as possible, minus `padding` bytes, which are reserved. It then returns 1. On failure, the call returns 0. Normally, *glibc* performs such shrinking automatically whenever the freeable memory reaches `M_TRIM_THRESHOLD` bytes. It uses a padding of `M_TOP_PAD`.

You'll almost never want to use these two functions for anything other than debugging or educational purposes. They are not portable and expose low-level details of *glibc*'s memory allocation system to your program.

Debugging Memory Allocations

Programs can set the environment variable `MALLOC_CHECK_` to enable enhanced debugging in the memory subsystem. The additional debugging checks come at the expense of less efficient memory allocations, but the overhead is often worth it during the debugging stage of application development.

Because an environment variable controls the debugging, there is no need to recompile your program. For example, you can simply issue a command like the following:

```
$ MALLOC_CHECK_=1 ./rudder
```

If `MALLOC_CHECK_` is set to 0, the memory subsystem silently ignores any errors. If it is set to 1, an informative message is printed to `stderr`. If it is set to 2, the program is immediately terminated via `abort()`. Because `MALLOC_CHECK_` changes the behavior of the running program, setuid programs ignore this variable.

Obtaining Statistics

Linux provides the `mallinfo()` function for obtaining statistics related to the memory allocation system:

```
#include <malloc.h>

struct mallinfo mallinfo (void);
```

A call to `mallinfo()` returns statistics in a `mallinfo` structure. The structure is returned by value, not via a pointer. Its contents are also defined in `<malloc.h>`:

```
/* all sizes in bytes */

struct mallinfo {
        int arena;    /* size of data segment used by malloc */
        int ordblks;  /* number of free chunks */
        int smblks;   /* number of fast bins */
        int hblks;    /* number of anonymous mappings */
        int hblkhd;   /* size of anonymous mappings */
        int usmblks;  /* maximum total allocated size */
        int fsmblks;  /* size of available fast bins */
        int uordblks; /* size of total allocated space */
        int fordblks; /* size of available chunks */
        int keepcost; /* size of trimmable space */
};
```

Usage is simple:

```
struct mallinfo m;

m = mallinfo ();

printf ("free chunks: %d\n", m.ordblks);
```

Linux also provides the `malloc_stats()` function, which prints memory-related statistics to `stderr`:

```
#include <malloc.h>

void malloc_stats (void);
```

Invoking `malloc_stats()` in a memory-intensive program yields some big numbers:

```
Arena 0:
system bytes     =  865939456
in use bytes     =  851988200
Total (incl. mmap):
system bytes     = 3216519168
in use bytes     = 3202567912
max mmap regions =      65536
max mmap bytes   = 2350579712
```

Stack-Based Allocations

Thus far, ball of the mechanisms for dynamic memory allocation that we have studied have used the heap or memory mappings to obtain dynamic memory. We should expect this because the heap and memory mappings are decidedly dynamic in nature. The other common construct in a program's address space, the stack, is where a program's *automatic variables* live.

There is no reason, however, that a programmer cannot use the stack for dynamic memory allocations. So long as the allocation does not overflow the stack, such an approach should be easy and should perform quite well. To make a dynamic memory allocation from the stack, use the `alloca()` system call:

```
#include <alloca.h>

void * alloca (size_t size);
```

On success, a call to `alloca()` returns a pointer to size bytes of memory. This memory lives on the stack and is automatically freed when the invoking function returns. Some implementations return NULL on failure, but most `alloca()` implementations cannot fail or are unable to report failure. Failure is manifested as a stack overflow.

Usage is identical to `malloc()`, but you do not need to (indeed, must not) free the allocated memory. Here is an example of a function that opens a given file in the system's configuration directory, which is probably */etc*, but is portably determined at compile time. The function has to allocate a new buffer, copy the system configuration directory into the buffer, and then concatenate this buffer with the provided filename:

```
int open_sysconf (const char *file, int flags, int mode)
{
        const char *etc = SYSCONF_DIR; /* "/etc/" */
        char *name;

        name = alloca (strlen (etc) + strlen (file) + 1);
        strcpy (name, etc);
        strcat (name, file);

        return open (name, flags, mode);
}
```

Upon return, the memory allocated with `alloca()` is automatically freed as the stack unwinds back to the invoking function. This means you cannot use this memory once the function that calls `alloca()` returns! However, because you don't have to do any cleanup by calling `free()`, the resulting code is a bit cleaner. Here is the same function implemented using `malloc()`:

```
int open_sysconf (const char *file, int flags, int mode)
{
        const char *etc = SYSCONF_DIR; /* "/etc/" */
        char *name;
        int fd;

        name = malloc (strlen (etc) + strlen (file) + 1);
        if (!name) {
                perror ("malloc");
                return -1;
        }
```

```
        strcpy (name, etc);
        strcat (name, file);
        fd = open (name, flags, mode);
        free (name);

        return fd;
    }
```

Note that you should not use `alloca()`-allocated memory in the parameters to a function call because the allocated memory will then exist in the middle of the stack space reserved for the function parameters. For example, the following is off-limits:

```
/* DO NOT DO THIS! */
ret = foo (x, alloca (10));
```

The `alloca()` interface has a checkered history. On many systems, it behaved poorly or gave way to undefined behavior. On systems with a small and fixed-sized stack, using `alloca()` was an easy way to overflow the stack and kill your program. On still other systems, `alloca()` did not even exist. Over time, the buggy and inconsistent implementations earned `alloca()` a bad reputation.

So, if your program must remain portable, you should avoid `alloca()`. On Linux, however, `alloca()` is a wonderfully useful and underutilized tool. It performs exceptionally well—on many architectures, an allocation via `alloca()` does as little as increment the stack pointer—and handily outperforms `malloc()`. For small allocations in Linux-specific code, `alloca()` can yield excellent performance gains.

Duplicating Strings on the Stack

A very common use of `alloca()` is to temporarily duplicate a string. For example:

```
/* we want to duplicate 'song' */
char *dup;

dup = alloca (strlen (song) + 1);
strcpy (dup, song);

/* manipulate 'dup'... */

return; /* 'dup' is automatically freed */
```

Because of the frequency of this need and the speed benefit that `alloca()` offers, Linux systems provide variants of `strdup()` that duplicate the given string onto the stack:

```
#define _GNU_SOURCE
#include <string.h>

char * strdupa (const char *s);
char * strndupa (const char *s, size_t n);
```

A call to strdupa() returns a duplicate of s. A call to strndupa() duplicates up to n characters of s. If s is longer than n, the duplication stops at n, and the function appends a null byte. These functions offer the same benefits as alloca(). The duplicated string is automatically freed when the invoking function returns.

POSIX does not define the alloca(), strdupa(), or strndupa() functions, and their record on other operating systems is spotty. If portability is a concern, use of these functions is highly discouraged. On Linux, however, alloca() and friends perform quite well and can provide an excellent performance boost, replacing the complicated dance of dynamic memory allocation with a mere adjustment of the stack frame pointer.

Variable-Length Arrays

C99 introduced *variable-length arrays* (VLAs), which are arrays whose geometry is set at runtime, not at compile time. GNU C has supported variable-length arrays for some time, but now that C99 has standardized them, there is greater incentive for their use. VLAs avoid the overhead of dynamic memory allocation in much the same way as alloca().

Their use is exactly what you would expect:

```
for (i = 0; i < n; ++i) {
        char foo[i + 1];

        /* use 'foo'... */
}
```

In this snippet, foo is an array of chars of variable size i + 1. On each iteration of the loop, foo is dynamically created and automatically cleaned up when it falls out of scope. If we used alloca() instead of a VLA, the memory would not be freed until the function returned. Using a VLA ensures that the memory is freed on every iteration of the loop. Thus, using a VLA consumes at worst n bytes, whereas alloca() would consume n * (n+1) / 2 bytes.

Using a variable-length array, we can rewrite our open_sysconf() function as follows:

```
int open_sysconf (const char *file, int flags, int mode)
{
        const char *etc; = SYSCONF_DIR; /* "/etc/" */
        char name[strlen (etc) + strlen (file) + 1];

        strcpy (name, etc);
        strcat (name, file);

        return open (name, flags, mode);
}
```

The main difference between `alloca()` and variable-length arrays is that memory obtained via the former exists for the duration of the function, whereas memory obtained via the latter exists until the holding variable falls out of scope, which can be before the current function returns. This could be welcome or unwelcome. In the `for` loop we just looked at, reclaiming the memory on each loop iteration reduces net memory consumption without any side effect (we did not need the extra memory hanging around). However, if for some reason we wanted the memory to persist longer than a single loop iteration, using `alloca()` would make more f158.60sense.

 Mixing `alloca()` and variable-length arrays in a single function can invite peculiar behavior. Play it safe and use one or the other in a given function.

Choosing a Memory Allocation Mechanism

The myriad memory allocation options discussed in this chapter may leave programmers wondering exactly what solution is best for a given job. In the majority of situations, `malloc()` is your best bet. Sometimes, however, a different approach provides a better tool. Table 9-2 summarizes guidelines for choosing an allocation mechanism.

Table 9-2. Approaches to memory allocation in Linux

Allocation approach	Pros	Cons
`malloc()`	Easy, simple, common.	Returned memory not necessarily zeroed.
`calloc()`	Makes allocating arrays simple, zeros returned memory.	Convoluted interface if not allocating arrays.
`realloc()`	Resizes existing allocations.	Useful only for resizing existing allocations.
`brk()` and `sbrk()`	Provides intimate control over the heap.	Much too low-level for most users.
Anonymous memory mappings	Easy to work with, sharable, allow developer to adjust protection level and provide advice; optimal for large mappings.	Suboptimal for small allocations; `malloc()` automatically uses anonymous memory mappings when optimal.
`posix_memalign()`	Allocates memory aligned to any reasonable boundary.	Relatively new and thus portability is questionable; overkill unless alignment concerns are pressing.
`memalign()` and `valloc()`	More common on other Unix systems than `posix_memalign()`.	Not a POSIX standard, offers less alignment control than `posix_memalign()`.
`alloca()`	Very fast allocation, no need to explicitly free memory; great for small allocations.	Unable to return error, no good for large allocations, broken on some Unix systems.
Variable-length arrays	Same as `alloca()`, but frees memory when array falls out of scope, not when function returns.	Useful only for arrays; `alloca()` freeing behavior may be preferable in some situations; less common on other Unix systems than `alloca()`.

Finally, let us not forget the alternative to all of these options: automatic and static memory allocations. Allocating automatic variables on the stack or global variables on the heap is often easier and does not require that the programmer manage pointers and worry about freeing the memory.

Manipulating Memory

The C language provides a family of functions for manipulating raw bytes of memory. These functions operate in many ways similarly to string-manipulation interfaces such as strcmp() and strcpy(), but they rely on a user-provided buffer size instead of the assumption that strings are null-terminated. Note that none of these functions can return errors. Preventing errors is up to the programmer—pass in the wrong memory region, and there is no alternative, except the resulting segmentation violation!

Setting Bytes

Among the collection of memory-manipulating functions, the most common is easily memset():

```
#include <string.h>

void * memset (void *s, int c, size_t n);
```

A call to memset() sets the n bytes starting at s to the byte c and returns s. A frequent use is zeroing a block of memory:

```
/* zero out [s,s+256) */
memset (s, '\0', 256);
```

bzero() is an older, deprecated interface introduced by BSD for performing the same task. New code should use memset(), but Linux provides bzero() for backward compatibility and portability with other systems:

```
#include <strings.h>

void bzero (void *s, size_t n);
```

The following invocation is identical to the preceding memset() example:

```
bzero (s, 256);
```

Note that bzero() (along with the other b interfaces) requires the header <strings.h> and not <string.h>.

Do Not Use memset() if You Can Use calloc()!

Avoid allocating memory with `malloc()` only to immediately zero the provided memory with `memset()`. While the result may be the same, foregoing the two functions for a single `calloc()`, which returns zeroed memory, is superior. Not only will you make one less function call, but `calloc()` may be able to obtain already zeroed memory from the kernel. In that case, you avoid manually setting each byte to 0, improving performance.

Comparing Bytes

Similar to `strcmp()`, `memcmp()` compares two chunks of memory for equivalence:

```
#include <string.h>

int memcmp (const void *s1, const void *s2, size_t n);
```

An invocation compares the first n bytes of s1 to s2 and returns 0 if the blocks of memory are equivalent, a value less than zero if s1 is less than s2, and a value greater than zero if s1 is greater than s2.

BSD again provides a now-deprecated interface that performs largely the same task:

```
#include <strings.h>

int bcmp (const void *s1, const void *s2, size_t n);
```

An invocation of bcmp() compares the first n bytes of s1 to s2, returning 0 if the blocks of memory are equivalent, and a nonzero value if they are different.

Because of structure padding (see "Other alignment concerns" on page 305 earlier in this chapter), comparing two structures for equivalence via memcmp() or bcmp() is unreliable. There can be uninitialized garbage in the padding that differs between two otherwise identical instances of a structure. Consequently, code such as the following is not safe:

```
/* are two dinghies identical? (BROKEN) */
int compare_dinghies (struct dinghy *a, struct dinghy *b)
{
        return memcmp (a, b, sizeof (struct dinghy));
}
```

Instead, programmers who wish to compare structures should compare each element of the structures, one by one. This approach allows for some optimization, but it's definitely more work than the unsafe memcmp() approach. Here's the equivalent code:

```
/* are two dinghies identical? */
int compare_dinghies (struct dinghy *a, struct dinghy *b)
{
        int ret;
```

```
        if (a->nr_oars < b->nr_oars)
                return -1;
        if (a->nr_oars > b->nr_oars)
                return 1;

        ret = strcmp (a->boat_name, b->boat_name);
        if (ret)
                return ret;

        /* and so on, for each member... */
}
```

Moving Bytes

memmove() copies the first n bytes of src to dst, returning dst:

```
#include <string.h>

void * memmove (void *dst, const void *src, size_t n);
```

Again, BSD provides a deprecated interface for performing the same task:

```
#include <strings.h>

void bcopy (const void *src, void *dst, size_t n);
```

Note that although both functions take the same parameters, the order of the first two is reversed in bcopy().

Both bcopy() and memmove() can safely handle overlapping memory regions (say, if part of dst is inside of src). This allows bytes of memory to shift up or down within a given region, for example. As this situation is rare, and a programmer would know if it were the case, the C standard defines a variant of memmove() that does not support overlapping memory regions. This variant is potentially faster:

```
#include <string.h>

void * memcpy (void *dst, const void *src, size_t n);
```

This function behaves identically to memmove(), except dst and src may not overlap. If they do, the results are undefined.

Another safe copying function is memccpy():

```
#include <string.h>

void * memccpy (void *dst, const void *src, int c, size_t n);
```

The memccpy() function behaves the same as memcpy(), except that it stops copying if the function finds the byte c within the first n bytes of src. The call returns a pointer to the next byte in dst after c, or NULL if c was not found.

Finally, you can use `mempcpy()` to step through memory:

```
#define _GNU_SOURCE
#include <string.h>

void * mempcpy (void *dst, const void *src, size_t n);
```

The `mempcpy()` function performs the same as `memcpy()`, except that it returns a pointer to the next byte after the last byte copied. This is useful if a set of data is to be copied to consecutive memory locations—but it's not so much of an improvement because the return value is merely `dst + n`. This function is GNU-specific.

Searching Bytes

The functions `memchr()` and `memrchr()` locate a given byte in a block of memory:

```
#include <string.h>

void * memchr (const void *s, int c, size_t n);
```

The `memchr()` function scans the n bytes of memory pointed at by s for the character c, which is interpreted as an `unsigned char`:

```
#define _GNU_SOURCE
#include <string.h>

void * memrchr (const void *s, int c, size_t n);
```

The call returns a pointer to the first byte to match c, or `NULL` if c is not found.

The `memrchr()` function is the same as the `memchr()` function, except that it searches backward from the end of the n bytes pointed at by s instead of forward from the front. Unlike `memchr()`, `memrchr()` is a GNU extension and not part of the C language.

For more complicated search missions, the awfully named function `memmem()` searches a block of memory for an arbitrary array of bytes:

```
#define _GNU_SOURCE
#include <string.h>

void * memmem (const void *haystack,
               size_t haystacklen,
               const void *needle,
               size_t needlelen);
```

The `memmem()` function returns a pointer to the first occurrence of the subblock `needle`, of length `needlelen` bytes, within the block of memory `haystack`, of length `haystacklen` bytes. If the function does not find `needle` in `haystack`, it returns `NULL`. This function is also a GNU extension.

Frobnicating Bytes

The Linux C library provides an interface for trivially convoluting bytes of data:

```
#define _GNU_SOURCE
#include <string.h>

void * memfrob (void *s, size_t n);
```

A call to memfrob() obscures the first n bytes of memory starting at s by exclusive-ORing (XORing) each byte with the numberf164.430 42. The call returns s.

The effect of a call to memfrob() can be reversed by calling memfrob() again on the same region of memory. Thus, the following snippet is a no-op with respect to secret:

```
memfrob (memfrob (secret, len), len);
```

This function is in no way a proper (or even a poor) substitute for encryption; its use is limited to the trivial obfuscation of strings. It is GNU-specific.

Locking Memory

Linux implements *demand paging*, which means that pages are paged in from disk as needed and paged out to disk when no longer needed. This allows the virtual address spaces of processes on the system to have no direct relationship to the total amount of physical memory, as secondary storage can provide the illusion of a nearly infinite supply of physical memory.

This paging occurs transparently, and applications generally need not be concerned with (or even know about) the Linux kernel's paging behavior. There are, however, two situations in which applications may wish to influence the system's paging behavior:

Determinism
> Applications with timing constraints require deterministic behavior. If some memory accesses result in page faults—which incur costly disk I/O operations—applications can overrun their timing needs. By ensuring that the pages it needs are always in physical memory and never paged to disk, an application can guarantee that memory accesses will not result in page faults, providing consistency, determinism, and improved performance.

Security
> If secrets are kept in memory, the secrets can be paged out and stored unencrypted on disk. For example, if a user's private key is normally stored encrypted on disk, an unencrypted copy of the key in memory can end up in the swap file. In a high-security environment, this behavior may be unacceptable. Applications for which this might be a problem can ask that the memory containing the key always remain in physical memory.

Of course, changing the kernel's paging behavior can result in a negative impact on overall system performance. One application's determinism or security may improve, but while its pages are locked into memory, another application's pages will be paged out instead. The kernel, if we trust its algorithms, chooses the optimal page to page out —that is, the page least likely to be used in the future—so when you change its behavior, it has to swap out a suboptimal page.

Locking Part of an Address Space

POSIX 1003.1b-1993 defines two interfaces for "locking" one or more pages into physical memory, ensuring that they are never paged out to disk. The first locks a given interval of addresses:

```
#include <sys/mman.h>

int mlock (const void *addr, size_t len);
```

A call to mlock() locks the virtual memory starting at addr and extending for len bytes into physical memory. On success, the call returns 0; on failure, the call returns –1 and sets errno as appropriate.

A successful call locks all physical pages that contain [addr,addr+len) in memory. For example, if a call specifies only a single byte, the entire page in which that byte resides is locked into memory. The POSIX standard dictates that addr should be aligned to a page boundary. Linux does not enforce this requirement, silently rounding addr down to the nearest page if needed. Programs requiring portability to other systems, however, should ensure that addr sits on a page boundary.

The valid errno codes include:

EINVAL
> The parameter len is negative.

ENOMEM
> The caller attempted to lock more pages than the RLIMIT_MEMLOCK resource limit allows (see "Locking Limits" on page 328).

EPERM
> The RLIMIT_MEMLOCK resource limit was 0, but the process did not possess the CAP_IPC_LOCK capability (again, see "Locking Limits" on page 328).

 A child process does not inherit the locked status of memory across a fork(). Due to the copy-on-write behavior of address spaces in Linux, however, a child process's pages are effectively locked in memory until the child writes to them.

As an example, assume that a program holds a decrypted string in memory. A process can lock the page containing that string with code such as the following:

```
int ret;

/* lock 'secret' in memory */
ret = mlock (secret, strlen (secret));
if (ret)
        perror ("mlock");
```

Locking All of an Address Space

If a process wants to lock its entire address space into physical memory, `mlock()` is a cumbersome interface. For such a purpose—common to real-time applications—POSIX defines a system call that locks an entire address space:

```
#include <sys/mman.h>

int mlockall (int flags);
```

A call to `mlockall()` locks all of the pages in the current process's address space into physical memory. The `flags` parameter, which is a bitwise OR of the following two values, controls the behavior:

MCL_CURRENT
> If set, this value instructs `mlockall()` to lock all currently mapped pages—the stack, data segment, mapped files, and so on—into the process's address space.

MCL_FUTURE
> If set, this value instructs `mlockall()` to ensure that all pages mapped into the address space in the future are also locked into memory.

Most applications specify a bitwise OR of both values.

On success, the call returns 0; on failure, it returns −1 and sets `errno` to one of the following error codes:

EINVAL
> The parameter `flags` is negative.

ENOMEM
> The caller attempted to lock more pages than the `RLIMIT_MEMLOCK` resource limit allows (see the later section "Locking Limits" on page 328).

EPERM
> The `RLIMIT_MEMLOCK` resource limit was 0, but the process did not possess the `CAP_IPC_LOCK` capability (again, see "Locking Limits" on page 328).

Unlocking Memory

To unlock pages from physical memory, again allowing the kernel to swap the pages out to disk as needed, POSIX standardizes two more interfaces:

```
#include <sys/mman.h>

int munlock (const void *addr, size_t len);
int munlockall (void);
```

The system call `munlock()` unlocks the pages starting at `addr` and extending for `len` bytes. It undoes the effects of `mlock()`. The system call `munlockall()` undoes the effects of `mlockall()`. Both calls return 0 on success, and on error return −1 and set `errno` to one of the following:

EINVAL
> The parameter `len` is invalid (`munlock()` only).

ENOMEM
> Some of the specified pages are invalid.

EPERM
> The `RLIMIT_MEMLOCK` resource limit was 0, but the process did not possess the `CAP_IPC_LOCK` capability (see "Locking Limits").

Memory locks do not nest. Therefore, a single `mlock()` or `munlock()` will unlock a locked page, regardless of how many times the page was locked via `mlock()` or `mlock all()`.

Locking Limits

Because locking memory can affect the overall performance of the system—indeed, if too many pages are locked, memory allocations can fail—Linux places limits on how many pages a process may lock.

Processes possessing the `CAP_IPC_LOCK` capability may lock any number of pages into memory. Processes without this capability may lock only `RLIMIT_MEMLOCK` bytes. By default, this resource limit is 32 KB—large enough to lock a secret or two in memory, but not large enough to adversely affect system performance. (Chapter 6 discusses resource limits and how to retrieve and change this value.)

Is a Page in Physical Memory?

For debugging and diagnostic purposes, Linux provides the `mincore()` function, which can be used to determine whether a given range of memory is in physical memory or swapped out to disk:

```
#include <unistd.h>
#include <sys/mman.h>

int mincore (void *start,
             size_t length,
             unsigned char *vec);
```

A call to `mincore()` provides a vector delineating which pages of a mapping are in physical memory at the time of the system call. The call returns the vector via `vec` and describes the pages starting at `start` (which must be page-aligned) and extending for `length` bytes (which need not be page-aligned). Each byte in `vec` corresponds to one page in the range provided, starting with the first byte describing the first page and moving linearly forward. Consequently, `vec` must be at least large enough to contain `(length - 1 + page size) / page size` bytes. The lowest-order bit in each byte is 1 if the page is resident in physical memory and 0 if it is not. The other bits are currently undefined and reserved for future use.

On success, the call returns 0. On failure, it returns −1 and sets `errno` to one of the following:

EAGAIN
 Insufficient kernel resources are available to carry out the request.

EFAULT
 The parameter `vec` points at an invalid address.

EINVAL
 The parameter `start` is not aligned to a page boundary.

ENOMEM
 `[address,address+1)` contains memory that is not part of a file-based mapping.

Currently, this system call works properly only for file-based mappings created with `MAP_SHARED`. This greatly limits the call's use.

Opportunistic Allocation

Linux employs an *opportunistic allocation* strategy. When a process requests additional memory from the kernel—say, by enlarging its data segment or by creating a new memory mapping—the kernel *commits* to the memory without actually providing any physical storage. Only when the process writes to the newly allocated memory does the kernel *satisfy* the commitment by converting the commitment for memory to a physical allocation of memory. The kernel does this on a page-by-page basis, performing demand paging and copy-on-writes as needed.

This behavior has several advantages. First, lazily allocating memory allows the kernel to defer most of the work until the last possible moment—if indeed it ever has to satisfy the allocations. Second, because the requests are satisfied page-by-page and on demand, only physical memory in actual use need consume physical storage. Finally, the amount of committed memory can far exceed the amount of physical memory and even swap space available. This last feature is called *overcommitment*.

Overcommitting and OOM

Overcommitting allows systems to run many more, and much larger, applications than they could if every requested page of memory had to be backed by physical storage at the point of allocation instead of the point of use. Without overcommitment, mapping a 2 GB file copy-on-write would require the kernel to set aside 2 GB of storage. With overcommitment, mapping a 2 GB file requires storage only for each page of data to which the process actually writes. Likewise, without overcommitment, every fork() would require enough free storage to duplicate the address space, even though the vast majority of pages never undergo copy-on-writes.

What if, however, processes attempt to satisfy more outstanding commitments than the system has physical memory and swap space? In that case, one or more of the satisfactions must fail. Because the kernel has already committed to the memory—the system call requesting the commitment returned success—and a process is attempting to use that committed memory, the kernel's only recourse is to kill a process, freeing up available memory.

When overcommitment results in insufficient memory to satisfy a committed request, we say that an *out of memory* (OOM) condition has occurred. In response to an OOM condition, the kernel employs the *OOM killer* to pick a process "worthy" of termination. For this purpose, the kernel tries to find the least important process that is consuming the most memory.

OOM conditions are rare—hence the huge utility in allowing overcommitment in the first place. To be sure, however, these conditions are unwelcome, and the indeterministic termination of a process by the OOM killer is often unacceptable.

For systems where this is the case, the kernel allows the disabling of overcommitment via the file */proc/sys/vm/overcommit_memory*, and the analogous *sysctl* parameter `vm.overcommit_memory`.

The default value for this parameter, 0, instructs the kernel to perform a heuristic overcommitment strategy, overcommitting memory within reason, but disallowing egregious overcommitments. A value of 1 allows all commitments to succeed, throwing caution to the wind. Certain memory-intensive applications, such as those in the scientific field, tend to request so much more memory than they ever need satisfied that such an option makes sense.

A value of 2 disables overcommitments altogether and enables *strict accounting*. In this mode, memory commitments are restricted to the size of the swap area plus a configurable percentage of physical memory. The configuration percentage is set via the file */proc/sys/vm/overcommit_ratio* or the analogous *sysctl* parameter, which is vm.over commit_ratio. The default is 50, which restricts memory commits to the size of the swap area plus half of the physical memory. Because physical memory contains the kernel, page tables, system-reserved pages, locked pages, and so on, only a portion of it is actually swappable and guaranteed to be able to satisfy commitments.

Be careful with strict accounting! Many system designers, repulsed by the notion of the OOM killer, think strict accounting is a panacea. However, applications often perform many unnecessary allocations that reach far into overcommitment territory, and allowing this behavior was one of the main motivations behind virtual memory.

## CHAPTER 10

Signals

Signals are software interrupts that provide a mechanism for handling asynchronous events. These events can originate from outside the system, such as when the user generates the interrupt character by pressing Ctrl-C, or from activities within the program or kernel, such as when the process executes code that divides by zero. As a primitive form of interprocess communication (IPC), one process can also send a signal to another process.

The key point is not just that the events occur asynchronously—the user, for example, can press Ctrl-C at any point in the program's execution—but also that the program handles the signals asynchronously. The signal-handling functions are registered with the kernel, which invokes the functions asynchronously from the rest of the program when the signals are delivered.

Signals have been part of Unix since the early days. Over time, however, they have evolved, most noticeably in terms of reliability, as signals once could get lost, and in terms of functionality, as signals may now carry user-defined payloads. At first, different Unix systems made incompatible changes to signals. Thankfully, POSIX came to the rescue and standardized signal handling. This standard is what Linux provides and is what we'll discuss here.

In this chapter, we'll start with an overview of signals and a discussion of their use and misuse. We'll then cover the various Linux interfaces that manage and manipulate signals.

Most nontrivial applications interact with signals. Even if you deliberately design your application to not rely on signals for its communication needs—often a good idea!— you'll still be forced to work with signals in certain cases, such as when handling program termination.

Signal Concepts

Signals have a very precise lifecycle. First, a signal is *raised* (we sometimes also say it is *sent* or *generated*). The kernel then *stores* the signal until it is able to deliver it. Finally, once it is free to do so, the kernel *handles* the signal as appropriate. The kernel can perform one of three actions, depending on what the process asked it to do:

Ignore the signal
> No action is taken. There are two signals that cannot be ignored: SIGKILL and SIGSTOP. The reason for this is that the system administrator needs to be able to kill or stop processes, and it would be a circumvention of that right if a process could elect to ignore a SIGKILL (making it unkillable) or a SIGSTOP (making it unstoppable).

Catch and handle the signal
> The kernel will suspend execution of the process's current code path and jump to a previously registered function. The process will then execute this function. Once the process returns from this function, it will jump back to wherever it was when it caught the signal. SIGINT and SIGTERM are two commonly caught signals. Processes catch SIGINT to handle the user generating the interrupt character—for example, a terminal might catch this signal and return to the main prompt. Processes catch SIGTERM to perform necessary cleanup, such as disconnecting from the network or removing temporary files, before terminating. SIGKILL and SIGSTOP cannot be caught.

Perform the default action
> This action depends on the signal being sent. The default action is often to terminate the process. This is the case with SIGKILL, for instance. However, many signals are provided for specific purposes that concern programmers in particular situations, and these signals are ignored by default because many programs are not interested in them. We will look at the various signals and their default actions shortly.

Traditionally, when a signal was delivered, the function that handled the signal had no information about what had happened except for the fact that the particular signal had occurred. Nowadays, the kernel can provide a lot of context to programmers who wish to receive it. Signals, as we shall see, can even pass user-defined data.

Signal Identifiers

Every signal has a symbolic name that starts with the prefix *SIG*. For example, SIGINT is the signal sent when the user presses Ctrl-C, SIGABRT is the signal sent when the process calls the abort() function, and SIGKILL is the signal sent when a process is forcefully terminated.

These signals are all defined in a header file included from `<signal.h>`. The signals are simply preprocessor definitions that represent positive integers—that is, every signal is also associated with an integer identifier. The name-to-integer mapping for the signals is implementation-dependent and varies among Unix systems, although the first dozen or so signals are usually mapped the same way (`SIGKILL` is infamously *signal 9* for example). A portable program will always use a signal's human-readable name, and never its integer value.

The signal numbers start at 1 (generally `SIGHUP`) and proceed linearly upward. There are about 31 signals in total, but most programs deal regularly with only a handful of them. There is no signal with the value 0, which is a special value known as the *null signal*. There's really nothing important about the null signal—it doesn't deserve a special name—but some system calls (such as `kill()`) use a value of 0 as a special case.

 You can generate a list of signals supported on your system with the command *kill -l*.

Signals Supported by Linux

Table 10-1 lists the signals that Linux supports.

Table 10-1. Signals

Signal	Description	Default action
SIGABRT	Sent by abort()	Terminate with core dump
SIGALRM	Sent by alarm()	Terminate
SIGBUS	Hardware or alignment error	Terminate with core dump
SIGCHLD	Child has terminated	Ignored
SIGCONT	Process has continued after being stopped	Ignored
SIGFPE	Arithmetic exception	Terminate with core dump
SIGHUP	Process's controlling terminal was closed (most frequently, the user logged out)	Terminate
SIGILL	Process tried to execute an illegal instruction	Terminate with core dump
SIGINT	User generated the interrupt character (Ctrl-C)	Terminate
SIGIO	Asynchronous I/O event	Terminate[a]
SIGKILL	Uncatchable process termination	Terminate
SIGPIPE	Process wrote to a pipe but there are no readers	Terminate
SIGPROF	Profiling timer expired	Terminate
SIGPWR	Power failure	Terminate
SIGQUIT	User generated the quit character (Ctrl-\)	Terminate with core dump

Signal	Description	Default action
SIGSEGV	Memory access violation	Terminate with core dump
SIGSTKFLT	Coprocessor stack fault	Terminate[b]
SIGSTOP	Suspends execution of the process	Stop
SIGSYS	Process tried to execute an invalid system call	Terminate with core dump
SIGTERM	Catchable process termination	Terminate
SIGTRAP	Break point encountered	Terminate with core dump
SIGTSTP	User generated the suspend character (Ctrl-Z)	Stop
SIGTTIN	Background process read from controlling terminal	Stop
SIGTTOU	Background process wrote to controlling terminal	Stop
SIGURG	Urgent I/O pending	Ignored
SIGUSR1	Process-defined signal	Terminate
SIGUSR2	Process-defined signal	Terminate
SIGVTALRM	Generated by setitimer() when called with the ITIMER_VIRTUAL flag	Terminate
SIGWINCH	Size of controlling terminal window changed	Ignored
SIGXCPU	Processor resource limits were exceeded	Terminate with core dump
SIGXFSZ	File resource limits were exceeded	Terminate with core dump

[a] The behavior on other Unix systems, such as BSD, is to ignore this signal.

[b] The Linux kernel no longer generates this signal; it remains only for backward compatibility.

Several other signal values exist, but Linux defines them to be equivalent to other values: SIGINFO is defined as SIGPWR,[1] SIGIOT is defined as SIGABRT, and SIGPOLL and SIGLOST are defined as SIGIO.

Now that we have a table for quick reference, let's go over each of the signals in detail:

SIGABRT

The abort() function sends this signal to the process that invokes it. The process then terminates and generates a core file. In Linux, assertions such as assert() call abort() when the conditional fails.

SIGALRM

The alarm() and setitimer() (with the ITIMER_REAL flag) functions send this signal to the process that invoked them when an alarm expires. Chapter 11 discusses these and related functions.

1. Only the Alpha architecture defines this signal. On all other machine architectures, this signal does not exist.

SIGBUS

The kernel raises this signal when the process incurs a hardware fault other than memory protection, which generates a SIGSEGV. On traditional Unix systems, this signal represented various irrecoverable errors, such as unaligned memory access. The Linux kernel, however, fixes most of these errors automatically, without generating the signal. The kernel does raise this signal when a process improperly accesses a region of memory created via mmap() (see Chapter 9 for a discussion of memory mappings). Unless this signal is caught, the kernel will terminate the process and generate a core dump.

SIGCHLD

Whenever a process terminates or stops, the kernel sends this signal to the process's parent. Because SIGCHLD is ignored by default, processes must explicitly catch and handle it if they are interested in the lives of their children. A handler for this signal generally calls wait(), discussed in Chapter 5, to determine the child's pid and exit code.

SIGCONT

The kernel sends this signal to a process when the process is resumed after being stopped. By default, this signal is ignored, but processes can catch it if they want to perform an action after being continued. This signal is commonly used by terminals or editors that wish to refresh the screen.

SIGFPE

Despite its name, this signal represents any arithmetic exception, and not solely those related to floating-point operations. Exceptions include overflows, underflows, and division by zero. The default action is to terminate the process and generate a core file, but processes may catch and handle this signal if they want. Note that the behavior of a process and the result of the offending operation are undefined if the process elects to continue running.

SIGHUP

The kernel sends this signal to the session leader whenever the session's terminal disconnects. The kernel also sends this signal to each process in the foreground process group when the session leader terminates. The default action is to terminate, which makes sense—the signal suggests that the user has logged out. Daemon processes "overload" this signal with a mechanism to instruct them to reload their configuration files. Sending SIGHUP to Apache, for example, instructs it to reread *httpd.conf*. Using SIGHUP for this purpose is a common convention but not mandatory. The practice is safe because daemons do not have controlling terminals and thus should never normally receive this signal.

SIGILL

The kernel sends this signal when a process attempts to execute an illegal machine instruction. The default action is to terminate the process and generate a core dump. Processes may elect to catch and handle SIGILL, but their behavior is undefined after its occurrence.

SIGINT

This signal is sent to all processes in the foreground process group when the user enters the interrupt character (usually Ctrl-C). The default behavior is to terminate; however, processes can elect to catch and handle this signal and generally do so to clean up before terminating.

SIGIO

This signal is sent when a BSD-style asynchronous I/O event is generated. This style of I/O is rarely used on Linux. (See Chapter 4 for a discussion of advanced I/O techniques that are common to Linux.)

SIGKILL

This signal is sent from the kill() system call; it exists to provide system administrators with a surefire way of unconditionally killing a process. This signal cannot be caught or ignored, and its result is always to terminate the process.

SIGPIPE

If a process writes to a pipe but the reader has terminated, the kernel raises this signal. The default action is to terminate the process, but this signal may be caught and handled.

SIGPROF

The setitimer() function, when used with the ITIMER_PROF flag, generates this signal when a profiling timer expires. The default action is to terminate the process.

SIGPWR

This signal is system-dependent. On Linux, it represents a low-battery condition (such as in an uninterruptible power supply, or UPS). A UPS monitoring daemon sends this signal to *init*, which then responds by cleaning up and shutting down the system—hopefully before the power goes out!

SIGQUIT

The kernel raises this signal for all processes in the foreground process group when the user provides the terminal quit character (usually Ctrl-\). The default action is to terminate the processes and generate a core dump.

SIGSEGV

This signal, whose name derives from *segmentation violation*, is sent to a process when it attempts an invalid memory access. This includes accessing unmapped memory, reading from memory that is not read-enabled, executing code in memory that is not execute-enabled, or writing to memory that is not write-enabled. Processes may catch and handle this signal, but the default action is to terminate the process and generate a core dump.

SIGSTOP

This signal is sent only by kill( ). It unconditionally stops a process and cannot be caught or ignored.

SIGSYS

The kernel sends this signal to a process when it attempts to invoke an invalid system call. This can happen if a binary is built on a newer version of the operating system (with newer versions of system calls) but then runs on an older version. Properly built binaries that make their system calls through *glibc* should never receive this signal. Instead, invalid system calls should return –1 and set errno to ENOSYS.

SIGTERM

This signal is sent only by kill( ); it allows a user to gracefully terminate a process (the default action). Processes may elect to catch this signal and clean up before terminating, but it is considered rude to catch this signal and not terminate promptly.

SIGTRAP

The kernel sends this signal to a process when it crosses a break point. Generally, debuggers catch this signal, and other processes ignore it.

SIGTSTP

The kernel sends this signal to all processes in the foreground process group when the user provides the suspend character (usually Ctrl-Z).

SIGTTIN

This signal is sent to a process that is in the background when it attempts to read from its controlling terminal. The default action is to stop the process.

SIGTTOU

This signal is sent to a process that is in the background when it attempts to write to its controlling terminal. The default action is to stop the process.

SIGURG

The kernel sends this signal to a process when out-of-band (OOB) data has arrived on a socket. Out-of-band data is beyond the scope of this book.

SIGUSR1 *and* SIGUSR2

These signals are available for user-defined purposes; the kernel never raises them. Processes may use SIGUSR1 and SIGUSR2 for whatever purpose they like. A common use is to instruct a daemon process to behave differently. The default action is to terminate the process.

SIGVTALRM

The setitimer() function sends this signal when a timer created with the ITIMER_VIRTUAL flag expires. Chapter 11 discusses timers.

SIGWINCH

The kernel raises this signal for all processes in the foreground process group when the size of their terminal window changes. By default, processes ignore this signal, but they may elect to catch and handle it if they are aware of their terminal's window size. A good example of a program that catches this signal is *top*—try resizing its window while it is running and watch how it responds.

SIGXCPU

The kernel raises this signal when a process exceeds its soft processor limit. The kernel will continue to raise this signal once per second until the process exits or exceeds its hard processor limit. Once the hard limit is exceeded, the kernel sends the process a SIGKILL.

SIGXFSZ

The kernel raises this signal when a process exceeds its file size limit. The default action is to terminate the process, but if this signal is caught or ignored, the system call that would have resulted in the file size limit being exceeded returns –1 and sets errno to EFBIG.

Basic Signal Management

With the signals out of the way, we'll now turn to how you manage them from within your program. The simplest and oldest interface for signal management is the signal() function. Defined by the ISO C89 standard, which standardizes only the lowest common denominator of signal support, this system call is very basic. Linux offers substantially more control over signals via other interfaces, which we'll cover later in this chapter. Because signal() is the most basic and, thanks to its presence in ISO C, quite common, we'll cover it first:

```
#include <signal.h>

typedef void (*sighandler_t)(int);

sighandler_t signal (int signo, sighandler_t handler);
```

A successful call to signal() removes the current action taken on receipt of the signal signo and instead handles the signal with the signal handler specified by handler. signo is one of the signal names discussed in the previous section, such as SIGINT or SIGUSR1. Recall that a process can catch neither SIGKILL nor SIGSTOP, so setting up a handler for either of these two signals makes no sense.

The handler function must return void, which makes sense because (unlike with normal functions) there is no standard place in the program for this function to return. The function takes one argument, an integer, which is the signal identifier (for example, SIGUSR2) of the signal being handled. This allows a single function to handle multiple signals. A prototype has the form:

```
void my_handler (int signo);
```

Linux uses a typedef, sighandler_t, to define this prototype. Other Unix systems directly use the function pointers; some systems have their own types, which may not be named sighandler_t. Programs seeking portability should not reference the type directly.

When it raises a signal to a process that has registered a signal handler, the kernel suspends execution of the program's regular instruction stream and calls the signal handler. The handler is passed the value of the signal, which is the signo originally provided to signal().

You may also use signal() to instruct the kernel to ignore a given signal for the current process or to reset the signal to the default behavior. This is done using special values for the handler parameter:

SIG_DFL
> Set the behavior of the signal given by signo to its default. For example, in the case of SIGPIPE, the process will terminate.

SIG_IGN
> Ignore the signal given by signo.

The signal() function returns the previous behavior of the signal, which could be a pointer to a signal handler, SIG_DFL, or SIG_IGN. On error, the function returns SIG_ERR. It does not set errno.

Waiting for a Signal, Any Signal

Useful for debugging and writing demonstrative code snippets, the POSIX-defined pause() system call puts a process to sleep until it receives a signal that either is handled or terminates the process:

```
#include <unistd.h>

int pause (void);
```

pause() returns only if a signal is received, in which case the signal is handled, and pause() returns −1 and sets errno to EINTR. If the kernel raises an ignored signal, the process does not wake up.

In the Linux kernel, pause() is one of the simplest system calls. It performs only two actions. First, it puts the process in the interruptible sleep state. Next, it calls schedule() to invoke the Linux process scheduler to find another process to run. As the process is not actually waiting for anything, the kernel will not wake it up unless it receives a signal. This whole ordeal consumes only two lines of C code.[2]

Examples

Let's look at a couple of simple examples. This first one registers a signal handler for SIGINT that simply prints a message and then terminates the program (as SIGINT would do anyway):

```
#include <stdlib.h>
#include <stdio.h>
#include <unistd.h>
#include <signal.h>

/* handler for SIGINT */
static void sigint_handler (int signo)
{
        /*
         * Technically, you shouldn't use printf() in a
         * signal handler, but it isn't the end of the
         * world. I'll discuss why in the section
         * "Reentrancy."
         */
        printf ("Caught SIGINT!\n");
        exit (EXIT_SUCCESS);
}

int main (void)
{
        /*
         * Register sigint_handler as our signal handler
         * for SIGINT.
         */
        if (signal (SIGINT, sigint_handler) == SIG_ERR) {
                fprintf (stderr, "Cannot handle SIGINT!\n");
                exit (EXIT_FAILURE);
        }

        for (;;)
                pause ();

        return 0;
}
```

2. Thus, pause() is only the second-simplest system call. The joint winners are getpid() and gettid(), each only one line.

In the following example, we register the same handler for SIGTERM and SIGINT. We also reset the behavior for SIGPROF to the default (which is to terminate the process) and ignore SIGHUP (which would otherwise terminate the process):

```c
#include <stdlib.h>
#include <stdio.h>
#include <unistd.h>
#include <signal.h>

/* handler for SIGINT and SIGTERM */
static void signal_handler (int signo)
{
        if (signo == SIGINT)
                printf ("Caught SIGINT!\n");
        else if (signo == SIGTERM)
                printf ("Caught SIGTERM!\n");
        else {
                /* this should never happen */
                fprintf (stderr, "Unexpected signal!\n");
                exit (EXIT_FAILURE);
        }
        exit (EXIT_SUCCESS);
}

int main (void)
{
        /*
         * Register signal_handler as our signal handler
         * for SIGINT.
         */
        if (signal (SIGINT, signal_handler) == SIG_ERR) {
                fprintf (stderr, "Cannot handle SIGINT!\n");
                exit (EXIT_FAILURE);
        }

        /*
         * Register signal_handler as our signal handler
         * for SIGTERM.
         */
        if (signal (SIGTERM, signal_handler) == SIG_ERR) {
                fprintf (stderr, "Cannot handle SIGTERM!\n");
                exit (EXIT_FAILURE);
        }

        /* Reset SIGPROF's behavior to the default. */
        if (signal (SIGPROF, SIG_DFL) == SIG_ERR) {
                fprintf (stderr, "Cannot reset SIGPROF!\n");
                exit (EXIT_FAILURE);
        }

        /* Ignore SIGHUP. */
        if (signal (SIGHUP, SIG_IGN) == SIG_ERR) {
```

```
                fprintf (stderr, "Cannot ignore SIGHUP!\n");
                exit (EXIT_FAILURE);
        }

        for (;;)
                pause ();

        return 0;
}
```

Execution and Inheritance

On fork, the child process inherits the signal actions of its parent. That is, the child copies the registered actions (ignore, default, handle) for each signal from its parent. Pending signals are *not* inherited, which makes sense: the pending signal was sent to a specific pid, decidedly not the child.

When a process is created via one of the *exec* family of system calls, all signals are set to their default actions unless the parent process is ignoring them; in that case, the newly imaged process will also ignore those signals. Put another way, any signal caught by the process before *exec* is reset to the default action after *exec*, and all other signals remain the same. This makes sense because a freshly executed process does not share the address space of its parent, and thus any registered signal handlers may not exist. Pending signals are inherited. Table 10-2 summarizes the inheritance.

Table 10-2. Inherited signal behavior

Signal behavior	Across forks	Across execs
Ignored	Inherited	Inherited
Default	Inherited	Inherited
Handled	Inherited	Not inherited
Pending signals	Not inherited	Inherited

This behavior on process execution has one notable use: when the shell executes a process "in the background" (or when another background process executes another process), the newly executed process should ignore the interrupt and quit characters. Thus, before a shell executes a background process, it should set SIGINT and SIGQUIT to SIG_IGN. It is therefore common for programs that handle these signals to first check to make sure they are not ignored. For example:

```
/* handle SIGINT, but only if it isn't ignored */
if (signal (SIGINT, SIG_IGN) != SIG_IGN) {
        if (signal (SIGINT, sigint_handler) == SIG_ERR)
                fprintf (stderr, "Failed to handle SIGINT!\n");
}

/* handle SIGQUIT, but only if it isn't ignored */
```

```
if (signal (SIGQUIT, SIG_IGN) != SIG_IGN) {
        if (signal (SIGQUIT, sigquit_handler) == SIG_ERR)
                fprintf (stderr, "Failed to handle SIGQUIT!\n");
}
```

The need to set a signal behavior to check the signal behavior highlights a deficiency in the `signal()` interface. Later, we will study a function that does not have this flaw.

Mapping Signal Numbers to Strings

In our examples thus far, we have hardcoded the names of the signals. But sometimes it is more convenient (or even a requirement) that you be able to convert a signal number to a string representation of its name. There are several ways to do this. One is to retrieve the string from a statically defined list:

```
extern const char * const sys_siglist[];
```

`sys_siglist` is an array of strings holding the names of the signals supported by the system, indexed by signal number.

An alternative is the BSD-defined `psignal()` interface, which is common enough that Linux supports it, too:

```
#include <signal.h>

void psignal (int signo, const char *msg);
```

A call to `psignal()` prints to `stderr` the string you supply as the `msg` argument, followed by a colon, a space, and the name of the signal given by `signo`. If `msg` is omitted, only the signal name is printed. If `signo` is invalid, the printed message will say so.

A better interface is `strsignal()`. It is not standardized, but Linux and many non-Linux systems support it:

```
#define _GNU_SOURCE
#include <string.h>

char * strsignal (int signo);
```

A call to `strsignal()` returns a pointer to a description of the signal given by `signo`. If `signo` is invalid, the returned description typically says so (some Unix systems that support this function return NULL instead). The returned string is valid only until the next invocation of `strsignal()`, so this function is not thread-safe.

Going with `sys_siglist` is usually your best bet. Using this approach, we could rewrite our earlier signal handler as follows:

```
static void signal_handler (int signo)
{
        printf ("Caught %s\n", sys_siglist[signo]);
}
```

Sending a Signal

The kill() system call, the basis of the common *kill* utility, sends a signal from one process to another:

```
#include <sys/types.h>
#include <signal.h>

int kill (pid_t pid, int signo);
```

In its normal use (i.e., if pid is greater than 0), kill() sends the signal signo to the process identified by pid.

If pid is 0, signo is sent to every process in the invoking process's process group.

If pid is –1, signo is sent to every process for which the invoking process has permission to send a signal, except itself and *init*. We will discuss the permissions regulating signal delivery in the next subsection.

If pid is less than –1, signo is sent to the process group -pid.

On success, kill() returns 0. The call is considered a success so long as a single signal was sent. On failure (no signals sent), the call returns –1 and sets errno to one of the following:

EINVAL
> The signal specified by signo is invalid.

EPERM
> The invoking process lacks sufficient permissions to send a signal to any of the requested processes.

ESRCH
> The process or process group denoted by pid does not exist or, in the case of a process, is a zombie.

Permissions

In order to send a signal to another process, the sending process needs proper permissions. A process with the CAP_KILL capability (usually one owned by root) can send a signal to any process. Without this capability, the sending process's effective or real user ID must be equal to the real or saved user ID of the receiving process. Put more simply, a user can send a signal only to a process that he or she owns.

 Unix systems, including Linux, define an exception for SIGCONT: a process can send this signal to any other process in the same session. The user ID need not match.

If `signo` is 0 (the aforementioned null signal) the call does not send a signal, but it still performs error checking. This is useful to test whether a process has suitable permissions to send the provided process or processes a signal.

Examples

Here's how to send `SIGHUP` to the process with process ID 1722:

```
int ret;

ret = kill (1722, SIGHUP);
if (ret)
        perror ("kill");
```

This snippet is effectively the same as the following invocation of the *kill* utility:

```
$ kill -HUP 1722
```

To check that we have permission to send a signal to 1722 without actually sending any signal, we could do the following:

```
int ret;

ret = kill (1722, 0);
if (ret)
        ; /* we lack permission */
else
        ; /* we have permission */
```

Sending a Signal to Yourself

The `raise()` function is a simple way for a process to send a signal to itself:

```
#include <signal.h>

int raise (int signo);
```

This call:

```
raise (signo);
```

is equivalent to the following call:

```
kill (getpid (), signo);
```

The call returns 0 on success and a nonzero value on failure. It does not set `errno`.

Sending a Signal to an Entire Process Group

Another convenience function makes it easy to send a signal to all processes in a given process group in the event that negating the process group ID and using `kill()` is deemed too taxing:

```
#include <signal.h>

int killpg (int pgrp, int signo);
```

This call:

```
killpg (pgrp, signo);
```

is equivalent to the following call:

```
kill (-pgrp, signo);
```

This holds true even if `pgrp` is 0, in which case `killpg( )` sends the signal `signo` to every process in the invoking process's group.

On success, `killpg()` returns 0. On failure, it returns –1 and sets `errno` to one of the following values:

EINVAL
> The signal specified by `signo` is invalid.

EPERM
> The invoking process lacks sufficient permissions to send a signal to any of the requested processes.

ESRCH
> The process group denoted by `pgrp` does not exist.

Reentrancy

When the kernel raises a signal, a process can be executing code anywhere. For example, it might be in the middle of an important operation that, if interrupted, would leave the process is an inconsistent state—say, with a data structure only half updated or a calculation only partially performed. The process might even be handling another signal.

Signal handlers cannot tell what code the process is executing when a signal hits; the handler can run in the middle of anything. It is thus very important that any signal handler your process installs be very careful about the actions it performs and the data it touches. Signal handlers must take care not to make assumptions about what the process was doing when it was interrupted. In particular, they must practice caution when modifying global (that is, shared) data. Indeed, it is a good idea for a signal handler never to touch global data; in an upcoming section, however, we will look at a way to temporarily block the delivery of signals as a way to allow safe manipulation of data shared by a signal handler and the rest of a process.

What about system calls and other library functions? What if your process is in the middle of writing to a file or allocating memory, and a signal handler writes to the same file or also invokes `malloc()`? Or what if a process is in the middle of a call to a function that uses a static buffer, such as `strsignal()`, when a signal is delivered?

Some functions are clearly not reentrant. If a program is in the middle of executing a nonreentrant function and a signal occurs and the signal handler then invokes that same nonreentrant function, chaos can ensue. A *reentrant function* is a function that is safe to call from within itself (or concurrently, from another thread in the same process). In order to qualify as reentrant, a function must not manipulate static data, must manipulate only stack-allocated data or data provided to it by the caller, and must not invoke any nonreentrant function.

Guaranteed-Reentrant Functions

When writing a signal handler, you have to assume that the interrupted process could be in the middle of a nonreentrant function (or anything else, for that matter). Thus, signal handlers must make use only of functions that are reentrant.

Various standards have decreed lists of functions that are *signal-safe*: reentrant and thus safe to use from within a signal handler. Most notably, POSIX.1-2003 and the Single UNIX Specification dictate a list of functions that are guaranteed to be reentrant and signal-safe on all compliant platforms. Table 10-3 lists the functions.

Table 10-3. Functions guaranteed to be safely reentrant for use in signals

abort()	accept()	access()
aio_error()	aio_return()	aio_suspend()
alarm()	bind()	cfgetispeed()
cfgetospeed()	cfsetispeed()	cfsetospeed()
chdir()	chmod()	chown()
clock_gettime()	close()	connect()
creat()	dup()	dup2()
execle()	execve()	_Exit()
_exit()	fchmod()	fchown()
fcntl()	fdatasync()	fork()
fpathconf()	fstat()	fsync()
ftruncate()	getegid()	geteuid()
getgid()	getgroups()	getpeername()
getpgrp()	getpid()	getppid()
getsockname()	getsockopt()	getuid()
kill()	link()	listen()
lseek()	lstat()	mkdir()
mkfifo()	open()	pathconf()
pause()	pipe()	poll()
posix_trace_event()	pselect()	raise()

read()	readlink()	recv()
recvfrom()	recvmsg()	rename()
rmdir()	select()	sem_post()
send()	sendmsg()	sendto()
setgid()	setpgid()	setsid()
setsockopt()	setuid()	shutdown()
sigaction()	sigaddset()	sigdelset()
sigemptyset()	sigfillset()	sigismember()
signal()	sigpause()	sigpending()
sigprocmask()	sigqueue()	sigset()
sigsuspend()	sleep()	socket()
socketpair()	stat()	symlink()
sysconf()	tcdrain()	tcflow()
tcflush()	tcgetattr()	tcgetpgrp()
tcsendbreak()	tcsetattr()	tcsetpgrp()
time()	timer_getoverrun()	timer_gettime()
timer_settime()	times()	umask()
uname()	unlink()	utime()
wait()	waitpid()	write()

Many more functions are safe, but Linux and other POSIX-compliant systems guarantee the reentrancy of only these functions.

Signal Sets

Several of the functions we will look at later in this chapter need to manipulate sets of signals, such as the set of signals blocked by a process or the set of signals pending to a process. The *signal set operations* manage these signal sets:

```
#include <signal.h>

int sigemptyset (sigset_t *set);

int sigfillset (sigset_t *set);
int sigaddset (sigset_t *set, int signo);

int sigdelset (sigset_t *set, int signo);

int sigismember (const sigset_t *set, int signo);
```

sigemptyset() initializes the signal set given by set, marking it empty (all signals excluded from the set). sigfillset() initializes the signal set given by set, marking it full (all signals included in the set). Both functions return 0. You should call one of these two functions on a signal set before further using the set.

`sigaddset()` adds `signo` to the signal set given by `set`, while `sigdelset()` removes `signo` from the signal set given by `set`. Both return 0 on success or –1 on error, in which case `errno` is set to the error code `EINVAL`, signifying that `signo` is an invalid signal identifier.

`sigismember()` returns 1 if `signo` is in the signal set given by `set`, 0 if it is not, and –1 on error. In the latter case, `errno` is again set to `EINVAL`, signifying that `signo` is invalid.

More Signal Set Functions

The preceding functions are all standardized by POSIX and found on any modern Unix system. Linux also provides several nonstandard functions:

```
#define _GNU_SOURCE
#define <signal.h>

int sigisemptyset (sigset_t *set);

int sigorset (sigset_t *dest, sigset_t *left, sigset_t *right);

int sigandset (sigset_t *dest, sigset_t *left, sigset_t *right);
```

`sigisemptyset()` returns 1 if the signal set given by `set` is empty and 0 otherwise.

`sigorset()` places the union (the binary OR) of the signal sets `left` and `right` in `dest`. `sigandset()` places the intersection (the binary AND) of the signal sets `left` and `right` in `dest`. Both return 0 on success and –1 on error, setting `errno` to `EINVAL`.

These functions are useful, but programs desiring POSIX compliance should avoid them.

Blocking Signals

Earlier we discussed reentrancy and the issues raised by signal handlers running asynchronously, at any time. We discussed functions not to call from within a signal handler because they themselves are not reentrant.

But what if your program needs to share data between a signal handler and elsewhere in the program? What if there are portions of your program's execution during which you do not want any interruptions, including from signal handlers? We call such parts of a program *critical regions*, and we protect them by temporarily suspending the delivery of signals. We say that such signals are *blocked*. Any signals that are raised while blocked are not handled until they are unblocked. A process may block any number of signals; the set of signals blocked by a process is called its *signal mask*.

POSIX defines, and Linux implements, a function for managing a process's signal mask:

```
#include <signal.h>

int sigprocmask (int how,
                 const sigset_t *set,
                 sigset_t *oldset);
```

The behavior of `sigprocmask()` depends on the value of how, which is one of the following flags:

SIG_SETMASK
> The signal mask for the invoking process is changed to set.

SIG_BLOCK
> The signals in set are added to the invoking process's signal mask. In other words, the signal mask is changed to the union (binary OR) of the current mask and set.

SIG_UNBLOCK
> The signals in set are removed from the invoking process's signal mask. In other words, the signal is changed to the intersection (binary AND) of the current mask, and the negation (binary NOT) of set. It is illegal to unblock a signal that is not blocked.

If oldset is not NULL, the function places the previous signal set in oldset.

If set is NULL, the function ignores how and does not change the signal mask, but it does place the signal mask in oldset. In other words, passing a null value as set is the way to retrieve the current signal mask.

On success, the call returns 0. On failure, it returns –1 and sets errno to either EINVAL, signifying that how was invalid, or EFAULT, signifying that set or oldset was an invalid pointer.

Blocking SIGKILL or SIGSTOP is not allowed. `sigprocmask()` silently ignores any attempt to add either signal to the signal mask.

Retrieving Pending Signals

When the kernel raises a blocked signal, it is not delivered. We call such signals *pending*. When a pending signal is unblocked, the kernel then passes it off to the process to handle.

POSIX defines a function to retrieve the set of pending signals:

```
#include <signal.h>

int sigpending (sigset_t *set);
```

A successful call to sigpending() places the set of pending signals in set and returns 0. On failure, the call returns −1 and sets errno to EFAULT, signifying that set is an invalid pointer.

Waiting for a Set of Signals

A third POSIX-defined function allows a process to temporarily change its signal mask and then wait until a signal is raised that either terminates or is handled by the process:

```
#include <signal.h>

int sigsuspend (const sigset_t *set);
```

If a signal terminates the process, sigsuspend() does not return. If a signal is raised and handled, sigsuspend() returns −1 after the signal handler returns, setting errno to EINTR. If set is an invalid pointer, errno is set to EFAULT.

A common sigsuspend() usage scenario is to retrieve signals that might have arrived and been blocked during a critical region of program execution. The process first uses sigprocmask() to block a set of signals, saving the old mask in oldset. After exiting the critical region, the process then calls sigsuspend(), providing oldset for set.

Advanced Signal Management

691.170bThe signal() function that we studied at the beginning of this chapter is very basic. Because it is part of the standard C library and therefore has to reflect minimal assumptions about the capabilities of the operating system on which it runs, it can offer only a lowest common denominator to signal management. As an alternative, POSIX standardizes the sigaction() system call, which provides much greater signal management capabilities. Among other things, you can use it to block the reception of specified signals while your handler runs, and to retrieve a wide range of data about the system and process state at the moment a signal was raised:

```
#include <signal.h>

int sigaction (int signo,
               const struct sigaction *act,
               struct sigaction *oldact);
```

A call to sigaction() changes the behavior of the signal identified by signo, which can be any value except those associated with SIGKILL and SIGSTOP. If act is not NULL, the system call changes the current behavior of the signal as specified by act. If oldact is not NULL, the call stores the previous (or current, if act is NULL) behavior of the given signal there.

The `sigaction` structure allows for fine-grained control over signals. The header `<sys/signal.h>`, included from `<signal.h>`, defines the structure as follows:

```
struct sigaction {
        void (*sa_handler)(int);    /* signal handler or action */
        void (*sa_sigaction)(int, siginfo_t *, void *);
        sigset_t sa_mask;           /* signals to block */
        int sa_flags;               /* flags */
        void (*sa_restorer)(void);  /* obsolete and non-POSIX */
};
```

The `sa_handler` field dictates the action to take upon receiving the signal. As with `signal()`, this field may be `SIG_DFL`, signifying the default action, `SIG_IGN`, instructing the kernel to ignore the signal for the process, or a pointer to a signal-handling function. The function has the same prototype as a signal handler installed by `signal()`:

```
void my_handler (int signo);
```

If `SA_SIGINFO` is set in `sa_flags`, `sa_sigaction`, and not `sa_handler`, dictates the signal-handling function. This function's prototype is slightly different:

```
void my_handler (int signo, siginfo_t *si, void *ucontext);
```

The function receives the signal number as its first parameter, a `siginfo_t` structure as its second parameter, and a `ucontext_t` structure (cast to a `void` pointer) as its third parameter. It has no return value. The `siginfo_t` structure provides an abundance of information to the signal handler; we will look at it shortly.

Note that on some machine architectures (and possibly other Unix systems), `sa_handler` and `sa_sigaction` are in a union, and you should not assign values to both fields.

The `sa_mask` field provides a set of signals that the system should block for the duration of the execution of the signal handler. This allows programmers to enforce proper protection from reentrancy among multiple signal handlers. The signal currently being handled is also blocked unless the `SA_NODEFER` flag is set in `sa_flags`. You cannot block `SIGKILL` or `SIGSTOP`; the call will silently ignore either in `sa_mask`.

The `sa_flags` field is a bitmask of zero, one, or more flags that change the handling of the signal given by `signo`. We already looked at the `SA_SIGINFO` and `SA_NODEFER` flags; other values for `sa_flags` include the following:

SA_NOCLDSTOP
> If `signo` is `SIGCHLD`, this flag instructs the system to not provide notification when a child process stops or resumes.

SA_NOCLDWAIT

If `signo` is SIGCHLD, this flag enables *automatic child reaping*: children are not converted to zombies on termination, and the parent need not (and cannot) call `wait()` on them. See Chapter 5 for a lively discussion of children, zombies, and `wait()`.

SA_NOMASK

This flag is an obsolete non-POSIX equivalent to `SA_NODEFER` (discussed earlier in this section). Use `SA_NODEFER` instead of this flag, but be prepared to see this value turn up in older code.

SA_ONESHOT

This flag is an obsolete non-POSIX equivalent to `SA_RESETHAND` (discussed later in this list). Use `SA_RESETHAND` instead of this flag, but be prepared to see this value turn up in older code.

SA_ONSTACK

This flag instructs the system to invoke the given signal handler on an *alternative signal stack*, as provided by `sigaltstack()`. If you do not provide an alternative stack, the default is used—that is, the system behaves as if you did not provide this flag. Alternative signal stacks are rare, although they are useful in some Pthreads applications with smaller thread stacks that might be overrun by some signal handler usage. We do not further discuss `sigaltstack()` in this book.

SA_RESTART

This flag enables BSD-style restarting of system calls that are interrupted by signals.

SA_RESETHAND

This flag enables "one-shot" mode. The behavior of the given signal is reset to the default once the signal handler returns.

The `sa_restorer` field is obsolete and no longer used in Linux. It is not part of POSIX, anyhow. Pretend that it is not there, and do not touch it.

`sigaction()` returns 0 on success. On failure, the call returns −1 and sets `errno` to one of the following error codes:

EFAULT

`act` or `oldact` is an invalid pointer.

EINVAL

`signo` is an invalid signal, SIGKILL, or SIGSTOP.

The siginfo_t Structure

The `siginfo_t` structure is also defined in <sys/signal.h>, as follows:

```
typedef struct siginfo_t {
        int si_signo;        /* signal number */
        int si_errno;        /* errno value */
        int si_code;         /* signal code */
        pid_t si_pid;        /* sending process's PID */
        uid_t si_uid;        /* sending process's real UID */
        int si_status;       /* exit value or signal */
        clock_t si_utime;    /* user time consumed */
        clock_t si_stime;    /* system time consumed */
        sigval_t si_value;   /* signal payload value */
        int si_int;          /* POSIX.1b signal */
        void *si_ptr;        /* POSIX.1b signal */
        void *si_addr;       /* memory location that caused fault */
        int si_band;         /* band event */
        int si_fd;           /* file descriptor */
};
```

This structure is rife with information passed to the signal handler (if you're using sa_sigaction in lieu of sa_sighandler). With modern computing, many consider the Unix signal model an awful method for performing IPC. Perhaps the problem is that these folks are stuck using signal() when they should be using sigaction() with SA_SIGINFO. The siginfo_t structure opens the door for wringing a lot more functionality out of signals.

There's a lot of interesting data in this structure, including information about the process that sent the signal and about the cause of the signal. Here is a detailed description of each of the fields:

si_signo
> The signal number of the signal in question. In your signal handler, the first argument provides this information as well (and avoids a pointer dereference).

si_errno
> If nonzero, the error code associated with this signal. This field is valid for all signals.

si_code
> An explanation of why and from where the process received the signal (for example, from kill()). We will go over the possible values in the following section. This field is valid for all signals.

si_pid
> For SIGCHLD, the pid of the process that terminated.

si_uid
> For SIGCHLD, the owning uid of the process that terminated.

si_status
> For SIGCHLD, the exit status of the process that terminated.

si_utime

For SIGCHLD, the user time consumed by the process that terminated.

si_stime

For SIGCHLD, the system time consumed by the process that terminated.

si_value

A union of si_int and si_ptr.

si_int

For signals sent via sigqueue() (see "Sending a Signal with a Payload" on page 361), the provided payload typed as an integer.

si_ptr

For signals sent via sigqueue() (see "Sending a Signal with a Payload" on page 361), the provided payload typed as a void pointer.

si_addr

For SIGBUS, SIGFPE, SIGILL, SIGSEGV, and SIGTRAP, this void pointer contains the address of the offending fault. For example, in the case of SIGSEGV, this field contains the address of the memory access violation (and is thus often NULL!).

si_band

For SIGPOLL, out-of-band and priority information for the file descriptor listed in si_fd.

si_fd

For SIGPOLL, the file descriptor for the file whose operation completed.

si_value, si_int, and si_ptr are particularly complex topics because a process can use them to pass arbitrary data to another process. Thus, you can use them to send either a simple integer or a pointer to a data structure (note that a pointer is not much help if the processes do not share an address space). These fields are discussed in the upcoming section "Sending a Signal with a Payload" on page 361.

POSIX guarantees that only the first three fields are valid for all signals. The other fields should be accessed only when handling the applicable signal. You should access the si_fd field, for example, only if the signal is SIGPOLL.

The Wonderful World of si_code

The si_code field indicates the cause of the signal. For user-sent signals, the field indicates how the signal was sent. For kernel-sent signals, the field indicates why the signal was sent.

The following si_code values are valid for any signal. They indicate how/why the signal was sent:

SI_ASYNCIO

The signal was sent due to the completion of asynchronous I/O (see Chapter 5).

SI_KERNEL

The signal was raised by the kernel.

SI_MESGQ

The signal was sent due to a state change of a POSIX message queue (not covered in this book).

SI_QUEUE

The signal was sent by sigqueue() (see the next section).

SI_TIMER

The signal was sent due to the expiration of a POSIX timer (see Chapter 11).

SI_TKILL

The signal was sent by tkill() or tgkill(). These system calls are used by threading libraries and are not covered in this book.

SI_SIGIO

The signal was sent due to the queuing of SIGIO.

SI_USER

The signal was sent by kill() or raise().

The following si_code values are valid for SIGBUS only. They indicate the type of hardware error that occurred:

BUS_ADRALN

The process incurred an alignment error (see Chapter 9 for a discussion of alignment).

BUS_ADRERR

The process accessed an invalid physical address.

BUS_OBJERR

The process caused some other form of hardware error.

For SIGCHLD, the following values identify what the child did to generate the signal sent to its parent:

CLD_CONTINUED

The child was stopped but has resumed.

CLD_DUMPED

The child terminated abnormally.

CLD_EXITED
> The child terminated normally via exit().

CLD_KILLED
> The child was killed.

CLD_STOPPED
> The child stopped.

CLD_TRAPPED
> The child hit a trap.

The following values are valid for SIGFPE only. They explain the type of arithmetic error that occurred:

FPE_FLTDIV
> The process performed a floating-point operation that resulted in division by zero.

FPE_FLTOVF
> The process performed a floating-point operation that resulted in an overflow.

FPE_FLTINV
> The process performed an invalid floating-point operation.

FPE_FLTRES
> The process performed a floating-point operation that yielded an inexact or invalid result.

FPE_FLTSUB
> The process performed a floating-point operation that resulted in an out-of-range subscript.

FPE_FLTUND
> The process performed a floating-point operation that resulted in an underflow.

FPE_INTDIV
> The process performed an integer operation that resulted in division by zero.

FPE_INTOVF
> The process performed an integer operation that resulted in an overflow.

The following si_code values are valid for SIGILL only. They explain the nature of the illegal instruction execution:

ILL_ILLADR
> The process attempted to enter an illegal addressing mode.

ILL_ILLOPC
> The process attempted to execute an illegal opcode.

ILL_ILLOPN
The process attempted to execute on an illegal operand.

ILL_PRVOPC
The process attempted to execute a privileged opcode.

ILL_PRVREG
The process attempted to execute on a privileged register.

ILL_ILLTRP
The process attempted to enter an illegal trap.

For all of these values, `si_addr` points to the address of the offense.

For `SIGPOLL`, the following values identify the I/O event that generated the signal:

POLL_ERR
An I/O error occurred.

POLL_HUP
The device hung up or the socket disconnected.

POLL_IN
The file has data available to read.

POLL_MSG
A message is available.

POLL_OUT
The file is capable of being written to.

POLL_PRI
The file has high-priority data available to read.

The following codes are valid for `SIGSEGV`, describing the two types of invalid memory accesses:

SEGV_ACCERR
The process accessed a valid region of memory in an invalid way—that is, the process violated memory-access permissions.

SEGV_MAPERR
The process accessed an invalid region of memory.

For either of these values, `si_addr` contains the offending address.

For `SIGTRAP`, these two `si_code` values identify the type of trap hit:

TRAP_BRKPT
The process hit a break point.

TRAP_TRACE
> The process hit a trace trap.

Note that si_code is a value field and not a bit field.

Sending a Signal with a Payload

As we saw in the previous section, signal handlers registered with the SA_SIGINFO flag are passed a siginfo_t parameter. This structure contains a field named si_value, which is an optional payload passed from the signal generator to the signal receiver.

The sigqueue() function, defined by POSIX, allows a process to send a signal with this payload:

```
#include <signal.h>

int sigqueue (pid_t pid,
              int signo,
              const union sigval value);
```

sigqueue() works similarly to kill(). On success, the signal identified by signo is queued to the process or process group identified by pid, and the function returns 0. The signal's payload is given by value, which is a union of an integer and a void pointer:

```
union sigval {
        int sival_int;
        void *sival_ptr;
};
```

On failure, the call returns −1 and sets errno to one of the following:

EAGAIN
> The invoking process has reached the limit on enqueued signals.

EINVAL
> The signal specified by signo is invalid.

EPERM
> The invoking process lacks sufficient permissions to send a signal to any of the requested processes. The permissions required to send a signal are the same as with kill() (see "Sending a Signal" on page 346).

ESRCH
> The process or process group denoted by pid does not exist or, in the case of a process, is a zombie.

As with kill(), you may pass the null signal (0) for signo to test permissions.

Signal Payload Example

This example sends the process with pid 1722 the `SIGUSR2` signal with a payload of an integer that has the value 404:

```
sigval value;
int ret;

value.sival_int = 404;

ret = sigqueue (1722, SIGUSR2, value);
if (ret)
        perror ("sigqueue");
```

If process 1722 handles `SIGUSR2` with an `SA_SIGINFO` handler, it will find `signo` set to `SIGUSR2`, `si->si_int` set to 404, and `si->si_code` set to `SI_QUEUE`.

A Flaw in Unix?

Signals have a bad reputation among many Unix programmers. They are an old, antiquated mechanism for kernel-to-user communication and are, at best, a primitive form of IPC. In a world of multithreading programs and event loops, signals feel anachronistic. In a system that has so impressively weathered time and that finds itself sporting the original programming paradigm it introduced on day one, signals are a rare misstep. I would not take the challenge of rethinking signals lightly, but a more expressive, easily extensible, thread-safe, and file descriptor based solution seems a proper start.

Nonetheless, for better or worse, we are stuck with signals. They are the only way to receive many notifications (such as the notification of an illegal opcode execution) from the kernel. Additionally, signals are how Unix (and thus Linux) terminates processes and manages the parent/child relationship. Thus, programmers must understand them and use them.

One of the primary reasons for signals' derogation is that it is hard to write a proper signal handler that is safe from reentrancy concerns. If you keep your handlers simple, however, and use only the functions listed in Table 10-3 (if you use any!), they should be safe.

Another chink in signals' armor is that many programmers still use `signal()` and `kill()`, rather than `sigaction()` and `sigqueue()`, for signal management. As the last two sections have shown, signals are significantly more powerful and expressive when `SA_SIGINFO`-style signal handlers are used. Although I myself am no fan of signals, working around their flaws and using Linux's advanced signal interfaces eases much of the pain (if not the whining).

## CHAPTER 11

Time

Time serves various purposes in a modern operating system, and many programs need to keep track of it. The kernel measures the passage of time in three different ways:

Wall time (or real time)

> This is the actual time and date in the real world—that is, the time as one would read it on a clock on the wall. Processes use the wall time when interfacing with the user or timestamping an event.

Process time

> This is the time that a process spends executing on a processor. It can be a measurement of the time the process itself spent executing (*user time*) or the time the kernel spent working on the process's behalf (*system time*). Processes care about process time for profiling, auditing, and statistical purposes, for example, measuring how much processor time a given algorithm took to complete. Wall time is misleading for such uses because, given the multitasking nature of Linux, wall time is generally greater than process time. Conversely, given multiple processors and a threaded process, the process time can actually exceed the wall time for a given operation!

Monotonic time

> This time source is strictly linearly increasing. Most operating systems, Linux included, use the system's uptime (time since boot) for this purpose. The wall time can change—for example, because the user may set it or because the system continually adjusts the time to combat clock skew—and additional imprecision can be introduced through, say, leap seconds. The system uptime, on the other hand, is a deterministic and unchangeable representation of time. The important aspect of a monotonic time source is not the current value but the guarantee that the time source is strictly linearly increasing and thus useful for calculating the difference in time between two samplings.

These three measurements of time can be represented in one of two formats:

Relative time

This is a value relative to some benchmark, such as the current instant: for example, *5 seconds from now*, or *10 minutes ago*. Monotonic time is useful for calculating relative time.

Absolute time

This represents time without any such benchmark: say, *noon on 25 March 1968*. Wall time is ideal for calculating absolute time.

Both relative and absolute forms of time have uses. A process might need to cancel a request in 500 milliseconds, refresh the screen 60 times per second, or note that 7 seconds have elapsed since an operation began. All of these call for relative time calculations. Conversely, a calendar application might save the date for the user's toga party as 8 February, a filesystem will write out the full date and time when a file is created (rather than "5 seconds ago"), and the user's clock displays the Gregorian date, not the number of seconds since the system booted.

Unix systems represent absolute time as the number of elapsed seconds since the *epoch*, which is defined as 00:00:00 UTC on the morning of 1 January 1970. UTC (Coordinated Universal Time) is roughly GMT (Greenwich Mean Time) or Zulu time. Curiously, this means that in Unix, even absolute time is, at a low level, relative. Unix introduces a special data type for storing "seconds since the epoch," which we will look at in the next section.

Operating systems track the progression of time via the *software clock*, a clock maintained by the kernel in software. The kernel instantiates a periodic timer, known as the *system timer*, that pops at a specific frequency. When a timer interval ends, the kernel increments the elapsed time by one unit, known as a *tick* or a *jiffy*. The counter of elapsed ticks is known as the *jiffies counter*. Previously a 32-bit value, jiffies is a 64-bit counter as of the 2.6 Linux kernel.[1]

On Linux, the frequency of the system timer is called HZ because a preprocessor define of the selfsame name represents it. The value of HZ is architecture-specific and not part of the Linux ABI. Thus, programs cannot depend on or expect any given value. Historically, the x86 architecture used a value of 100, meaning the system timer ran 100 times per second (that is, the system timer had a frequency of 100 hertz). This gave each jiffy a value of 0.01 seconds. With the release of the 2.6 Linux kernel, the kernel developers bumped the value of HZ to 1000, giving each jiffy a value of 0.001 seconds. However,

---

1. The Linux kernel now supports "tickless" operation, so this is no longer strictly true.

in version 2.6.13 and later, HZ is 250, providing each jiffy a value of 0.004 seconds.[2] There is a trade-off inherent in the value of HZ: higher values provide higher resolution but incur greater timer overhead.

Although processes should not rely on any fixed value of HZ, POSIX defines a mechanism for determining the system timer frequency at runtime:

```
long hz;

hz = sysconf (_SC_CLK_TCK);
if (hz == -1)
        perror ("sysconf"); /* should never occur */
```

This interface is useful when a program wants to determine the resolution of the system's timer, but it is not needed for converting system time values to seconds because most POSIX interfaces export measurements of time that are already converted or that are scaled to a fixed frequency, independent of HZ. Unlike HZ, this fixed frequency is part of the system ABI; on x86, the value is 100. POSIX functions that return time in terms of clock ticks use CLOCKS_PER_SEC to represent the fixed frequency.

Occasionally, events conspire to turn off a computer. Sometimes, computers are even unplugged; yet, upon boot, they have the correct time. This is because most computers have a battery-powered *hardware clock* that stores the time and date while the computer is off. When the kernel boots, it initializes its concept of the current time from the hardware clock. Likewise, when the user shuts down the system, the kernel writes the current time back to the hardware clock. The system's administrator may synchronize time at other points via the *hwclock* command.

Managing the passage of time on a Unix system involves several tasks, only some of which any given process is concerned with: they include setting and retrieving the current wall time, calculating elapsed time, sleeping for a given amount of time, performing high-precision measurements of time, and controlling timers. This chapter covers this full range of time-related chores. We'll begin by looking at the data structures with which Linux represents time.

Time's Data Structures

As Unix systems evolved, implementing their own interfaces for managing time, multiple data structures came to represent the seemingly simple concept of time. These data structures range from the simple integer to various multifield structures. We'll cover them here before we dive into the actual interfaces.

---

2. HZ is also now a compile-time kernel option, with the values 100, 250, 300, and 1000 supported on the x86 architecture. Regardless, user space cannot depend on any particular value for HZ.

The Original Representation

The simplest data structure is `time_t`, defined in the header `<time.h>`. The intention was for `time_t` to be an opaque type. However, on most Unix systems, including Linux, the type is a simple typedef to the C `long` type:

```
typedef long time_t;
```

`time_t` represents the number of elapsed seconds since the epoch. "That won't last long before overflowing!" is a typical response. In fact, it will last longer than you might expect, but it indeed will overflow while plenty of Unix systems are still in use. With a 32-bit `long` type, `time_t` can represent up to 2,147,483,647 seconds past the epoch. This suggests that we will have the Y2K mess all over again—in *2038*! With luck, however, come 22:14:07 on Monday, 18 January 2038, most systems and software will be 64-bit.

And Now, Microsecond Precision

Another issue with `time_t` is that a lot can happen in a single second. The `timeval` structure extends `time_t` to add microsecond precision. The header `<sys/time.h>` defines this structure as follows:

```
#include <sys/time.h>

struct timeval {
        time_t        tv_sec;     /* seconds */
        suseconds_t   tv_usec;    /* microseconds */
};
```

`tv_sec` measures seconds, and `tv_usec` measures microseconds. The confusing `suseconds_t` is normally a typedef to an integer type.

Even Better: Nanosecond Precision

Not content with microsecond resolution, the `timespec` structure ups the ante to nano-second resolution. The header `<time.h>` defines this structure as follows:

```
#include <time.h>

struct timespec {
        time_t tv_sec;     /* seconds */
        long   tv_nsec;    /* nanoseconds */
};
```

Given the choice, interfaces prefer nanosecond to microsecond resolution In addition, the `timespec` structure dropped the silly `suseconds_t` business in favor of a simple and unpretentious `long`. Consequently, since the introduction of the `timespec` structure, most time-related interfaces have switched to it and thus have gained greater precision. However, as we will see, one important function still uses `timeval`.

In practice, neither structure usually offers the stated precision because the system timer is not providing nanosecond or even microsecond resolution. Nonetheless, it's preferable to have the resolution available in the interface so it can accommodate whatever resolution the system does offer.

Breaking Down Time

Some of the functions that we will cover convert between Unix time and strings or programmatically build a string representing a given date. To facilitate this process, the C standard provides the tm structure for representing "broken-down" time in a more human-readable format. This structure is also defined in <time.h>:

```
#include <time.h>

struct tm {
        int tm_sec;          /* seconds */
        int tm_min;          /* minutes */
        int tm_hour;         /* hours */
        int tm_mday;         /* the day of the month */
        int tm_mon;          /* the month */
        int tm_year;         /* the year */
        int tm_wday;         /* the day of the week */
        int tm_yday;         /* the day in the year */
        int tm_isdst;        /* daylight savings time? */
#ifdef _BSD_SOURCE
        long tm_gmtoff;      /* time zone's offset from GMT */
        const char *tm_zone; /* time zone abbreviation */
#endif /* _BSD_SOURCE */
};
```

The tm structure makes it easier to tell whether a time_t value of, say, 314159 is a Sunday or a Saturday (it is the former). In terms of space, it is obviously a poor choice for representing the date and time, but it is handy for converting to and from user-oriented values.

The fields are as follows:

tm_sec
> The number of seconds after the minute. This value normally ranges from 0 to 59, but it can be as high as 61 to indicate up to two leap seconds.

tm_min
> The number of minutes after the hour. This value ranges from 0 to 59.

tm_hour
> The number of hours after midnight. This value ranges from 0 to 23.

tm_mday

The day of the month. This value ranges from 0 to 31. POSIX does not specify the value 0; however, Linux uses it to indicate the last day of the preceding month.

tm_mon

The number of months since January. This value ranges from 0 to 11.

tm_year

The number of years since 1900.

tm_wday

The number of days since Sunday. This value ranges from 0 to 6.

tm_yday

The number of days since 1 January. This value ranges from 0 to 365.

tm_isdst

A special value indicating whether daylight savings time (DST) is in effect at the time described by the other fields. If the value is positive, DST is in effect. If it is 0, DST is not in effect. If the value is negative, the state of DST is unknown.

tm_gmtoff

The offset in seconds of the current time zone from Greenwich Mean Time. This field is present only if _BSD_SOURCE is defined before including <time.h>.

tm_zone

The abbreviation for the current time zone—for example, EST. This field is present only if _BSD_SOURCE is defined before including <time.h>.

A Type for Process Time

The type clock_t represents clock ticks. It is an integer type, often a long. Depending on the interface, the ticks that clock_t represent are the system's actual timer frequency (HZ) or CLOCKS_PER_SEC.

POSIX Clocks

Several of the system calls discussed in this chapter utilize *POSIX clocks*, a standard for implementing and representing time sources. The type clockid_t represents a specific POSIX clock, five of which Linux supports:

CLOCK_REALTIME

The system-wide real time (wall time) clock. Setting this clock requires special privileges.

CLOCK_MONOTONIC
A monotonically increasing clock that is not settable by any process. It represents the elapsed time since some unspecified starting point, such as system boot.

CLOCK_MONOTONIC_RAW
Similar to CLOCK_MONOTONIC, except the clock is not eligible for slewing (correction for clock skew). That is, if the hardware clock runs faster or slower than wall time, it won't be adjusted when read via this clock. This clock is Linux-specific.

CLOCK_PROCESS_CPUTIME_ID
A high-resolution, per-process clock available from the processor. For example, on the x86 architecture, this clock uses the timestamp counter (TSC) register.

CLOCK_THREAD_CPUTIME_ID
Similar to the per-process clock, but unique to each thread in a process.

POSIX requires only CLOCK_REALTIME. Therefore, while Linux reliably provides all five clocks, portable code should rely only on CLOCK_REALTIME.

Time Source Resolution

POSIX defines the function clock_getres() for obtaining the resolution of a given time source:

```
#include <time.h>

int clock_getres (clockid_t clock_id,
                  struct timespec *res);
```

A successful call to clock_getres() stores the resolution of the clock specified by clock_id in res if it is not NULL and returns 0. On failure, the function returns −1 and sets errno to one of the following two error codes:

EFAULT
res is an invalid pointer.

EINVAL
clock_id is not a valid time source on this system.

The following example outputs the resolution of the five time sources discussed in the previous section:

```
clockid_t clocks[] = {
        CLOCK_REALTIME,
        CLOCK_MONOTONIC,
        CLOCK_PROCESS_CPUTIME_ID,
        CLOCK_THREAD_CPUTIME_ID,
        CLOCK_MONOTONIC_RAW,
        (clockid_t) −1 };
```

```
        int i;

        for (i = 0; clocks[i] != (clockid_t) -1; i++) {
                struct timespec res;
                int ret;

                ret = clock_getres (clocks[i], &res);
                if (ret)
                        perror ("clock_getres");
                else
                        printf ("clock=%d sec=%ld nsec=%ld\n",
                                clocks[i], res.tv_sec, res.tv_nsec);
        }
```

On a modern x86 system, the output resembles the following:

```
clock=0 sec=0 nsec=4000250
clock=1 sec=0 nsec=4000250
clock=2 sec=0 nsec=1
clock=3 sec=0 nsec=1
clock=4 sec=0 nsec=4000250
```

Note that 4,000,250 nanoseconds is 4 milliseconds, which is 0.004 seconds. In turn, 0.004 seconds is the resolution of the x86 system clock given an HZ value of 250, as we discussed in the first section of this chapter. Thus, we see that both CLOCK_REALTIME and CLOCK_MONOTONIC are tied to jiffies and the resolution provided by the system timer. Conversely, both CLOCK_PROCESS_CPUTIME_ID and CLOCK_PROCESS_CPUTIME_ID utilize a higher-resolution time source—on this x86 machine, the TSC, which we see provides nanosecond resolution.

On Linux (and most other Unix systems), all of the functions that use POSIX clocks require linking the resulting object file with *librt*. For example, if compiling the previous snippet into a complete executable, you might use the following command:

```
$ gcc -Wall -W -O2 -lrt -g -o snippet snippet.c
```

Getting the Current Time of Day

Applications have several reasons for desiring the current time and date: to display it to the user, to calculate relative or elapsed time, to timestamp an event, and so on. The simplest and historically most common way of obtaining the current time is the time() function:

```
#include <time.h>

time_t time (time_t *t);
```

A call to time() returns the current time represented as the number of seconds elapsed since the epoch. If the parameter t is not NULL, the function also writes the current time into the provided pointer.

On error, the function returns –1 (typecast to a time_t) and sets errno appropriately. The only possible error is EFAULT, noting that t is an invalid pointer.

For example:

```
time_t t;

printf ("current time: %ld\n", (long) time (&t));
printf ("the same value: %ld\n", (long) t);
```

A Consistent but Inaccurate View of Time

time_t's representation of "seconds elapsed since the epoch" is not the actual number of seconds that have passed since that fateful moment in time. The Unix calculation assumes leap years are all years divisible by four and ignores leap seconds altogether. The point of the time_t representation is not that it is accurate, but that it is consistent—and it is.

A Better Interface

The function gettimeofday() extends time() by offering microsecond resolution:

```
#include <sys/time.h>

int gettimeofday (struct timeval *tv,
                  struct timezone *tz);
```

A successful call to gettimeofday() places the current time in the timeval structure pointed at by tv and returns 0. The timezone structure and the tz parameter are obsolete; neither should be used on Linux. Always pass NULL for tz.

On failure, the call returns –1 and sets errno to EFAULT; this is the only possible error, signifying that tv or tz is an invalid pointer.

For example:

```
struct timeval tv;
int ret;

ret = gettimeofday (&tv, NULL);
if (ret)
        perror ("gettimeofday");
else
        printf ("seconds=%ld useconds=%ld\n",
                (long) tv.sec, (long) tv.tv_usec);
```

The timezone structure is obsolete because the kernel does not manage the time zone, and *glibc* refuses to use the timezone structure's tz_dsttime field. We will look at manipulating the time zone in a subsequent section.

An Advanced Interface

POSIX provides the clock_gettime() interface for obtaining the time of a specific time source. More useful, however, is that the function allows for nanosecond precision:

```
#include <time.h>

int clock_gettime (clockid_t clock_id,
                   struct timespec *ts);
```

On success, the call returns 0 and stores the current time of the time source specified by clock_id in ts. On failure, the call returns –1 and sets errno to one of the following:

EFAULT
    ts is an invalid pointer.

EINVAL
    clock_id is an invalid time source on this system.

The following example obtains the current time of all four of the standard time sources:

```
clockid_t clocks[] = {
        CLOCK_REALTIME,
        CLOCK_MONOTONIC,
        CLOCK_PROCESS_CPUTIME_ID,
        CLOCK_THREAD_CPUTIME_ID,
        CLOCK_MONOTONIC_RAW,
        (clockid_t) -1 };
int i;

for (i = 0; clocks[i] != (clockid_t) -1; i++) {
        struct timespec ts;
        int ret;

        ret = clock_gettime (clocks[i], &ts);
        if (ret)
                perror ("clock_gettime");
        else
                printf ("clock=%d sec=%ld nsec=%ld\n",
                        clocks[i], ts.tv_sec, ts.tv_nsec);
}
```

Getting the Process Time

The times() system call retrieves the process time of the running process and its children, in clock ticks:

```
#include <sys/times.h>

struct tms {
        clock_t tms_utime;    /* user time consumed */
        clock_t tms_stime;    /* system time consumed */
        clock_t tms_cutime;   /* user time consumed by children */
        clock_t tms_cstime;   /* system time consumed by children */
};

clock_t times (struct tms *buf);
```

On success, the call fills the provided tms structure pointed at by buf with the process time consumed by the invoking process and its children. The reported times are broken into user and system time. *User time* is the time spent executing code in user space. *System time* is the time spent executing code in kernel space—for example, during a system call, or a page fault. The reported times for each child are included only after the child terminates, and the parent invokes waitpid() (or a related function) on the process. The call returns the number of clock ticks, monotonically increasing, elapsed since an arbitrary but fixed point in the past. This reference point was once system boot— thus, the times() function returned the system uptime in ticks—but the reference point is now about 429 million seconds before system boot. The kernel developers implemented this change to catch kernel code that could not handle the system uptime wrapping around and hitting zero. The absolute value of this function's return is thus worthless; relative changes between two invocations, however, continue to have value.

On failure, the call returns –1 and sets errno as appropriate. On Linux, the only possible error code is EFAULT, signifying that buf is an invalid pointer.

Setting the Current Time of Day

While previous sections have described how to retrieve times, applications occasionally also need to set the current time and date to a provided value. This is almost always handled by a utility designed solely for this purpose, such as *date*.

The time-setting counterpart to time() is stime():

```
#define _SVID_SOURCE
#include <time.h>

int stime (time_t *t);
```

A successful call to stime() sets the system time to the value pointed at by t and returns 0. The call requires that the invoking user have the CAP_SYS_TIME capability. Generally, only the root user wields this capability.

On failure, the call returns –1 and sets errno to EFAULT, signifying that t was an invalid pointer, or EPERM, signifying that the invoking user did not possess the CAP_SYS_TIME capability.

Usage is very simple:

```
time_t t = 1;
int ret;

/* set time to one second after the epoch */
ret = stime (&t);
if (ret)
        perror ("stime");
```

We will look at functions that make it easier to convert human-readable forms of time to a time_t in a subsequent section.

Setting Time with Precision

The counterpart to gettimeofday() is settimeofday():

```
#include <sys/time.h>

int settimeofday (const struct timeval *tv,
                  const struct timezone *tz);
```

A successful call to settimeofday() sets the system time as given by tv and returns 0. As with gettimeofday(), passing NULL for tz is the best practice. On failure, the call returns –1 and sets errno to one of the following:

EFAULT
    tv or tz points at an invalid region of memory.

EINVAL
    A field in one of the provided structures is invalid.

EPERM
    The calling process lacks the CAP_SYS_TIME capability.

The following example sets the current time to a Saturday in the middle of December 1979:

```
struct timeval tv = { .tv_sec  = 31415926,
                      .tv_usec = 27182818 };
int ret;

ret = settimeofday (&tv, NULL);
if (ret)
        perror ("settimeofday");
```

An Advanced Interface for Setting the Time

Just as clock_gettime() improves on gettimeofday(), clock_settime() obsolesces settimeofday():

```
#include <time.h>

int clock_settime (clockid_t clock_id,
                   const struct timespec *ts);
```

On success, the call returns 0, and the time source specified by `clock_id` is set to the time specified by `ts`. On failure, the call returns −1 and sets `errno` to one of the following:

EFAULT
: `ts` is an invalid pointer.

EINVAL
: `clock_id` is an invalid time source on this system.

EPERM
: The process lacks the needed permissions to set the specified time source, or the specified time source may not be set.

On most systems, the only settable time source is `CLOCK_REALTIME`. Thus, the only advantage of this function over `settimeofday()` is that it offers nanosecond precision (along with not having to deal with the worthless `timezone` structure).

Playing with Time

Unix systems and the C language provide a family of functions for converting between broken-down time (an ASCII string representation of time) and `time_t`. `asctime()` converts a `tm` structure—broken-down time—to an ASCII string:

```
#include <time.h>

char * asctime (const struct tm *tm);
char * asctime_r (const struct tm *tm, char *buf);
```

It returns a pointer to a statically allocated string. A subsequent call to any time function may overwrite this string; `asctime()` is not thread-safe.

Thus, multithreaded programs (and developers who loathe poorly designed interfaces) should use `asctime_r()`. Instead of returning a pointer to a statically allocated string, this function uses the string provided via `buf`, which must be at least 26 characters in length.

Both functions return `NULL` in the case of error.

`mktime()` also converts a `tm` structure, but it converts it to a `time_t`:

```
#include <time.h>

time_t mktime (struct tm *tm);
```

`mktime()` also sets the time zone via `tzset()`, as specified by `tm`. On error, it returns –1 (typecast to a `time_t`).

`ctime()` converts a `time_t` to its ASCII representation:

```
#include <time.h>

char * ctime (const time_t *timep);
char * ctime_r (const time_t *timep, char *buf);
```

On failure, it returns NULL. For example:

```
time_t t = time (NULL);

printf ("the time a mere line ago: %s", ctime (&t));
```

Note the lack of newline. Perhaps inconveniently, `ctime()` appends a newline to its returned string.

Like `asctime()`, `ctime()` returns a pointer to a static string. As this is not thread-safe, threaded programs should instead use `ctime_r()`, which operates on the buffer provided by `buf`. The buffer must be at least 26 characters in length.

`gmtime()` converts the given `time_t` to a `tm` structure, expressed in terms of the UTC time zone:

```
#include <time.h>

struct tm * gmtime (const time_t *timep);
struct tm * gmtime_r (const time_t *timep, struct tm *result);
```

On failure, it returns NULL.

This function statically allocates the returned structure and is thus thread-unsafe. Threaded programs should use `gmtime_r()`, which operates on the structure pointed at by `result`.

`localtime()` and `localtime_r()` perform functions akin to `gmtime()` and `gmtime_r()`, respectively, but they express the given `time_t` in terms of the user's time zone:

```
#include <time.h>

struct tm * localtime (const time_t *timep);
struct tm * localtime_r (const time_t *timep, struct tm *result);
```

As with `mktime()`, a call to `localtime()` also calls `tzset()` and initializes the time zone. Whether `localtime_r()` performs this step is unspecified.

`difftime()` returns the number of seconds that have elapsed between two `time_t` values, cast to a `double`:

```
#include <time.h>

double difftime (time_t time1, time_t time0);
```

On all POSIX systems, `time_t` is an arithmetic type, and `difftime()` is equivalent to the following, excepting detection of overflow in the subtraction:

```
(double) (time1 - time0)
```

On Linux, because `time_t` is an integer type, there is no need for the cast to `double`. To remain portable, use `difftime()`.

Tuning the System Clock

Large and abrupt jumps in the wall clock time can wreak havoc on applications that depend on absolute time for their operation. Consider as an example *make*, which builds software projects as detailed by a *Makefile*. Each invocation of the program does not rebuild entire source trees; if it did, in large software projects, a single changed file could result in hours of rebuilding. Instead, *make* looks at the file modification timestamps of the source file (say, *wolf.c*) versus the object file (*wolf.o*). If the source file or any of its prerequisites, such as *wolf.h*, is newer than the object file, *make* rebuilds the source file into an updated object file. If the source file is not newer than the object, no action is taken.

With this in mind, consider what might happen if the user realized his clock was off by a couple of hours and ran *date* to update the system clock. If the user then updated and resaved *wolf.c*, we could have trouble. If the user has moved the current time backward, *wolf.c* will look older than *wolf.o*, even though it isn't, and no rebuild will occur.

To prevent such a debacle, Unix provides the `adjtime()` function, which gradually adjusts the current time in the direction of a given delta. The intention is for background activities such as Network Time Protocol (NTP) daemons, which constantly adjust the time in correction of clock skew, to use `adjtime()` to minimize their effects on the system. The periodic adjustment of the clock to correct for clock skew is called *slewing*:

```
#define _BSD_SOURCE
#include <sys/time.h>

int adjtime (const struct timeval *delta,
             struct timeval *olddelta);
```

A successful call to `adjtime()` instructs the kernel to slowly begin adjusting the time as stipulated by `delta`, and then returns 0. If the time specified by `delta` is positive, the kernel speeds up the system clock by `delta` until the correction is fully applied. If the time specified by `delta` is negative, the kernel slows down the system clock until the correction is applied. The kernel applies all adjustments such that the clock is always monotonically increasing and never undergoes an abrupt time change. Even with a negative `delta`, the adjustment will not move the clock backward; instead, the clock slows down until the system time converges with the corrected time.

If `delta` is not `NULL`, the kernel stops processing any previously registered corrections. However, the part of the correction already made, if any, is maintained. If `olddelta` is not `NULL`, any previously registered and yet unapplied correction is written into the provided `timeval` structure. Passing a `NULL delta` and a valid `olddelta` allows retrieval of any ongoing correction.

The corrections applied by `adjtime()` should be small. The ideal use case is NTP, which applies only small corrections (but a handful of seconds). Linux maintains minimum and maximum correction thresholds of a few thousand seconds in either direction.

On error, `adjtime()` returns –1 and sets `errno` to one of these values:

EFAULT
> `delta` or `olddelta` is an invalid pointer.

EINVAL
> The adjustment delineated by `delta` is too large or too small.

EPERM
> The invoking user does not possess the `CAP_SYS_TIME` capability.

RFC 1305 defines a significantly more powerful and correspondingly more complex clock-adjustment algorithm than the gradual correction approach undertaken by `adjtime()`. Linux implements this algorithm with the `adjtimex()` system call:

```
#include <sys/timex.h>

int adjtimex (struct timex *adj);
```

A call to `adjtimex()` reads kernel time-related parameters into the `timex` structure pointed at by `adj`. Optionally, depending on the `modes` field of this structure, the system call may additionally set certain parameters.

The header `<sys/timex.h>` defines the `timex` structure as follows:

```
struct timex {
        int modes;              /* mode selector */
        long offset;            /* time offset (usec) */
        long freq;              /* frequency offset (scaled ppm) */
        long maxerror;          /* maximum error (usec) */
        long esterror;          /* estimated error (usec) */
        int status;             /* clock status */
        long constant;          /* PLL time constant */
        long precision;         /* clock precision (usec) */
        long tolerance;         /* clock frequency tolerance (ppm) */
        struct timeval time;    /* current time */
```

```
        long tick;           /* usecs between clock ticks */
    };
```

The modes field is a bitwise OR of zero or more of the following flags:

ADJ_OFFSET
    Set the time offset via offset.

ADJ_FREQUENCY
    Set the frequency offset via freq.

ADJ_MAXERROR
    Set the maximum error via maxerror.

ADJ_ESTERROR
    Set the estimated error via esterror.

ADJ_STATUS
    Set the clock status via status.

ADJ_TIMECONST
    Set the phase-locked loop (PLL) time constant via constant.

ADJ_TICK
    Set the tick value via tick.

ADJ_OFFSET_SINGLESHOT
    Set the time offset via offset once with a simple algorithm like adjtime().

If modes is 0, no values are set. Only a user with the CAP_SYS_TIME capability may provide a nonzero modes value; any user may provide 0 for modes, retrieving all of the parameters but setting none of them.

On success, adjtimex() returns the current clock state, which is one of the following:

TIME_OK
    The clock is synchronized.

TIME_INS
    A leap second will be inserted.

TIME_DEL
    A leap second will be deleted.

TIME_OOP
    A leap second is in progress.

TIME_WAIT
    A leap second just occurred.

TIME_BAD
>The clock is not synchronized.

On failure, `adjtimex()` returns −1 and sets `errno` to one of the following error codes:

EFAULT
>`adj` is an invalid pointer.

EINVAL
>One or more of `modes`, `offset`, or `tick` is invalid.

EPERM
>`modes` is nonzero, but the invoking user does not possess the `CAP_SYS_TIME` capability.

The `adjtimex()` system call is Linux-specific. Applications concerned with portability should prefer `adjtime()`.

RFC 1305 defines a complex algorithm, so a complete discussion of `adjtimex()` is outside the scope of this book. For more information, see the RFC.

Sleeping and Waiting

Various functions allow a process to sleep (suspend execution) for a given amount of time. The first such function, `sleep()`, puts the invoking process to sleep for the number of seconds specified by `seconds`:

```
#include <unistd.h>

unsigned int sleep (unsigned int seconds);
```

The call returns the number of seconds *not* slept. Thus, a successful call returns 0, but the function may return other values between 0 and `seconds` inclusive (if, say, a signal interrupts the nap). The function does not set `errno`. Most users of `sleep()` do not care about how long the process actually slept and, consequently, do not check the return value:

```
sleep (7);      /* sleep seven seconds */
```

If sleeping the entire specified time is truly a concern, you can continue calling `sleep()` with its return value until it returns 0:

```
unsigned int s = 5;

/* sleep five seconds: no ifs, ands, or buts about it */
while ((s = sleep (s)))
        ;
```

Sleeping with Microsecond Precision

Sleeping with whole-second granularity is pretty lame. A second is an eternity on a modern system, so programs often want to sleep with subsecond resolution. Enter `usleep()`:

```
/* BSD version */
#include <unistd.h>

void usleep (unsigned long usec);

/* SUSv2 version */
#define _XOPEN_SOURCE 500
#include <unistd.h>

int usleep (useconds_t usec);
```

A successful call to `usleep()` puts the invoking process to sleep for `usec` microseconds. Unfortunately, BSD and the Single UNIX Specification disagree on the prototype of the function. The BSD variant receives an `unsigned long` and has no return value. The SUS variant, however, defines `usleep()` to accept a `useconds_t` type and return an `int`. Linux follows SUS if `_XOPEN_SOURCE` is defined as `500` or higher. If `_XOPEN_SOURCE` is undefined or set to less than `500`, Linux follows BSD.

The SUS version returns `0` on success and `-1` on error. Valid `errno` values are `EINTR`, if the nap was interrupted by a signal, or `EINVAL`, if `usecs` was too large (on Linux, the full range of the type is valid, and thus this error will never occur).

According to the specification, the `useconds_t` type is an unsigned integer capable of holding values as high as 1,000,000.

Due to the differences between the conflicting prototypes and the fact that some Unix systems may support one or the other, but not both, it is wise never to explicitly include the `useconds_t` type in your code. For maximum portability, assume that the parameter is an `unsigned int`, and do not rely on `usleep()`'s return value:

```
void usleep (unsigned int usec);
```

Usage is then:

```
unsigned int usecs = 200;

usleep (usecs);
```

This works with either variant of the function, and checking for errors is still possible:

```
errno = 0;
usleep (1000);
if (errno)
        perror ("usleep");
```

Most programs, however, do not check for or care about usleep() errors.

Sleeping with Nanosecond Resolution

Linux deprecates the usleep() function, replacing it with nanosleep(), which provides nanosecond resolution and a smarter interface:

```
#define _POSIX_C_SOURCE 199309
#include <time.h>

int nanosleep (const struct timespec *req,
               struct timespec *rem);
```

A successful call to nanosleep() puts the invoking process to sleep for the time specified by req and then returns 0. On error, the call returns –1 and sets errno appropriately. If a signal interrupts the sleep, the call can return before the specified time has elapsed. In that case, nanosleep() returns –1, and sets errno to EINTR. If rem is not NULL, the function places the remaining time to sleep (the amount of req not slept) in rem. The program may then reissue the call, passing rem for req (as shown later in this section).

Here are the other possible errno values:

EFAULT
    req or rem is an invalid pointer.

EINVAL
    One of the fields in req is invalid.

In the basic case, usage is simple:

```
struct timespec req = { .tv_sec = 0,
                        .tv_nsec = 200 };

/* sleep for 200 ns */
ret = nanosleep (&req, NULL);
if (ret)
        perror ("nanosleep");
```

And here is an example using the second parameter to continue the sleep if interrupted:

```
struct timespec req = { .tv_sec = 0,
                        .tv_nsec = 1369 };
struct timespec rem;
int ret;

/* sleep for 1369 ns */
retry:
ret = nanosleep (&req, &rem);
if (ret) {
        if (errno == EINTR) {
                /* retry, with the provided time remaining */
```

```
                req.tv_sec = rem.tv_sec;
                req.tv_nsec = rem.tv_nsec;
                goto retry;
        }
        perror ("nanosleep");
}
```

Finally, here's an alternative approach (perhaps more efficient, but less readable) toward the same goal:

```
struct timespec req = { .tv_sec = 1,
                        .tv_nsec = 0 };
struct timespec rem, *a = &req, *b = &rem;

/* sleep for 1s */
while (nanosleep (a, b) && errno == EINTR) {
        struct timespec *tmp = a;
        a = b;
        b = tmp;
}
```

nanosleep() has several advantages over sleep() and usleep():

- Nanosecond, as opposed to second or microsecond, resolution
- Standardized by POSIX.1b
- Not implemented via signals (the pitfalls of which are discussed later)

Despite deprecation, many programs prefer to use usleep() rather than nanosleep(). Because +nanosleep() is a POSIX standard and does not use signals, new programs should prefer it (or the interface discussed in the next section) to sleep() and usleep().

An Advanced Approach to Sleep

As with all of the classes of time functions we have thus far studied, the POSIX clocks family provides the most advanced sleep interface:

```
#include <time.h>

int clock_nanosleep (clockid_t clock_id,
                     int flags,
                     const struct timespec *req,
                     struct timespec *rem);
```

clock_nanosleep() behaves similarly to nanosleep(). In fact, this call:

```
ret = nanosleep (&req, &rem);
```

is the same as this call:

```
ret = clock_nanosleep (CLOCK_REALTIME, 0, &req, &rem);
```

The difference lies in the `clock_id` and `flags` parameters. The former specifies the time source to measure against. Most time sources are valid, although you cannot specify the CPU clock of the invoking process (e.g., `CLOCK_PROCESS_CPUTIME_ID`); doing so would make no sense because the call suspends execution of the process, and thus the process time stops increasing.

What time source you specify depends on your program's goals for sleeping. If you are sleeping until some absolute time value, `CLOCK_REALTIME` may make the most sense. If you are sleeping for a relative amount of time, `CLOCK_MONOTONIC` definitely is the ideal time source.

The `flags` parameter is either `TIMER_ABSTIME` or `0`. If it is `TIMER_ABSTIME`, the value specified by `req` is treated as absolute and not relative. This solves a potential race condition. To explain the value of this parameter, assume that a process, at time `T+0`, wants to sleep until time `T+1`. At `T+0`, the process calls `clock_gettime()` to obtain the current time (`T+0`). It then subtracts `T+0` from `T+1`, obtaining `Y`, which it passes to `clock_nano sleep()`. Some amount of time, however, will have passed between the moment at which the time was obtained and the moment at which the process goes to sleep. Worse, what if the process was scheduled off the processor, incurred a page fault, or something similar? There is always a potential race condition in between obtaining the current time, calculating the time differential, and actually sleeping.

The `TIMER_ABSTIME` flag nullifies the race by allowing a process to directly specify `T+1`. The kernel suspends the process until the specified time source reaches `T1 + 1`. If the specified time source's current time already exceeds `T+1`, the call returns immediately.

Let's look at both relative and absolute sleeping. The following example sleeps for 1.5 seconds:

```
struct timespec ts = { .tv_sec = 1, .tv_nsec = 500000000 };
int ret;

ret = clock_nanosleep (CLOCK_MONOTONIC, 0, &ts, NULL);
if (ret)
        perror ("clock_nanosleep");
```

Conversely, the next example sleeps until an absolute value of time—which is exactly one second from what the `clock_gettime()` call returns for the `CLOCK_MONOTONIC` time source—is reached:

```
struct timespec ts;
int ret;

/* we want to sleep until one second from NOW */
ret = clock_gettime (CLOCK_MONOTONIC, &ts);
if (ret) {
        perror ("clock_gettime");
        return;
```

```
        }

        ts.tv_sec += 1;
        printf ("We want to sleep until sec=%ld nsec=%ld\n",
                ts.tv_sec, ts.tv_nsec);
        ret = clock_nanosleep (CLOCK_MONOTONIC, TIMER_ABSTIME,
                               &ts, NULL);
        if (ret)
                perror ("clock_nanosleep");
```

Most programs need only a relative sleep because their sleep needs are not very strict. Some real-time processes, however, have very exact timing requirements and need the absolute sleep to avoid the danger of a potentially devastating race condition.

A Portable Way to Sleep

Recall from Chapter 2 our friend select():

```
#include <sys/select.h>

int select (int n,
            fd_set *readfds,
            fd_set *writefds,
            fd_set *exceptfds,
            struct timeval *timeout);
```

As mentioned in that chapter, select() provides a portable way to sleep with sub-second resolution. For a long time, portable Unix programs were stuck with sleep() for their naptime needs: usleep() was not widely available, and nanosleep() was as of yet unwritten. Developers discovered that passing select() 0 for n, NULL for all three of the fd_set pointers, and the desired sleep duration for timeout resulted in a portable and efficient way to put processes to sleep:

```
struct timeval tv = { .tv_sec = 0,
                      .tv_usec = 757 };

/* sleep for 757 us */
select (0, NULL, NULL, NULL, &tv);
```

If portability to older Unix systems is a concern, using select() may be your best bet.

Overruns

All of the interfaces discussed in this section guarantee that they will sleep *at least as long as requested* (or return an error indicating otherwise). They will never return success without the requested delay elapsing. It is possible, however, for an interval *longer* than the requested delay to pass.

This phenomenon may be due to simple scheduling behavior—the requested time may have elapsed, and the kernel may have woken up the process on time, but the scheduler may have selected a different task to run.

There exists a more insidious cause, however: *timer overruns*. This occurs when the granularity of the timer is coarser than the requested time interval. For example, assume the system timer ticks in 10 ms intervals and a process requests a 1 ms sleep. The system is able to measure time and respond to time-related events (such as waking up a process from sleep) only at 10 ms intervals. If, when the process issues the sleep request, the timer is 1 ms away from a tick, everything will be fine—in 1 ms, the requested time (1 ms) will elapse, and the kernel will wake up the process. If, however, the timer hits right as the process requests the sleep, there won't be another timer tick for 10 ms. Subsequently, the process will sleep an extra 9 ms! That is, there will be nine 1 ms overruns. On average, a timer with a period of X has an overrun rate of $X/2$.

The use of high-precision time sources, such as those provided by POSIX clocks, and higher values for HZ, minimize timer overrun.

Alternatives to Sleeping

If possible, you should avoid sleeping. Often, you cannot, and that's fine—particularly if your code is sleeping for less than a second. Code that is laced with sleeps in order to "busy-wait" for events is usually of poor design. Code that blocks on a file descriptor, allowing the kernel to handle the sleep and wake up the process, is better. Instead of the process spinning in a loop until the event hits, the kernel can block the process from execution and wake it up only when needed.

Timers

Timers provide a mechanism for notifying a process when a given amount of time elapses. The amount of time before a timer *expires* is called the *delay*, or the *expiration*. How the kernel notifies the process that the timer has expired depends on the timer. The Linux kernel offers several types. We will study them all.

Timers are useful for several reasons. Examples include refreshing the screen 60 times per second or canceling a pending transaction if it is still ongoing after 500 milliseconds.

Simple Alarms

alarm() is the simplest timer interface:

```
#include <unistd.h>

unsigned int alarm (unsigned int seconds);
```

A call to this function schedules the delivery of a SIGALRM signal to the invoking process after seconds of real time have elapsed. If a previously scheduled signal was pending, the call cancels the alarm, replaces it with the newly requested alarm, and returns the number of seconds remaining in the previous alarm. If seconds is 0, the previous alarm, if any, is canceled, but no new alarm is scheduled.

Successful use of this function thus also requires registering a signal handler for the SIGALRM signal. (Signals and signal handlers were covered in the previous chapter.) Here is a code snippet that registers a SIGALRM handler, alarm_handler(), and sets an alarm for five seconds:

```
void alarm_handler (int signum)
{
        printf ("Five seconds passed!\n");
}

void func (void)
{
        signal (SIGALRM, alarm_handler);
        alarm (5);

        pause ();
}
```

Interval Timers

Interval timer system calls, which first appeared in 4.2BSD, have since been standardized in POSIX and provide more control than alarm():

```
#include <sys/time.h>

int getitimer (int which,
               struct itimerval *value);

int setitimer (int which,
               const struct itimerval *value,
               struct itimerval *ovalue);
```

Interval timers operate like alarm(), but optionally can automatically rearm themselves and operate in one of three distinct modes:

ITIMER_REAL
> Measures real time. When the specified amount of real time has elapsed, the kernel sends the process a SIGALRM signal.

ITIMER_VIRTUAL
> Decrements only while the process's user-space code is executing. When the specified amount of process time has elapsed, the kernel sends the process a SIGVTALRM.

ITIMER_PROF
   Decrements both while the process is executing, and while the kernel is executing
   on behalf of the process (for example, completing a system call). When the specified
   amount of time has elapsed, the kernel sends the process a SIGPROF signal. This
   mode is usually coupled with ITIMER_VIRTUAL so that the program can measure
   user and kernel time spent by the process.

ITIMER_REAL
   Measures the same time as alarm(); the other two modes are useful for profiling.

The itimerval structure allows the user to specify the amount of time until the timer
expires, as well as the expiration, if any, with which to rearm the timer upon expiration:

```
struct itimerval {
        struct timeval it_interval;  /* next value */
        struct timeval it_value;     /* current value */
};
```

Recall from earlier that the timeval structure provides microsecond resolution:

```
struct timeval {
        long tv_sec;   /* seconds */
        long tv_usec;  /* microseconds */
};
```

setitimer() arms a timer of type which with the expiration specified by it_value.
Once the time specified by it_value elapses, the kernel rearms the timer with the time
provided by it_interval. Thus, it_value is the time remaining on the current timer.
Once it_value reaches zero, it is set to it_interval. If the timer expires, and
it_interval is 0, the timer is not rearmed. Similarly, if an active timer's it_value is set
to 0, the timer is stopped and not rearmed.

If ovalue is not NULL, the previous values for the interval timer of type which are
returned.

getitimer() returns the current values for the interval timer of type which.

Both functions return 0 on success and –1 on error, in which case errno is set to one of
the following:

EFAULT
   value or ovalue is an invalid pointer.

EINVAL
   which is not a valid interval timer type.

The following code snippet creates a SIGALRM signal handler (again, see Chapter 10) and
then arms an interval timer with an initial expiration of five seconds, followed by a
subsequent interval of one second:

```
void alarm_handler (int signo)
{
        printf ("Timer hit!\n");
}

void foo (void)
{
        struct itimerval delay;
        int ret;

        signal (SIGALRM, alarm_handler);

        delay.it_value.tv_sec = 5;
        delay.it_value.tv_usec = 0;
        delay.it_interval.tv_sec = 1;
        delay.it_interval.tv_usec = 0;
        ret = setitimer (ITIMER_REAL, &delay, NULL);
        if (ret) {
                perror ("setitimer");
                return;
        }

        pause ();
}
```

Some Unix systems implement `sleep()` and `usleep()` via `SIGALRM`. `alarm()` and `setitimer()` also use `SIGALRM`. Therefore, programmers must be careful not to overlap calls to these functions; the results are undefined. For the purpose of brief waits, programmers should use `nanosleep()`, which POSIX dictates will not use signals. For timers, programmers should use `setitimer()` *or* `alarm()`.

Advanced Timers

The most powerful timer interface, not surprisingly, hails from the POSIX clocks family.

With POSIX clocks–based timers, the acts of instantiating, initializing, and ultimately deleting a timer are separated into three different functions: `timer_create()` creates the timer, `timer_settime()` initializes the timer, and `timer_delete()` destroys it.

 The POSIX clocks family of timer interfaces is undoubtedly the most advanced but also the newest (ergo the least portable) and most complicated to use. If simplicity or portability is a prime motivator, `setitimer()` is most likely a better choice.

Creating a timer

To create a timer, use `timer_create()`:

```
#include <signal.h>
#include <time.h>

int timer_create (clockid_t clockid,
                  struct sigevent *evp,
                  timer_t *timerid);
```

A successful call to `timer_create()` creates a new timer associated with the POSIX clock `clockid`, stores a unique timer identification in `timerid`, and returns 0. This call merely sets up the conditions for running the timer; nothing actually happens until the timer is armed, as shown in the following section.

The following example creates a new timer keyed off the `CLOCK_PROCESS_CPUTIME_ID` POSIX clock and stores the timer's ID in `timer`:

```
timer_t timer;
int ret;

ret = timer_create (CLOCK_PROCESS_CPUTIME_ID,
                    NULL,
                    &timer);
if (ret)
        perror ("timer_create");
```

On failure, the call returns –1, `timerid` is undefined, and the call sets `errno` to one of the following:

EAGAIN
> The system lacks sufficient resources to complete the request.

EINVAL
> The POSIX clock specified by `clockid` is invalid.

ENOTSUP
> The POSIX clock specified by `clockid` is valid, but the system does not support using the clock for timers. POSIX guarantees that all implementations support the `CLOCK_REALTIME` clock for timers. Whether other clocks are supported is up to the implementation.

The `evp` parameter, if non-`NULL`, defines the asynchronous notification that occurs when the timer expires. The header `<signal.h>` defines the structure. Its contents are supposed to be opaque to the programmer, but it has at least the following fields:

```
#include <signal.h>

struct sigevent {
        union sigval sigev_value;
        int sigev_signo;
        int sigev_notify;
        void (*sigev_notify_function)(union sigval);
        pthread_attr_t *sigev_notify_attributes;
```

```
};

union sigval {
        int sival_int;
        void *sival_ptr;
};
```

POSIX clocks–based timers allow much greater control over how the kernel notifies the process when a timer expires, allowing the process to specify exactly which signal the kernel will emit, or even allowing the kernel to spawn a thread and execute a function in response to timer expiration. A process specifies the behavior on timer expiration via sigev_notify, which must be one of the following three values:

SIGEV_NONE

A "null" notification. On timer expiration, nothing happens.

SIGEV_SIGNAL

On timer expiration, the kernel sends the process the signal specified by sigev_signo. In the signal handler, si_value is set to sigev_value.

SIGEV_THREAD

On timer expiration, the kernel spawns a new thread (within this process) and has it execute sigev_notify_function, passing sigev_value as its sole argument. The thread terminates when it returns from this function. If sigev_notify_attributes is not NULL, the provided pthread_attr_t structure defines the behavior of the new thread.

If evp is NULL, as it was in our earlier example, the timer's expiration notification is set up as if sigev_notify were SIGEV_SIGNAL, sigev_signo were SIGALRM, and sigev_value were the timer's ID. Thus, by default, these timers notify in a manner similar to POSIX interval timers. Via customization, though, they can do much, much more!

The following example creates a timer keyed off CLOCK_REALTIME. When the timer expires, the kernel will issue the SIGUSR1 signal and set si_value to the address storing the timer's ID:

```
struct sigevent evp;
timer_t timer;
int ret;

evp.sigev_value.sival_ptr = &timer;
evp.sigev_notify = SIGEV_SIGNAL;
evp.sigev_signo = SIGUSR1;
ret = timer_create (CLOCK_REALTIME,
                    &evp,
                    &timer);
if (ret)
        perror ("timer_create");
```

Arming a timer

A timer created by `timer_create()` is unarmed. To associate it with an expiration and start the clock ticking, use `timer_settime()`:

```
#include <time.h>

int timer_settime (timer_t timerid,
                   int flags,
                   const struct itimerspec *value,
                   struct itimerspec *ovalue);
```

A successful call to `timer_settime()` arms the timer specified by `timerid` with the expiration `value`, which is an `itimerspec` structure:

```
struct itimerspec {
        struct timespec it_interval;  /* next value */
        struct timespec it_value;     /* current value */
};
```

As with `setitimer()`, `it_value` specifies the current timer expiration. When the timer expires, `it_value` is refreshed with the value from `it_interval`. If `it_interval` is 0, the timer is not an interval timer and will disarm once `it_value` expires.

Recall from earlier that the `timespec` structure provides nanosecond resolution:

```
struct timespec {
        time_t  tv_sec;    /* seconds */
        long    tv_nsec;   /* nanoseconds */
};
```

If `flags` is `TIMER_ABSTIME`, the time specified by `value` is interpreted as absolute (as opposed to the default interpretation, where the value is relative to the current time). This modified behavior prevents a race condition during the steps of obtaining the current time, calculating the relative difference between that time, and a desired future time, and arming the timer. See the discussion in the earlier section, "An Advanced Approach to Sleep" on page 383 for details.

If `ovalue` is non-NULL, the previous timer expiration is saved in the provided `itimer spec`. If the timer was previously disarmed, the structure's members are all set to 0.

Using the `timer` value initialized earlier by `timer_create()`, the following example creates a periodic timer that expires every second:

```
struct itimerspec ts;
int ret;

ts.it_interval.tv_sec = 1;
ts.it_interval.tv_nsec = 0;
ts.it_value.tv_sec = 1;
ts.it_value.tv_nsec = 0;
```

```
ret = timer_settime (timer, 0, &ts, NULL);
if (ret)
        perror ("timer_settime");
```

Obtaining the expiration of a timer

You can get the expiration time of a timer without resetting it via `timer_gettime()`:

```
#include <time.h>

int timer_gettime (timer_t timerid,
                    struct itimerspec *value);
```

A successful call to `timer_gettime()` stores the expiration time of the timer specified by `timerid` in the structure pointed at by `value` and returns 0. On failure, the call returns −1 and sets `errno` to one of the following:

EFAULT
    `value` is an invalid pointer.

EINVAL
    `timerid` is an invalid timer.

For example:

```
struct itimerspec ts;
int ret;

ret = timer_gettime (timer, &ts);
if (ret)
        perror ("timer_gettime");
else {
        printf ("current sec=%ld nsec=%ld\n",
                ts.it_value.tv_sec, ts.it_value.tv_nsec);
        printf ("next sec=%ld nsec=%ld\n",
                ts.it_interval.tv_sec, ts.it_interval.tv_nsec);
}
```

Obtaining the overrun of a timer

POSIX defines an interface for determining how many, if any, overruns occurred on a given timer:

```
#include <time.h>

int timer_getoverrun (timer_t timerid);
```

On success, `timer_getoverrun()` returns the number of additional timer expirations that have occurred between the initial expiration of the timer and notification to the process—for example, via a signal—that the timer expired. For instance, in our earlier example, where a 1 ms timer ran for 10 ms, the call would return 9.

According to POSIX, if the number of overruns is equal to or greater than DE
LAYTIMER_MAX, the call returns DELAYTIMER_MAX. Unfortunately, Linux does not imple-
ment this behavior: instead, once the number of timer overruns exceeds DELAYTIM
ER_MAX, it wraps back to zero and starts anew.

On failure, the function returns –1 and sets errno to EINVAL, the lone error condition,
signifying that the timer specified by timerid is invalid.

For example:

```
int ret;

ret = timer_getoverrun (timer);
if (ret == -1)
        perror ("timer_getoverrun");
else if (ret == 0)
        printf ("no overrun\n");
else
        printf ("%d overrun(s)\n", ret);
```

Deleting a timer

Deleting a timer is easy:

```
#include <time.h>

int timer_delete (timer_t timerid);
```

A successful call to timer_delete() destroys the timer associated with timerid and
returns 0. On failure, the call returns –1, and errno is set to EINVAL, the lone error
condition, signifying that timerid is not a valid timer.

GCC Extensions to the C Language

The GNU Compiler Collection (GCC) provides many extensions to the C language, some of which have proven to be of particular value to system programmers. The majority of the additions to the C language that we'll cover in this appendix offer ways for programmers to provide additional information to the compiler about the behavior and intended use of their code. The compiler, in turn, utilizes this information to generate more efficient machine code. Other extensions fill in gaps in the C programming language, particularly at lower levels.

GCC provides several extensions now available in the latest C standard, ISO C11. Some of these extensions function similarly to their C11 cousins, but ISO C11 implemented other extensions rather differently. New code should use the standardized variants of these features. We won't cover such extensions here; we'll discuss only GCC-unique additions.

GNU C

The flavor of C supported by GCC is often called GNU C. In the 1990s, GNU C filled in several gaps in the C language, providing features such as complex variables, zero-length arrays, inline functions, and named initializers. But after nearly a decade, C was finally upgraded, and with the standardization of ISO C99 and then ISO C11, GNU C extensions grew less relevant. Nonetheless, GNU C continues to provide useful features, and many Linux programmers still use a subset of GNU C—often just an extension or two—in their C99- or C11-compliant code.

One prominent example of a GCC-specific code base is the Linux kernel, which is written strictly in GNU C. Recently, however, Intel has invested engineering effort in allowing the Intel C Compiler (ICC) to understand the GNU C extensions used by the kernel. Consequently, many of these extensions are now growing less GCC-specific.

Inline Functions

The compiler copies the entire code of an "inline" function into the site where the function is called. Instead of storing the function externally and jumping to it whenever it is called, it runs the contents of the function directly. Such behavior saves the overhead of the function call and allows for potential optimizations at the call site because the compiler can optimize the caller and callee together. This latter point is particularly valid if the parameters to the function are constant at the call site. Naturally, however, copying a function into each and every chunk of code that invokes it can have a detrimental effect on code size. Therefore, functions should be inlined only if they are small and simple or are not called in many different places.

For many years, GCC has supported the `inline` keyword, instructing the compiler to inline the given function. C99 formalized this keyword:

```
static inline int foo (void) { /* ... */ }
```

Technically, however, the keyword is merely a hint—a suggestion to the compiler to consider inlining the given function. GCC further provides an extension for instructing the compiler to *always* inline the designated function:

```
static inline __attribute__ ((always_inline)) int foo (void) { /* ... */ }
```

The most obvious candidate for an inline function is a preprocessor macro. An inline function in GCC will perform as well as a macro and receives type checking. For example, instead of this macro:

```
#define max(a,b) ({ a > b ? a : b; })
```

one might use the corresponding inline function:

```
static inline max (int a, int b)
{
        if (a > b)
                return a;
        return b;
}
```

Programmers tend to overuse inline functions. Function call overhead on most modern architectures—x86 in particular—is very, very low. Only the most worthy of functions should receive consideration!

Suppressing Inlining

In its most aggressive optimization mode, GCC automatically selects functions that appear suitable for inlining and inlines them. This is normally a good idea, but sometimes the programmer knows that a function will perform incorrectly if inlined. One example of this is when using `__builtin_return_address` (discussed later in this appendix). To suppress inlining, use the `noinline` keyword:

```
__attribute__ ((noinline)) int foo (void) { /* ... */ }
```

Pure Functions

A "pure" function is one that has no side effects and whose return value reflects only the function's parameters or nonvolatile global variables. Any parameter or global variable access must be read-only. Loop optimization and subexpression elimination can be applied to such functions. Functions are marked as pure via the pure keyword:

```
__attribute__ ((pure)) int foo (int val) { /* ... */ }
```

A common example is strlen(). Given identical inputs, this function's return value is invariant across multiple invocations, and thus it can be pulled out of a loop and called just once. For example, consider the following code:

```
/* character by character, print each letter in 'p' in uppercase */
for (i = 0; i < strlen (p); i++)
        printf ("%c", toupper (p[i]));
```

If the compiler does not know that strlen() is pure, it would need to invoke the function with each iteration of the loop.

Smart programmers—as well as the compiler, if strlen() were marked pure—would write or generate code like this:

```
size_t len;

len = strlen (p);
for (i = 0; i < len; i++)
        printf ("%c", toupper (p[i]));
```

Parenthetically, even smarter programmers (such as this book's readers) would write:

```
while (*p)
        printf ("%c", toupper (*p++));
```

It is illegal and indeed makes no sense for a pure function to return void, as the return value is the sole point of such functions. An example of a nonpure function is random().

Constant Functions

A "constant" function is a stricter variant of a pure function. Such functions cannot access global variables and cannot take pointers as parameters. Thus, the constant function's return value reflects nothing but the passed-by-value parameters. Additional optimizations, on top of those possible with pure functions, are possible for such functions. Math functions, such as abs(), are examples of constant functions (presuming they don't save state or otherwise pull tricks in the name of optimization). A programmer marks a function constant via the const keyword:

```
__attribute__ ((const)) int foo (int val) { /* ... */ }
```

As with pure functions, it makes no sense for a constant function to return void.

Functions That Do Not Return

If a function does not return, perhaps because it invariantly calls exit(), the programmer can mark the function with the noreturn keyword, enlightening the compiler to that fact:

```
__attribute__ ((noreturn)) void foo (int val) { /* ... */ }
```

In turn, the compiler can make additional optimizations, with the understanding that under no circumstances will the invoked function ever return. It does not make sense for such a function to return anything but void.

Functions That Allocate Memory

If a function returns a pointer that can never alias[1] existing memory—almost assuredly because the function just allocated fresh memory, and is returning a pointer to it—the programmer can mark the function as such with the malloc keyword, and the compiler can in turn perform suitable optimizations:

```
__attribute__ ((malloc)) void * get_page (void)
{
        int page_size;

        page_size = getpagesize ();
        if (page_size <= 0)
                return NULL;

        return malloc (page_size);
}
```

Forcing Callers to Check the Return Value

Not an optimization, but a programming aid, the warn_unused_result attribute instructs the compiler to generate a warning whenever the return value of a function is not stored or used in a conditional statement:

```
__attribute__ ((warn_unused_result)) int foo (void) { /* ... */ }
```

1. A memory *alias* occurs when two or more pointer variables point at the same memory address. This can happen in trivial cases where a pointer is assigned the value of another pointer and also in more complex, less obvious cases. If a function is returning the address of newly allocated memory, no other pointers to that same address should exist.

This allows the programmer to ensure that all callers check and handle the return value from a function where the value is of particular importance. Functions with important but oft-ignored return values, such as `read()`, make excellent candidates for this attribute. Such functions cannot return `void`.

Marking Functions as Deprecated

The `deprecated` attribute instructs the compiler to generate a warning at the call site whenever the function is invoked:

```
__attribute__ ((deprecated)) void foo (void) { /* ... */ }
```

This helps wean programmers off deprecated and obsolete interfaces.

Marking Functions as Used

Occasionally, no code visible to a compiler invokes a particular function. Marking a function with the `used` attribute instructs the compiler that the program uses that function, despite appearances that the function is never referenced:

```
static __attribute__ ((used)) void foo (void) { /* ... */ }
```

The compiler therefore outputs the resulting assembly language and does not display a warning about an unused function. This attribute is useful if a static function is invoked only from handwritten assembly code. Normally, if the compiler is not aware of any invocation, it will generate a warning, and potentially optimize away the function.

Marking Functions or Parameters as Unused

The `unused` attribute tells the compiler that the given function or function parameter is unused and instructs it not to issue any corresponding warnings:

```
int foo (long __attribute__ ((unused)) value) { /* ... */ }
```

This is useful if you're compiling with `-W` or `-Wunused` and you want to catch unused function parameters, but you occasionally have functions that must match a predetermined signature (as is common in event-driven GUI programming or signal handlers).

Packing a Structure

The `packed` attribute tells the compiler that a type or variable should be packed into memory using the minimum amount of space possible, potentially disregarding alignment requirements. If specified on a `struct` or `union`, all variables therein are so packed. If specified on just one variable, only that specific object is packed.

The following packs all variables within the structure into the minimum amount of space:

```
struct __attribute__ ((packed)) foo { ... };
```

As an example, a structure containing a char followed by an int would most likely find the integer aligned to a memory address not immediately following the char, but, say, three bytes later. The compiler aligns the variables by inserting bytes of unused padding between them. A packed structure lacks this padding, potentially consuming less memory but failing to meet architectural alignment requirements.

Increasing the Alignment of a Variable

As well as allowing packing of variables, GCC also allows programmers to specify an alternative minimum alignment for a given variable. GCC will then align the specified variable to *at least* this value, as opposed to the minimum required alignment dictated by the architecture and ABI. For example, this statement declares an integer named beard_length with a minimum alignment of 32 bytes (as opposed to the typical alignment of 4 bytes on machines with 32-bit integers):

```
int beard_length __attribute__ ((aligned (32))) = 0;
```

Forcing the alignment of a type is generally useful only when dealing with hardware that may impose greater alignment requirements than the architecture itself, or when you are hand-mixing C and assembly code and you want to use instructions that require specially aligned values. One example where this alignment functionality is utilized is for storing oft-used variables on processor cache lines to optimize cache behavior. The Linux kernel makes use of this technique.

As an alternative to specifying a certain minimum alignment, you can ask that GCC align a given type to the largest minimum alignment that is ever used for any data type. For example, this instructs GCC to align parrot_height to the largest alignment it ever uses, which is probably the alignment of a double:

```
short parrot_height __attribute__ ((aligned)) = 5;
```

This decision generally involves a space/time trade-off: variables aligned in this manner consume more space, but copying to or from them (along with other complex manipulations) may be faster because the compiler can issue machine instructions that deal with the largest amount of memory.

Various aspects of the architecture or the system's toolchain may impose maximum limits on a variable's alignment. For example, on some Linux architectures, the linker is unable to recognize alignments beyond a rather small default. In that case, an alignment provided using this keyword is rounded down to the smallest allowed alignment. For example, if you request an alignment of 32, but the system's linker is unable to align to more than 8 bytes, the variable will be aligned along an 8-byte boundary.

Placing Global Variables in a Register

GCC allows programmers to place global variables in a specific machine register, where the variables will then reside for the duration of the program's execution. GCC calls such variables *global register variables.*

The syntax requires that the programmer specify the machine register. The following example uses ebx:

```
register int *foo asm ("ebx");
```

The programmer must select a variable that is not function-clobbered: that is, the selected variable must be usable by local functions, saved and restored on function call invocation, and not specified for any special purpose by the architecture or operating system's ABI. The compiler will generate a warning if the selected register is inappropriate. If the register is appropriate—ebx, used in this example, is fine for the x86 architecture—the compiler will in turn stop using the register itself.

Such an optimization can provide huge performance boosts if the variable is frequently used. A good example is with a virtual machine. Placing the variable that holds, say, the virtual stack frame pointer in a register might lead to substantial gains. On the other hand, if the architecture is starved of registers to begin with (as the x86 architecture is), this optimization makes little sense.

Global register variables cannot be used in signal handlers or by more than one thread of execution. They also cannot have initial values because there is no mechanism for executable files to supply default contents for registers. Global register variable declarations should precede any function definitions.

Branch Annotation

GCC allows programmers to annotate the expected value of an expression—for example, to tell the compiler whether a conditional statement is likely to be true or false. GCC, in turn, can then perform block reordering and other optimizations to improve the performance of conditional branches.

The GCC syntax for branch notation is horrendously ugly. To make branch annotation easier on the eyes, we use preprocessor macros:

```
#define likely(x)    __builtin_expect (!!(x), 1)
#define unlikely(x)  __builtin_expect (!!(x), 0)
```

Programmers can mark an expression as likely or unlikely true by wrapping it in likely() or unlikely(), respectively.

The following example marks a branch as unlikely true (that is, likely to be false):

```
int ret;

ret = close (fd);
if (unlikely (ret))
        perror ("close");
```

Conversely, the following example marks a branch as likely true:

```
const char *home;

home = getenv ("HOME");
if (likely (home))
        printf ("Your home directory is %s\n", home);
else
        fprintf (stderr, "Environment variable HOME not set!\n");
```

As with inline functions, programmers have a tendency to overuse branch annotation. Once you start anointing expressions, you might be tempted to mark *all* expressions. Be careful, though—you should mark branches as likely or unlikely only if you know *a priori* and with little doubt that the expressions will be true or false *nearly all of the time* (say, with 99 percent certainty). Seldom-occurring errors are good candidates for unlikely(). Keep in mind that a false prediction is worse than no prediction at all.

Getting the Type of an Expression

GCC provides the typeof() keyword to obtain the type of a given expression. Semantically, the keyword operates the same as sizeof(). For example, this expression returns the type of whatever x points at:

```
typeof (*x)
```

We can use this to declare an array, y, of those types:

```
typeof (*x) y[42];
```

A popular use for typeof() is to write "safe" macros that can operate on any arithmetic value and evaluate their parameters only once:

```
#define max(a,b) ({               \
        typeof (a) _a = (a); \
        typeof (b) _b = (b); \
        _a > _b ? _a : _b; \
})
```

Getting the Alignment of a Type

GCC provides the keyword *alignof* to obtain the alignment of a given object. The value is architecture- and ABI-specific. If the current architecture does not have a required alignment, the keyword returns the ABI's recommended alignment. Otherwise, the keyword returns the minimum required alignment.

The syntax is identical to `sizeof()`:

```
__alignof__(int)
```

Depending on the architecture, this probably returns 4, as 32-bit integers are generally aligned along 4-byte boundaries.

alignof() in C11 and C++11

C11 and C++11 introduced `alignof()`, which works identically to `alignof()` but is standardized. If writing a C11 or C++11 program, prefer `alignof()`.

The keyword works on lvalues, too. In that case, the returned alignment is the minimum alignment of the backing type, not the actual alignment of the specific lvalue. If the minimum alignment was changed via the `aligned` attribute (described earlier, in "Increasing the Alignment of a Variable" on page 400), that change is reflected by `__alignof__`.

For example, consider this structure:

```
struct ship {
        int year_built;
        char cannons;
        int mast_height;
};
```

along with this code snippet:

```
struct ship my_ship;

printf ("%d\n", __alignof__(my_ship.cannons));
```

The *alignof* in this snippet will return 1, even though structure padding probably results in `cannons` consuming 4 bytes.

The Offset of a Member Within a Structure

GCC provides a built-in keyword for obtaining the offset of a member of a structure within that structure. The `offsetof()` macro, defined in `<stddef.h>`, is part of the ISO C standard. Most definitions are horrid, involving obscene pointer arithmetic and code unfit for minors. The GCC extension is simpler and potentially faster:

```
#define offsetof(type, member)   __builtin_offsetof (type, member)
```

A call returns the offset of `member` within `type`—that is, the number of bytes, starting from zero, from the beginning of the structure to that member. For example, consider the following structure:

```
struct rowboat {
        char *boat_name;
        unsigned int nr_oars;
        short length;
};
```

The actual offsets depend on the size of the variables and the architecture's alignment requirements and padding behavior. On a 32-bit machine, we might expect calling offsetof() on struct rowboat with boat_name, nr_oars, and length to return 0, 4, and 8, respectively.

On a Linux system, the offsetof() macro should be defined using the GCC keyword and need not be redefined.

Obtaining the Return Address of a Function

GCC provides a keyword for obtaining the return address of the current function, or one of the callers of the current function:

```
void * __builtin_return_address (unsigned int level)
```

The parameter level specifies the function in the call chain whose address should be returned. A value of 0 asks for the return address of the current function, a value of 1 asks for the return address of the caller of the current function, a value of 2 asks for *that* function's caller's return address, and so on.

If the current function is an inline function, the address returned is that of the calling function. If this is unacceptable, use the noinline keyword (described earlier, in "Suppressing Inlining" on page 396) to force the compiler not to inline the function.

There are several uses for the __builtin_return_address keyword. One is for debugging or informational purposes. Another is to unwind a call chain in order to implement introspection, a crash dump utility, a debugger, and so on.

Note that some architectures can return only the address of the invoking function. On such architectures, a nonzero parameter value can result in a random return value. Thus, any parameter other than 0 is nonportable and should be used only for debugging purposes.

Case Ranges

GCC allows case statement labels to specify a range of values for a single block. The general syntax is as follows:

```
case low ... high:
```

For example:

```
switch (val) {
case 1 ... 10:
        /* ... */
        break;
case 11 ... 20:
        /* ... */
        break;
default:
        /* ... */
}
```

This functionality is quite useful for ASCII case ranges, too:

```
case 'A' ... 'Z':
```

Note that there should be a space before and after the ellipsis. Otherwise, the compiler can become confused, particularly with integer ranges. Always do the following:

```
case 4 ... 8:
```

and never this:

```
case 4...8:
```

Void and Function Pointer Arithmetic

In GCC, addition and subtraction operations are allowed on pointers of type void and pointers to functions. Normally, ISO C does not allow arithmetic on such pointers because the size of a "void" is a nonsensical concept and is dependent on what the pointer is actually pointing to. To facilitate such arithmetic, GCC treats the size of the referential object as one byte. Thus, the following snippet advances a by one:

```
a++;        /* a is a void pointer */
```

The option -Wpointer-arith causes GCC to generate a warning when these extensions are used.

More Portable and More Beautiful in One Fell Swoop

Let's face it, the *attribute* syntax is not pretty. Some of the extensions we've looked at in this chapter require preprocessor macros to make their use palatable, but all of them can benefit from a sprucing up in appearance.

With a little preprocessor magic, this is not hard. Further, in the same action, we can make the GCC extensions portable by defining them away in the case of a non-GCC compiler (whatever that is).

To do so, stick the following code snippet in a header and include that header in your source files:

```
#if __GNUC__ >= 3
# undef  inline
# define inline          inline __attribute__ ((always_inline))
# define __noinline      __attribute__ ((noinline))
# define __pure          __attribute__ ((pure))
# define __const         __attribute__ ((const))
# define __noreturn      __attribute__ ((noreturn))
# define __malloc        __attribute__ ((malloc))
# define __must_check    __attribute__ ((warn_unused_result))
# define __deprecated    __attribute__ ((deprecated))
# define __used          __attribute__ ((used))
# define __unused        __attribute__ ((unused))
# define __packed        __attribute__ ((packed))
# define __align(x)      __attribute__ ((aligned (x)))
# define __align_max     __attribute__ ((aligned))
# define likely(x)       __builtin_expect (!!(x), 1)
# define unlikely(x)     __builtin_expect (!!(x), 0)
#else
# define __noinline      /* no noinline */
# define __pure          /* no pure */
# define __const         /* no const */
# define __noreturn      /* no noreturn */
# define __malloc        /* no malloc */
# define __must_check    /* no warn_unused_result */
# define __deprecated    /* no deprecated */
# define __used          /* no used */
# define __unused        /* no unused */
# define __packed        /* no packed */
# define __align(x)      /* no aligned */
# define __align_max     /* no align_max */
# define likely(x)       (x)
# define unlikely(x)     (x)
#endif
```

For example, the following marks a function as pure, using our shortcut:

```
__pure int foo (void) { /* ... */ }
```

If GCC is in use, the function is marked with the pure attribute. If GCC is not the compiler, the preprocessor replaces the __pure token with a no-op. Note that you can place multiple attributes on a given definition, and thus you can use more than one of these defines on a single definition with no problems.

Easier, prettier, and portable!

Bibliography

This bibliography presents recommended reading related to system programming, broken down into four subcategories. None of these works are required reading. Instead, they represent my take on the top books on the given subject matter. If you find yourself pining for more information on the topics discussed here, these are my favorites.

Some of these books address material with which this book assumes the reader is already conversant, such as the C programming language. Other texts included make great supplements to this book, such as the works covering *gdb*, Git, or operating system design. Whatever the case, I recommend them all. Of course, these lists are certainly not exhaustive—please do explore other resources.

Books on the C Programming Language

These books document the C programming language, the lingua franca of system programming. If you do not code C as well as you speak your native tongue, one or more of the following works (coupled with a lot of practice!) ought to help you in that direction. If nothing else, the first title—universally known as *K&R*—is a treat to read. Its brevity reveals the simplicity of C.

The C Programming Language, 2nd ed. Brian Kernighan and Dennis Ritchie. Prentice Hall, 1988. This book, written by the author of the C programming language and his then coworker, is the bible of C programming.

C in a Nutshell. Peter Prinz and Tony Crawford. O'Reilly Media, 2005. A great book covering both the C language and the standard C library.

C Pocket Reference. Peter Prinz and Ulla Kirch-Prinz. Translated by Tony Crawford. O'Reilly Media, 2002. A concise reference to the C language, handily updated for ANSI C99.

Expert C Programming. Peter van der Linden. Prentice Hall, 1994. A wonderful discussion of lesser-known aspects of the C programming language, elucidated with an amazing wit and sense of humor. This book is rife with non sequiturs and jokes.

C Programming FAQs: Frequently Asked Questions, 2nd ed. Steve Summit. Addison-Wesley, 1995. This beast of a book contains more than 400 frequently asked questions (with answers) on the C programming language. Many of the FAQs beg obvious answers in the eyes of C masters, but some of the weightier questions and answers should impress even the most erudite of C programmers. Note there is an online version that has likely been more recently updated.

Books on Linux Programming

The following texts cover Linux programming, including discussions of topics not covered in this book and Linux programming tools.

Unix Network Programming, Volume 1: The Sockets Networking API. W. Richard Stevens et al. Addison-Wesley, 2003. The definitive tome on the socket API; unfortunately not specific to Linux, but fortunately recently updated for IPv6.

UNIX Network Programming, Volume 2: Interprocess Communications. W. Richard Stevens. Prentice Hall, 1998. An excellent discussion of interprocess communication (IPC).

PThreads Programming. Bradford Nichols et al. O'Reilly Media, 1996. A deeper reference to the POSIX threading API, Pthreads, supplementing this book.

Managing Projects with GNU Make. Robert Mecklenburg. O'Reilly Media, 2004. An excellent treatment on GNU Make, the classic tool for building software projects on Linux.

Version Control with Subversion. Ben Collins-Sussman et al. O'Reilly Media, 2004. A comprehensive take on Subversion, the successor of CVS for revision control and source code management on Unix systems, by three of Subversion's own authors.

Version Control with Git. Jon Loeliger et al. O'Reilly Media, 2012. A excellent introduction to Git, the sometimes confusing but always powerful distributed revision control system.

GDB Pocket Reference. Arnold Robbins. O'Reilly Media, 2005. A handy pocket guide to *gdb*, Linux's debugger.

Linux in a Nutshell. Ellen Siever et al. O'Reilly Media, 2009. A whirlwind reference to all things Linux, including many of the tools comprising Linux's development environment.

Books on the Linux Kernel

The two titles listed here cover the Linux kernel. Reasons for investigating this topic are threefold. First, the kernel provides the system call interface to user space and is thus the core of system programming. Second, the behaviors and idiosyncrasies of a kernel shed light on its interactions with the applications it runs. Finally, the Linux kernel is a wonderful chunk of code, and these books are fun.

Linux Kernel Development. Robert Love. Addison-Wesley, 2010. My own effort in this category is ideally suited to system programmers who want to know about the design and implementation of the Linux kernel. Not an API reference, this book offers a great discussion of the algorithms used and decisions made by the Linux kernel.

Linux Device Drivers. Jonathan Corbet et al. O'Reilly Media, 2005. This is a great guide to writing device drivers for the Linux kernel, with excellent API references. Although aimed at device drivers, the discussions will benefit programmers of any persuasion, including system programmers merely seeking more insight into the machinations of the Linux kernel. A great complement to my own Linux kernel book.

Books on Operating System Design

These two works, not specific to Linux, address operating system design in the abstract. As I've stressed in this book, a strong understanding of the system on which you develop can only improve your output.

Operating System Concepts. Abraham Silberschatz et al. Prentice Hall, 2012. An excellent introduction to operating systems, their history, and their underlying algorithms. Includes an excellent set of case studies.

UNIX Systems for Modern Architectures. Curt Schimmel. Addison-Wesley, 1994. This book, less on Unix than modern processor and cache architectures, is an excellent introduction to how operating systems cope with the complexities of modern systems. Although growing a bit dated, I still highly recommend it.

Index

Symbols

#define (preprocessor), 21
-pthread flag, 227
. (dot) directory, 260
.. (dot-dot) directory, 260
/ (root) directory, 259
/dev/random, 281
/dev/urandom, 281
/dev/zero (BSD), 311
/etc/manifest, 72
/root directory, 259
1:1 threading, 215–217
\n (new-line character), 75

A

ABIs, 6
abort() system call, 154, 334, 336
    malloc() debugging and, 315
absolute pathname, 12, 259
    current working directories and, 260
absolute section (process), 16
absolute time, 364
access control lists (ACLs), 20
adjtime() function (time), 377
adjtimex() system call, 378
advice
    on file I/O, 118–121
    on file mapping, 115–118

advice parameter (madvise() system call), 116
alarm() function, 336
    timers and, 386
alarm_handler() function (time), 387
alloca() system call, 316–320
Alpha systems and creat() system call, 32
American National Standards Institute (ANSI),
    8
anti-lock braking systems (as real-time system),
    190
Anticipatory I/O scheduler, 127
Apache, 2
APIs, 5
append mode, 38
    writing files in, 78
application binary interface (ABI), 6
application programming interface (API), 5
arithmetic exception signal, 337
    si_code values for, 359
arrays
    dynamically allocating, 298
    zero-length, 287
asctime() function (time), 375
async-safe functions, 20
asynchronous I/O, 123
    events, handling, 333–362
    operations, 121–123
    threads vs., 214
atexit() function (processes), 149, 151

We'd like to hear your suggestions for improving our indexes. Send email to index@oreilly.com.

atomic operations, 222

B

background process group, 168
backups, open() call and, 28
bash, 2
bash instance, 168
batch real-time policy, 194
bcmp() function (BSD), 322
bcopy() function (BSD), 323
Beagle search structure (GNOME), 292
binaries, 211
binary data
    reading, 76
    writing, 77, 79
binary interface, defining, 6
block boundaries, 69
block devices, 14
    files, 14
block number, 124
    sorting I/O by, 132–135
block size, 69
    effects on performance, 68
block started by symbol (bss), 16
blocking
    read() calls and, 33
    signals, 351–353
blocking I/O, 213
blocks, 16
break point signal, 307, 339
brk() system call, 307, 313
broken links, 13
BSD
    /dev/zero in, 311
    data alignment in, 304
    dirfd() function, 269
    file ownership in, 29
    process group function support in, 172
    signaling asynchronous I/O events, 338
    waiting for processes in, 158–160
bss section (process), 16
bss segment memory region, 295
buddy memory allocation scheme, 308
buffer size, 69
buffered I/O, 67–90
    streams, 73–83
    thread safety, 86–89
    user-, 67–70

buffers
    controlling, 84–86
    directories in, 261
    representation of, 66
    setting type of, in stdio interface, 84
buffer_head data structure, 66
busy waiting, 201
bytes
    comparing, 322
    frobnicating, 325
    moving, 323
    searching, 324
    setting, 321
    stacklen, 324
bzero() function (BSD), 321

C

C language
    compilers for, 4
    int type, 139
    libraries, 3
    long type, 81
    standards, 8
    stdin, stdout, stderr libraries, 25
    storing extended attribute values as strings,
        252
The C Programming Language (Ritchie, Ker-
    nighan), 8
C++
    libstdcxx, 5
    malloc() and, 297
cache effect (process migration), 186
calloc() function (memory), 298, 311, 322
    data alignment and, 303–305
    freeing memory after, 301
cancellation points (threads), 231
capabilities system, 19
CAP_CHOWN capability, 248
CAP_DOWNER capability
    changing permissions and, 246
    removing directories and, 268
CAP_IPC_LOCK capability, 328
CAP_KILL capability, 346
CAP_SYS_ADMIN capability, 252
CAP_SYS_IPC capability, 206
CAP_SYS_NICE capability, 183
    getpriority()/setpriority() and, 185
    real-time processes and, 207
    setting scheduling policy and, 196

Z

zero device, 280
zero padding, 46–48
zero page (process), 16

zero-length arrays, 287
zombie processes, 18, 162
    waiting on, 151
Zulu time, 364

About the Author

Robert Love has been using and contributing to Linux since its earliest days, including significant contributions to the Linux kernel and GNOME desktop environment. Robert is Staff Software Engineer at Google, where he was a member of the team that designed and shipped Android. He currently works on Google's web search infrastructure. Robert holds a B.S. in Computer Science and a B.A. in Mathematics from the University of Florida. He lives in Boston.

Colophon

The image on the cover of *Linux System Programming* is a man in a flying machine. Well before the Wright brothers achieved their first controlled heavier-than-air flight in 1903, people around the world attempted to fly by simple and elaborate machines. In the second or third century, Zhuge Liang of China reportedly flew in a Kongming lantern, the first hot air balloon. Around the fifth or sixth centuries, many Chinese people purportedly attached themselves to large kites to fly through the air.

It is also said that the Chinese created spinning toys that were early versions of helicopters, the designs of which may have inspired Leonardo da Vinci in his initial attempts at a solution to human flight. da Vinci also studied birds and designed parachutes, and in 1845, he designed an ornithopter, a wing-flapping machine meant to carry humans through the air. Though he never built it, the ornithopter's birdlike structure influenced the design of flying machines throughout the centuries.

The flying machine depicted on the cover is more elaborate than James Means's model soaring machine of 1893, which had no propellers. Means later printed an instruction manual for his soaring machine, which in part states that "the summit of Mt. Willard, near the Crawford House, N.H., will be found an excellent place" to experiment with the machines.

But such experimentation was often dangerous. In the late nineteenth century, Otto Lilienthal built monoplanes, biplanes, and gliders. He was the first to show that control of human flight was within reach, and he gained the nickname "father of aerial testing," as he conducted more than 2,000 glider flights, sometimes traveling more than a thousand feet. He died in 1896 after breaking his spine during a crash landing.

Flying machines are also known as mechanical birds and airships, and are occasionally called by more colorful names such as the Artificial Albatross. Enthusiasm for flying machines remains high, as aeronautical buffs still build early flying machines today.

The cover image and chapter opening graphics are from the Dover Pictorial Archive. The cover font is Adobe ITC Garamond. The text font is Adobe Minion Pro; the heading font is Adobe Myriad Condensed; and the code font is Dalton Maag's Ubuntu Mono.

www.ingramcontent.com/pod-product-compliance
Ingram Content Group UK Ltd.
Pitfield, Milton Keynes, MK11 3LW, UK
UKHW010607280325
456822UK00002B/5